D1376482

Rock Eras

Rock Eras
Interpretations of Music and Society, 1954-1984

Jim Curtis

Bowling Green State University Popular Press
Bowling Green, Ohio 43403

Language is a social fact.
—Saussure

"It's Only Rock and Roll (But I Like It)"
—The Rolling Stones

Cover design by Gary Dumm

For Beth,
who loves Elvis and the Beach Boys and the Beatles and Boy George and...

Contents

Preface

While working on this book, I have thought of it as a piece of music because it has themes and variations, recurring motifs, and maybe even rhythm. Yet, for most of my life I have written about subjects which have nothing to do with music at all, so my love of rock 'n' roll may need some explanation. The thing is, it all started down home.

I was born on April 16, 1940, in Florence, Alabama, birthplace of W.C. Handy and Sam Phillips, and a neighbor of the future home of Fame Studios in Muscle Shoals. In 1943, my family moved to Tupelo, Mississippi, which was about five miles from East Tupelo, where Elvis Presley was going to Lawhon Elementary School. Tupelo is named for a gum tree, as in the title of Van Morrison's "Tupelo Honey," and is mentioned in Bobby Gentry's "Ode to Billy Joe." (Tupelo is north of Meridian, the birthplace of Jimmy Rodgers and Steve Forbert). Although Tupelo is in the hill country about 70 or 80 miles from the delta, one great blues singer, Howlin' Wolf, lived briefly in Tupelo, and another one, Mississippi John Hurt, recorded a song called "Tupelo Blues." When I was little, I played with Tammy Wynette, who is my second cousin. At least my father tells me that I played with her; I don't remember her at all. I do remember, though, that I saw Elvis in concert at the Mississippi-Alabama Fair and Dairy Show when he came back to Tupelo in the fall of 1956.

I have a direct connection to Elvis and the rise of rockabilly in Memphis through my cousin Charles Underwood (I do remember him—he once showed me a leather guitar cover he had made for Elvis). Charles wrote "Ubangi Stomp," which was a hit for Warren Smith on Sun Records in 1956. In 1962, after he moved to Hollywood, he engineered Bobby Pickett's "Monster Mash" and Herb Alpert's "The Lonely Bull."

So, I have some personal connections with popular music in America. The title of Bill Malone's fine book *Southern Music, American Music* stresses the point that much of American popular music comes from the South—whether it be the early minstrel shows, jazz, gospel, blues, bluegrass, country and western, or rock 'n' roll. And many of the important innovators in those styles came from Mississippi.

But, like my cousin Charles, I didn't stay in the South. Although I had other places to go and other things to do, my love of music stayed with me. By now, I've had enough time to clarify to myself what I believe about music, and what I don't believe. It seems helpful to state those beliefs at the outset.

1

Music is a form of communication, and the simplest form of communication is a conversation between two people. A conversation is neither what one person says, nor what the other person says—it's the interaction between the two of them. The same thing happens in music. The excitement of music occurs when an interaction between the performers and the audience takes place. This excitement is neither in the psyches of the performers, nor in the psyches of the people in the audience. What counts is what happens between the performers and the audience.

Popular music *always* has an audience. That is why it is called "popular". Although virtually everything that has ever been written about rock 'n' roll has to do with the performers, their personalities, what they eat for breakfast, their sex lives, and so forth, I believe that the audience is the great unknown in our understanding of the music. After all, without an audience there are no popular performers, and certainly no stars. No one makes people go to concerts and buy records; they must do these things because they want to. The music must satisfy certain needs which these people have, and I believe that we can never understand the music without understanding the needs which the audience brings to the music. Of course, these needs are never conscious or fully articulated, as in the piece of show biz wisdom which says, "Give 'em what they want before they know they want it."

Popular music always has an audience, and that audience is situated in a particular environment which feels comfortable for enjoying that particular style of music. I call this the "implied audience."

Still, no one—not even the guy in the Kinks' "Rock 'N' Roll Fantasy"—listens to music all the time. We go to class, watch TV, fall in love, fall out of love, get married, get divorced, and go through lots of monkey business in addition to listening to music. We all live in a large, complicated, confusing society which affects us in ways which we are only beginning to understand. Inevitably, these activities affect the kinds of music which we like and which we don't like.

All the performers discussed in this book meet two criteria. First, they are, or were, very popular. Most of them have been popular for a long time. This enduring popularity means that an interaction takes place between these performers and their audiences; in turn, that means that their music tells us something about the society in which it appeared. To paraphrase Ferdinand de Saussure, the founder of modern linguistics, popular music is a social fact, like language. Therefore its significance is not, and cannot be, restricted to a single person. Just as a language which only one person can speak is not a language, so music which only one person likes is not popular music.

Second, all the performers discussed in this book were innovators. They sang in a new way, or they played an instrument in a new way, or they combined styles in a new way. Innovation often occurs in popular music when there is an interaction between technological innovation and performers from a socio-ethnic group not active in the previous period. This is why I will be giving a good deal of attention to the socio-ethnic origins of the performers and the entrepreneurs. After all, America is a nation of immigrants, and popular music is primarily created by immigrants.

If there is any factor which is more ignored in popular music than the audience, it is technology. Rock 'n' roll could never have come to mean what it does to a world-wide audience today without a complex network of recording studios, pressing plants, radio stations, and sound reproduction equipment. No one person planned or created this network; it evolved over a number of years, responding to forces of the marketplace and of government regulation as it did so. If, as I believe, the great performers are great because of their intuitive understanding of how to use technology to make music, then we need to understand that technology as something more than passive machinery. I have not yet read anything that offers a more provocative, more useful way of understanding technology than Marshall McLuhan's book, *Understanding Media* and I will be drawing on his work throughout this book.

Since I will be dealing here only with very popular, very innovative performers, I am going to leave a lot of people out. No one needs to write another version of *The Rolling Stone Illustrated History of Rock and Roll*. As the subtitle of this book indicates, this is not a history of rock 'n' roll, it is a book of interpretations of that history, with emphasis on the patterns which kept recurring in the years 1954-1984.

I am also interested in the way rock history relates to the history of Anglo-American popular music, of which it constitutes an essential part. I discuss some of the issues involved in this interaction in my chapter, "Bing, the Chairman, and the King." But even after rock took over popular music, it never silenced sentimental ballads completely. Rather, the dialectic between "sweet" and "hot" music continued in a new form. Since the twenties, there has been a tension between "sweet" music (Paul Whiteman, Glenn Miller, Liberace, Barry Manilow) and "hot" music (Louis Armstrong, Fletcher Henderson, Little Richard, Van Halen). Musicologist Charles Hamm has called people who like "sweet" music "the fourth audience"—in addition to the audiences for rock, soul, and country and western[1]. I have paid little attention to this music because, although it certainly is popular, it is rarely innovative.

I believe that anything as important as rock 'n' roll must have some more general meaning for our society. Rock 'n' roll interacts with the great themes of American life such as the frontier, for instance. But more generally, rock 'n' roll is one more manifestation of the Romantic movement, which has been affecting Western society at least since the beginning of the nineteenth century.

To make the point, I'd like to pose a riddle by describing an actual performance situation, and then asking the reader to identify the act involved.

The crowds began gathering outside the theater four hours before the performance was scheduled to start, and police were hard put to maintain order. Rumors began to circulate that people had been killed in the crush. The management had oversold the house, so that when people with reserved seats arrived, they couldn't even get in, much less claim their seats. The lucky ones inside booed the opening act, and hysteria broke out when the star act of the evening finally appeared[2].

So who was it? Elvis? The Beatles? Michael Jackson?

The correct answer is: "none of the above." The star act was an actor named William Henry West Betty, better known as Master Betty. The venue was London's Covent Garden Theatre, and the date was December 1, 1804. At the time of his spectacular London debut in a now forgotten tragedy, *Barbarossa*, Master Betty was all of thirteen years old. In effect, he was the first rock star, the first performer who evoked not just acclaim but hysteria while a teenager. His spectacular success (which his biographer calls "Bettymania") represents an early expression of the Romantic cult of unspoiled youth, natural spontaneity, and direct expression of emotion, rather than maturity and experience, which, in one way or another, describes the popularity of every rock star beginning with Elvis.

Since I believe so much in these various forms of interaction, what I don't believe is anything that denies interaction. I don't believe in purity, for instance. Virtually all the forms of creativity which have ever come out of this nation of immigrants have consisted of an adaptation of styles and forms taken from somewhere else. That is to say, creativity in America is inherently impure, an amalgam of diverse parts, and the creativity often manifests itself in the ability to make the parts interact. These generalizations apply to American architecture, to American literature, and to American painting, and they apply to rock 'n' roll as well. Since I believe this, I don't believe in the purity of any one style or period of rock 'n' roll. I don't believe in the purity of Elvis' Sun sessions, I don't believe in the purity of Dylan's acoustic period, and I don't believe in the purity of The Clash's political commitment.

Since I don't believe in purity, I also don't believe that there is any point in cutting myself off from the society which produced the music I love by denouncing its commercialism. I agree completely with what Michael Lydon said on this point:

From the start, rock has been commercial in its very essence. An American creation on the level of the hamburger or the billboard, it was never an art form that just happened to make money, nor a commercial undertaking that sometimes became art. Its art was synonymous with its business...everybody has the message: rock-and-roll sells[3].

I believe anyone who cannot, or will not, accept the commercialism of rock 'n' roll simply cannot understand it. I do not mean by this that I condone the exploitation of artists, especially black artists, by record companies and promoters; but for better or for worse, rock 'n' roll would never have affected America, England, and the world as it has without its commercial success.

Since I don't believe in purity, I also don't believe in making value judgements. If rock 'n' roll is primarily a social fact, as I believe it is, then there is no point in passing judgements on whether Dylan was overrated in the sixties, or whether disco was superficial. What matters is that both Dylan and disco were very popular, and I want to get on with the business of working out the implications of that popularity.

As my comment about the relationship between rock 'n' roll and earlier American popular music indicates, I don't believe in the kind of randomness which Elvis suggested to an interviewer one time. Going into his best aw-shucks-I'm-just-a-simple-country-boy shuffle, he opined, "I was lucky. I came along at the right time." That's true enough; he did "come along at the right time." The trouble is, *all* popular performers come along at the right time. So, we could make the history of rock 'n' roll sound like this: "First there was black rhythm 'n' blues; then Elvis and Chuck Berry and Buddy Holly and Little Richard and Jerry Lee Lewis came along; then the Motown groups and the girl groups and the Beach Boys came along; then the Beatles and the rest of the British Invasion came along and...." It all sounds as though we were sitting in the bleachers on New Year's Day in Pasadena, watching the floats in the Rose Bowl Parade go by. When people say that major acts "just came along at the right time," they imply that these acts were not affected by earlier performers, and that the audience is not affected by them either. I believe that both performers and audiences are affected by the music they grew up with, as well as other things, so that to explain the success of a given act, you need to make the social and cultural context of that success as specific as possible. That is a major goal of mine throughout this book.

Ever since that unforgettable day in 1954 when I first heard LaVern Baker's "Tweedle Dee" on a heavy 78 rpm record, I have learned a lot of things about rock 'n' roll and the society which produced it. It may help the reader if I mention a few of them at the outset. First and foremost, there was McLuhan's *Understanding Media*, a book which changed by life. And I am still thinking about what I read in Leslie Fiedler's *Love and Death in the American Novel*, as well as in Claude Levi-Strauss's *Structural Anthropology*.

More specifically, I think I first sensed the possibility of this book when I was reading Greil Marcus's *Mystery Train*. In his chapter on The Band, Marcus suggests that the group could make us hear, for a moment, the unity of American music, an unpredictable resolution of a "common inheritance."[4] That phrase has stayed with me, and has challenged me to explain just what that "common inheritance" is and how it gets resolved. In his book, *The Story of Rock*, Carl Belz points out that no one has ever been able to offer explanations such as these. And Henry Pleasants' perceptive *The Great American Popular Singers* gave me a useful model for analyzing popular vocal styles. So perhaps it is not too much to say that the diverse origins of this book match the diverse origins of the music which it interprets.

Finally, I need to thank the University of Missouri-Columbia, and especially Richard Wallace, Interim Dean of the College of Arts and Science, for granting me a year of Research Leave, during which I wrote most of this book. Very few institutions, and very few administrators, would have supported such an unusual project, and I deeply appreciate the belief in my work which this decision involved. I would also like to thank Jeanmarie Fraser, who was always willing to do another computer search for me, and Jeaneice Brewer and Carolyn Collings, who handled the numerous inter-library loans which I requested. *Rock Eras* is a richer and fuller book because of their readiness to help. My wife, Donna, helped me learn to write on a word processor, and how to do many other things as well. As for the shortcomings of the book. I take sole responsibility for them.

Columbia, Missouri

Notes

[1]Charles Hamm,The Fourth Audience," *Popular Music,* I (1983), pp. 123-141.

[2]I have compiled these facts about Betty's London debut from Sandra K. Norton, *William Henry West Betty: Romatic Child Actor,* unpublished dissertation, University of Missouri-Columbia, 1976, pp. 63-66.

[3]Michael Lydon, "Rock for Sale," in *Side-Saddle on the Golden Calf,* George H. Lewis, ed. (Pacific Palisades, CA: Goodyear Publishing Co., 1972), p. 314.

[4]Greil Marcus, *Mystery Train, Images of America in Rock 'N' Roll Music* (New York: Dutton, 1976), p. 34.

Some Principles

I do not believe that we can fully appreciate rock 'n' roll by talking only about the music and the performers and nothing else. It seems to me that the music has such vital connections with society and with technology that any full appreciation of it depends on an understanding of how society and technology operate in general. Thus, I am beginning here with a brief statement of the principles which inform this book.

Classics of any kind, whether they are songs or performances, mean more than their authors or performers intend them to mean. If they did not, they wouldn't interest us after the particular circumstances giving rise to them have disappeared. Since this is so, we can validly find meanings in classics which would not have made sense to the authors or performers. The conscious attitudes of creative people who work by intuition and feeling do not determine—and thus limit—our perceptions.

We have here the first of the many binary oppositions in this book, the opposition between conscious and unconscious meanings. Binary oppositions of this kind have begun to appear more and more frequently in the work of people who want to understand the interrelationships between the arts and society. This has happened in large part because French anthropologist Claude Levi-Strauss and other Structuralists have worked with them so successfully.

There is nothing mysterious about binary oppositions; even advertisers use them, as in the way Sears advertises its "plain pocket jeans." Plain pocket jeans acquire meaning in contrast to the designed jeans made by Calvin Klein, Gloria Vanderbilt, Jordache, and the others who put their names on the right back pocket to justify their higher prices. In the same way, binary oppositions operate in society to create meaning through contrast.

We can think of binary oppositions in two different ways. One way is to think of each term of the opposition as interacting with the other to form a whole. I call such an opposition a binary pair. The other way is to think of neither term as interacting with the other. I call such an opposition a dichotomy. We can often understand major innovations in music and elsewhere as resolutions of dichotomies into binary pairs.

The settling of America offers a case in point which may make the discussion less abstract. In the seventeenth century, the Puritans fled what they perceived as the godlessness of England in order to found "a city on a hill," as the famous phrase has it. They believed themselves different from those whom they had left behind, and sought to found a society which would accordingly differ from all others. Then, as Richard Slotkin points out in *Regeneration*

7

Through Violence, the Puritans found a land inhabited by people with darker skins, different mores, and many gods instead of one. As a result, they had a pervasive sense of their own differentness both from Europeans and from native Americans, and they bequeathed this sense of differentness to modern America. It is as though the Puritans said to the world, "We are what we are in ourselves, and you are different from us." Thus, we have as the primal opposition in American history:

SELF/OTHER

This opposition has had various meanings at various times in American history. Expressed as a dichotomy, self/other manifests itself as racism. After all, a major justification for slavery was that blacks were different from, i.e., inferior to, whites. More recently, the House Un-American Activities Committee provided a convenient example of what happens when politicians treat self/other as a dichotomy. Expressed as a binary pair, though, self/other expresses the cosmopolitan attitude best symbolized by the Statue of Liberty.

Another opposition often treated as a dichotomy in American life is high culture/popular culture, as in "Roll Over Beethoven." Like Chuck Berry, most Americans have chosen popular culture over high culture; I believe, however, that we don't have to choose. One man who didn't choose was Marshall McLuhan, from whom the principles of this book derive[1]. In his book *Understanding Media* we find sentences such as this one, "The advent of electric media released art from this strait jacket [of the printed word] at once, creating the world of Paul Klee, Picasso, Braque, Einstein, the Marx Brothers, and James Joyce"[2]. To someone who thinks of popular culture and high culture as a dichotomy, this grouping may seem startling, for it resolves that dichotomy into a binary pair by including the Marx Brothers among such mandarins of twentieth-century high culture as Picasso. McLuhan was *not* saying that the Marx Brothers' movies— *Duck Soup* (1933), for example—were in some sense "as good as" a painting by Picasso, for the very comparison is spurious. Rather, he was saying that both high culture, as well as popular culture, in the twentieth century constitute creative responses to their times.

We can say that both high culture and popular culture have their own validity by distinguishing them in the following way. If we associate high culture with time, and popular culture with space, then it appears that people appreciate works of high culture for long periods of time, but that works of popular culture disseminate more rapidly in space. That is to say, people may not appreciate the Rolling Stones a century after Mick Jagger's death as much as people appreciated Beethoven a century after *his* death. But the Rolling Stones have had an incomparably greater impact on their times than Beethoven had on his because so many more people have heard their music.

If we wish, we can learn to take both high culture and popular culture by relating them both to the social environments in which they appeared. Beethoven's music depended largely on the patronage of European nobles like Count Razumovsky, while the Rolling Stones' music belongs to an era when performers depend on popular acceptance. Naturally, the musical styles are different because they lived at different times.

To return to McLuhan, I take three key principles from him. First, history occurs as a series of social processes. That is to say, if we wish to understand historical events and historical figures, we cannot take them in isolation; rather, we must first define the larger process in which they take part.

Second, social processes are structured by the dominant media complex operating in the society at that time. Like McLuhan, I believe that technology is not passive and neutral because we learn—or internalize, to use the technical term—the relationships it creates just as we learn to speak our native language. And, just as we express ourselves by speaking that language, so we express those technological relationships in what we do and in what we create. When we act upon our environment, we extend ourselves through technology, which is more than TV sets and airplanes. To quote McLuhan again:

It is necessary to see literacy as typographic technology, applied not only to the rationalizing of the entire procedures of production and marketing, but to law and education and city planning as well. The principles of continuity, uniformity, and repeatability have, in England and America, long permeated every phase of communal life. In those areas a child learns literacy from traffic and street, from every car and toy and garment[3].

As this passage implies, McLuhan argues that people who become literate unconsciously acquire a mindset that involves the principles of uniformity and repeatability of the letters on the printed page, and that this process occurs independently of the meaning of the separate words. This is what he meant by his famous, and infamous, phrase,"The medium is the message." To summarize some complex matters, for McLuhan, literacy creates dichotomies such as the mind/body dichotomy which has so long bedevilled Western thought. In contrast to the hot dichotomies of literacy and mechanical technology, we now have the cool binary pairs of electrical technology, the technology which created rock 'n' roll. This new technology is creating what Walter Ong has called "secondary orality," a stage in the evolution of consciousness which has affinities with primary orality, but is not the same thing. Not surprisingly, many creative people in the twentieth century have come from areas which have what Ong calls "residual orality."

Third, McLuhan's comment about the way electricity released art from its strait jacket implies a relationship between creativity and technology. For McLuhan, creativity and technology constitute a binary pair, so that we can use each one to interpret the other. I think this assumption is essential, for I believe that technology is as natural a part of our environment as the weather, and that the great performers respond to it intuitively. Ignoring technology in writing about rock 'n' roll is like wondering why people are coming into the house wearing raincoats without bothering to ask whether it is raining outside.

We know that the styles of American popular music have changed, but very few people who write about music offer anything more than a chronological explanation of change; they say, in effect, as the times change so do musical styles. I believe that there is more to it than this, that change occurs in patterns which we can describe in simple language. Naturally, these patterns are never completely consistent and uniform; they always have exceptions and inconsistencies. The patterns which I discuss in this book merely describe tendencies, nothing more. Yet, after we make these allowances, patterns can hold up well enough to satisfy our profoundly human need to make sense of our lives.

Since rock 'n' roll has depended on electric media from its very beginning, I want to take the Laws of Media which McLuhan published in 1977 as a means of organizing the patterns in rock 'n' roll history. But the very word "laws" causes problems because it may suggest the kind of cause and effect relationship that the laws of physics describe. McLuhan never thought of his laws in this way; he thought of them as probes or metaphors. They are more like propositions to be tested, and that's what I want to do. In the pages that follow, I will treat media as interrelated complexes of images and styles; when one element of a complex changes, the others usually change as well. These complexes resemble a piece of music which cannot be divided up into parts without destroying the whole.

In music and clothing, fashions change rapidly, and one attractive feature of McLuhan's Laws is that they assume change as a constant. They embody in their inherently dynamic structure the assumption that things are constantly changing into other things, in the same way things happen in what we call real life. Since music itself is inherently dynamic, the general principles and the material at hand fit together nicely.

A final general point about McLuhan: Much of his work is exciting, not so much for the information it gives us, as for the possibilities it suggests. So, in any application of his work, the persuasiveness comes, not from any one statement, but from the cumulative effect of a series of internally consistent statements. Although something which explains one particular thing may not be a principle, something which explains a number of different things in different periods probably has some more general meaning.

McLuhan thinks of media evolution in the following way: he assumes that the appearance of a new medium does not annihilate previous media; rather, it causes a re-organization of previously existing relationships. In his provocative way, McLuhan cast his Laws not in verifiable propositions, but in the form of four questions which we can ask about any new medium:

What does it enhance?   What does it obsolesce?
What does it retrieve that had been obsolesced earlier?

What does it reverse into when pushed to the limits of its potential?[4]

In his work on media history, Paul Levinson has arranged these four questions into tetrad wheels, which show the dynamics of the process.

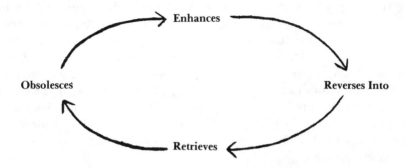

As a practical application of a tetrad wheel, consider Levinson's tetrad wheel for radio:

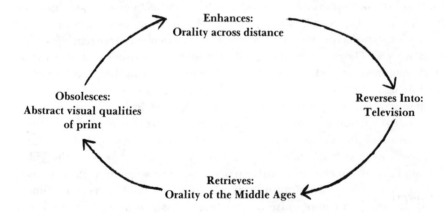

To put this tetrad wheel into propositional form, radio enhanced orality by broadcasting the sound of a human voice over great distances. It obsolesced the abstract visual qualities of print, which had previously provided the only means of disseminating information over great distances (notice that this does *not* mean that people stopped publishing newspapers; it means, rather, that radio caused people to think of newspapers in a new way). Radio retrieved the orality of the Middle Ages, which is to say that it did not create orality as a new phenomenon. And finally, radio reverses into television.

In the private communication on which I am drawing here, Levinson also says, "An especially interesting feature of the tetrad wheels, I think, is that the horizontal axis [obsolescence-reversal] is the ground, and the vertical axis [intensification-retrieval] is the figure"[5]. This figure/ground opposition, a recurring feature of McLuhan's thought, assumes that we perceive by contrast, that what we perceive—the figure—becomes perceptible against something— the ground—which contrasts with it, but which we don't associate with it.

For the purposes of this book, rock 'n' roll is the figure, and we have usually perceived it against the ground of television. Despite the epochal appearances of Elvis and the Beatles on the Ed Sullivan Show (and the memorable night when George Harrison appeared unannounced on The Smothers Brothers Comedy Hour), television did not play a significant role in the development of rock 'n' roll until MTV. For one thing, the very size of the picture has precluded the total involvement in the music which means so much. For another, it is characteristic of the highly visual society in which we live that engineers have devoted much more attention to the quality of the picture than to the quality of the sound.

Levinson also makes the point that, in working with the tetrad wheels, we need to keep in mind what he calls "the consistency of effect"; that is to say, there is no such thing as "the" set of answers to these questions, for there are as many possible tetrad wheels for each technology as technology has effects. So the tetrads which I offer here amount to compressions, or summaries, of numerous tetrads, since each one has elements from many possible tetrad wheels. They do not plot the development of a single strand, such as the development of rock 'n' roll in purely musical terms, because I want to make as many different kinds of connections as I can. In order to do this, I want to add some additional questions of my own to McLuhan's four questions.

My first question is: In what period did this medium operate as a force for innovation? In our media-saturated society, we have radio (AM, FM, and CB), television (with its various permutations such as network, cable, video discs, and games), and movies—just to name a few. A new medium may obsolesce another medium's capacity for innovation, which lasts only for a certain time.

I also want to compromise the pristine formalism of McLuhan's Laws by adding people to them. On one side of the medium, we have the performers, and thus a second question: What were the socio-ethnic origins of the performers who made the innovations? The sense of place remains problematic and troubling in such a mobile society as America, but I am still Southern enough to believe that it matters who your people are, and where you came from. These things may matter mostly in the negative sense that they give you something to run from, and they may matter in ways which you never fully understand. But they *do* matter, so I include an element in the overall pattern, something which I call "sociology," an account of the social, ethnic, and/ or class origins of the performers.

On the other side of the medium we have the audience, which is in a particular situation, and which I will call the "implied audience." Although people can listen to the same piece of music in different places, one of them usually feels better than others, and when the music changes, that place changes as well. It will become apparent that, in America, the crucial opposition in the situation of the audience is the opposition between public space and private space.

Now to get to rock 'n' roll at last: I believe that we can use McLuhan's augmented Laws to divide rock 'n' roll history (so far, anyhow) into three ten-year periods beginning in 1954, when rock 'n' roll began. The British invasion came in 1964, and disco appeared in 1974. In each of these ten-year periods, the first five years were a period of intense innovation, and ended in death. Buddy Holly died in 1959; the tumultuous year of 1969 gave us the Tate-La Bianca murders and the Rolling Stones' free concert at Altamont; in 1979, 11 teenagers died as they tried to get into a concert by The Who in Cincinnati. Logically, the second five years was a period of assimilation in each of the three decades.

Since television served as a ground against which we perceived rock 'n' roll, each of these three major periods followed a major crisis in American political life, a crisis which involved us all, because we saw it on television. In 1953, we watched the Army-McCarthy hearings; in 1963, we watched President Kennedy's funeral (and for years afterward asked each other where we were when we first heard the news); and in 1973, we watched the Watergate hearings. Each of these crises gave the lie to the lessons which we had learned in tenth-grade civics classes, and the recurring conflict between the American dream and the American reality caused a tension which the music released. In each case, of course, it was a different kind of music which we enjoyed in a different kind of space.

There was a great deal of American popular music before rock 'n' roll, of course. Like rock 'n' roll, that music often makes sense in terms of its socio-ethnic composition and its use of technology. This generalization especially applies to the great performers, and we can understand the continuity between rock 'n' roll and what went before it by applying it to the greatest of the great—Bing Crosby, Frank Sinatra, and Elvis Presley.

Notes

[1] I have discussed McLuhan's work in detail in *Culture as Polyphony. An Essay on the Nature of Paradigms* (Columbia: U. of Missouri Press, 1978).

[2] Marshall McLuhan, *Understanding Media. The Extensions of Man* (New York: McGraw-Hill, 1964), p. 54.

[3] *Ibid.*, p. 300.

[4] Marshall McLuhan. "Laws of the Media," *et cetera*, Vol. 34, No. 2 (June, 1977), p. 175.

[5] Letter to the author from Paul Levinson, dated 10 April 1981.

SECTION I

Bing, the Chairman, and the King

Two factors have revolutionized twentieth-century America: the appearance of technological innovations and the flood of immigrants from eastern and southern Europe. Naturally, these factors have revolutionized twentieth-century American popular culture as well, and have shaped the careers of the three greatest popular singers of our time. For there are only three great ones, if we consider singers as singers, and disregard the singer-songwriter-instrumentalists from Chuck Berry to Bruce Springsteen; they are Bing Crosby, Frank Sinatra, and Elvis Presley. Each man can claim a superlative: Bing was the best loved, Frank was the greatest artist, and Elvis was the greatest social phenomenon. Their careers have definite patterns which link them together than Elvis', but Frank and Elvis are much more alike as personalities.

The crucial fact that unites them is that all three were immigrants in different ways. Before we consider the meaning of immigration and assimilation for each of them, let us pause to note historian Gilbert Ostrander's comments on the general significance of immigration:

The century of America's first machine age was also the century of the great European exodus, and the European migration to America during the century after 1820 equaled three times the total population of the United States in 1820. German and Irish immigrants arrived in the north-eastern United States by the hundreds of thousands annually from the 1840's on: beginning in the 1880's, they were joined by the "New Immigration" from southeastern and central Europe; and beginning early in the twentieth century, American cities absorbed the mass migration of Negroes from the southern countryside as well. This ethnic assimilation, compounded by technological revolution, had comprehensively transformed the American national character by the eve of World War II[1].

German and Irish immigration in the 1840's gave rise to the first organized expression of innocence (or nativism, as it is called in politics), the Know-Nothing Party. But of far greater consequence was the Jewish immigration, which amounted to 1.5 million between 1880 and 1910. These Jews came from the urban areas of eastern Europe (Minsk, Kiev, Warsaw, and so forth), and tended to stay in the urban areas of America; barred from many professions and possessing a vigorous tradition in the performing arts, they had an

15

extraordinary effect on popular culture (as well as on science and high culture, of course).

Repressed minorities need to have a shrewd sense of what the majority public likes in order to survive, so it doesn't seem surprising that Jewish immigrants such as Adolph Zukor, Louis B. Mayer, Samuel Goldwyn (born Samuel Goldfisch in the Warsaw ghetto), and the Warner brothers dominated the movie studios from the twenties through the fifties. Then, too, there were the great Jewish songwriters such as Irving Berlin, Jerome Kern, and George and Ira Gershwin. In McLuhan's terms, the extraordinary success of Jews in American show business does not mean that they have a natural sense of rhythm, any more than blacks do. Rather, their success comes from the energy released by the fragmentation of a traditional, oral society during assimilation into the literate environment of American life.

It was the music that Irving Berlin and the others wrote that McLuhan was referring to when he noted that the word "melody" comes from the Greek *"melos modos,* 'the road round,'...a continuous, connected, and repetitive structure that is not used in the 'cool' art of the Orient"[2]. This continuity occurs only in literate societies. Musicologist Charles Hamm describes such music as "tonal" (it begins and ends on a certain tone), uses triadic chords, and is goal-oriented in that each given piece moves toward a climax. The climax in "The Star-Spangled Banner," for instance, occurs on the word "free" in the line "O'er the land of the free." These characteristics occur in most post-Renaissance Western music, whether it is popular music, or Beethoven[3].

It is important to understand that the music of Beethoven shares this characteristically literate structure with the music of Irving Berlin, because the first great rock 'n' rollers-like the first great jazzmen-came from areas characterized by what Walter Ong has called "residual orality," and they challenged and changed that structure. They did so because they came from a society which had internalized literacy to a lesser degree than Yankee America.

Although he does not use the term "oral society," Henry Pleasants is implying what that term means for performance styles when he speaks of a singer who:

...could not see artistic value in moving cleanly from, say, C to G, when his intuition sensed melodic and rhetorical substance in uncharted pitches between the authorized modes. So, while accepting the European diatonic major and minor modes, and a European four-beats-to-the-bar-rhythm, he bent the notes and shifted the rhythmic accentuation to suit his communicative purpose, achieving a rhetorical elegance previously unknown in Western music[4].

Considering the importance of black performers in twentieth-century America, Pleasants calls this an "Afro-American" idiom, and the first great performer who used it, the first true superstar of modern America, was Al Jolson, whose life and career show some of the patterns which are repeated and varied in the lives and careers of Bing, Frank, and Elvis.

Al Jolson was born Asa Yoelson in Srednicke, in Russian Lithuania. His father was a rabbi who emigrated to America in 1890, at the height of the Jewish immigration. Thus, Al Jolson's life shows a working out of what I call the three-generation" theory[5], in which the fragmentation of an oral society, and the expression of that fragmentation in a famous person, takes three generations. I first noticed this pattern while reading Erik Erikson's *Young Man Luther*. Erikson shows that Martin Luther's grandfather lived the traditional life of a German peasant, his father made the break from farming to become a miner, and Luther began the Reformation. This pattern seems to have been inherent in the breakup of traditional societies in the West, for it also appears in the lives of Adolph Hitler and Joseph Stalin.

The three-generation pattern appears clearly in Al Jolson's life. His grandfather lived a traditional life in a poverty-ridden nineteenth-century *stettl*, his father moved to America, and Jolson left an estate of $4,000,000 when he died at his Palm Springs home in 1950. But the fragmentation in attitudes which show-business success on this scale requires means a secularization of values as well. As with Martin Luther (and with Hitler, too, for that matter), tension usually arises between the father and the grandson on this point. It disturbed Jolson's devout father a great deal that his son was singing secular music, and it is most appropriate that this conflict appears in *The Jazz Singer* (1928). (This same conflict between cantoral and secular singing appears in the careers of Jews who wanted to become opera singers as well—as the life of Richard Tucker shows.) In fact, Pleasants claims to hear traces of cantoral diction in Jolson's singing. But, paradoxically for the man who starred in the first talkie, Jolson could not deal with, or accept, technology; and thus he limited his own fame. As someone once said, "he needed the contact with a live audience like a diabetic needs insulin." He never reached the stature of Bing, Frank, and Elvis.

While discussing Bing, Frank, and Elvis, I want to define "talent," that amorphous quality usually measured by popularity (just as popularity is defined by talent), as the merger of the two factors which I mentioned at the beginning. "Talent" can be defined as the process of the merger of the socio-ethnic group from which the performer came, and the performer's intuitive ability to sense the possibilities of new technology. By general agreement, Bing Crosby had a lot of talent.

Bing Crosby was born in Tacoma, Washington, May 2, 1904 (or 1901—there is some disagreement about the year) into a Catholic family. His forbears presumably came over from Ireland during the wave of immigration in the mid-nineteenth century, so his life does not conform to the three-generation pattern, as Jolson's does. But the Irish connection proved important for him because the Irish have a long-established tradition of performance on which he could, and did, draw. As a matter of fact, one of Bing's uncles, a certain George Harrigan, had a fine Irish tenor voice, and became a local singing star in the Tacoma-Seattle area. Catholicism creates few of the conflicts between secular and sacred performance that Jews such as Jolson experienced. We also need to remember that Bing attended Gonzaga High School in Spokane, a Jesuit institution where public speaking was a priority subject, and elocution competitions were held regularly. Bing attributed much of his later success, his confidence in public, his ability to project his voice, and so forth, to this early training.

But Bing did not have to project his voice as Jolson had. He became famous for his crooning style, of course, and that crooning style depended on the presence of a microphone. A full explanation of its meaning requires a brief digression here.

Technology does more than fragment oral societies; it also determines the styles of the music which the great performers create. Occasionally, a detail will serve as a part for the whole, and explain, in the most general terms of course, the major features of an era. Consider, for example, the importance of the trumpet for jazz in the twenties (Kid Ory, Louis Armstrong, and Bix Beiderbecke), and then of the trombone and saxophone (Tommy Dorsey and Lester Young) for the big bands in the thirties and forties. A holistic explanation of the instrumental lineup of these bands has to do with the situation in which people listened to the music. Now, the nightclubs and dance halls in which people listened to jazz and swing did not always have the acoustics of Carnegie Hall, and the audience did not always concentrate on the music. So brasses and reeds, not strings, predominated because they could produce and sustain the necessary volume.

The same thing applies to recording techniques. As one historian of the record industry has put it, "The enormous volume capacities of the brass and percussion instruments had been ideally suited to the recording facilities of the day, but of course they had not been able to approach the subtle sound of the violin with its soft overtones."[6] Since recording technology before 1925 could not accommodate stringed instruments, it could also not accommodate crooners.

The popularity of Bing's distinctive style was a response to the invention of the microphone and of electrical recording techniques in the middle twenties, when the changeover from the crude acoustic microphones to the increasingly sensitive electric microphones began. Pleasants says that Bing "was, in effect, overheard by the microphone."[7] Bing didn't sing at the microphone, as Jolson did, he sang *into* it. Particularly on Bing's early recordings for Okeh, and the other small labels in the early thirties, he "sounds as if he were leaning over the piano in your own parlor singing to you,"[8] as a radio announcer of the time put it. As a matter of fact, Bing's only failure as a performer came when he and his partner Al Rinker were playing the Paramount Theater in New York with Paul Whiteman's band. As Bing's biographer explains the situation, "These were the days before microphones on stage and the Paramount was much larger than any theater they had played before. The audience just couldn't hear them..."[9]

Technology in the form of the microphone, in effect, displaced the music and changed the relationship between performer and audience. Before the twenties, when people listened to a band and a singer, they had been occupying public space in a concert hall or theater designed for that purpose. Now, people could listen to a band and a singer in private space, in their houses and apartments, by simply turning on the radio or record player. This crucial change in the stylistic history of popular music did not happen once and for all, however; a constantly changing dialectic between public and private space continues to operate in popular music even today.

For Bing, the presence of the microphone meant that he could croon, not belt, so that, in effect, he was the last of the parlor singers. People heard his radio programs every week in their parlors. They thought of him as a friend of the family, not a star. His style seemed so simple that they believed anybody could do it; it reinforced the impression that he was really one of them. This simplicity and familiarity enabled him to convey a whole society's despair in "Brother, Can You Spare A Dime?" And, of course, his celebration of our biggest holiday, "White Christmas," remains the most popular record ever made. Clearly, then, Bing democratized popular singing (his immediate predecessor, Rudy Vallee, had gone to Yale, after all).

Bing helped to move the locus of popular music from New York to the West Coast, away from connotations of elitism. Bing was also a true innocent in that he disliked the trappings of show business; he wore casual, comfortable clothes, and his passion for golf at times seriously hampered the development of his career. Yet, we notice that Bing's lack of ambition also comes from his need, possibly unconscious, to play the prosperous Irish squire. After he sowed his wild oats in the twenties, he settled down with a nice Catholic girl, was a stern disciplinarian to his children, and went to horse races whenever he could.

Francis Albert Sinatra was born on December 12, 1915 in Hoboken, New Jersey. His life conforms to the three-generation pattern very well indeed. Because his paternal grandfather lived in Sicily, Frank thinks of himself as Sicilian. His parents came to this country and achieved a certain level of middle-class success. Like Martin Luther's parents, Frank's parents wanted him to choose a safe career; they strongly opposed his desire to enter show business.

Until the publication of the autobiography on which he is supposedly working, the most informative statements about his performance style that Frank has made are in an article, "Me and My Music," which appeared in *Life* in 1965. In it, he explicitly links himself with an Italian tradition of performance, in the same way that Bing had a family precedent for singing in his uncle. Frank says that he searched for a distinctive style of his own and "What I finally hit on was more the *bel canto* Italian school of singing, without making a point of it."[10] As Pleasants explains, *bel canto* exploits *rubato*, the practice of stealing time from one note in a phrase and giving it to another, and it is Frank's *rubato* that creates his distinctive phrasing, as when he holds the word "go" in the first line of "You Go To My Head." But his impeccable, distinctive style balances *rubato* with *legato,* the smooth passage from one note to another. As it happens, Frank tells us that he learned this *legato* from an odd musical couple, Tommy Dorsey and Jascha Heifetz.

In the middle of a phrase, while the tone was still being carried through the trombone, he'd go *shhh* and take a quick breath and play another four bars with that breath. Why couldn't a singer do that too? Fascinated, I began listening to other soloists. I bought every Jascha Heifetz record I could find and listened to him play the violin hour after hour. His constant bowing, where you never heard a break, carried the melody straight on through, just like Dorsey's trombone[11].

Here we have the *melos modos,* the flowing continuity to which McLuhan referred, which no singer had ever developed so consciously or masterfully.

But Frank could never have sung to very many people in this way without the microphone, and he knows it.

One thing that was tremendously important was learning the use of the microphone. Many singers never learned to use one. They never understood, and still don't, that a microphone is their instrument. It's *like they were part of the orchestra,* but instead of playing a saxophone they're playing a microphone[12].

For all of Frank's desire to sing as though he were part of the orchestra, he surely knows that, by their very nature, the big bands limited the importance of the singer. Their popularity had caused them to grow, so that by 1940, when Frank joined the Tommy Dorsey Orchestra, it numbered 19 musicians. Several of those musicians, most obviously Tommy himself, were virtuoso performers in their own right. Such size precluded the exciting improvisations of jazz in the twenties and required elaborate orchestrations which subordinated the singer to an overall effect. The fact that Tommy would not allow Frank's name to appear on the records that Frank made with his orchestra tells us a lot about the role of the singer in big bands. There was merely an indication of "Vocal Chorus," and that anonymous vocal chorus usually followed an instrumental introduction of at least 32 bars.

Frank thus found himself in a paradoxical situation in the early forties. On one hand, by using the microphone, he could sing over the brass and reed section on which he had modelled his style, but on the other, the arrangement treated him like the proverbial cog in a machine. As a result of this tension, Frank broke with Tommy after staying with him for two and half years. The microphone isolated the singer from the backup group, and thus began a trend which affects popular music even today.

Like most stylistic innovations, Frank's emergence from the big band had a precedent, and one which demonstrated that high culture and popular culture evolve in similar ways. The microphone was to the big band what the heavy nineteenth-century piano was to the symphony orchestra. In terms of performers, Frank was to twentieth-century popular culture what Franz Liszt was to nineteenth-century high culture. As the nineteenth century progressed, changes in the manufacture of pianos produced a bigger piano than the one which Mozart had played. This instrument could maintain very high tensions on the strings, and thus produce greater volume. This greater volume isolated the soloist from the symphony, and created the possibility for Liszt's virtuoso displays. Similarly, the microphone gave the singers more volume, and isolated them from the big bands. Liszt could thus dominate an orchestra when he played a concert just as Frank could dominate a big band when he sang. Arnold Shaw calls Frank a "twentieth-century Romantic," and so he was, just as Liszt was a nineteenth-century Romantic. Both men exploited technological innovations which made it possible for them to display their personalities and egos (Not coincidentally, both men had a similar effect on women).

The years with Dorsey formed both Frank's style and his repertory; they gave him his phrasing and his songs which he has been singing for forty years now: "I'll Never Smile Again" (his first big song, from 1940), "The Song Is You," "Night and Day," and so forth. But because of the tension between the singer and the big band, Frank did not sing at his best with Dorsey. His voice, while clearly The Voice, sounds thin and unexciting on his 1940 recording of "Fools Rush In," with the Dorsey band.

Frank's greatest musical achievements came some twenty years later, from about 1955 to 1965—that is to say, from the time Elvis burst into national prominence to the British Invasion. As Arnold Shaw reminds us in his biography of Frank, in the 1957 *Down Beat* readers poll, he outpointed his nearest contender for the top male singer by ten to one; he won the *Metronome* poll so overwhelmingly that the editors commented, "Sinatra literally devoured this one; there was no chance for anyone else." They put him on their cover as Mr. Personality, while *Jazz 1957* named him and Billie Holliday as Singers of the Year[13].

In 1962, Frank released no fewer than four albums which went gold: *This Is Sinatra; Frank Sinatra Sings for Only the Lonely; Songs for Swingin' Lovers;* and *Nice 'N' Easy*. Nelson Riddle, a big band veteran and a former trombonist, arranged these albums, even including "Fools Rush In," (which Frank had first recorded 22 years earlier) on *Nice 'N' Easy*. The title of a slightly later album, *Sinatra and Strings*, tells us what makes these albums great music.

The improved recording studios which created rock 'n' roll also created Frank's best work. The microphones could pick up the lush strings which had replaced the brasses and reeds without letting them compete with him, or interfering with his exquisite phrasing. If the big band sound was predicated on public performance, these albums were for home listening—preferably on the living room couch. In the phrase of the day, Frank was singing classic makeout music.

Just as Liszt was not the first or only nineteenth-century piano virtuoso, Frank was not the first or only singing star who emerged from a big band. Although they were the greatest at what they did, and had the greatest public impact, they appeared as the culmination of a clear evolution. Bing had sung with Paul Whiteman before beginning a solo career, and Frank had many contemporaries whose careers resemble his. Virtually all the white popular singers of the post-war era, such as Doris Day and Perry Como, began their careers with big bands, and then broke with them.

The third of our great performers is Elvis Presley, who was born on January 8, 1935, in Tupelo, Mississippi into a Southern fundamentalist family; his parents belonged to the Pentecostal Church. To understand the magnitude of his popular impact, let us consider the following statistics:

—Elvis' first movie, *Love Me Tender* (1956), recouped its production costs *in three days;* no other movie before or since has ever done that.
—Elvis is the only major movie star whose every movie made money. Bing may have won an Academy Award for *Going My Way* (1949), and Frank may have won one for *From Here to Eternity* (1953), but by the bottom line by which Hollywood lives, Elvis is the greatest movie star ever.
—In his 22-year recording career, from 1955 to 1977, Elvis placed 737 records on Billboard's 100. That averages out to about 3 songs per month, *every month,* for 22 years. No other group or performer has ever had such a constant string of hits.

It is facts like these that we need to explain, and explain by resorting to more than vague generalities like "Elvis came along at the right time."

Everyone knows that Elvis was born in Tupelo, that his parents were poor, and that he moved to Memphis when he was thirteen. But no one seems to have noticed that his life conforms to the pattern of assimilation which occurs in immigrant families. His grandfather worked as a sharecropper, his father moved from the country to the city (first to Tupelo, and then to Memphis), and the son became famous. We can thus consider him an immigrant like Al Jolson and Frank Sinatra, in whose lives the three-generation pattern also appears. Indeed, sociologist Lewis Killiam has argued forcefully that we should consider white Southerners—especially poor white Southerners, the "poor white trash," from whom Elvis came—as a minority group like blacks or Italians[14].

If Al Jolson, Bing Crosby, Frank Sinatra, and Elvis Presley all descended from immigrants, and if the traditions of the homeland significantly affected their lives and careers, may we not find some general similarities among Russia, Ireland, Sicily, and the South? I think we may. The South's most perceptive journalist, Marshall Frady, has written, "But no matter how tatty a commonplace it became, the final truth is that the South *did* long constitute something like another country within the map of the United States. It amounted to something like America's Ireland or America's Sicily.[15]

Indeed, if we compare Russia, Ireland, Sicily, and the South, we find that all four regions have been poor, have been largely dependent on agriculture, and therefore subject to famine, as in the cases of Russia and Ireland. Many people have understandably wanted to leave, and emigration has repeatedly depleted their populations. Another reason for leaving has been that all four regions have had violent histories, replete with racial and sectional strife; this to say that they all treat self/other as a dichotomy, that they define themselves as different from neighboring regions. As a result, the oppositions, Russia and the West, Ireland and England, Sicily and northern Italy, and the South and the North all have the same resonance; and these defensive attitudes have given rise to similar mythologies.

Elvis was an immigrant, but he was a *WASP* immigrant, and this apparent contradiction offers a key to his fabulous success. As Pleasants puts it, "Adult white Americans who can have had little, if any, knowledge of the black origins of Elvis' songs, or of his way with them, sensed an exotic, alien atavistic presence, something from outside their own culture and traditional environment."[16] Elvis thus had the exotic appeal of a foreigner—that is, someone from a more oral society—as Rudolph Valentino had had. But at the same time he was a *WASP* from the interior of America, where most people lived. These people could, and ultimately did, identify him with God, motherhood, and country, as they never could with any other performer.

Elvis and Frank dominated American popular music during the period 1954-1959 as no other two performers have ever dominated any period before or since. To understand the links between them is to gain insight into the complexity of American music in the fifties.

Elvis' television debut may serve as a case in point. Everyone knows, more or less, that Elvis sang on the Ed Sullivan Show on September 9, 1956; what people forget is that he first appeared on national television on January 28 of that year on *Stage Show*, for which none other than Tommy and Jimmy Dorsey served as hosts. It was, of course, the Dorsey brothers for whom Frank had sung in the early forties, and Elvis attracted Tommy Dorsey's attention for very much the same reasons as Frank had. On that program, Elvis sang "Blue Suede Shoes," and the Dorsey orchestra backed him up when he introduced "Heartbreak Hotel." Elvis' appearance with the Dorseys dramatizes the continuity between the big bands and rock 'n' roll, as well as between Frank and Elvis.

Moreover, Elvis and Frank once appeared on the same program. When Elvis returned from the Army in 1960, Frank hosted a television special, "Welcome Home, Elvis." Later, in the seventies, Elvis began to include the song "My Way" in his concerts, which Paul Anka had written for Frank in 1968—as if to acknowledge his affinity in stature with Frank. Like Frank, Elvis did not play an instrument (in any serious way, at least), and he did not usually write his own material. So we may say that Elvis represented, not so much the beginning of something new, as the culmination of a developmental process which had begun in the late twenties with Bing.

Elvis and Frank had a number of hits with similar themes. These two major sex symbols, profoundly romantic men who drove women crazy in performance, often sang songs in which they vowed fidelity and abject submission to one woman (Cf. the first big hit for Johnny Cash: "I Walk the Line"). This powerful combination of physical appeal and emotional commitment produced the following pairs of songs:

Elvis:	Frank:
"Any Way You Want Me'	"All of Me"
"Don't Be Cruel"	"Prisoner of Love"
"Loving You"	"You'll Always Be the One I Love"
"A Fool Such As I"	"Fools Rush In"
	(and "I'm a Fool to Want You")
"I'm Gonna Sit Right Down	"I'm Gonna Sit Right Down
and Cry Over You"	and Write Myself A Letter"

To be sure, these immensely desirable men won't wait forever ("It's Now or Never" and "Don't Wait Too Long"), but generally they want to settle down ("Wear My Ring Around Your Neck" and "Love and Marriage").

Elvis and Frank were self-made men, and they created themselves with their clothing before they made themselves rich and famous with their singing. More indicatively than anything else, their attitude toward clothing distinguished them from Bing. While Bing took little interest in clothing, preferring a hat (to hide his baldness) and old golf outfits, Frank and Elvis both became dandies as young men.

Even as a teenager, Frank acquired the nickname "Slacksey" because he kept his slacks neatly pressed all the time. And Arnold Shaw tells us that when he was travelling with the Tommy Dorsey Orchestra:

Band members were...impressed by his cleanliness. Despite the rigors of travelling and no matter how rushed the trip was, he would not sit down to eat at a dirty table. Nor could band members understand how, after long hours in the bus, Frank would emerge with his clothes immaculate. He insisted on showers, sometimes two or three a day when facilities were available[17].

Shaw also mentions that Frank used to wash his hands so frequently that it became a standing joke. Frank seems to have had some of the immigrant's guilt about breaking with the old ways.

Here is how Johnny Burnette describes the way Elvis dressed when he was the same age: "Whenever I saw him, and that was often, he'd be wearing purple pants with black stripes down the side, white buck shoes and a pink sports jacket. He'd always have his shirt collar turned up and would wear his hair real long."[18] The difference between Frank and Elvis continued even when they had enough money to buy anything they wanted. Frank's idea of an appropriate outfit for a concert went no further than a custom-made tuxedo. But Elvis ordered Nudie, the Hollywood tailor to the stars, to whip up his famous gold lame suit. And later, in the seventies, he wore for his concerts in Las Vegas the spangled white jump-suit-like outfits with the high collars which served as surrogate crowns for the King of Rock 'N' Roll. Less obvious than the sartorial differences is the fact that Frank and Elvis belong to readily identifiable types of dandies.

At about the same Master Betty was knocking them dead in the London theaters, Beau Brummell was making his name a symbol for fastidious dressing. This arch Romantic was the progenitor of what we might call conformist dandies, of whom Frank is an excellent example. Contrary to popular belief, Beau had a horror of attracting attention to himself; he wore the same clothing as everyone else—only his was of better material and more finely cut. He specifically anticipates Frank in his mania for cleanliness, which was a most revolutionary attitude in 1800. Elvis, on the other hand, belongs to the eccentric dandies like Oscar Wilde, who wanted to flaunt their individuality. Elvis would wear a pink sport coat and turned up collar; Wilde wore a green velvet coat with a drooping lily in his buttonhole. As a poor white Southerner, Elvis had much the same need to distinguish himself, to create an identity, as Wilde, a gay Irishman in England.[19]

Elvis' clothing, if nothing else, qualified him to sing Carl Perkins' "Blue Suede Shoes." This song strikes a genuinely new note in American popular music, a privative quality in someone whose dandyism expresses his sense of self as something discrete from society. The song takes on great force because it is set in a hillbilly ambience—Elvis' accent would tell us that even without the reference to keeping liquor in a "fruit jar"—at a time when white middle-class society generally considered poor whites as second-class citizens. "Blue Suede Shoes" does not imply revolt, if we think of revolt in the European sense of social involvement; it proclaims revolt as a withdrawal from society, and thus an intensification of a private sense of the self. "Blue Suede Shoes" evoked just what teenagers were feeling in 1956, and they went wild over the song.

Redneck though he was, Elvis was never just a good ole boy. Linda Ray Pratt catches the ambivalence in his life and in his image very well when she writes that, "The paradox of Elvis was that he was able simultaneously to reveal the reality of the modern South while concealing it in a myth of the American Dream. He was at once both 'King' and outsider.[20] With this ambivalence in mind, we can begin to specify what we mean when we say that "Elvis came along at the right time."

Speaking very generally, we can identify two major traditions in the history of twentieth-century American popular music. These two traditions arose in different parts of the country among different ethnic groups, and produced different kinds of music. Each one has predominated for part of the twentieth century.

First, there was the New York tradition which we usually refer to as Tin Pan Alley. Although there were important exceptions such as Cole Porter, most of its greatest songwriters were Jewish immigrants from Eastern Europe (It is interesting to note that Irving Berlin, the man who wrote "God Bless America," was born in Russia). In addition to Berlin, the major names include Jerome Kern, George and Ira Gerschwin, Richard Rogers and Lorenz Hart (and Rodgers' second lyricist Oscar Hammerstein). With the advent of the talkies, a number of these men moved to Hollywood to score musicals. So, since throughout this book I will be associating musical styles with their places of origins, I prefer to call Tin Pan Alley the New York-Hollywood tradition. As this tradition matured with such great shows as *Porgy and Bess* (1935), and such great movie musicals as *Forty-Second Street* (1933), the songs often had a dramatic function in that they revealed character or set up conflicts. Yet, even when they did not, as in the case of the Jerome Kern songs which Flo Ziegfeld inserted into his reviews, they were presented in a theatrical setting.

Musically, the New York-Hollywood tradition derived from nineteenth-century high culture, and generally followed its harmonic practices. To state a complex matter very briefly, this music was tonal in that it began and ended on a certain tone, was polyphonic in that it sounded notes together as chords, and was goal-oriented in that it progressed toward a clearly audible climax.

The second great tradition in American popular music is the Southern tradition. It arose in the South during the Reconstruction, and spread northward from New Orleans and the Mississippi delta to Chicago, and westward into Texas and Oklahoma. This was the tradition of Southern blacks, with its African emphasis on percussion rather than melody, but it was also the music of Southern whites as well. This music tends to employ the pentatonic scale of folk musics the world over, and consequently has ambiguous keys and usually lacks a definite climax. As a result, it has an emotional resonance rather than a narrative structure. This quality fitted in well with its setting, for it was performed in brothels, bars, and dance halls—in fact, almost anywhere except in theaters.

This Southern tradition embraced considerably greater variety than the New York-Hollywood tradition, including as it did jazz and gospel and the blues and country music. It was from this tradition, and as an amalgam of this tradition, that rock 'n' roll in the persons of Elvis, Jerry Lee Lewis, Chuck Berry, and Little Richard appeared. We can say, then, that the larger significance of the rock revolution was that in about 1954 the Southern tradition began to challenge the national dominance of the New York-Hollywood tradition.

This change did not come about overnight, and it never came about completely. Throughout the fifties, and indeed until Beatlemania, the New York-Hollywood tradition continued to turn out very successful songs from hit plays and movies. I want to argue that the ambivalence of the relationship between these two great traditions in the fifties is the key to the ambivalence in Elvis. Although it was Elvis' fate to begin the transition from the dominance of one of America's great musical traditions in popular music to the other, he himself never completed this transition. His affinities with both of these traditions enabled him to pull unprecedented audiences, and to evoke unprecedented adulation. Because he has so many affinities with Frank, Elvis is as much the last great crooner as he is the first great rocker. To think of him as either one or the other is to diminish his stature, and to refuse to recognize him for what he was.

We can personalize Elvis' ambivalence by thinking of him in 1952, when, at the age of seventeen, he was just another redneck who was not even very well liked by other rednecks. What performers was he listening to? Typically, he was listening to representatives of both the New York-Hollywood tradition, and the Southern tradition as well. His musical ambivalence stretched between Dean Martin on one hand and the Blackwood Brothers on the other.

Elvis' admiration for Dean Martin in 1952 may seem puzzling at first, but upon consideration it makes sense. Like Elvis, Dean was an outsider, and, Italian, but one who had made it big, and who had received the acceptance by the world outside Tupelo and Memphis for which Elvis yearned. Dean served more as a role model for Elvis than as an immediate influence on him.

Although the early Elvis doesn't sound anything like Dean does on any of his hits from the early fifties, like "If" and "Sway," the later Elvis used a similar throwaway delivery. Moreover, Dean's devil-may-care stage persona may have contributed something to the loose, wise-cracking Elvis of the Las Vegas stage shows. The fact that Dean and Elvis, for all their differences, both played Las Vegas reminds us that they were two of the four performers who made it in the fifties, and who went on to become megastars. The other two were Dean's sometime partner, Jerry Lewis, and Liberace (I do hope that someday someone will write something on Liberace as Elvis' alter ego). All four of them gravitated to Hollywood and Las Vegas. When Elvis went to Hollywood, he made movies which were no more ambitious than the ones which Dean had made with Jerry Lewis, such at *The Stooge* (1952).

Thus, for Elvis in 1952, Dean was more of a symbol than anything else— a symbol of the New York-Hollywood tradition, which turned out crooners. If we listen carefully to the legendary Sun sessions of 1954 and 1955, where rock 'n' roll begins, we can hear the part of Elvis which felt the attraction of this tradition. The most obvious case in point is that, in addition to the songs recorded by black jump bands and white country artists, Elvis recorded the Rodgers and Hart classic from 1933, "Blue Moon" (Perhaps he had heard the version which Mel Torme recorded in 1949). He sings it in the same hard, brilliant tenor which he uses for he first version of "I Love You Because." But if Elvis was the last of the great crooners, he was the first of the great rockers, so the Sun sessions have a schizophrenic quality, On "I'll Never Let You Go," Elvis croons the first part, and then he and the boys segue into a rockabilly version of the second chorus. Like so much else in Elvis' career, this song shows that he never decided between the Southern tradition he grew up with and the New York-Hollywood tradition which promised to make his dreams come true.

Rockabilly was a distinctly Southern style, so we now need to ask, "What was Southern about Elvis?" In one of the most famous lines in show biz history, Sam Phillips said, "If I could find a white man who could sing like a black man, I'd make a million dollars." People often take Elvis' success to mean that Sam had found the man he was looking for, and that Elvis was just another white who stole black music. Even in the early seventies, Greil Marcus realized that, "It is probably time to say that this is nonsense; the mysteries of black and white in American music are just not that simple."[22] Among other things, we can wonder just how much black music Elvis knew. He knew the sound of black jump bands, and some black gospel, but probably not much more than that. He might have heard some B.B. King and Muddy Waters records, but they don't seem to have affected him. I cannot believe that the giants of down home blues such as Son House, Charley Patton, and Robert Johnson were anything more than names to him. Richard Middleton is certainly right when he says that, "The rough tone, spontaneous, irregular rhythms, and 'dirty' intonation that most blues singers would have used are for the most part conspicuously absent from Elvis's performance."[23] The "deep blues," as Robert Palmer calls the work of these men from the Delta, never had more than limited popular appeal, even among blacks, and Elvis wanted popularity and acceptance above all.

The evidence of the Sun sessions certainly supports this judgement. Elvis, bassist Bill Black, drummer D.J. Fontana, and guitarist Scotty Moore cut songs like Big Boy Crudup's "That's All Right"; Arthur Gunter's "Baby Let's Play House," which had been a local hit on Excello in Nashville; and Ray Brown's "Good Rockin' Tonight," which had done well for Winonie Harris. On none of these songs does Elvis sound like any identifiable black singer; while his voice has the microtonal richness of the bluesmen, he is already his own man.

Elvis and the boys didn't sweeten up black songs to make them acceptable to white audiences, as Pat Boone soon started doing; they fundamentally re-cast them, as a comparison between Elvis' and Winonie Harris' "Good Rockin' Tonight" shows. Winonie's version is a fine jump band record which sounds a lot like a Count Basie arrangement, with lots of gutsy brass. Scotty's electric semi-solid guitar substitutes for the whole brass section on Elvis' version, which gives the song a lighter quality. If the song is less powerful, it is correspondingly more hypnotic.

A comparison of Elvis' "Hound Dog" with the original by Big Mama Thornton shows an even more striking contrast. Big Mama sings "Hound Dog" like the novelty song "How Much Is That Doggie in the Window?" which was a hit at the time. She plays with the song, and even pretends to howl like a hound. She simply doesn't take it seriously. It's hard to believe that Elvis is singing the same song because he breathes fire and passion into what she took for a joke. By any applicable criterion, Elvis' version is better, stronger, and more deeply felt than hers.

The Sun sessions transform country and western songs no less radically. Elvis' acoustic guitar works with the bass and drums to form a rhythm section which gave Scotty the freedom to create the sound of rock 'n' roll. His guitar has a more fluid, more supple sound than the steel guitar on the Hank Williams records which everybody was listening to at the time.

Nothing was more characteristically Southern about Elvis than his love of white gospel music in general, and of the Blackwood Brothers in particular. In fact, the first time I ever saw Elvis he was not performing; he was in the audience, just like I was. We had both gone to East Tupelo—this was at about the time of the Sun sessions—to hear the Blackwood Brothers. So it seems perfectly reasonable to me that the Million Dollar Quartet at Sun Records—

Elvis, Jerry Lee Lewis, Carl Perkins,and Johnny Cash would sing hymns during breaks in recording sessions. Charles Wolfe nicely points up the inability of people in the North to understand the Southern context of rock 'n' roll: "Thus, while preachers across the land thundered against the rock and roll revolution, the instigators of the new sound debated original sin with (Sam) Phillips or gathered around the piano to do another chorus of Jesus, Jesus, Jesus,"[24]

For to be Southern is to be an evangelical Protestant, just as to be Irish is to be a Catholic—even if one does not go to church. This religious homogeneity which made the South the Bible Belt resulted from the fact that very few Catholic and Jewish immigrants settled in the South. In most Southern towns, the neighborhood church (Baptist, Methodist, or Church of Christ) served—and to a great extent still serves—as a social and cultural, as well as a religious, center. In a region which had very few theaters, dance halls, and bars, gospel singing was one form of truly popular music which people enjoyed, and which the preachers couldn't denounce as immoral. Indeed, gospel singing became so popular in the South after World War II that it turned into a fairly lucrative profession.

Here I need to notice a difference between black gospel and white gospel. The persecutions which blacks suffered gave their gospel singing a transcendent, other-worldly emphasis. To maintain their belief in a better world after death, blacks made a sharp distinction between sacred music and profane music. If gospel singing was God's music, then the blues was the devil's music; black preachers warned their congregations against it.

By contrast, the advantages which whites enjoyed in the South enabled them to take a more relaxed attitude toward gospel singing. White gospel had a greater openness to secular music than black gospel, although the distinction remained a strong one for many people. Thus, "Gospel Boogie," the first big gospel hit, sung by the Homeland Harmony Quartet on the White Church label in 1948, aroused considerable controversy, even though it did sell about 200,000 copies. It used boogie woogie piano runs rather like those in the Andrews Sisters' "Boogie Woogie Bugle Boy," and, predictably, preachers attacked it on moral grounds. Despite its success, the song received general acceptance among gospel audiences only after Pat Boone recorded it as "A Wonderful Time Up There" in 1958.[25]

Thanks in large part to the success of Wally Fowler's Oak Ridge Quartet, which had a program on WSM, Nashville's clear channel station, and to Wally's "all-night singings," gospel music had become professionalized by the early fifties. The 1953 *Billboard* "Country and Western Artists' Directory" listed no less than 23 full-time gospel groups[26]. The most important of these groups for Elvis, and the one which was a harbinger for musical trends far outside the South, was the Blackwood Brothers.

Three of the four Blackwood Brothers were actually brothers, and had been born in Mississippi. By the late forties, they had learned the lesson of "Gospel Boogie," and had created a hot, eclectic quartet sound. Wolfe says that, "The Blackwood Brothers records issued...in 1948-9 contain such striking features as an echo chamber, a bass singing boogie riffs, use of nonsense rhythmic phrases, two tenors making daring octave jumps for a dramatic crescendo effect and numerous harmonic devices that were probably borrowed from popular black 'jubilee' groups like the Golden Gate Quartet."[27] Both here and in his statement that "The technique of a high tenor being cushioned against close harmony, a favorite with black gospel quartets, was appropriated by the Blackwoods,"[28] Wolfe seems to me to be exaggerating the significance of black influence on the Blackwoods, just as people have exaggerated the significance of black influence on Elvis. James Blackwood, the tenor and the leader of the group, always sounded to me like the people I heard singing in church, only a lot better. I can't think of a single song in which he used melisma, the vocal embellishment in which the singer stretches a single syllable over several different notes. It was the combination of the clear tenor lead, the backup harmonies, often with an emphatic bass, and the boogie beat that made the Blackwoods so exciting.

The Blackwoods anticipated rock groups of the late sixties, and not just in their use of the echo chamber. As the Beach Boys and the Rolling Stones later did, they recorded on their own label, and had complete artistic control over their product. In fact, the Blackwood Brothers and the Statesmen Quartet, the two dominant white gospel groups of the fifties, strikingly anticipate the Beatles and the Rolling Stones. The Blackwoods, with their restrained stage presence and sweet harmonies played the Beatles to the Statesmen's Rolling Stones. The Statesmen took more musical chances, and had a generally rowdier show. (And gospel groups may even have had their own groupies. I remember seeing the Statesmen with two girls from my high school one Sunday afternoon.) So it's not so startling as it might seem to hear the line, "And let the glory hallelujahs rock and roll," in the Statesmen's "Some Glad Day."

By 1951, the Blackwoods were starting to reach a larger audience, and they signed with RCA Victor; in 1954, they had a national hit, "Have You Talked to the Man Upstairs?" It is not surprising, then, that when Elvis was asked to join the Blackwoods, he gave the offer serious thought even though he was already starting to tear up the charts.[29] Joining the Blackwoods was about as much as a kid from Hume High could have hoped for—they even toured in their own bus! However, Elvis did record several albums of hymns, and used three gospel groups as backup singers[30]—The Jordanaires (1956-67); the Imperials (1969-71); and J.D. Sumner and the Stamps Quartet (1972-77). They all made distinct contributions to the sound of his records (J.D. Sumner, who played a significant role in Elvis' career, had sung bass with the Blackwood Brothers). On his second appearance on the Ed Sullivan show, in 1957, he sang "Peace in the Valley." And so it goes. There can be no doubt as to the significance of white gospel singing for Elvis personally and for the social context in which he created his music.

It is for this reason that I do not accept the distinction which Richard Middleton makes in the form of two unfortunate neologisms. He finds "boogification" and "gospelization" in Elvis' singing. By "boogification," he means Elvis' practice of singing a single note as a triplet, and giving a quaver to the off-beat; this produces the syncopation which gives his records their very physical quality. As for "gospelization," it is "an equivalent in the area of pitch to what boggification does in the area of rhythm. In both cases the squareness and regularity of the lyrical tradition of white popular song are broken up, on the one hand through off-beat accents and rhythmic complexity, on the other, through 'off-tune' melodic patterns."[31]

There is no need to make this awkward distinction while discussing Elvis' singing because we can find ample precedent for what he did in the work of the Blackwood Brothers and the Statesmen. Although rockabilly was a true synthesis which drew on black jump bands, country and western groups, and white gospel without being dependent on any of them, we can say that Elvis used two aspects of white gospel. Caught between the two traditions as he was, he could hear in the tenors of James Blackwood and of Jake Hess (of the Statesmen) echoes of the new York-Hollywood practice of hitting notes squarely; this similarity promised a welcome resolution of the tensions which he experienced. But behind those tenors, he could hear the boogie-woogie piano pounding away (as I recall, Hovie Lister of the Statesmen had an especially rhythmic left hand). In effect, rockabilly replaced the piano with a guitar, and just as Frank had learned to sing by imitating Tommy Dorsey's horn, so Elvis sang by imitating boogie woogie piano. That is certainly not all he did, but boogie woogie phrasing was crucial to the way he sang.

You can hear this clearly on "All Shook Up," which begins with a phrase which would not seem out of place in a gospel song, "Well bless my soul." By hitting these notes, and the four monosyllabic words, squarely, Elvis converts them into triplets: 1) un-well-uh; 2) bless-uh-my; 3) y-soul-uh. When you convert four words into three triplets, you break up the words in a fresh, exciting way. As Middleton says of this kind of syncopation, "The effect is physical, demanding movement, jerking the body into activity."[32] Middleton is correct in calling "All Shook Up" a "mannerist" song, for the technique keeps overpowering the silly images of the song to produce an unsettling effect. This kept happening to Elvis, of course; since he could both croon and rock, he didn't always know when to do what.

By using gospel influences to make secular music, Elvis was bringing about a secularization of what was originally a religious form. He certainly did not begin the secularization of white gospel, as the success of "Gospel Boogie" attests, and he certainly did not do it completely. Given the extraordinary significance of gospel, both black and white, in the South, and given the equally extraordinary significance of the Southern singers who became famous by secularizing gospel techniques, the nature of secularization deserves a word or two of explanation.

Most people who have studied the subject agree that secularization accompanies the modernization of traditional societies, or the fragmentation of oral societies by literacy, as McLuhan would have put it. I will be using the transposition theory of secularization, which interprets secularization not as a simple denial of religion, but as a transposition of religious themes, images, and situations into secular ones.

As an ongoing process, secularization releases social energy, often in the form of creative energy. Two book titles may illustrate how secularization occurs. Goethe's novel *The Sorrows of Young Werther* (1774), uses a word for "sorrows" which had previously been used only for the sufferings of Christ. Goethe gives his hero's sufferings a new intensity by implicitly comparing them to those of Christ (secularization is one of the clearest of the many links between European Romanticism and rock 'n' roll). A more typically American example comes from 1900, when industrialist Andrew Carnegie wrote a book about philanthropy and called it *The Gospel of Wealth*.

A final point: The presence of secularization distinguishes the Southern tradition from the New York-Hollywood tradition. With the exception of *The Jazz Singer* (1928), which shows the process of Al Jolson's secularization from cantor's son to secular star, hardly any of the songs, and hardly any of the performers, in the New York-Hollywood tradition show the tension between the sacred and the profane which informs the work and the lives of so many Southern performers.

Elvis' controversial, intensely physical performance style, which earned him the name "Elvis the Pelvis" in the repressed fifties, represents a form of secularization even more distinctly than his vocal style which it complements so well. Since Elvis could not find a satisfactory performance style for secular music in his immediate society, he secularized the one he knew best. He tells it like this:

There were these singers [in the Pentecostal church in Tupelo which he attended with his parents], perfectly fine singers, but nobody responded to them. Then there were the preachers and they cut up all over the place, jumping on the piano, moving every which way. The crowd responded to them. I guess I learned from them[34].

Elvis exaggerates when he says that no one paid any attention to the gospel singers. What he doesn't quite want to say is that in church the preacher was the star, the headliner, and that the singers were only the warmup act. Since Elvis always wanted to be a star, he followed his impulse to imitate the performance style of the preachers. Down home, we used to say that an especially fervent preacher was "on fire for the Lord"; the skinny kid who noticed how much attention the preachers got grew into a man who recorded "Burning Love," and got the women in the audience to understand that he was on fire for them.

But it is not enough to identify the sources of a performance style, for to do that, and leave it at that, is to ignore the audience. To take the audience into consideration in Elvis' case, it is necessary to understand how technology had re-organized the performance setting since the thirties.

The big band singers hardly ever played an instrument; they were specialists who did nothing but sing, and they depended on a large group of musicians. After all, brass and reed instruments were needed to produce and sustain adequate volume to fill the ballrooms in which the big bands played, and no one can play a saxophone and sing at the same time. Yet, in 1957, Elvis played, not a ballroom, but the Cotton Bowl Stadium. As Michael Lydon has said:

A string quartet plays chamber music; electric quartets, even trios, can play stadium music. Gigantic audiences are common in rock 'n' roll because electricity has made such massive concerts possible, and rock 'n' roll musicians play music that moves multitudes [35].

Lydon makes a very suggestive reference to the string quartet here, for the violin appeared as a response to the need for greater volume than medieval lutes and early instruments could produce. In very much the same way, the electric guitar (to be discussed in more detail later) produced so much more volume than the acoustic guitar that it greatly increased the potential size of audiences.

Since electricity made it possible for three or four musicians to produce far more volume than Tommy Dorsey's twenty-man band could have, it eliminated the visual clutter which the musicians, instruments, and instrument stands had created on stage. As electricity cleared the stage, Elvis filled the void with the visceral performance style of Pentecostal preachers. No singing star had ever moved as he did because no singing star had ever come from a background which had provided a precedent for such frenzy, and no singing star had needed to fill the stage in this way.

The effect of technology on performance is also related to the clothing which performers wear on stage. At least for Frank and Elvis, a relationship exists between the singer's attitude toward clothing and the meaning of technology for his performance style: The greater the dependence on technology, the greater the need to compensate for the distance from the audience by clothing. Neither Frank nor Elvis made a conscious strategy out of this relationship; rather, it came from the intuitive feel for what would work, and what wouldn't work, that made them stars.

The different meanings of technology appear even at the beginnings of their careers. Frank got his first break when Harry James heard him sing at the Rustic Cabin (near Alpine, New Jersey) in March of 1939; Sam Phillips first heard Elvis, not in a live performance, but on a record at the Sun Studios in Memphis in late 1953. The rest is history.

If electricity isolated Elvis on stage, his Southern heritage isolated him off stage because he let it limit him. The essence of being a good ole boy, which Southerners still believe Elvis was, is not to change; his Southern roots, which gave him invaluable precedents as a performer, gave him no precedents which helped him mature as a man. The careers of Frank and Elvis offer obvious contrasts in this regard.

When Frank achieved the stardom he wanted so much, he entered the world of big-time show biz. He married the glamorous Ava Gardner; he socialized with other major stars, and made movies with them, such as *On the Town* (1949), with Gene Kelly, and *High Society* (1956), with Bing. By 1945, he had turned into a political activist; he spoke out against racial prejudice, and recorded "The House I Live In," an eloquent plea for tolerance. These activities led to his association with, and participation in, the inaugurations of Presidents Kennedy and Reagan. No wonder they called him the Chairman of the Board.

Elvis, on the other hand, did not seek out a career in show business. It came to him when Sam Phillips heard the now famous record which he had made for him mother's birthday. As soon as he could, Elvis bought the ultimate Southern status symbol, and the only one which really mattered in the South, a big house with white columns in front. He made Graceland the cocoon which Colonel Tom encouraged him to weave about him. In Hollywood, he played adolescent sex games with starlets and bimbos; when he married, he married a very ordinary girl. He never went to Hollywood parties, or became friends with major stars, although he could have done both. The King of Rock 'N' Roll made himself into a Sun King, a world unto himself. His isolation was at once his great glory as a performer and his greatest limitation as a man.

Notes

[1]Gilbert M. Ostrander, *American Civilization in the First Machine Age: 1890-1940* (New York: Harper and Row, 1970), p. 4.

[2]McLuhan, *Understanding Media, p. vi.*

[3]See Charles Hamm, "The Acculturation of Musical Styles," in *Contemporary Music and Music Cultures* (Englewood Cliffs: Prentice-Hall, 1975), p. 129.

[4]Henry Pleasants, *The Great American Popular Singers* (New York: Simon and Schuster, 1975), p. 26.

[5]For more detail on the three-generation theory, see *Culture as Polyphony*, pp. 131-132.

[6]C.A. Schicke, *Revolution in Sound* (Boston and Toronto: Little, Brown, 1974), p. 72.

[7]Pleasants, *The Great American Popular Singers*, p. 136.

[8]Quoted in *ibid*, p. 134.

[9]Charles Thompson, *Bing. The Authorized Biography* (New York: David McKay Company, 1975), p. 27.

[10]Frank Sinatra, "Me and My Music," *Life*, 18 March, 1965, p. 86

[11] *Ibid.*

[12] *Ibid.*, p. 87.

[13]See Arnold Shaw, *Sinatra. Twentieth-Century Romantic* (New York: Holt Rinehart and Winston, 1968), p. 237.

[14]See Lewis Killian, *White Southerners* (New York: Random House, 1970).

[15]Marshall Frady, *Southerners, A Journalist's Odyssey* (New York: New American Library, 1980), p. xiv.

[16]Pleasants, *The Great American Popular Singers*, p. 272.

[17]Quoted in Shaw, *Sinatra,* p. 237.

[18]Quoted in Paul Lichter, *The Boy Who Dared to Rock, The Definitive Elvis* (Garden City: Dolphin Books, 1978), p. 14.

[19]On Brummell, Wilde, and other dandies, see Ellen Moers, *The Dandy, Brummell to Beerbohm* (New York: The Viking Press, 1960).

[20]Linda Ray Pratt, "Elvis, or the Ironies of a Southern Identity," in *Elvis: Images and Fancies,* Jac J. Thorpe, ed. (Jackson: University Press of Mississippi, 1979), p. 41.

[21]I am drawing here on Hamm's contrasts between the two traditions in "The Acculturation of Musical Styles," in *Contemporary Music and Music Cultures.*

[22]Greil Marcus, *Mystery Train, Images of America in Rock 'N' Roll Music* (New York: E.P. Dutton, 1976), p. 180.

[23]Richard Middleton, "All Shook Up? Innovation and Continuity in Elvis Presley's Vocal Style," in *Elvis: Images and Fancies,* p. 153.

[24]Charles K. Wolfe, "Presley and the Gospel Tradition," in *ibid.*

[25]See Charles K. Wolfe, "Gospel Goes Uptown: White Gospel Music, 1945-1955," in *Folk Music and Modern Sound,* William Ferris and Mary L. Hart, eds. (Jackson: University Press of Mississippi, 1982), pp. 80-100.

[26] *Ibid.,* p. 98.

[27]Charles K. Wolfe, " 'Gospel Boogie': White Southern Gospel Music in Transition, 1945-1955," in *Popular Music.I,* Richard Middleon and David Horn, eds. (Cambridge: Cambridge U. Press, 1981), p. 77.

[28]*Ibid.*

[29]See Wolfe's account of this remarkable story in "Presley and the Gospel Tradtion," p. 139; J.D. Sumner, who recounted it, discreetly said that Elvis was offered a place "in a major quartet," but it could only have been the Blackwood Brothers.

[30]Despite Elvis' love of gospel singing, I doubt that he would have recorded these albums if a number of hymn-like songs had not appeared on the charts in the fifties, For more on this, see Chapter 4.

[31]See Middleton,"All Shook Up," p. 155.

[32] *Ibid.,* p. 153.

[33]Quoted in Lichter, *The Boy Who Dared to Rock,* p. 8.

[34]In the seventies, Elvis became a preacher of sorts when he gave long, rambling talks on various occult subjects to the Memphis Mafia.

[35]Michael Lydon, *Boogie Lightning* (New York; The Dial Press, 1974), p. 56.

SECTION II
1954-1964

Chapter 1:
Why 1954-1964?

All schemes of periodization, including the one I am using here, have a certain arbitrary quality. In particular, it may seem arbitrary to date the beginning of the rock 'n' roll era as the spring of 1954. "Wanted", by Perry Como, stood at the top of the singles chart in April of that year, and the soundtrack from *The Glenn Miller Story* (1954) headed the album chart. *Life* magazine for April 12 advertised two-tone hardtop Studebaker convertibles, and reported that, the previous week, the largest television audience in history, some eighty million people, had watched a 90-minute special which featured scenes and songs from Rodgers and Hammerstein musicals. Still, I agree with Arnold Shaw that "If one had to pick the recording session at which rock 'n' roll was born it would be the date of April 12, 1954 at Pythian Temple on Manhattan's West Side at which Bill Haley and the Comets cut 'Rock Around the Clock.' "[1] Bill Haley's "Rock Around the Clock," stilted as it now seems, offered teenagers their first chance to hear rock 'n' roll out loud when it played as the titles rolled for *Blackboard Jungle* (1955). About three months later, on July 5, 1954, there occurred another, far more important session: Elvis' first Sun session. And in September, Alan Freed began his controversial stint as a deejay at WINS in New York.

So, in the spring of 1954, rock 'n' roll came into being and began its rapid evolution, with lots of attendant hoopla. In fact, when we think of "the fifties" what we really mean is the period 1954-1959, the first great period of musical innovation in rock 'n' roll history. On April 24, 1959-almost exactly five years to the day after the "Rock Around the Clock" session—Your Hit Parade broadcast its last show, implicitly admitting that rock 'n' roll had established itself as dominant. More ominous, though, is the death which people associated with 1959—that of Buddy Holly, on February 2. As the traditional litany has it, in 1959, Elvis was in the Army, Chuck Berry was in jail, Jerry Lee Lewis was in disgrace, and Buddy Holly was dead. Without these powerful innovators, a period came to an end.

Although Alan Freed did not literally die in 1959, he certainly died professionally. A riot broke out at his rhythm revue in Boston on May 3, 1959, and the pressure on Freed from the payola investigations intensified during that summer. As Arnold Passman says "On November 21, 1959, he was dismissed from WABC because he refused 'on principle' to sign a statement that he had never received funds or gifts to promote records. Two days later, 'by mutual consent,' WNEW-TV cancelled his video dance show'"[2]. Although this complex, self-destructive man continued to work in radio for some time, and died in 1965, he was no longer a major force in music.

The years 1959-1964 saw the rise of girl groups, the Motown sound, and surf music. Although Motown groups such as the Supremes and the Miracles had lots of hits after 1964, they did not necessarily produce the most innovative sounds. These came, of course, from the British Invasion, led by the Beatles, who, in April of 1964, had the top five songs on the singles charts. No one had ever done that before, and perhaps no one will ever do that again. Clearly, those songs marked the end of one era and the beginning of a new one.

For a holistic understanding of rock 'n' roll in 1954-59, we need to understand the ground against which it emerged, and which gave it a particular verve. Television has served as the ground for the figure of rock 'n' roll in all periods, but the intensity of rock 'n' roll fever derived in part from the fact that it served as a release from political tensions. These tensions were caused by the man who was the biggest television star of the spring of 1954, a man who stood for the opposite of whatever rock 'n' roll means—Senator Joseph McCarthy.

When McLuhan stated in *Understanding Media* that television had destroyed McCarthy, few people believed him, but he lived to see his comment become a commonplace. During the Army-McCarthy hearings, which lasted from April 22 to June 27, weekly polls showed that McCarthy's support steadily eroded. Since these hearings did not feature any serious debates about Communism, the erosion of McCarthy's support suggests to me that the real issue had little to do with Communism. The real issue was what I have called the self/other opposition, an opposition which has much to do with rock 'n' roll.

It is futile to personalize, and thus to limit, McCarthyism to the neuroses of a single man; to understand rock 'n' roll as an expression of the fifties, we need to understand what needs McCarthyism satisfied, and what it meant for the future. McCarthyism continued the isolationism of the thirties which sought to separate America from the rest of the world, as Americans always do when they treat the self/other opposition as a dichotomy. After the war, America had to accept her role as a world power, while still yearning for isolation. The Cold War simply identified the "other" term of this dichotomy as Communists.

Such dichotomies have the greatest impact in print which allows people to imagine the "other"—however defined—as different, inferior, and less than human. Hence, McCarthy relied on references to lists and documents which contained the number of Communists in the State Department, the Army, and so forth. But the television image allows no such abstraction, and as they watched the hearings, people saw, not demons, but confused and intimidated people; not a righteous crusader, but a hard—"hot," in McLuhan's terms—domineering man. As a reporter put it, "The American people could not believe just how ugly that ugly man was until they saw him, finally, on television during the

Army-McCarthy hearings."[3] The process thus reversed itself, as historical processes often do, and the cool television image showed McCarthy himself as an "other," and the public gradually learned to dislike him.

When the Senate finally rebuked McCarthy on December 2, it did not, of course, address the more general issues which had made McCarthyism possible; they remain with us. That brings us to rock 'n' roll, and Pleasants' reference to Elvis as an "atavistic presence" foreign to the American middle class. Elvis and the other Southern rockers sounded to adults who took the self/other dichotomy for granted as "others"—as threatening, lower-class outsiders. McCarthy had railed against the enemy within, and it seemed to many that these rockers represented another version of that enemy. Conversely, the kids felt all the more intensely about the music, because it offered a release from the vague but real tensions of McCarthyism which made little sense to them.

After McCarthy's demise, it became harder to scare young people with the bugaboo of the "other." Although ministers, politicians, and other authority figures liked to call rock 'n' roll a Communist conspiracy, it sounded weak. It sounded even weaker when Elvis turned out to be a God-fearing, patriotic young man who entered the army with nary a murmur. In transforming his image into that of a fun-loving American boy, he prepared us for the Beach Boys, who had none of his Southern intensity and redneck origins. His image began to resemble that of Dick Clark, who had never had to change his image (or his appearance); his Pepsodent smile and neat tie reassured everyone that the music was nothing more than youthful high jinks.

The Army-McCarthy hearings, and McCarthyism in general, defined the terms of the controversies which would rage around rock 'n' roll for the next fifteen years, until by 1969, it had grown so powerful and had such general appeal among those under the mythical age of thirty that it had to be assimilated into the American way of life—that is, the music had to become "self," not "other."

At last, then, the whole complex for the period 1954-1959 looks like this:

Media	Sociology	Enhances	Obsolesces
45 rpm singles/ AM radio	Poor Southerners	Aural perception	Big Bands and Rural Blues
Retrieves Sexuality	Reverses Into Rock		

The remaining chapters in this section will deal in greater detail with these relationships.

Notes

[1] Arnold Shaw, *The Rockin' Fifties: The Decade That Transformed the Pop Music*

Scene (New York: Hawthorn Books, 1974), p. 136.

[2]Arnold Passman, *The Deejays* (New York: Macmillan, 1971), p. 237.

[3]Alfred Friendly, of the Washington *Post,* quoted in John G. Adams, *Without Precedent. The Story of the Defeat of McCarthyism* (New York: W.W. Norton, 1983), p. 293.

Chapter 2:
Media Interplay and Its
Implications for Youth Culture

The principle that television served as a ground for the figure of rock 'n' roll has many implications, most of them indirect. In the fifties, television was so important that, for all practical purposes, the media mix consisted of television on one hand, and everything else on the other.

In the Lovin' Spoonful's "Nashville Cats," John Sebastian refers to hearing a "yellow Sun record"; we listened to fifties rock 'n' roll on 45 rpm records, sometimes on our own record players with the distinctive thick spindles, and sometimes on AM radio. This particular media mix defined many things about the music, such as the length of the songs, and where we listened to them. But it came about as a result of two external factors which had nothing to do with the music—World War II and the FCC.

Just as World War I delayed widespread commercial radio broadcasting (with the result that radio took America by storm in the winter of 1921-22), so World War II delayed widespread television broadcasting. The war effort artificially delayed television development, since the government had issued patents for the new medium in the thirties, and in fact RCA chairman David Sarnoff opened the World's Fair in 1939 with a television broadcast. But only after the war did media change begin to occur in ways which affected the whole country. By 1948, all three networks had regular national broadcasting, even if not all major cities had stations. Politicians recognized the power of television, and the Democrats and Republicans decided to hold their conventions in Philadelphia because that city had good television linkage.[1]

The Federal Communications Commission, a government agency notoriously vulnerable to pressure from politicians and corporation executives, has given American media history an odd stop-start quality because of its seemingly arbitrary decisions. One of these occurred in 1948 when the FCC refused to grant any more licenses for television stations until engineers had resolved certain interference problems. When the FCC began to grant licenses again in 1952, television swept the country rapidly. In doing so, it took over virtually all the comedy and variety programming from radio, which was left with hours of free air time. As a result, many radio stations began to play much more popular music than they had in the past; some of them even began to play rock 'n' roll.

41

People had been playing recorded music over the radio virtually since the invention of the medium, but artists such as Bing Crosby protested that they were losing record sales because listeners could enjoy their music for free. In 1940, a court held that when a radio station bought a record, it could do anything it wanted to with it, even play it on the air. This decision made possible Martin Block's famous "Make Believe Ballroom," from WNEW in New York, and "In 1942, the Federal Communications Commission reported that music in one form or another accounted for more than 75 per cent of air time. Of this, 48.2 per cent of all stations were using music 100 per cent."[2] However, these figures may deceive us unless we remember that most of the all-music stations were located in rural areas, and/or had relatively low power. As a result, not as many people were listening to music as it might seem. Those who did listen to music on the radio tended to listen at the beginning and end of the day. In fact, many major celebrities of the fifties, such as Steve Allen, Ernie Kovacs and Dave Garroway got their start by doing morning music and talk shows on the radio.

The number of radio stations doubled between the end of the war in 1945 and 1950. Since there was not enough network programming to go around, many of these new stations relied on recorded music. Thus, the postwar period witnessed the rise of the disc jockey as a celebrity separate from the station—a phenomenon analogous to the rise of the singer separate from the band (sometimes, the careers of a disc jockey and a singer would become interrelated, as with Williams B. Williams at WNEW, a long-time admirer of Frank Sinatra). Like so many other things in American popular culture, the all-disc jockey station seems to have begun in Los Angeles, at KLAC, and people began to use the term "personality radio."

The beginning of rock 'n' roll coincided with the end of personality radio, but the major disc jockeys played a crucial role in 1954 and 1955 because of their autonomy and their location. Several of them, such as Bill Randle at WERE in Cleveland, Bob Clayton at WHDH in Boston, and Ed McKenzie at WJBK in Detroit worked at stations in major northeastern markets; they thus had the opportunity, and the power, to play rockabilly outside the South. Bill Randle, for instance, broke Elvis in the north before anyone else.

In the days before stations compiled playlists, the personality disc jockeys followed their personal tastes, and could play the suggestive records by black groups, such as the infamous "Work With Me Annie" by Hank Ballard and the Midnighters, and "Honey Love" by Clyde McPhatter and the Drifters. These songs caused such an uproar about "leerics" that you would have thought that Seymour Simons and Gerald Marks had never written "All of Me" in 1931. The difference was that, whereas the smooth melodies of Tin Pan Alley songs made sex seem a little abstract, the beat of rhythm 'n' blues made it urgent and intense. Which is to say that it retrieved the sexuality of music.

But the personalities on the records tended to overpower the personalities on the radio, and in 1955 Todd Storz introduced the Top 40 format on KDWH in Omaha. The Top 40 format, as developed by radio innovator Gordon

McLendon, soon took over big-city AM stations, and is obviously of major importance to the history of rock 'n' roll. The story goes that the idea for the format occurred to Storz when he was sitting in a bar in Omaha, and noticed that people kept playing certain songs over and over again. It happened that there were 40 slots on the jukebox, and Storz decided to use 40 songs on his playlist. Top 40 radio thus represented an assimilation of the jukebox to the radio, a change which had far-reaching implications for the implied audience.

Although many people still like to "drop the coin right into the slot," as Chuck Berry put it in "School Days," the heyday of the jukebox coincided with that of the big band, from about 1937 to about 1948. Since people listened and danced to jukeboxes in public places such as restaurants and bars, there was an obvious fit between the jukeboxes and the big band records on them, which were oriented towards performance in public space (in this sense, jukeboxes resemble the music machines such as orchestrions and player pianos which did so much to popularize ragtime, which was also a style oriented toward public space).

But when Top 40 radio became a "50,000 watt jukebox of the air," as it has been called, it tended to create an implied audience in private space. Transistors created smaller radios, which made it possible for people to listen, not just in the living room, but anywhere in the house. The kids listened to Top 40 while they were doing their homework in their rooms and while they were cruising in the family car. In 1959, there were 156 million radios in working condition in America (more than three times the number of television sets); and of this number, 26%, or something over 40 million, were in cars.[3] That number had grown from 6 million car radios in 1946.[4] As in Chuck Berry's "No Particular Place to Go," the classic implied audience for fifties rock 'n' roll was a teenage couple cruising in the very private space of the car, listening to 45 rpm singles on an AM radio.

In the process of freeing up air time for rock 'n' roll on AM radio stations, television also created an identity crisis for them, because they could no longer pull the listeners who tuned in to hear Jack Benny or Fred Allen. Gordon McLendon solved this problem by creating recorded jingles for station identifications ("Ninety three KHJ") and playing them over and over. Thus it happened that television forced Top 40 stations to begin making more imaginative use of tape than the musicians were, and brought on the distinguishing features which make a Top 40 station immediately identifiable.

The use of tape by Top 40 stations forms another connection between World War II and media history. During the war, the Germans had perfected tape recorders, which the Allies captured in 1945, and which then went on the market in 1947. The economy and simplicity of tape, as opposed to vinyl masters, offered obvious advantages for recording.

Top 40 radio took innovative popular music from prime time television (although what we would now call MOR music continued on television with *The Perry Como Show* and its ilk). Television could accomodate innovative music only when it was not in prime time, and when television itself was a secondary medium: *American Bandstand.* The well-known fact that even when performers appeared on *Bandstand* they lip-synced to the record shows how completely the record had replaced the live performance. When *Bandstand* went national on August 4, 1957, it became something like a visual Top 40 station with a national audience, and began to create a national consensus in clothing, dances, and music.

Television's prominence starting in 1948 also solves another problem about the early years of rock 'n' roll. Most people know that, in the fifties, white kids often became bored with Patty Page and Perry Como, and that when turning the dial, came upon black stations playing rhythm 'n' blues. These white kids thus greatly increased the audience for what people had previously called "race music." The mystery is, where did these black stations get the money to go on the air? The solution is that, after 1948, the standard radio formats lost much of their allure, and white investors realized that they could make money by reaching the black audience which they had formerly ignored.

So much for radio. What about the records themselves? After records changed over from cylinders to discs, the heavy 78 rpm record remained standard until 1948, when a Hungarian immigrant named Peter Goldmark invented the long-playing 33 1/3 record for Columbia. Columbia hailed this as a great boon for classical music, which had especially suffered from the frequent interruptions that changing the 78s had caused (as a result, live radio broadcasts of classical music, such as those of Arturo Toscanini with the NBC Symphony, kept their positions in network programming). But at the same time, in the fateful year of 1948, RCA Victor introduced the 45 rpm record. There followed the so-called "war of the speeds," which lasted from 1948 to 1950, when RCA gave in. Admitting that the 33 1/3 lp worked better for classical music, and having no idea what it was doing, it began publicizing the 45 rpm record as the appropriate medium for popular music. The company certainly had no awareness that in so doing it was giving popular music a media identity which it had never had before.

Carl Belz was the first to remind us that the appearance of the light, durable 45s created a new, more casual attitude toward the music, since we could flip through the records, stack them, or carry them around, much more easily.[5] But we also need to integrate these new records into the overall media situation of the fifties. Before World War II, there had been three major electronic media: movies, radio, and records. The studios controlled the movies, the networks controlled radio, and the major labels controlled records. By 1954, this more or less monolithic structure had begun to crumble. People did not just automatically go to the movies anymore; they could choose between movies in public space, and television, in private space—and they often chose television. People generally defined their musical tastes by buying 45 rpm singles or 33 1/3 rpm albums. Of the three major media, only radio was not clearly opposed to another medium, and it had a schizophrenic identity; it was split between

Top 40 stations and those who resisted rock 'n' roll in the name of "good music."

It is difficult to exaggerate the significance of the media revolution of the fifties, for it transformed every aspect of American life, from politics to sex. But it didn't do so immediately, of course; indeed, the implications of this great change are still working themselves out. Although media themselves have no content, they affect the mythological oppositions of the society; and the most radical changes affect the primal opposition, that of self/other, which gives a society its identity. Media change in the fifties makes the most sense when we think of it in terms of this opposition.

Before America became a media-saturated society, the sense of identity, the "self" term of the opposition self/other, generally derived from place. As D.W. Meinig has pointed out, America has identified herself with three symbolic landscapes—the New England village, the Midwestern Main Street memorialized at Disneyland (which opened July 17, 1955), and the California suburbs. But none of these landscapes can accomodate anyone except affluent White Anglo-Saxon Protestants; the blacks, Jews, Eastern Europeans, and hillbillies who have created so much of American popular culture, destroy the coherence of these places because they represent the "other" as a term of a dichotomy.

The media revolution of the fifties made possible the beginning of the integration of such groups into American life, and it did so because it displaced music. That is to say, it relieved the music of its dependence on a place for its performance, and thus on external factors. Before the fifties, black musicians usually performed in bars, taverns, and brothels, and such places tend to run afoul of the law in one way or another. Thus, for instance, the authorities broke up Storyville, New Orleans' red light district in 1917, and thereby changed the history of jazz. Something similar happened in Kansas City two decades later, when the demise of the graft-ridden Pendergast political machine in the late thirties created hard times for the unregulated bars in which Count Basie, Mary Lou Williams, and Joe Turner had started out. Liquor laws usually prove crucial in placing and displacing music; only after 1934 did the laws allow club owners in Manhattan to serve drinks, so that they could afford to hire a band. Even than, it took all of John Hammond's persistence to get them to give gigs to the black bands that made 52nd Street famous as "Swing Street." But the economic conditions which made the music possible also silenced it, when strippers replaced musicians there in the early fifties.

But the combination of 45 rpm singles and AM radio in the Top 40 format did not depend on place. All aspects of the business such as recording, manufacture, distribution, and purchase, became less expensive, and more decentralized. In its reliance on *Billboard's* charts, Top 40 radio created a national musical consensus; at the other extreme, the kids could carry their records on vacations, so that they could spread the word of a new hit from one area to another.

The demise of the radio networks and the proliferation of stations meant that kids could have access to more different kinds of music than their counterparts had had in the past. Although many of these white middle-class kids might have felt uncomfortable at the thought of going to a black bar to listen to rhythm 'n' blues (even if they knew where one was), they had no difficulty in turning the dial to a radio station which played rhythm 'n' blues.

For it was the *kids* who listened to the music; with their own media, and the money to spend on them, they became conscious of themselves as teenagers. As the following tables show, the names of groups and the names of songs express this consciousness:

Table I
Groups With Teen Names in 1956

The Teen Queens, "Eddie My Love"
Frankie Lymon and the Teenagers, "Why Do Fools Fall In Love"
The Six Teens, "A Casual Look"

Table II
Fifties Hits With "Teen" In Their Titles

1955 "Teen-Age Prayer," Gale Storm
1957 "Teen Angel," Mark Dinning
     "A Teenager's Romance," Ricky Nelson
     "Teenage Crush," Tommy Sands
1958 "Sweet Little Sixteen," Chuck Berry
     "Sixteen Candles," The Crests
1959 "Teen Beat," Sandy Nelson
     "Teenager in Love," Dion and the Belmonts

For the first time, teenagers singing for teenagers about being teenagers constituted a major force in American popular music. This is how it happened that several groups had one big hit, and then disappeared again. A number of the groups were from New York, whether they were whites like Dion and the Belmonts, or blacks like Frankie Lymon and the Teenagers. In either case, the simplicity of recording on tape made it possible for them to go into a studio, cut a song which lasted for three minutes, and become stars for six months. But as Bill Graham has said, you learn what kind of people musicians are only after they make it, and in some cases instant stardom overwhelmed these poor kids. Often they knew only two or three songs, and hadn't had the time to develop a performance style. More seriously, some of them went from living in coldwater walkups to making $1,000 dollars a week almost overnight.[7] Predictably, they turned to drugs, which either killed them, as with Frankie Lymon, or interrupted their careers for long periods, as with Dion. Yet their very amateurishness came across as innocence, and solidified their rapport with the audience.

But Frankie Lymon and the Teenagers, as well as other such groups, needed only to know a few songs, because the cheap 45s enabled the kids to listen to the same performances over and over again. Before the fifties, the song was the thing, not the performance. When Cole Porter's great "Night and Day" came out, Paul Whiteman, Andre Kostelanetz, Benny Goodman, Bing Crosby, and the Tommy Dorsey Orchestra all had hits with it. This phenomenon continued all through the big band years, and well into the fifties. In November of 1951, there were no less than three hit versions of the song "Sin"—Eddy Howard's, the Four Aces', and Savannah Churchill's. This tendency, along with the related matter of cover records, recurred sporadically for several years, and finally disappeared with a bang in February of 1957, when "Young Love," by both Tab Hunter and Sonny James, and "Banana Boat Song" by both Harry Belafonte and the Tarriers were on the charts at the same time.

In the fifties, then, youth culture and the media were interdependent. Because music became *the* expression of youth culture, we want to understand the nature of youth culture as a social phenomenon in the most general sense. Historian Gilman Ostrander has even coined a term for it: "technical filiarchy." Ostrander means by this the fact that "The technological age belonged to youth, because the age was constantly outdistancing the comprehension of those elders who, in preindustrial times, had been able to think of themselves as better."[8] Although techological filiarchy began in the nineteenth century, it took on increasing importance in the twentieth. This is why we must pause to consider briefly the social meaning of the technological innovations of the man ultimately responsible for the Motown Sound, Henry Ford.

Henry Ford put his assembly line into operation on January 14, 1914. As we know, it revolutionized the nature of work in our time, and made him so popular that he could easily have been elected president if he had wanted the office. Thanks to the time and motion studies which he commissioned and the special tools which he had built, workers greatly increased their own productivity because they stood in one place and did one thing all day. Since the assembly line required only limited mechanical skills, it obsolesced seniority and the apprentice system. Even young men could make a decent living by working on the line. As James Flink has put it:

Mass production had two clear benefits from the point of view of the worker. One was that the resulting higher wages and lower prices raised the worker's standard of living appreciably. The other was that new opportunities for remunerative industrial employment were opened to the immigrant, the Black migrant to the northern city, the physically handicapped, and the educable mentally retarded.[9]

Henry Ford generally has the reputation of a bigot, but since he didn't need workers with special training, he became the first equal opportunity employer, the person most responsible for integrating into the landscape of American industrial life those people who represented the "other," and specifically blacks, of course. By 1923, Ford employed about 5,000 blacks, more than any other large American corporation and roughly half the number employed in the entire automobile industry.[10]

In the twenties, the assembly line affected organizations other than corporations. As Robert and Helen Lynd wrote in *Middletown,* their classic study of Muncie, Indiana, which appeared in 1929:

The school, like the factory, is a thoroughly regimented world. Immovable seats in orderly rows fix the sphere of activity for each child. For all, from the timid six-year-old entering school for the first time to the most assured senior, the general routine is much the same.[11]

The schools and the corporations resembled each other in more than the uniformity of the physical environment, though. Both institutions were growing rapidly; high school enrollment doubled, from 2 million to 4 million between 1920 to 1930.[12] And just as Ford's assembly line obsolesced seniority, so the famous Cardinal Principles of Secondary Education of 1918 obsolesced the elitist high schools of the pre-war era. These principles democratized high school by emphasizing social proficiency as conducive to "worthy home membership", instead of Latin and mathematics.

Yet it was also during the twenties, when more and more young people were spending more and more time in schools and factories, that the first great revolution of electrical media took place. Radio, the movies, the car, and the telephone, all offered greater possibilities for enjoyment of the immediate moment. This really means that as people became urbanized in the twenties, technology tended to split their time into the dichotomy of work and play, and intensified each half. Work, whether at the school or at the factory, involved repetition and uniformity; it thus created the need for the immediacy of experience which popular culture offered.

Movie historian Larry May has rightly emphasized what the first great movie stars, Douglas Fairbanks and Mary Pickford, did to create youth culture in America. As the man who made sports respectable for the middle classes, Fairbanks once said, "We read so much of work and success that someone needs to preach the glory of play."[13] Fairbanks showed here a remarkable insight into the way play, or leisure pursuits in general, served to stabilize the social order unbalanced by the new media.

But, from the very beginning, movies threatened the Victorian world which believed that an idle mind was the devil's workshop. Still, the movies prevailed, and they did so because, as May puts it, "The potential conflict between expressive play and self-denial dissolved in the youth cult...At a time when expression of eroticism and spontaneity was linked to the vices of the upper and lower orders, youth provided an answer."[14] The cult of perpetual youth which Fairbanks and Pickford began in Hollywood had such a pervasive effect because it fitted so well into American mythology. When Pickford said, "The impulses of youth are natural and good,"[15] she was making a statement which Americans could understand. Since we have usually thought of our country as young, unlike the older countries of Europe, we readily assimilate youth to something like innocence. Because of this association, the movies of "Doug" and "Mary," as people called them in the twenties, created something new, a narcissistic youth culture which glorified play, as an attitude which had strong justifications in American mythology.

The youth culture of the fifties thus had an important precedent in the youth culture of the twenties. But, if the most widespread medium of the youth culture of the twenties was film, the most widespread medium of youth culture of the fifties was the 45 rpm record, as we know. Virtually all the kids of high school age were in high school, and not working in factories—something which intensified their awareness of being teenagers. In the dichotomy work/play, then, "work" was school, and "play" was music, as in "School Days."

To the assembly line, which had obsolesced seniority and experience in the twenties, there corresponded the electric guitar, which obsolesced the often lengthy apprenticeship which aspiring blues singers in the delta had served. It was much easier to learn to play credibly on the electric guitar than on the acoustic guitar, just as it was easier to record on tape than on vinyl. It was the interplay of all these media, then, that created the particular kind of youth culture which appeared in the fifties.

Notes

[1]I have taken a good deal of the information in this chapter from Eric Barnouw, *The Golden Web, A History of Broadcasting in the United States*, Vol. II, 1933 to 1953 (New York: Oxford U. Press, 1968); and *The Image Empire. A History of Broadcasting in the United States*, Vol. III, From 1953 (New York: Oxford U. Press, 1970).

[2]Arnold Passman, *The Deejays* pp. 89-90.

[3]Irving Settel, *A Pictorial History of Radio* (New York: The Citadel Press, 1960), p. 159.

[4]Peter Fornatale and Joshua E. Mills, *Radio in the Television Age* (Woodstock, NY: The Overlook Press, 1980), p. 20.

[5]See Eric Belz, *The Story of Rock*, 2nd ed. (New York: Oxford U. Press, 1972).

[6]See D.W. Meinig, "Symbolic Landscapes," in *The Interpretation of Ordinary Landscapes*, D.W. Meinig, ed. (New York: Oxford U. Press, 1979), pp. 164-194.

[7]See Philip Groia's often moving account of these groups in *They All Stood on the Corner, New York City's Rhythm and Blues Groups of the 1950's* (Setauket, NY: The Edmond Publishing Co., 1973).

[8]Gilman M. Ostrander, *American Civilization in the First Machine Age: 1890-1940*, p. 273.

[9]James J. Fling, *The Car Culture* (Cambridge: The MIT Press, 1975), p. 84.

[10]Ibid., p. 85.

[11]Robert and Helen Lynd, *Middletown* (New York: Harcourt, Brace, and Company, 1929), p. 188.

[12]See figure 2-4 in Lindley J. Stiles, Lloyd E. McCleary, and Roy C. Turnbaugh, *Secondary Education in the United States* (New York: Harcourt, Brace and World, 1962), p. 26.

[13]Quoted in Larry May, *Screening Out the Past* (New York: Oxford U. Press, 1980), p. 114.

[14] *Ibid.*, pp. 114-5.

[15]Quoted in *ibid.*, p. 125.

[16]See figure 2-4 in Stiles *et al.*, *Secondary Education in the United States*, p. 26.

Chapter 3:
Socio-Ethnic Origins of the
Performers and Entrepreneurs

Elvis was not alone: The major solo acts, both black and white, in fifties rock 'n' roll came from the South, and the South had something to do with the way they performed. There were no major white rockers from the North in the fifties: the great black groups, from Hank Ballard and the Midnighters to the Platters, who came from the North, sang in a variety of styles. Here the fascination lies not in relating the styles to their regional origins, but in understanding the collaboration between black performers and Jewish entrepreneurs.

Table I shows the overwhelming importance of Southern rockers in the fifties.

Table I
Birthplaces of Major Solo Acts in
Fifties Rock "N" Roll

Brook Benton: Camden, South Carolina
Chuck Berry: San Jose, California (Moved to St. Louis at the age of three)
Ray Charles: Albany, Georgia
Bo Diddley: McComb, Mississippi
Fats Domino: New Orleans, Louisiana
Buddy Holly: Lubbock, Texas
Jerry Lee Lewis: Ferriday, Louisiana
Carl Perkins: Jackson, Tennessee
Elvis Presley: Tupelo, Mississippi
Lloyd Price: New Orleans, Louisiana
Little Richard: Macon, Georgia
Gene Vincent: Norfolk, Virginia

This list does not include every solo act, of course, but it includes the heart of the music. Even the reaction against rock 'n' roll came from the South, in the form of Pat Boone, born in Jacksonville, Florida.

Two of the major performers on the list, Chuck Berry and Buddy Holly, require a separate comment. It seems odd to think that Chuck was born in San Jose, because of his references to St. Louis in "Back in U.S.A." and other songs. Although St. Louis is not a Southern town, it is on the way from the Delta to Chicago, and was an important rhythm 'n' blues town in the thirties, when it was noted for its piano players such as "Stump" Johnson. Chuck grew up in the religious atmosphere which blacks took out of the South with them: His father is a Baptist minister.

As for Buddy Holly, we must begin by ignoring the scene in *The Buddy Holly Story* in which a minister denounces the music which Buddy had played the night before at the skating rink. This scene no doubt went into the script as part of the mythology which says that fifties rock 'n' roll expressed youthful rebellion against parents and society. The *audience* may have perceived it that way, but the performers rarely did. In fact, Buddy Holly was a model son, and a good Southern boy. He remained a devout Baptist to the end of his life, paying the church 10% of the royalties for "Peggy Sue," "That'll Be the Day," and his other classics as a tithe. Just before he died he was thinking of recording gospel songs, as Elvis had done.

Buddy was close to his parents, and his biographer, Jonathan Goldrosen, cites the following astounding statement by his mother:

We never minded having him practicing at our house with his friends. He was trying to be a success, of course, so we were all for him. Anyway, I liked the sort of music he was listening to. You see, some of those parents were really down on their kids and made fun of their music—but the music Buddy was playing wasn't so very different from what we were used to, as far as we were concerned.[1]

Not only was Buddy not a rebel (except that he didn't share Texas bigotry), he made music very much like what he heard around him, the music of Hank Williams and Jimmy Rodgers. An echo of Rodgers' yodelling appears in Buddy's distinctive way of singing with a catch in his voice, as in his delivery of the phrase "Peggy Su-ue." When Buddy's mother—a remarkable woman who suggested to him the phrase "Maybe Baby"—said that his music "wasn't so very different from what we were used to," she was responding to the Crickets' combination of electric guitar, stand-up bass, and drums which produced a lighter sound than that which, say, Scotty Moore and D. J. Fontana produced on Elvis' records. Out there in Lubbock, Buddy probably hadn't heard much blues, so his sound retained a country and western flavor, even if it did have a broader appeal.

Many of the black performers from the South—most notably Ray Charles, of course—have their music roots in gospel, a phenomenon which will be considered in the next chapter. Of the white Southerners, Jerry Lee Lewis offers the most fascinating stylistic melange. Jerry was born in Ferriday, Louisiana, which is on the lower Mississippi across from Natchez, and thus in the heart of the South's rich lumber-growing region. Arnold Shaw points out that, in the twenties, the South produced almost half the nation's lumber. As a result, there arose the need for entertainment:

What local ballrooms were to the big bands of the 30's and the borscht circuit was to a generation of comics, the lumber, levee turpentine, and sawmill camps of the South were to the bluesmen who progressed from rural to urban styling.[2]

The rough atmosphere of these crudely built camps way out in the woods seems to have fostered a bawdy style, as the brothels of Storyville had done a generation before. The camps produced, for instance, the legendary Speckled Red (born Rufus Perryman), whose mneomonic and highly erotic ditty "The Dirty Dozens" is now lost to history. It was this style that Jerry inherited in, for example, "Whole Lotta Shakin' Goin, On," which makes Fat Domino's piano on "Blueberry Hill" seem pretty tame.

Although Jerry did not hear Speckled Red, Little Brother Montgomery, or Sunnyland Slim, the major performers from the Ferriday area, he heard those who played in their tradition, as he himself says:

When I was a young man, I used to go to Haney's Big House, a local dance hall where Negro bands and combos played. Afterward, I'd try to do the songs I heard and pick up on their style. But I also liked singers like Hank Williams and Red Foley, who was my favorite. I created my own style from all of these, I'd say.[3]

So far, this sounds like a familiar pattern in American popular music, one in which a gifted white kid is drawn to black music, and adapts its style and flair for a white audience. But there's more to it than this, for if the similarities between Elvis and Frank offer a study of the meaning of immigration in American life, we have a remarkable analogy to it in Jerry's fascination with Al Jolson. He says it began like this:

When I was about twelve, I walked into a theater in Ferriday, Louisiana where I was born. Before the picture went on, they played a record. I never stayed for the picture (The Jolson Story). That record hit me so hard I rushed out, ran all the way home, sat down at the piano, and tried to sing "Down Among the Sheltering Pines" exactly as Al Jolson had done it. And would you believe it? Although I heard the song just once, I knew every word. The way Jolson did it, each word stood out like an electrified stop sign. I've never forgotten those words—and I've never stopped admiring Al Jolson.[4]

As we know, Jolson limited his own success by his antipathy for records and radio; Jerry had no such antipathy, but there is a similarity in their intense performance styles. Jerry's overwhelming live shows did not earn him the nickname "The Killer" for nothing. In the fifties, only a Southerner could match Jolson's intensity.

Another problem with *The Buddy Holly Story* is that it leaves out the significance of Norman Petty, the man who owned the recording studio in Clovis, New Mexico, where Buddy Holly began recording. That a major hit like "Peggy Sue" would be recorded in Clovis, New Mexico (or even that there would *be* a recording studio in Clovis, New Mexico) was a prime indicator of the extent of media decentralization in the fifties. The most important WASP entrepreneur, though, was Sam Phillips, the owner of Sun Records who had said "If I could find a white man who could sing like a black, I could make a million dollars," not long before Elvis walked in the door. Robert Palmer exonerates him from the charge of racism, though, emphasizing that when Phillips set up in the recording business in 1949, he recorded black groups exclusively, and cut "Rocket 88" with the Rhythm Kings featuring Ike Turner.[5] But by the early fifties, he was losing the talented black artists to Chess Records in Chicago, to which we now turn.

With the Chess brothers, Leonard and Phil, we have the most striking example of the association of Eastern European Jews and Southern blacks combining their separate talents to create great music. Before considering this matter in more detail, we should recall the Chess brothers and the other Jewish entrepeneurs in show business. On the East Coast, William Paley, the most important and influential executive in the history of American popular culture, headed CBS; on the West Coast, all the movie moguls, like Harry Cohn and Samuel Goldwyn were Jews. But they were men of a very different kind from the Chess brothers because they represented the show business establishment to which Bing and Frank belonged; they wanted to have nothing to do with black performers.

By contrast, Leonard Chess had great empathy with the blacks he recorded, like Muddy Water, Little Water, Howlin' Wolf, and the others. The immigrant from Poland and the immigrants from the delta found something in common in that they shared the kinds of beliefs which characterize oral societies the world over. As Malcolm Chisholm, an engineer who worked with Chess, says of him, "He lived in one of those exclusively Jewish villages in Poland until he was seven, and there was a tremendous amount of superstition involved in that. I think Leonard picked up a great many more superstitions from the blacks with whom he lived and worked, and whom he rather liked, although he didn't admit it much."[6]

Actually, Leonard Chess was following the footsteps of another Chicago man, Abe Saperstein, who created one of America's great institutions of black entertainment in 1927 when he changed the name of a local basketball team from the Savoy Hot Five to the Harlem Globetrotters and took it on the road. Speaking of Harlem, the most important venue for black entertainers, one of the most important in the history of American popular culture, is the Apollo Theater, which Frank Schiffman and Leo Brecher took over in 1935. To this day it remains in the Schiffman family, which has managed to win the trust and respect of many blacks. Clearly, the difficulties of running the Apollo—for anyone, let alone a Jew—are such that no one would undertake it as a purely business venture. The Schiffmans, like the Chesses, have had a dedication to black culture which transcends dollars and cents. Musing on this, Jack Schiffman has written, "It may be because we are Jews and identify ourselves with the struggles of all minority groups.[7]

Like Elvis, Leonard Chess and Frank Schiffman were not alone; a number of Eastern European Jews managed the small labels in New York and Los Angeles which put out most of the black rhythm 'n' blues/rock 'n' roll records of the fifties. These men had a remarkable commitment to the music, and to the culture it expressed, as former record executive Johnny Sippel pointed out to Arnold Shaw:

Origins of Performers and Entrepreneurs

Ralph Bass (of Savoy Records) was one of a group of men who were white and intelligent, even learned, and who became so involved in R & B they went black—and I mean *Black*. They talked black, affected black mannerisms, and some of them married black women. The younger of the Mesner brothers, owners of Aladdin, did. So did Monte Kay, who wed Diahann Carroll when she was a complete unknown and mixed marriages were a no-no. Ralph Bass divorced a white wife to marry a black gal.

Just think of it! Paul Reiner of Black & White Records, Herman Lubinsky of Savoy, Freddie Mendelsohn of Regent and Herald, Leonard Chess of Chess and Checkers, Jerry Wexler of Atlantic, Art Rupe of Specialty—all of them were bright, well read if not erudite, and all of them became so profoundly enmeshed in R & B, they literally changed color. And all of them happened to be Jewish.[8]

Clearly, for such men, the recording business was something more than just a business: they made it into a way of life. Indeed, Freddie Mendelsohn, of Herald Records, made a most un-businesslike decision when he chose to begin recording gospel almost exclusively (Gospel great James Cleveland records with him). Since black gospel music has the most limited appeal of any style of black music, he could hardly have hoped to make much money from the change.

Chess was the only Jewish-owned label between the coasts which recorded black music. Savoy, Black & White (a name indicating a hope of crossover hits?), and Specialty were in Los Angeles, while Atlantic, Groove, and Baton were in New York—and Herald was just across the river in Newark. The presence of record companies in New York and Los Angeles hardly seems to attest to the decentralization of media which I have been emphasizing. But here we need to keep in mind the situation of the implied listeners, who were black. In the fifties, America was still very much a segregated society; blacks couldn't go to most theaters, clubs, and restaurants; so, as Ahmet Ertegun shrewdly noted, "Black people had to find entertainment in their homes—and the record was it."[9] Although blacks constituted a minority within American society, and a *poor* minority at that, they bought records out of all proportion to their numbers and earning power. Thus, it was one of the ironic and unforeseen consequences of the civil rights movement and the increasing acceptance of black music that the small labels which had sustained it during the fifties gradually went out of business.

No such distinctions apply to innovation in radio in the fifties, for it occurred far from either coast, and was carried out, quite consistently, by WASPs. David MacFarland, the historian of Top 40 radio, cites financial reasons for this fact:

Top 40 developed first in the middle markets because they were the markets that (a) could support the expense of the software, hardware, and personnel investment that the pioneers believed was necessary, and (b) because the large-market stations were too expensive to buy.[10]

It seems to me that MacFarland is confusing necessary and sufficient causes here. Before innovators could innovate, they obviously had to obtain control of one or more radio stations, and money required that those stations be removed from major markets. But once they had the stations, nothing forced them to engage in an unconscious collaboration in developing Top 40.

If we speak of pioneer innovators in Top 40, we must speak of three men: Todd Storz, Gordon McLendon, and Gerald Bartell. Todd Storz and his father bought KOWH in Omaha in 1949, and with a music-and-news format, he made it the number one station by 1953—even though it had only 500 watts, and was a day-time station. Gordon McLendon was born in Paris, Texas, and his father had a string of movie theaters in the area. By June of 1954, he had made KLIF number one in Dallas. Finally, Gerald Bartell, who was born in Chicago, pooled money with relatives to buy WOKY in Milwaukee, which he put in the top three by October of 1952. All of these men were bright, well-educated scions of wealthy families, and were thus able to exercise considerable control despite their youth. In these respects, they resemble William Paley, but I suspect that they were able to do what they did because Omaha, Dallas, and Milwaukee were far from media centers, so that no one could tell them what couldn't be done.

What it comes to, then, is that the performers and entrepreneurs who created fifties rock 'n' roll were outsiders. Many of the performers were born during the depression, and the desperation of that period found a release in the intensity of their music. In the North, the collaboration between blacks and Jews, as the two major groups of outsiders, has enormous significance (notice that two of the partners at Atlantic, Nesuhi and Ahmet Ertegun, were not Jews, but were outsiders in a more radical sense—they were the sons of the Turkish ambassador in Washington). And midwestern businessmen put the records on the air in their Top 40 format. While New York and Los Angeles remained major entertainment centers, they had little to do with rock 'n' roll.

Notes

[1]Quoted in Jonathan Goldrosen, *The Buddy Holly Story* (New York: Quick Fox, 1975), p. 24.

[2]Arnold Shaw, *Honkers and Shouters. The Golden Years of Rhythm and Blues* (New York: Collier Books, 1978), p. 29

[3]Quoted in Arnold Shaw, *The Rockin' 50's* (New York: Hawthorn Books, 1974), p. 191

[4]Quoted in *ibed.*, p. 190.

[5]Robert Palmer, *Deep Blues* (New York: The Viking Press, 1981), p. 218 ff.

[6]Quoted in Shaw, *Honkers and Shouters*, p. 162.

[7]Jack Schiffman, *Uptown, The Story of Harlem's Apollo Theatre* (New York: Cowles Book Company, 1971), p. 174.

[8]Quoted in Shaw, *Honkers and Shouters*, p. 343.

[9]Quoted in *ibid.*, p. 343.

[10]David MacFarland, *The Development of the Top 40 Radio Format*, unpublished dissertation, University of Wisconsin, 1972. The factual information in the next paragraph comes from MacFarland.

Chapter 4:
The Beginnings of Secularization
in Black Music

Just as Elvis was not alone in coming from the South, so he was not alone in drawing on religious modes in his performance style. And it is here that his affinities with black culture show up, for the impetus of secularization explains a good deal about the dynamics of black music as it began to reach a large white audience in the fifties. To understand how this happened, we need to keep in mind the differences in the way blacks and whites have thought about religion, especially in the South.

Historically for Southern whites, religious and secular music have constituted a binary pair in that there was little, if any, tension between them. Thus, it seemed perfectly reasonable to Elvis to record albums of hymns, and, as we know, Buddy Holly wanted to do so as well. For years, the Grand Ole Opry has often included a "sacred number," and some country and western standards such as the Carter Family's "Will the Circle Be Unbroken" *are* hymns, although they don't appear in hymnals.

But the persecution of blacks gave evangelical Protestantism, with its promise of salvation and transcendence of the cares of this world, an intensity which it did not always have among whites, and which it retained even after they left the South. James Baldwin made the point eloquently in *The Fire Next Time,* when he recalled the Harlem church in which he had grown up: "Perhaps we were, all of us—pimps, whores, racketeers, church members, and children—bound together by the nature of our oppression, and the specific and peculiar complex of risks we had to run; if so, within these limits we sometimes achieved with each other a freedom that was close to love."[1]

Because blacks needed the church as refuge more than whites did, they tended to make a dichotomy of the distinction between sacred and profane music in that one excluded the other. To be sure, the prolific composer Thomas Dorsey, who wrote great hymns such as "Precious Lord Take My Hand," also wrote blues songs such as "It's Tight Like That." Mahalia Jackson is more typical, though, in her refusal to sing at the Apollo Theater, no matter how much the Schiffman family urged her to. This insistence on a distinction between the sacred and the profane caused many blacks to call the blues "the devil's music."

The emphasis in evangelical Protestantism on converting sinners and witnessing for the Lord determined a great deal about the style of gospel singing. Gospel singers want to "shout the church," as they put if—to affect the audience, to move it to shouts and tears. Thus, gospel singers express a continual awareness of their reciprocal relationship with the audience; this interaction, known as call and response, ultimately derives from African traditions which do not make a dichotomy between the audience and the performer as Western traditions do.

The male quartet in popular music, which usually consists of a lead singer and three backup singers, is a gospel form by origin, at least among blacks. And something like the call and response interplay between the singers and the church takes place between the lead singer and the backup singers. Thus, for instance, Julius Cheeks, the great lead singer for the Sensational Nightingales, cries out, "Help me sing it, boys," to the rest of the quartet on "I Want to Go," and "Let me hear you say it again, boys," on "Prayed Too Late." But the arrangements show a good deal of flexibility, because occasionally the Nightingales sing some of the words *before* Cheeks does.

As far as vocal style is concerned, one identifying characteristic of gospel singing is melisma, the practice of stretching a single syllable over several notes (gospel singers call such ornamentation "curlicues"). There is, of course, great variety among the various gospel groups; Julius Cheeks' voice has a hoarse, throaty intensity which gives conviction to his witness, as opposed to that of Claude Jeters, lead singer of the Swan Silvertones, who has a smoother voice. But they both identify themselves as gospel singers by their use of melisma, as when Cheeks sings "swift" as "swi-i-ift" and "strong" as "stro-ong" in their classic "To the End," just as Jeter sings "whisper" as "whispe-er" and "times" as "ti-i-imes" on "You Can Just Whisper a Prayer."

Gospel music is usually the first kind of music that blacks listen to, and it often makes a lasting impact. To cite James Baldwin again, "There is no music like that music, no drama like the drama of the saints rejoicing, the sinner moaning, the tambourines racing, and all those voices coming together and crying holy unto the Lord."[2] But northern cities had their secularizing effect on the large numbers of blacks who had moved into them during and after World War II, just as they had a similar effect on the Eastern European Jews like Al Jolson who had moved into them at the turn of the century. Still, the change from the sacred to the profane did not preclude a stylistic continuity. Falsetto is another characteristic of gospel singing, and in a way that epitomizes the secularization process in black music, the teenaged James Cleveland's falsetto on "I Can Depend on Jesus," with the Gospelaires anticipates Frankie Lymon's falsetto on "Why Do Fools Fall In Love?" (Not to mention my very favorite trash song from the fifties, his "No, I'm Not a Juvenile Delinquent").

One great performer, Ray Charles, and one great fifties group, the Platters, may represent the stylistic and thematic changes which secularization entailed in gospel music as radio and 45 rpm singles created a larger white audience for black music than it had ever had before. The fact that Ray, who grew up in tiny, remote Greenville, Georgia, and the Platters, from urban Los Angeles, both drew on gospel to create some of the most popular records of the fifties indicates just how pervasive this process was.

In his autobiography *Brother Ray,* Ray says that, in addition to his acquaintances among jazz and blues musicians:

I also knew many gospel men and women. Some were friends of mine, others just acquaintances. Among them were the best singers I had ever heard in my life. And the very cream of the crop—for me at least—were cats like Ira Tucker of the Dixie Hummingbirds, Archie Brownlee of the Five Blind Boys of Mississippi, and Claude Jeters of the Swan Silvertones. These guys have voices which could shake down your house and smash all the furniture in it. Jesus, could they wail! They sang for real, and I loved their music as much as any music in the world.[3]

Of course, Ray's style is not pure gospel style; it is not pure anything—that is its glory. But he drew on gospel in crucial ways when he decided to stop imitating Nat "King" Cole and develop his own style. As he says, "Now, I'd been singing spirituals since I was three, and I'd been hearing the blues for just as long. These were my main two musical currents. So what could be more natural than to combine them?"[4] And combine them he did, in his first big song among white audiences, "Hallelujah I Love Her So."

"Hallelujah" is a shout of religious joy common in Southern churches, both black and white. In this song, Ray substitutes *eros* for *agape,* to use the theological terms; he substitutes earthly love for salvation as a source for joy. His song "Just for a Thrill" makes a similar substitution, by which the sufferings which the woman causes the man correspond to the sufferings which the machinations of the Devil cause the Christian. Although he bends the notes in a bluesy way, as a gospel singer generally wouldn't, Ray uses melisma in a way which suggests that he learned a good deal from listening to Claude Jeters and the others. In "Come Rain or Come Shine" he sings "pain" as "pa-a-ain" and "shine" as "shi-i-ine." He also plays with falsetto on "I've Got A Woman."

Ray's neo-boogie woogie "What'd I Say?" involves a call and response relationship with the Raelets, who repeat "hey...ho" after him. And even the studio version includes audience response which urges him to "sing it again." Then, too, on "Drown In My Own Tears," he shouts "all ri-i-ight" in approval of the Raelets. But Ray uses this interplay, not to evoke a state of grace, but to create a sense of excitement. Ray's arrangement, too, is consistent with this secularization, and not just in its longer instrumental breaks, for it clearly sets him apart as the leader and the lead singer. Dynamic interplay of the kind that often happens between Claude Jeters and the other Swan Silvertones hardly ever happens between Ray and the Raelets.

But if Ray limits this interplay, it disappears altogether on the much smoother, much whiter sound of the Platters' great hits of the fifties. The backup singers, three men and a woman, don't sing a word on "The Magic Touch," they simply complement the lush strings by repeating "oo-oo." Indeed, the arrangement takes the isolation of lead singer Tony Williams to its logical conclusion, for he sings the last line a capella. Of course, "The Magic Touch" represents an extreme example, but the backup singers actually sing words only occasionally, to build up to the grand finale, as on "Heaven On Earth," and "I'm Sorry."

What isolates, emphasizes. If Tony Williams has lost all interplay with his musical environment, he compensates by taking his use of melisma almost to the point of caricature. Again and again, sometimes in almost every line, his clear, pure tenor voice adds two or three syllables to a word. Probably the most famous instance occurs in the second chorus of "Only You," when he sings "oh-oh-only you," with a heart-stopping catch, almost a sob in his voice. These two bars alone evoke a great deal of classic fifties pop music.

As is the case with Ray's music, there is a noteworthy consistency among the arrangements, the vocal styles, and the lyrics. The Platters sing secular hymns in which highly romanticized love, cued by the massed violins, has replaced salvation as a source of happiness. The titles alone of two of their great hits are indicative: "My Prayer" and "Heaven On Earth." Although "My Prayer" comes from the thirties, it fits in with their other songs, for the singer prays, not for salvation, but "to be with you." Likewise, "Heaven On Earth" will come into being when the singer is with his beloved. "I'm Sorry" has no religious imagery, but amounts to a secular confession, addressing a woman, not God, the singer asks for forgiveness, not grace. "Only You," however, has a certain ambiguity; given the Platters' other songs, we sense that the singer is addressing his beloved, but he might be addressing God in the line, "Only you can make this world seem right."

The white teenagers who bought Ray's records and the Platters' platters hardly thought about their gospel qualities. I suspect that most teenage boys were like me in imagining themselves singing "Only You" to their steady girlfriends. And although I had heard a lot of gospel singing—white gospel singing, to be sure—it never occurred to me to associate the dionysian qualities of "Hallelujah I Love Her So" with anything I had ever heard in church.

The black reaction to Ray's music was very different, and very negative. Ray recalls that, "I got letters accusing me of bastardizing God's work. A big-time preacher in New York scolded me before his congregation."[5] And it wasn't just people like preachers, who might have been defending their own territory. No less a performer than Big Bill Broonzy expressed his shock and dismay at Ray's work: "Ray Charles is mixin' the blues with spirituals. That's wrong...He's got a good voice but it's a church voice. He should be singing in church."[6]

But Ray has always had a strong belief in himself and in his music, and the criticisms didn't bother him. Sam Cooke's experience in combining the sacred and profane in music proved much more painful. Sam began singing with the Soul Stirrers, and was trained by R. H. Harris, who organized the group. Sam subsequently had great success as a pop singer, of course, with hits like "Chain Gang" and the classic "Twistin' the Night Away." But in the sixties, he began to think that he might want to sing with the Soul Stirrers again; when he appeared on stage with them at their anniversary program in Chicago, people began shouting (in Harris' censored version), "Get that Blues singer down. Get that no good so-and-so-down. This is a *Christian* program"[7] (the fact that these people could called Sam a "blues singer" indicates that they simply divided black music into two categories, the sacred and the profane, gospel and the blues). Naturally, Sam felt deeply hurt. He had failed to understand the differences in attitude between his white audience and his black audience.

Secularization appears in the work of many black performers in the fifties besides Ray Charles and the Platters, of course. Almost any hit by a doo-wop group from the early or middle fifties offers striking examples of melisma by the lead singer. Anyone who doubts this might listen to "Earth Angel," by the Penguins (note the similarity to "Heaven on Earth"); "In the Still of the Night," by the Five Satins; or "I'll Be Home," by the Flamingos. Given his gospel training, Sam Cooke predictably stretches syllables over several notes again and again on "You Send Me."

Gospel singing is nothing if not a lived experience, since the singer is making a witness for the Lord. So secularization affected the lives of the Southerners who drew on gospel in their performance styles. Elvis became a secular preacher in his long, rambling orations to the Memphis Mafia in the seventies. The young Jerry Lee Lewis was a real preacher for a time, and his rousing performances showed that he learned as much from fundamentalist preachers as Elvis did. And we already know the price Sam Cooke paid for taking up secular music. Roy Hamilton and Little Richard experienced much personal anquish because they had done so, and ultimately give it up entirely. On the other hand, Chuck Berry, the son of a Baptist preacher, made the transition with no difficulty; growing up in St. Louis, rather than in a closely knit small Southern town, probably made all the difference for him.

A number of hits from the fifties merged the sacred and the profane; in addition to "Earth Angel" and "Heaven On Earth," Mark Dinning's "Teen Angel" and Bobby Helm's "My Special Angel" come from this period. But as Table I shows, several hits of the fifties are hymns which have nothing to do with romantic love.

Table I

Hymn-Like Hits of the Fifties

1953 "I Believe," Frankie Laine
  "Crying in the Chapel," Sonny Till and the Orioles
1954 "You'll Never Walk Alone," Roy Hamilton
1958 "He's Got the Whole World in His Hands," Laurie London
1959 "The Battle Hymn of the Republic," The Mormon Tabernacle Choir

There is great variety in this group of songs, and they are performed in a variety of different styles. But both the arrangements and the lyrics have this in common: they affirm that order exists in the world. It seems reasonable to suppose that the media revolution of the fifties, with its unsettling implications, created the need for reassurance which these songs met. In particular, the popularity of the most important secular hymn in American history, "The Battle Hymn of the Republic," is another way of saying the same thing, that these songs expressed the way popular music, which had not yet become synonymous with rock 'n' roll, was creating a national community of the young which was becoming conscious of itself as a community. And self-conscious communities of any kind often take on religious overtones in America.

Notes

[1] James Baldwin, *The Fire Next Time* (New York: The Dial Press, 1963), p. 55.
[2] *Ibid.,* p. 47.
[3] Ray Charles and David Ritz, *Brother Ray* (New York: The Dial Press, 1977), p. 120.
[4] *Ibid.,* p. 149.
[5] *Ibid.,* p. 151.
[6] Arnold Shaw, *The World of Soul* (New York: Cowles Book Company, 1970), p. 284.
[7] Quoted in Tony Heilbut, *The Gospel Sound* (New York: Simon and Schuster, 1971), p. 121.

Chapter 5:
Cover Records

Covering records, the practice whereby one group recorded another group's hit single, was a characteristic phenomenon of the fifties. For instance, in an effort to maintain his popularity against the threat of rock 'n' roll, Perry Como covered Gene and Eunice's "Kokomo," in 1955, and the Crew-Cuts covered "Sh-Boom" by the Chords, and "Earth Angel" by the Penguins in the same year. Since such well-known examples as these involved whites who took a hit by a black group on a small label, and whitened its sound in order to record it on a major label, cover records have understandably become associated with racism and exploitation. In "Black Roots, White Fruits" of their book *Rock "N" Roll Is Here To Pay*, Steve Chapple and Reebe Garofalo vehemently denounce the practice of cover records, and cite some horror stories of black artists whom the major record companies defrauded.[1] This certainly happened, and we already know about Elvis' shameful treatment of Arthur "Big Boy" Crudup. I have no desire to defend the greed and callousness of the major labels in the fifties; but without in any way defending them, I wish to discuss cover records as an aspect of the evolution of popular music caught up in a media revolution which no one understood.

For one thing, we need to remember that exploitation in the music business does not begin and end with white artists stealing from black artists. Would that it were that simple. Blacks are just as capable of exploiting blacks as whites are. In his book *The Gospel Sound*, Tony Heilbut makes the point that Thomas A. Dorsey "earned only a fraction of the money due him. He long ago gave up tracing the singers who plagiarized his material."[2] Since he primarily wrote black gospel songs, it was blacks, not whites, who did the plagiarizing. Although they have fewer opportunities, to be sure, black business people can exploit artists as well as white ones. Heilbut notes that, "Gospel promoters are notoriously crooked."[3]

Even when the major labels had hits with their cover versions of black recordings, not all blacks suffered equally. Drawing on his long experience as a music business insider, Arnold Shaw comments:

...Historians outside the music scene neglect the simple fact that the R & B record companies generally *owned* the copyrights that were covered. What they lost in sales of their own records, their publishing subsidiaries more than made up in royalties received on other records, performance earnings, foreign income, etc.[4]

Given the limited pressing and distribution facilities of small black records labels, cover records often proved a blessing in disguise. It was the performers who did not write their own material who suffered the most, such as Etta James, whose "Wallflower" was cleaned up and covered by Georgia Gibbs as "Dance With Me Henry."

Still, there was considerable variety in the cover versions of black performances. At one extreme, Pat Boone lightened Little Richard's "Tutti Frutti" to a whiter shade of pale. As another possibility, the Crew-Cuts made a career by getting down as well as white singers could hits like "Sh-Boom" by the Chords. And then there was Elvis. Chapple and Garofalo list "Hound Dog" as a cover of a black song, ignoring two crucial factors: 1) that Elvis completely re-worked the style of the song and changed its lyrics, and 2) that the song itself was written by the great songwriting team of Jerry Leiber and Mike Stoller.

Because some of the cover records, such as Pat Boone's, now seem so embarrassing, people seem to have forgotten that the major labels in New York were not just covering songs by black artists in the early fifties; they were also covering songs by white artists. Hank Williams is the obvious case in point. In November of 1951, for example, there were no less than three covers of his song "Sin" on the charts—one by Eddy Howard, one by the Four Aces, and one by Savannah Churchill. In 1953, Tony Bennett covered his "Cold, Cold Heart," and Jo Stafford covered his "Jambalaya." The executives must have thought that Hank's voice was too hillbilly, and the arrangements too simple, to satisfy a national audience, so they gave the songs to singers who would smooth them out, and to arrangers who would create a bigger sound.

It seems clear, then, that cover records appeared as a part of the transition from a recording with appeal limited either ethnically or regionally to a recording with national appeal. The media revolution abolished this distinction by February of 1957, the last month when two different recordings of the same song appeared on the charts. Both the "Banana Boat Song," Harry Belafonte's calypso hit, and its cover by the Tarriers sold well. But this classic instance of a white cover of a black song was not alone, for in the same month, there were two hit versions of "Young Love," Sonny James' country version, and Tab Hunter's teenage version. Here we have a white artist covering a song by another white artist. Racism alone does not explain cover records.

Before the media revolution took hold, show biz people distinguished between the song and the performance. They took songs from Broadway shows, for instance, and arranged them as singles. Thus, Tony Bennett, the Four Aces, and Tony Martin, all had single versions of "Stranger in Paradise," from *Kismet*, by Robert Wright and George Forrest, on the charts in January of 1954. However, as the media merged the song and the performance, show songs disappeared from the charts; the last one to make it to the top ten was the very sexist "Standing on the Corner," from Frank Loesser's *The Most Happy Fella*, which did well for the Four Lads in June of 1956. This process of merging the song and the performance is the process which caused the demise of *Your Hit Parade*, of course.

But the most fascinating thing about the fifties, at least as far as black music is concerned, is the way blacks retrieved white songs from the thirties, the classic era of the big bands and Tin Pan Alley, and gave them a rhythm 'n' blues feel. These artists so completely made them over, as Elvis did with "Hound Dog", that Table I may come as a surprise to some people.

TABLE I

Black Covers of White Songs from the Thirties

Artist	Year	Song and Origin
Ray Charles	1960	"Georgia on My Mind," Hoagy Carmichael. 1930
	1962	"You Are My Sunshine," Jimmie Davis, 1940
Fats Domino	1956	"Blueberry Hill," introduced by Gene Autry in the Movie *The Singing Hill*, 1941; a hit for Glenn Miller and His Orchestra (vocal by Ray Eberle) in the same year.
	1957	"My Blue Heaven," Walter Donaldson, 1927
	1963	"Red Sails in the Sunset," introduced by Ray Noble and His Orchestra, 1935
The Drifters	1954	"White Christmas," by Irving Berlin, 1944
	1960	"Save the Last Dance for Me," by Arthur Tracy, 1931
The Five Satins	1956	"In the Still of the Night," by Cole Porter, 1934; introduced by Nelson Eddy
The Flamingos	1956	"I Only Have Eyes for You" introduced by Dick Powell and Ruby Keeler in the movie *Dames*, 1935
Ray Hamilton	1954	"You'll Never Walk Alone" and "If I Loved You," from the Rodgers and Hammerstein musical *Carousel*, 1945
The Harptones	1953	"A Sunday Kind of Love," a hit in 1946 for Claude Thornhill and His Orchestra with vocal by Fran Warner
The Orioles	1953	"I Cover the Water Front," theme song of the movie of the same name, 1933
The Platters	1926	"My Prayer," a hit for Vera Lynn in 1939
	1958	"Smoke Gets In Your Eyes," from Jerome Kern's musical *Roberta*, 1933
	1960	"Harbor Lights," a hit for Rudy Vallee in 1937; revived by Sammy Kaye in 1950
The Spaniels	1954	"Goodnight Sweetheart, Goodnight," a hit for Rudy Vallee in 1931
Billy Ward and His Dominoes	1957	"Star Dust," by Hoagy Carmichael, 1929

The reader will have noted that I have listed the songs either by composer or by the artist who introduced them, depending on which seemed more important.

The presence of songs by great composers like Hoagy Carmichael, Cole Porter, and Rodgers and Hammerstein, and big bands like those of Claude Thornhill and Glenn Miller, means that these black artists took their material from the very heart of white popular culture. But, significantly, they did not draw on songs of the postwar period with which their white audience might have had distinct associations; rather, they drew on standards like "In the Still of the Night," or obscure songs like "Save the Last Dance for Me." It might seem that blacks would find very little to their liking in these songs, but two observations are in order here. First, as they became conscious of their white audience, they shrewdly chose songs which had a proven appeal to that audience. Second, when a style changes radically enough, it temporarily becomes dissociated from content. It is significant in this regard that The Platters covered the largest number of songs from the thirties and forties, because Tony Williams' extreme use of melisma could have made virtually any twentieth-century love song sound thrilling. As we know, he cultivated style for its own sake more than any other performer of his time.

Because of *Happy Days*, we associate "Blueberry Hill" so completely with the fifties that it is helpful to compare Fats Domino's version with Glenn Miller's. The big band version epitomizes what Frank Sinatra rebelled against when he left Tommy Dorsey in 1943. It begins with the usual long introduction by the brass and reeds; Ray Eberle's smooth vocal emphasizes the melodic continuity by holding the words ending in "-ill" which make the lyrics memorable: "thrillll"; "stillll," and so forth. Fats, on the other hand, substitutes his stride-like piano and a strong backbeat from his drummer for the band's brass and reeds. Instead of holding the rhyming words, he lets the piano fill in instead. By singing a phrase, and then letting the piano (or sometimes the saxophone) repeat it, he creates something like the identifying feature of black music, a call-and-response interplay. In short, Fats makes "Blueberry Hill" his own song as much as Elvis makes "Hound Dog" *his* own.

The analogy to such covers of white standards which occurs to anyone who knows art history is with cubism. A number of people have commented that we find only the most traditional subject matter—still lifes and portraits—in the great cubist paintings of Picasso and Braque. As in these performances by blacks, so with the paintings: the stylistic innovations carried the weight of the work, as though the non-innovative content maintained a certain equilibrium. Although the song itself does not come from the past, the same predominance of innovative style for its own sake, appears in the nonsense syllables of the first line of Little Richard's "Tutti Frutti," in the chorus of the Coasters' "Get A Job," and a number of other hits of the time.

In addition to these examples of musical interchange between the races, during the fifties, we also find a few instances of white covers of white songs, and black covers of black songs. One of Pat Boone's best records was "Love Letters in the Sand," a hit in 1958, in which he covered a song which had done well for Russ Columbo in 1931. As such, it fits in well with the black covers of songs from the thirties; since there was no obviously superior black version of the same song, it does not suffer by comparison. Best of all, no one was being exploited. And in the next year, Bobby Darin did well with a neo-jive version of a song, "Mack the Knife," from an unlikely source, *The Three Penny Opera*, by Brecht and Weill, 1928.

I also have two examples of hit songs which show, despite a radical difference in performance styles—or indeed because of that—the continuity in taking material from the thirties. Eddie Fisher's 1951 hit, "Lady of Spain," was introduced in England by Jack Payne and His Orchestra in 1931. Similarly, Elvis put a hillbilly version of "Blue Moon," the Rodgers and Hart classic from 1934, on his second album; however, it became a hit for him only in 1961. These tributes to the thirties from such unlikely and such different sources bear eloquent witness to the enduring appeal of Tin Pan Alley songs.

Finally, I know of only one successful cover from the fifties in which a black artist re-worked a black song; this was Fats Domino's "Corrina Corrina," a traditional folk blues associated with Cab Calloway in 1933 (to be sure, Chuck Berry recorded W.C. Handy's "St. Louis Blues" (1914), probably for sentimental reasons, but it wasn't a hit).

One generalization follows from all this. If we think of the songs which we now consider as classic rock 'n' roll, like "Hound Dog," and "Tutti Frutti", which were *not* covers of songs from the thirties and forties, which did not derive from gospel, and which were not taken from another medium, we realize that they were in a minority. To get a sense of the achievement of the great performers, we need to remember what a mixed bag the top ten charts were through the period 1954-59. A further thought suggests itself: since Chuck Berry and Buddy Holly almost always recorded original material in which style and content merged, this may explain why they had more direct influence than anyone else in the fifties on the subsequent course of rock 'n' roll history.

Notes

[1]See "Black Roots, White Fruits: Racism in the Music Industry," in Steve Chapple and Reebee Garofalo, *Rock 'N' Roll Is Here To Pay* (Chicago: Nelson-Hall, 1977), pp. 231-268.

[2]Tony Heilbut, *The Gospel Sound*, p. 71.

[3]*Ibid.*, p. 283.

[4]Arnold Shaw, *The Rockin' 50's*, pp. 128-129.

Chapter 6:
Electric Guitars, Chuck Berry,
and Buddy Holly

Just as brass instruments created the sound of jazz in the twenties and thirties, so stringed instruments have created the sound of rock 'n' roll since the fifties. Whereas in jazz, the trumpet, the saxophone, and the trombone have all had their virtuosos, the rock 'n' roll instrument which truly matters is the electric guitar. Thus, to understand rock 'n' roll, we must understand the electric guitar—how it came into being, and how it transformed popular music, even as it was being transformed itself. Only in this way can we understand the two most important guitarists of the fifties, Chuck Berry and Buddy Holly.

It is fitting that the electric guitar created rock 'n' roll, for there is hardly any classical repertoire for the guitar. In Europe, it was virtually always a vernacular instrument, whether it played the music of the people in the streets, or whether genteel ladies plucked its gut or silk strings in nineteenth-century parlors. Such acoustic guitars created their characteristically mellow sound when the vibrating strings resonated in the wooden body of the guitar itself. In America, this sound proved unsatisfactory, and musicians substituted steel strings. The metal gave a twangier sound with more bite, but it still decayed very rapidly— it had little sustain, to use the technical term—and guitar makers tried various expedients which would give it a bigger sound.

In the thirties, guitar makers experimented both with the body of the guitar, and with the strings. Thus, they added a metal resonator, which gave the sound more force; bluesman Son House played a resonator guitar. They also twinned the strings, producing a twelve-string guitar. The twelve-string guitar also had a bigger sound, but the large neck required a big man with big hand, like Leadbelly, to play it.

It was also during the thirties that the acoustic guitar took on a new meaning as a result of one of the many interactions between popular music and film. With the advent of sound, movie cowboys began to sing—and play the guitar. "With the example of Roy Rogers and Gene Autry, the guitar finally gained respectability in America. What had formerly been a folk instrument, confined largely to country musicians or to disreputable bluesmen, now became accepted in any family."[1]

Really, though, nothing but electricity could transform the guitar,so music and technology merged. Interestingly enough, the production history of the guitar roughly coincides with the production history of the television set. Experimentation with both media began in the twenties, and production began in the thirties; World War II delayed both of them. Then, between them, they defined the fifties. The difference, though, is that everybody knew that television was a new medium, and that it was one which required national standards. The electric guitar, however, developed in fits and starts from the acoustic guitar. And individual tinkerers in the tradition of Thomas Edison and Henry Ford could produce important results right away.

Although various stories circulate about people who put an electric pickup on an acoustic guitar in the twenties, most of them remain vague. We do know that the Rickenbacker Company put out the first commercially produced electric guitar in 1931. Like many electric guitars at the time, it was intended for the Hawaiian market. As guitar historians Tom and Mary Anne Evans tell us, "The aim in the 1930s was to produce an electric guitar which sounded like an acoustic guitar, only louder, so it was natural to approach the problem simply by putting a pickup on a f-hole guitar."[2] These guitars had two soundholes, in the form of a cursive *f* on either side of the strings (hence the name), rather than the traditional round hole under them. They were also larger than acoustic guitars, with arched tops and a hardwood neck; all these features gave the sound more sustain. They thus offer an example of what McLuhan calls "rear-view mirrorism," in that they treat something new as though it was something old—such as the first cars, which had sockets for buggy whips. The Gibson Company acknowledged this rear-view mirrorism, when it called its commercially successful electric-acoustic guitars the ES (for Electric Spanish) series.

Another way of manipulating the guitar's sound tended to separate black and white musicians during the thirties. This was slide, or bottleneck guitar, the use of a long, smooth instrument held against the strings by the left hand. Slide guitar gives the effect of an exaggerated glissando, and came to America from Hawaii. Blind Lemon Jefferson picked it up, presumably from the many Hawaiian records on the market in the twenties. He profoundly affected the style of electric guitar playing in the thirties, when Elmore James made his name with it. Inadvertently, slide guitar playing created a difference in black and white styles. Black bluesmen held the guitar Spanish style, while whites usually held it across their laps Hawaiian style, and called it steel guitar.

I suspect that the difference came about because of the differences in the role of the guitar in the blues and country traditions. In the blues, the guitar was the prime solo instrument, of course, and its dominance made musicians inclined to play slide guitar rather as they had played the more familiar style. In country music, however, the fiddle, not the guitar, predominated, and country musicians usually played in groups. As a result, the guitar often played the fills and introductions to which Hawaiian style was well suited.

Nick Tosches calls Bob Dunn, who joined Milton Brown and His Musical Brownies in 1934, the first amplified steel guitarist.[3] Dunn had fitted a home-make pickup to a Mexican acoustic guitar. Although Dunn was the first (and, Tosches thinks, the best) amplified guitarist in the thirties, he was not the only one. Remarkably, all the major amplified guitarists of the thirties were from Texas and Oklahoma, as the following table shows.

Birthplaces of Major Amplified Guitarists
of the Thirties

Charlie Christian	Dallas, Texas
Bob Dunn	Houston, Texas
Leon McAuliffe	Houston, Texas
Oscar Moore	Austin, Texas
T-Bone Walker	Linden, Texas

To be sure, John Ham.mond discovered Charlie Christian while he was living in Oklahoma City, and Leon McAuliffe played with Bob Wills and His Texas Playboys, who were usually based in Tulsa. The electric guitar became important in the Southwest partially because people could afford them (as blacks could not in the South), and partially because they needed them to play at the dances which the more Puritanical whites of the South rarely attended. Thus, like rock 'n' roll and Top 40 radio in the fifties, the electric guitar as a lead instrument appeared far from the media centers of New York and Los Angeles, where it would have had to battle the well-established tradition of brass and reed instruments.

Although the pioneer electric guitarists did not all play in the same style, one generalization about them holds. As we recall, it was in the late thirties that great singers like Frank Sinatra and Billie Holliday were training themselves to sing through a microphone as though they were part of the horn section of a big band; it's not surprising, then, that electric guitarists of the thirties sounded like horns, too (this was stylistic, as opposed to technological, rear-view mirrorism). After John Hammond discovered Charlie Christian playing his Gibson ES-150 in Oklahoma City, and got him a job with Benny Goodman:

He saw that notes could be sustained, and a saxophone style of single note playing which he so admired could be obtained, and of course the volume of the guitar could now equal that of any other instrument. In fact many early observers of Christian's playing actually thought at first they were listening to a saxophone.[4]

Charlie Christian became the most influential early electric guitarist not simply because he was a genius, but also because he played with Benny Goodman, and a lot of musicians heard him. Bob Dunn and Leon McAuliffe actually began playing in this style a little before him, and may have had some influence on him. Dunn's solos with Milton Brown's groups have a syncopated, horn-like quality, and Jesse Ashlock, who played the fiddle with Bob Wills, once commented,"We tried to do the same thing on strings they did on horns."[5] While electricity had given the guitar a new prominence, it did not give it an identity of its own.

It was easier for guitarists who played in small groups or as solo artists to innovate; hence the importance of Oscar Moore, and his mentor T-Bone Walker. Oscar played with the Nat King Cole Trio in Los Angeles from 1943 to 1947, and did much to establish the legitimacy of the guitar. The trio consisted of Nat's piano and vocals, Johnny Miller's acoustic bass, and Oscar's Gibson ES-150; it became a model for many later jazz combos.

But it was T-Bone Walker, author of the classic, deeply moving "Stormy Monday," who made the electric guitar a driving lead instrument. He didn't attempt to imitate a horn; his picking belongs only on a guitar. As Paul Oliver says,"His technique was dazzling with its runs and flamboyant arpeggios and ideally suited to an electric instrument."[6] Although T-Bone was well recorded (like Oscar Moore, he worked mostly in Los Angeles), so that we can appreciate his skill today, we have missed something essential about him, for, like Al Jolson, he was primarily a live performer. A great showman, he was the first to make the newly conspicuous and dominant guitar a part of his act by playing it while holding it between his legs or behind his back.

Still, this handful of virtuosos did not make a musical revolution immediately. Among both blacks and whites, in both the blues and country music tradition, the acoustic guitar had enormous appeal as a symbol of simplicity, directness, and thus that great American virtue, innocence. Muddy Waters started playing an electric guitar about 1943, in order to get the volume he needed in raucous South Side bars, but he preferred acoustic. And then there is the case of Bob Wills and the Texas Playboys, one of the truly revolutionary groups in the history of American popular music.

People usually say that Bob Wills played "Western swing," but this hybrid term simply indicates the impossibility of classifying him. He played the most traditional country instrument, the fiddle, but when he interpolates "Aa-haa" and"Ye-es," his intonations come directly from the field hollers of the black workers he grew up with in west Texas. As the Texas Playboys coalesced as a unit, they maintained more of a loose jazz feel than other country groups. He not only added an electric guitar in 1935, as we know, but also at about the same time he did something even more startling—he added a drummer. His drummer, "Smokey" Dacus, didn't think he'd fit in at first, but soon realized what Bob wanted—a punchy beat for dancing, and created it by using a brush with his left hand, for the downbeats, and hit a stick against a suitcase, on two and four. Bob's charisma and presence made this unlikely grouping, which at one time included both a tenor banjo and tenor saxophone, continually inventive without lapsing into self-indulgence.

You never knew what to expect from Bob Wills and the Texas Playboys. They sound like an East Coast big band on the first few bars of his trademark "San Antonio Rose" (even "Deep in the Heart of Texas" begins in the same way), and the ending. But in between, the fiddles and the steel guitar mark the origin of their music as the Southwest. On "Silver Bells," though, it's just the opposite; the fiddles begin it in a traditional way, and only later does a smooth horn section come in.

We recognize innovators by the resistance they encounter, and Bob encountered a lot of it, most noticeably and symbolically at the Grand Old Opry. When the Texas Playboys began setting up in Ryman Auditorium one time in the early forties with their twin lead fiddles, a steel guitar *and* electric guitar, and drums, it was too much for the traditionalists. Minnie Pearle quotes Roy Acuff, "The King of Country Music," as saying "They're spoiling the Opry—putting on those amplified instruments here."[7]

As the saying goes, nobody liked Bob but the people. The Texas Playboys had an infectious dance beat, easier to follow than that of traditional country string bands, but not as heavy as in black rhythm and blues. When we listen to his records now, we hear him as a clear precursor of the rockabilly sound of the fifties. In fact, he was Bill Haley's idol, and when Bill began his recording career in 1950, he called his group Bill Haley and the Four Aces of Western Swing. It is a remarkable tribute to Bob's openness that, in 1958, when an unholy alliance of politicans, ministers, and country musicians was denouncing rock 'n' roll, he welcomed it. In a newspaper interview he once said:

"Rock and Roll? Why, man, that's the same kind of music we've been playing since 1928!... What I mean is that people don't change much. We didn't call it 'rock and roll' back when we introduced it as our style in 1928, and we don't call it rock and roll the way we play it now. But it's just basic rhythm and has gone by a lot of different names in my time."[8]

Finally, there are intriguing connections between Bob and Buddy Holly. Bob was born in Turkey, Texas, which is only about sixty miles as the crow flies, from Lubbock, where Buddy was born. In 1957, Bob moved briefly to Abilene, about 150 miles from Lubbock, and it would be surprising if Buddy hadn't gone to one of his shows. As if this weren't enough, when Buddy decided that he needed another guitarist to make the Crickets a quartet, he picked Tommy Allsup, who had previously played with Johnnie Lee Wills, Bob's brother.

Returning to a consideration of the production history of the electric guitar, we notice that it came into its own in the post-war period, "When Gibson started production again after the Second World War, it found an enormous demand for amplified instruments which had not existed before the war. While electric Hawaiian guitars remained popular, the real growth was in the demand for electric-acoustic guitars, which rapidly superseded the unamplified arch-top guitars of 30s."[9] The second thing to notice is the dependence of the electric guitar, like so many other technological devices of the late forties, on the electronics industry which the war had created in Los Angeles. It was in Los Angeles that Leo Fender formed the Fender Electrical Instrument Co. in 1947. In that same year, also in Los Angeles, Fred Bigsby built what Donald Brosnac calls the first modern electric guitar for Merle Travis. This guitar had a maple body—hard woods such as maple create more sustain—with the insides carved out. Thus, the sound was created both within the body, and outside it, by the amplifiers, and is called a semi-solid body.

Semi-solid body guitars created the sound of fifties rock 'n' roll. Bill Haley played a Gibson L7, Scotty Moore played a Gibson, and Link Wray played a Gibson Les Paul on his instrumental "Rumble." Such guitars combine some of the mellow sound of an acoustic with the sustain of an electric. Thus, we can add these guitars to the list of other features of fifties rock 'n' roll as a transitional style which I have already discussed.

Link Wray's Gibson Les Paul brings up the name of the great visionary of the electric guitar, Les Paul. Like most visionaries, he was so far ahead of his time that people couldn't understand what he was doing. As early as 1941, he understood that putting an electric pickup on a guitar obsolesced the guitar body as it had existed for centuries, since the sound came from the amplifiers, not from the body. Acting on this understanding, he took a 4″ x 4″ piece of lumber and attached it to a guitar neck. This was the guitar proper, and although he sawed apart a guitar body, and glued each half to the lumber, he did so purely for the convenience of holding and playing it. Since the guitar now externalized the sound, what was required was a completely rigid, solid body constructed of a very hard wood, and later plastic or metal. It appeared in the form of the legendary Fender Stratocaster of 1953, and later versions. Since the body no longer produced the sound, it no longer had to look like a guitar body, and in 1958, Gibson produced the "Flying V," which Bo Diddley played. But rear-view mirrorism continued, for, in the same year, Gretsch produced its Tennessean, a hollow-body guitar without sound holes; but since people expected them on a guitar, it had *painted* f-holes.

Thus, rock 'n' rollers in the fifties played two distinctively different kinds of guitars. Gibson semi-solid bodies with a mellow sound, and solid bodies such as the Stratocaster, with a brighter sound. The two greatest singer-songwriter-guitarists of the fifties, Chuck Berry and Buddy Holly, can be distinguished by, among other things, their choice of guitars. Chuck played a Gibson ES-175, and Buddy played a Stratocaster. As we consider each of them in turn, it will become apparent that other things about their music are consistent with this difference.

Chuck recorded at Chess Records in Chicago, where blues greats like Muddy Waters, Howlin' Wolf, and Little Walter recorded. Buddy recorded at Norman Petty's studio in Clovis, New Mexico, which had produced some rockabilly hits, but had no musical giants like the ones at Chess. Thus, Chuck was writing and recording in a clearly defined cultural context, and we can usually understand his music by thinking about how he changed and assimilated the music of various precursors. This is hardly the case at all with Buddy.

Chuck's situation at Chess offers an instructive contrast with Elvis's situation at Sun. Chuck soon transcended the urban blues sound of Chess, just as Elvis soon transcended the rockabilly sound of Sun. But they did so in very different ways. Since Elvis did not write his own material, he was lucky enough to have an understanding producer in Sam Phillips who would let him develop his own style more or less through sheer musical intuition. Though this style did owe a lot to blues and to white gospel, it was uniquely his own.

As a singer-songwriter-guitarist, Chuck was the more assimilative; he himself has said that his two principal early influences were Louis Jordan and Nat King Cole, and to this list we must add Hank Williams.

I would never have thought about Chuck's relationship to Hank Williams if a friend of mine had not mentioned one time that when he was a teenager in Philadelphia in the fifties, he and his friends thought of Chuck as a country and western singer. After I got over my astonishment, I began to think about what that meant, aside from the fact that "Memphis" has a coy country and western sentimentalism (actually, "Memphis" probably derives from "The Naughty Lady of Shady Lane," which was a big hit for the Mills Brothers in 1954). One might begin by saying that Hank had what Chuck created; Hank epitomized what Chuck created. It is as though Chuck combined Hank's abilities as a singer-songwriter-guitarist, in such a way as to create a music with the national appeal of Frankie Laine's and Jo Stafford's covers of Hank's songs. But Chuck did not compromise or imitate because he had a national audience with a specific identity—teenagers—just as Hank had had a regional audience with a specific identity—hillbillies. Hank's audience came into being through a combination of geography and clear-channel radio stations; Chuck's audience was created by population demographics of the baby boom and by the media revolution which created Top 40 radio. Both these groups lived at the behest of a larger authority—parents for teenagers, and the northern establishment for hillbillies—and their good times threatened this authority. Their lyrics acknowledge the presence of this larger group, as in Hank's "Settin' the Woods on Fire." The man tells the woman he invites to go dancing with him that the next day he'll "be back plowin'," just as in "Sweet Little Sixteen," the girl will be "back in class again" after she's had her fling (and the high school kid in "School Days" is "hopin' to pass"). The teenager's experience of school corresponds to the redneck's experience of farm work. Both men deal with the frustrations of this situation with humor, as in Hank's witty, deliberately absurd rhymes in "Settin' the Woods on Fire," and the girl's stuck seat belt in "No Particular Place to Go," a deft metaphor for the sexual frustration of the fifties. The fact that people rarely used seat belts in the fifties makes this situation a matter of choice on Chuck's part, and hence all the more indicative.

One other similarity between Hank and Chuck is anomalous, but worth noting. While both of them spoke for, and to, their audience with a fine intuitive sense, they also dabbled in other regional styles. Thus, Hank wrote a fine tribute to Cajun music, "Jambalaya," and Chuck wrote a tribute to Caribbean music, "Havana Moon." In both songs, the music respects these ethnic roots, and the lyrics use the patois of the area.

Still, Chuck was a black man singing to white teenagers, while Hank, who had grown up poor and white in the South, was singing to people just like him. So it is reasonable to ask how Chuck came to terms with black music. What did he keep, and what did he discard?

Some of Chuck's music has a very black sound, as on "Wee Wee Hours." Chuck doesn't play guitar at all on this song, which has a bluesy piano lead, and the slow, heavily accentuated backbeat by the drums which marked the rhythm and blues style of the late forties and early fifties (Southern disc jockeys used to call it "droopy drawers music"). "Thirty Days," with its reference to a gypsy woman is still a very black song, but not so bluesy. It is a song for adults, for the singer is married to the woman, and threatens to see a judge about a warrant. On "Too Much Monkey Business," the singer is also an adult; he has fought in the Korean War, and his woman wants him to get married, settle down, and—notoriously—write a book.

But "Thirty Days" and "Two Much Monkey Business" have Chuck's good-natured wit, as in the threat to take his problem to the United Nations, and differ noticeably from what the true bluesmen were recording at Chess. Chuck's songs are in a steady, predictable 4/4 time, with none of Muddy Waters' inventive stop time rhythms, In his lyrics, Chuck used rhymed couplets, rather than the *aab* scheme of traditional blues. Neither here nor anywhere else does Chuck use the sexual braggadoccio of so many great blues songs, such as Muddy's famous "I'm Your Hoochie Coochie Man," or of his fellow Chess artist Bo Diddley's "I'm a Man." The blues was music for adults, and blues singers treated sex with an adult intensity, which would have put off teenagers.

As to the sound, there is a bit of bluesy vibrato in the guitar break on "Johnny B. Goode," and on "School Days." In "Johnny B. Goode," and "No Particular Place to Go," he sets up a call and response relationship between his voice and his guitar, very much like what Fats Domino does with his voice and his piano on "Blueberry Hill." Blues singers didn't need any backup vocals, and Chuck used them only on "Too Pooped to Pop" (an eclectic record, his only one with a sax break and a cha cha beat), and "Almost Grown," which has doo wop vocals. But he never used the harmonica on any of his records, although Little Walter was recording for Chess at the time. Instead, he used what became the standard rock 'n' roll grouping of electric lead guitar, bass, and drums, with the difference that he kept a brittle, bluesy piano.

The black music which meant the most to Chuck was the music of two men who had enjoyed great success with white audience—Louis Jordan, the first black to have a million seller, "Choo Choo Ch'Boogie," in 1946; and Nat King Cole, the first black to have his own television program, *The Nat King Cole Show*, which ran on NBC from 1956 to 1957. Like Chuck's, Louis' songs were in rhymed couplets, with lots of fast patter and humor. In Louis' "Saturday Night Fish Fry," as in Chuck's "Round and Round," the police break up what is obviously an after-hours party at a black club.

But if Louis tommed a bit in his stage persona, Nat did not. Pleasants puts it well when he says that, "It may be doubted that Nat King Cole ever made a conscious decision to tailor his singing to white taste."[10] Although Chuck certainly addressed "Sweet Little Sixteen" to white teenagers, he was not pandering to them, because he lacked an intuitive feel for the blues idiom— he was from St. Louis, after all, not the Delta. We might also recall here that

Ray Charles started out playing country and western, and then taught himself to imitate Nat perfectly. With Chuck, it's not a matter of singing what we would now call MOR ballads, as Nat did, but a matter of orientation.

Chuck intuitively understood the new media complex of the fifties. His songs are radio songs, paced to the jingles and patter of the Top 40 station, and people often listened to them in their cars, as in "No Particular Place to Go," so everything is speeded up. The lines are shorter—often masterpieces of succinctness—and the guitar work is faster (the tempo is, in fact, so fast that he can get away with such approximate rhymes as "math/pass" in "School Days," and "Music/use it" in "Rock and Roll Music," which might have seemed merely inept on slower songs). The guitar, which gives these songs their drive, has a new and exciting prominence. A flashy guitar run grabs the listener's attention at the beginning of "No Particular Place to Go," "Back in the U.S.A.," and "Johnny B. Goode."

The guitar isn't simply more prominent and faster than it had been on earlier rhythm and blues and rockabilly records—it's also played in a higher register. The guitar breaks on "Roll Over Beethoven," for example, are quite high; Chuck is often playing from about the tenth fret on down. And he could do this only on an electric guitar. A prime reason the acoustic guitar, even with an electric pickup, remained a rhythm instrument for so long was that it was virtually impossible to get any volume on high notes. But on an electric guitar you can get volume as well as sustain on high notes and on the low notes fretted up toward the tuning machines, and Chuck exploits this range to declare the guitar's independence as a solo instrument. Thus, it was electricity that delivered the music from "the days of old," i.e., the big band era.

Chuck's lyrics, as well as his overall sound, show an awareness of the media revolution of the fifties. Although teenagers felt themselves to be an oppressed minority, they could feel for the first time that they weren't alone, as the nascent youth culture acquired some consciousness of itself as a national force. Chuck sensed this, and put it into his lyrics. The girl in "Sweet Little Sixteen," with whom guys all over the country want to dance, watches *American Bandstand* and collects autographs; the boy in "Anthony Boy" watches TV instead of doing his homework; Chuck appeals to his disc jockey on "Roll Over Beethoven," and of course Johnny B. Goode becomes a movie star.

Thus, Chuck was, in effect, engaged in a process of defining rock 'n' roll in an American, not a regional or ethnic, context. We need to remember here that most of Chuck's classics became hits in the late fifties, when various authority figures, in their own version of McCarthyism, were attacking the music as un-American and ungodly. In mythical terms, the music represented a Dionysian threat to Apollonian security; it was, in short, the "other" in a self/other dichotomy.

Chuck made it possible for rock 'n' roll to sustain itself by assimilating the conflicts of youth culture to what I have called the macrostructure of American mythology. After all, as the witty Lord Illingworth quips in Oscar Wilde's play *A Woman of No Importance*, "The youth of America is their only tradition. It has been going on now for three hundred years. To hear them talk, one would imagine they were in their first childhood."[11] From the beginning, America has defined itself as a young country in opposition to old Europe, as a democratic state in opposition to elitist, feudal Europe; the popular music of youth culture had an undeniably American quality by its very nature.

Thus, Chuck could write "Roll Over Beethoven," which is simultaneously an assertion of the power of rock 'n' roll and a highly traditional opposition of an infectious dance music with a back beat you can't lose—as what Walt Whitman called his "barbaric yawp"—to the elitist, text-oriented art music of Europe. In "Brown-Eyed Handsome Man," Chuck jokes that the Venus de Milo lost both her arms in a "rasslin' match" (wrestling was very big on TV in the fifties); he has here the same irreverent attitude to European art as his fellow Missourian Mark Twain, in *Innocents Abroad*. And Twain would have appreciated Chuck's enthusiasm for America in "Back in the U.S.A.," which is not Fourth of July patriotism, but a love of the vernacular America of hamburgers and jukeboxes.

The opposition of democracy and elitism is not simply a matter of the opposition of America and Europe, though, for American class structure has provided many examples here at home. Chuck uses it in "Maybelline," in which our hero drives a Ford, in opposition to his rival's Cadillac Coupe de Ville. And, of course, our hero as a man of the people passes the Cadillac in triumph. This treatment is consistent with the origin of the Ford, which was originally everyman's car in opposition to the cars of the early twentieth century, which only the wealthy could afford.

Moreover, Clark Gable's situation in Frank Capra's archetypal romantic comedy *It Happened One Night* (1934) anticipates our hero's situation in "Maybelline." Clark drives a Model T as the film's climax approaches, and is overtaken by the limousine in which Claudette Colbert's father is riding. In both *It Happened One Night* and "Maybelline," the man of the people wins. In the movie, he wins the girl, and in the song he wins the race.

That leaves "Johnny B. Goode," the first show biz song in rock 'n' roll. Johnny, as a guitar player from the oral culture of the south who becomes a movie star, resembles Elvis both in real life, and in his movies such as *Jailhouse Rock* and *Loving You*. Show biz thus offers teenagers the possibilities for self-fulfillment either as performers, as in "Johnny B. Goode," or as listeners, as in "Sweet Little Sixteen," and "School Days," which their society denies them.

In contrast to Chuck, Buddy did not write narrative songs, and although he addressed his music to other teenagers, he never mentions high school, or cars. Buddy's biographer John Goldrosen makes a good point when he says of "Words of Love," "Listened to today, the record seems to have little relation to its own time, or to any time."[12] The intimate, quiet quality of many of his songs ("Rave On" is an exception, obviously) gives them an odd resemblance to the great Tin Pan Alley love songs, for their lack of reference to time and place give them a universal quality.

The two prime characteristics of his vocal style are the Hank Williams hiccup, and the glide from one note to another. On "It Doesn't Matter Any More," he holds the word "you" over four different notes, and as Goldrosen notes, he begins "Rave On" with "well," which he makes into a rising six-syllable word. This is not melisma, because he hits each note distinctly, but what Goldrosen doesn't say is that it takes a strong, full voice to sing like that without breaking or cracking. The strength of Buddy's voice sounds forth full and clear in some of the records he made in New York as a singles act after he split with the Crickets, such as "It Doesn't Matter Any More," which has a violin arrangement instead of rock 'n' roll accompaniment. No other rock 'n' roller of the fifties except Elvis, whom Buddy met in Lubbock in 1955, could have sung like this—or would have wanted to.

Although Buddy played a Stratocaster, he didn't play only a Stratocaster; he strums an acoustic guitar on "Well All Right." Just before his death, Buddy was getting interested in Cajun music, as Hank Williams had done before him, and was thinking of recording an album of gospel songs. In short, he was as unclassifiable as Bob Wills, who gives a clue as to how we might talk about him. The intimacy of his songs, their timelessness, the sincerity of his delivery, and the strength of his voice, all suggest the term "country swing crooner."

Obviously, Buddy had as eclectic a musical sense as Bob Wills did, and both of them did the unexpected. Their use of drums offers a case in point. If Bob surprised people by putting in drums, Buddy surprised people by taking them out. "Peggy Sue" is probably Buddy's best-known song, and it has no drums at all; drummer Jerry Allison provided the rhythm for the song by slapping on his knees.

Both Buddy and Bob played for dances in the Southwest, but they recorded in very different contexts. Bob's recordings convey the flavor of the way his band played for dances; his interpolated comments and hollers retain the loose, crowd-pleasing quality which his public performances must have had. But while Buddy loved to perform—Gary Busey shows this wonderfully in *The Buddy Holly Story (1978)* he knew that he was making records for Top 40 stations to play, and he and the Crickets and Norman Petty often worked for long hours in getting the intonations and balance just right. They understood very well that people listen more closely to records than to live performances. Still, he thought of studio work and live performances as closely related. As Tommy Alsup once explained, "He knew it would help the popularity of his songs if local bands played them at high school dances and the like, so he rarely did anything that any little old band couldn't play."[13]

To clarify the nature of Buddy's music, it is useful here to consider the contrasts between him and Chuck in terms of a figure/ground opposition between the themes of the lyrics and the means used to produce the overall sound. We may consider as the figure of Chuck's work the themes of the lyrics, which over and over again deal with the meaning of media in a social context. But aside from his semi-solid body Gibson, he used no studio devices in producing the overall sound. Thus, an emphasis on technology in the figure balances a de-emphasis on technology in the ground.

We have just the opposite figure/ground contrast in Buddy's music. He concentrates on boy/girl relationships to the exclusion of almost everything else; his characteristic ambivalence about love, which Goldrosen and others have noted, keeps the songs from becoming sappy. The social setting of media thus does not appear at all in what I have been calling the figure of his music.

By contrast, however, technology pervades the quality of the ground, which produced the overall sound. Goldrosen is surely right when he says that, "Holly was probably the first rock 'n' roll artist to use vocal and instrumental overdubbing."[14] But in the early spring of 1957 in Clovis, New Mexico, Norman Petty didn't have a multi-track board, so they put down the rhythm track, and then recorded the vocal and guitar solos over that for "Words of Love." In technical terms, this means that the two tracks are a generation apart, with a consequent loss of fidelity. But as Goldrosen points out, the rhythm track recedes as a result, and gives the vocal its close, intimate quality. This overdubbed sound gives the record a slightly unreal quality (for 1957, at least), and thus makes it more removed from a social setting than ever.

Although "Words of Love" was the first song which Buddy overdubbed, it was not the last. Buddy sang a duet with himself on "Listen to Me," and again the intimacy of the lyrics (and Buddy's delivery of them) is well suited to the unusual effect of the overdubbing. "Listen to Me" sounds as if there is an echo added on the first vocal track, but not on the second. Norman Petty did not create the echo effect as Sam Phillips did at Sun, with a tape device which delayed the sound for a tenth of a second, and then played it back. Rather, he used the simple arrangement of playing the sound through a speaker on one side of an empty room, and then picking it up on another speaker on the other side of the room.

It is unsettling to notice that the social setting, so important in Chuck's music interrupted his career when—like so many black musicians before him— he got in trouble with the law; and it is equally unsettling to notice that technology, so important to Buddy's music in the form of his Stratocaster and Norman Petty's studio, killed him when his rented plane crashed that cold February night in 1959. It is a melodramatic exaggeration to say that an era ended abruptly in 1959, because Fats Domino, Ray Charles, the Everly Brothers, and other major acts of the fifties continued to perform and put records on the charts, but rock 'n' roll was clearly changing. In the next period, 1959-1964, a period of assimilation, the innovative records no longer came from the provinces, and the sound of the records changed as well.

Notes

[1]Tom and Mary Anne Evans, *Guitars. From the Renaissance to Rock* (New York and London: Paddington Press, 1977) p. 318.

[2] *Ibid.,* p. 341.

[3]Nick Tosches, *Country. The Biggest Music in America* (New York: Stein and Day, 1977), p. 187.

[4]Maurice J. Summerfield, *The Jazz Guitar. Its Evolution and Its Players* (Tyne and Wear: Summerfield, 1978), p. 15.

[5]Quoted in Charles R. Townsend, *San Antonio Rose. A Life of Bob Wills* (Urbana: U. of Illinois Press, 1976), p. 102

[6]Paul Oliver, *The Story of the Blues* (n.p.: Chilton Book Company, 1969), p. 144.

[7]Quoted in Tony Palmer, *All You Need Is Love* (New York: Grossman Publishers, 1976), p. 189.

[8]Quoted in Townsend, *San Antonio Rose,* p. 269.

[9]Evans and Evans, Guitars, p. 346.

[10]Pleasants, *The Great-American Popular Singers,* p. 220.

[11]Oscar Wilde, *The Plays of Oscar Wilde* (New York: The Modern Library, n.d.), p. 139.

[12]John Goldrosen, *Buddy Holly. His Life and Music* (Bowling Green: Popular Press 1975), p. 81.

[13]Quoted in *ibid.,* p. 92.

[14]*Ibid.,* p. 83.

Chapter 7:
The East Coast Rises Again

Grease, the most profitable movie musical of all time, takes place in 1959. The place is not given but we can guess that it takes place in a large Eastern city because of the way it sets up an opposition between Italians and Poles. The movie actually mutes this opposition by leaving out last names, but the libretto of the Broadway show indicates it clearly. The two important characters are Sandy Dumbrowski (Olivia Newton-John in the movie), and Eugene Florczyk, a skinny kid who wears glasses and who is out of it all, and who is therefore class valedictorian. They represent devotion to external social ideals, such as virginity and book learning, respectively. On the other hand, Danny is Danny Zuko, and as played by John Travolta, is obviously Italian. The libretto notes that his friend Sonny is "Italian-looking," and as played by Michael Tucci in the movie, he certainly does look Italian. Betty is Betty Rizzo, and Cha Cha is Cha Cha DiGregorio. The spontaneous, fun-loving Italians represent devotion to the self, not to social ideals. The opposition of these two ethnic groups in *Grease* thus corresponds to a recurring opposition in Americal culture in that it presents the Poles, Sandy and Eugene, as experience, and the Italians as innocence. In the end, of course, Sandy gets converted to innocence, as women who represent experience in American movies usually do.

Grease thus portrays something essential about a good deal of the music of the period 1959-1964—its urban, ethnic quality. With the exception of the Everly Brothers, hardly any Southern rockers of significance appeared after the first surge of the great performers of the mid-fifties. There was only one Pole, Bobby Vinton, but the Italians abounded. They came from Italian neighborhoods in the New York-New Jersey-Philadelphia area. A number of the new performers came from the Bronx, so we can begin there.

The best-known group from the Bronx was Dion and the Belmonts; they took their name from Belmont Avenue, a street in Bronx's Little Italy, and their names suggest just how Italian they were: Dion DiMucci, Angelo D'Alea, Carlo Mastangelo, and Fred Milano (in fact, we could think of "The Wanderer," as an expression of Italian Macho). Dion and the Belmonts, along with some other Italian singing groups which had only local hits, such as the Earls, the Regents, and the Consorts, hung out at the Cousin Music Shop on Fordham Road in the Bronx, which was owned by Lou Cichetti. Cichetti, who owned the Cousin record label, issued "Barbara Ann," by the Regents in 1961; the song became a valuable copyright when the Beach Boys made it a standard.[1]

One important Italian singles act came from the Bronx: Bobby Darin (Waldo Robert Cassotto).

Other boroughs had Italian talent, too, of course. Vito (Vito Picone) and the Elegants came from Staten Island; their "Little Star" was a hit both in America and in Italy. Randy (Dominick Safito) and the Rainbows (their hit was "Denise," in 1963) came from Brooklyn, as did Vito (Vito Balsamo) and the Salutations.

Moving across the Hudson to New Jersey, we find that the Four Seasons ("Sherry,"; "Big Girls Don't Cry") came from the Italian section of Newark; the three Seasons who sang were Frankie Valli, Bob Gaudio, and Tommy DeVito. Joey Dee and the Starliters rode the Twist craze to fame while they were playing the Peppermint Lounge in Manhattan in 1961 and recorded "The Peppermint Twist." Joey was Joe DiNicola and the group was from Passaic (incidentally, the Peppermint Lounge was owned by an Italian, Ralph Saggese). While she was not exactly a rocker, the most popular female vocalist of the period was Connie Frances ("Who's Sorry Now", "Lipstick on Your Collar," etc.). She was from Newark and was born Constance Francanero. And although Sandra Dee, "lousy with virginity," was neither a singer nor Italian, she was part of this pattern, too. She was from Bayonne, and her real name was Alexandra Zuck.

American Bandstand originated from Philadelphia, and Dick Clark's entertainment complex fostered the careers of two Italian Teen Idols, Frankie Avalon (Avallone) and Fabian Forte, both of whom were from South Philadelphia (Chubby Checker was from the same neighborhood). They both recorded for Chancellor Records, and were managed by their writers, Bob Marcucci and Peter DeAngelis. Bobby Rydell (remember the kids in _Grease_ go to Rydell High—presumably in memory of his "Swingin' School") was born Robert Ridarelli. In 1960, he showed his devotion to his Italian heritage when he recorded "Volare," which had been a minor hit in 1959 for Domenico Modugno, who had written it. And who can forget Annette Funicello, born in Utica, New York, who recorded "O Dio Mio" in 1960? "Volare" and "O Dio Mio" formed part of an Italian trend in popular music, which was not so completely youth music as it later became. For example, the theme music from _La Dolce Vita_ was a hit in 1960, and in 1961 Emilio Pericoli had a hit with "Al Di La." Finally, outside the New York area there was Freddie Cannon ("Tallahassie Lassie"), who was Fred Picariello, from Revere, Massachusetts.

But it is not enough to describe a pattern, such as the ethnic composition of singing groups, which appears at any given time; it is also necessary to explain it. During this period, a number of East Coast Italian singers got breaks because of a combination of factors. First, they grew up in an ethnic culture which had a strong musical tradition. Second, they could, and did, sing on streetcorners; the passersby gave them a ready and undemanding audience which rural and suburban kids lacked (when New York groups wanted to experiment with echo effects, they sang in the subway). Third, they lived in a center of the music industry, so that it was easy for them to meet agents and producers.

If this sounds a lot like what happened to Frank Sinatra, that is just the point. In this period of assimilation of the breakthrough of rock 'n' roll, the traditional patterns of American popular music re-appeared. If, in the period just before rock 'n' roll, we had Frank Sinatra, Perry Como, Tony Bennett, and Vic Damone, then in the period just after it we had Dion, Frankie Valli, and the rest of the young Italians.

The career of Bobby Darin, the first white singer to record for Atlantic, shows how the Italians linked rock 'n' roll to mainstream popular music at this time. He had "Splish Splash," a rock 'n' roll number as his first big hit in 1958, but he idolized Frank Sinatra as only an East Coast Italian singer could, so he began recording standards. He did well with "Mack the Knife", from Brecht and Weil's *Three-Penny Opera,* and in 1962 he left Atlantic, where he didn't fit in, to go to Capitol Records. While he was at Capitol, he recorded "Chementine" and "Baby Face," among others. Similarly, Dion and the Belmonts cut the Rodgers and Hart classic, "Where or When" in 1960. The next year Bobby Rydell tried his hand at "That Old Black Magic," which Harold Arlen and Johnny Mercer had written in 1942. It is probably not coincidental that Sinatra had recorded both songs in the fifties.

My friend Paul Levinson once commented that the history of American popular music consists of black musicians, Jewish songwriters, and Italian singers. Of course, that leaves out a lot of people—like Bix Beiderbecke, Cole Porter, and Jim Morrison; still, the last few pages show that it's a useful generalization nevertheless. The next chapter, on Motown, will discuss the blacks in Detroit, but for now we want to stay on the East Coast, and that means discussing Jewish songwriters.

"Discounting pockets of creativity in New Orleans and Detroit, the Brill Building accounted for much of the best rock popular between 1959 and 1964,"[2] states Greg Shaw on what he calls "Brill Building pop." What he neglects to say is that virtually all of the songwriters who worked in the Brill Building near Times Square were ambitious Jewish kids from the same area of Brooklyn. Before talking about the songwriters themselves, we need to understand the men who brought them together, so it makes sense to begin a survey of Jews in popular music where we began with the Italians—in the Bronx.

Two very different Jewish kids from the Bronx were seminal forces in rock 'n' roll throughout the sixties, although they were not performers—Don Kirshner and Phil Spector.

In one way or another, Don Kirshner has been responsible for a large number of hits, and for starting a large number of careers. He seems to have, not a musical gift, but something like it—a gift for recognizing what will sell, what combination of talent will sell in a particular medium. He worked with Italians like Bobby Darin, whom he met in a candy store in the Bronx, and Connie Frances, whom he knew when he was going to Upsala College in New Jersey. But Brill Building Pop resulted from Kirshner's coordination of the work of those talented Jewish kids from Brooklyn.

So they all took the subway from Brooklyn to Times Square every morning: Carole King (nee Klein) and Gerry Goffin, Cynthia Weil and Barry Mann, Neil Sedaka and Howard Greenfield, and Neil Diamond. As Jewish songwriters in New York, they thought of themselves as continuing the tradition of Tin Pan Alley greats like George and Ira Gershwin. In fact, Simon Frith has said, "There was little, formally, to distinguish the teenage pop songs which emerged from the Brill Building from similarly well-made love songs that had been pouring out of Tin Pan Alley for decades."[3] And the descriptions of Kirshner's offices, which were divided up into little cubicles with just enough room for a piano, a piano stool, and chair, sound very much like the descriptions of those turn-of-the-century offices which gave rise to the term Tin Pan Alley in the first place. Originally, Tin Pan Alley was on Fourteenth Street; when it moved uptown to follow the theaters, it moved—to the Brill Building.

However, we find no simple continuity between Tin Pan Alley and Don Kirshner's stable of songwriters, but a fascinating interplay of continuity and contrast. During the heyday of Tin Pan Alley, in the twenties and thirties, the Alleymen (as Ian Whitcomb calls them) were writing for Broadway, and with the advent of the talkies, Hollywood. They were adults writing for other adults, and their love of cultural references, clever word play, and so forth shows it. By contrast, Kirshner's songwriters were kids writing for other kids; none of them wrote for Broadway or Hollywood. They wanted to put out 45 rpm singles. So even if their music was formally similar to that of Tin Pan Alley, their simple, colloquial lyrics had hardly any similarity to the lyrics of Cole Porter.

We also have a second contrast with Tin Pan Alley. Earlier, when people wrote songs, they would see publishers, hoping to get them published. And song publishers in turn had people called "song pluggers" whose duties included trying to persuade band leaders to incorporate the songs into their repertoires. The potent combination of radio and phonograph had short-circuited this system, and the songs had only a negligible existence as sheet music. So. once Carole King had written a song with Goffin, she would make a demo record which Kirshner would then use to persuade a group or a singer—often people Kirshner was working with—to record the song. King thus had much more to do with the final record than if she had simply published the music, for everyone agrees that her musical instincts were so good that groups often copied her arrangements, and she in fact released her own version of one song which she wrote with Goffin under her own name ("It Might As Well Rain Until September," 1963).

Phil Spector recorded both in New York and in Los Angeles, where he made Gold Star Studios famous; I include him here because he fits in so well with the East Coast tradition of Jewish men who worked with black performers. Phil's first mentor was George Goldner, who recorded Frankie Lymon and the Teenagers and Little Anthony and the Imperials. Goldner also produced the first black record which made a significant crossover into the white market, "Gee," by the Crows. Like Herman Lubinsky of Savoy Records, Phil worked with black singers and married a black woman. Furthermore, Phil apprenticed with Leiber and Stoller while they were producing great tracks for the Coasters and the Drifters.

Phil took an important musical cue from "There Goes My Baby," which Leiber and Stoller produced for the Drifters in the spring of 1959. It was indicative that, as a period of assimilation began, "There Goes My Baby" softened its beat with a string section. Moreover, it used a particular beat, the bayon, which had a catchy Latin "bom bom-bom" riff. Phil used "the good old bayon," as he once called it, again and again. You hear it on "Da Doo Ron Ron," on "Be My Baby," and many other of his hits.

Although Phil has had a long and illustrious career, his moment came in the early sixties when he recorded the great girl groups such as the Crystals and the Ronettes. Not coincidentally, this was also the era of Alfred Hitchcock's *Psycho* (1960). I say "not coincidentally," because we need to think of Phil not as a record producer, but as an *auteur*. He is the only record producer who has ever been able to make fans think of records in terms of the producer, not the performers. Like Hitchcock, he dominated the performers so that they expressed his ideas, not their own talent. His records have a recognizable style, as the work of an *auteur* should; we might more usefully refer to his "wall of sound" as a "mass of sound," for he recorded everything in mono, with a single mike. By crowding the instruments together, he created an undifferentiated sound which intrigued us no matter how many times we heard the record. We kept asking, "How did he do that?", just like we did when we watched the shower scene in *Psycho*.

The movie analogy works in another way as well, for two of the great girl group songs, "Leader of the Pack," and "He's A Rebel," amount to commentaries on the two movies which did so much to create fifties youth culture, *The Wild One* (1953) and *Rebel Without A Cause* (1955). In both of those movies, the guy is clearly the star; the girl group songs shift the emphasis to the girl. "Leader of the Pack" has such a strongly cinematic quality that it begins with a conversation between two girls, and then the lead singer tells the story in a flashback.

When the girl group sound broke, it broke big. "Leader of the Pack," "He's A Rebel," "Da Doo Ron Ron," "My Boyfriend's Back," "Chapel of Love," and "Be My Baby" all went to #1 in the early sixties. So we need to ask why this happened at this particular time. I think that we cannot explain the appeal of the girl groups simply by listening to the records or praising Phil's genius. Rather, we need to turn to television, the ground against which rock 'n' roll was the figure. There was one television star in the early sixties who outshone all the others and who mesmerized the American people, especially the young people, night after night—John Kennedy. I believe that President Kennedy was so much the man of the hour and we were so infatuated with the way he was obsolescing the distinction between politics and show biz that we were not interested in other male heroes. But we were very receptive to young, nubile girls who sang about male heroes. So it makes sense to say that the girl groups enjoyed great success because they were properly positioned (to use a marketing term) between Phil Spector on one hand and President Kennedy on the other.

Finally, though, we need to think of Phil as a transitional figure caught between two great eras of music. He unwittingly revealed this when he marked the time on his greatest record, the Righteous Brothers' "You've Lost That Lovin' Feeling," as 3:05 instead of the correct 3:45. He had so many musical ideas that he was anticipating the concept albums of the sixties, with their longer cuts, yet paradoxically these albums obsolesced the role of the all-knowing producer—which was virtually the only role he could play in the studio.

The early sixties was not an era of strong musical personalities; it was a democratic era, a time when the kids themselves were stars when they danced. A King/Goffin dance song "The Loco-Motion," went to #1 in 1962; its lyrics emphasize that it is "easy to do," and it was in fact sung by King's maid. The success of this record exemplifies what we might call, for lack of any better word, the amateurish quality of the music in this period. There was certainly nothing amateurish about King and Goffin, but Little Eva was an amateur, and the number and importance of dance crazes such as the Twist, the Mashed Potato, and so on, indicates that a change was occurring in the relationship between the performers and the audience.

On November 6, 1961 *Life* breathlessly reported that "Now the Twist is the biggest dance craze since the Charleston,"[4] and in such periods the audience becomes more important than the performers. During dance crazes, the performers provide the occasion for the experience, rather than its cause. The high school hop in *American Graffiti* (1973) at which the kids seriously, even studiously, do the Stroll illustrates the point. The kids were participating in the music in a very narcissistic way, not being overwhelmed by it. In particular, the Twist was more narcissistic than jitterbugging, since the couples broke apart and danced without touching each other. But, as if to compensate for this, the exaggerated motion of the hips gave the dancing a more overtly sexual quality.

In this amateurish, i.e., democratic age, the Twist was a readily accessible dance, and became popular with adults as well as with kids. *Life's* spread on the Twist shows Senator Jacob Javits and other New York socialites at the Peppermint Lounge. Murray the K gave the obvious explanation for the way the Twist brought the young and old together, "It caught on among adults because it was the only dance they could do".[5] That is not to say, though, that the Twist did not derive from earlier dances, and in fact dance historians Marshall and Jean Stearns derive the following genealogy for it:

The swaying motion of the Twist was employed long ago in Africa and by the Negro folk in the South. This movement was used in the 1913 routine of a dance called Ballin' the Jack (as a youth in New Orleans, pianist Jelly Roll Morton sang of "Sis'...out on the levee doin' the double Twis' "); blues shouters of the twenties used it as they raised their arms to belt out a tune; and in the thirties it was inserted during the breakaway (where partners separated) of the Lindy.[6]

Like the electric guitar, then, the Twist came from the thirties.

A lot of kids from Philadelphia's ethnic neighborhoods got to dance on *American Bandstand*, which was broadcast nationally beginning in August of 1957, and the cameras spent half the program on the dances. To quote the Stearnses again, "In the foreground, these programs presented a group of authentically awkward dancers with whom any teen-ager could identify. The girls danced like girls, and unlike professional TV dancers, the boys really danced like boys."[7] Since local kids got so much camera time, *Bandstand* made Philadelphia the origin of fads in clothing for teenagers for the first time.

The success of *Bandstand* also meant that television set the tone for the music more than it ever had before. In America, television is the least spontaneous of all the major media (there is too much money involved for spontaneity), so the singers lip-synced their songs. It was difficult to project intensity on black and white television in the afternoon, so *Bandstand* produced the Teen Idols, who had no intensity to begin with.

The word "amateurish" applies literally to Fabian, as we realize when we hear his voice crack on "Tiger," but there's more to it than this. When the girls mobbed Fabian, they were acting out a learned experience which had more to do with their own need for excitement than with his performances. And if the safe, controlled environment of *Bandstand* produced Fabian, the safe, controlled environment of *Ozzie and Harriet* produced Ricky Nelson, virtually the only WASP Teen Idol.

If the Teen Idols were all personality (i.e., television exposure) and no performance, the black girl groups such as the Crystals, the Ronettes, the Shirelles and so on, were all performance and no personality. They didn't become celebrities because they rarely appeared on *Bandstand*, and the teen magazines which reported what Fabian had for breakfast didn't feature the girl groups, both because they were girls and because they were black. Their records did well, nevertheless, in part because their lyrics dealt with the generalized situation of being a teenager in love and/or in high school. "Will You Love Me Tomorrow," for instance, articulates a common anxiety of the time. Since the music existed only on the record, the fans could listen to it without wondering about the performers in any serious way.

Fans who could dissociate performance from personality in this way could also dissociate the music from any particular place. The kids on *Bandstand* were usually from Philadelphia, of course, but they were enough like kids in other places that it didn't matter much. Kids in Florida and Texas and California could imagine readily enough that they were dancing on *Bandstand;* after all, they danced to the same records at their own parties. Thus *Bandstand* helped to create an awareness of rock 'n' roll as a shared, national phenomenon, and the lyrics of hit songs both expressed and intensified that awareness. After "At the Hop," "Twistin' U.S.A." was a natural for Danny and the Juniors in 1960, and Chubby Checker made a successful cover of it in 1961. The lyrics of "Dancing in the Street" (1964) by Martha and the Vandellas also enumerate places around the country where people are dancing. And of course the Beach Boys made "Surfin' U.S.A."

But a unique example of the consciousness of the national quality of rock 'n' roll occurred in 1961, when Atlantic hired a singer named Tommy Facenda to record "High School U.S.A." The people at Atlantic divided the country into 28 regions, got the names of the biggest high schools in those areas, and worked them into the lyrics. I was in college in Nashville when "High School U.S.A." came out, and I remember feeling a thrill at hearing the name of Hillsboro High School on a record. I'm sure a lot of other people felt the same way—and I'm sure that no one cared who Tommy Facenda was. I know of no other example of a song which was a hit in regional versions.

The series of answer songs which were hits in 1960 also indicates the dissociation of the singer from the song. Several times a song whose title was a command or a question would be answered by another song. Answer songs rode on the coattails, as it were, of the popularity of the first song, and resembled parodies in that their success depended on a knowledge of the original. (And sometimes there were real parodies: In New York, a group which called itself the Detergents had a local hit with "The Leader of the Laundromat," a parody of the Shangri-Las' "The Leader of the Pack.") The first answer song in this period was Jeanne Black's "He'll Have to Stay," which responded to Jim Reeves' "He'll Have to Go." Marilyn Michaels answered Ray Peterson's "Tell Laura I Love Her" with "Tell Tommy I Miss Him,." and Damita Jo answered the Drifters' "Save the Last Dance for Me" with (predictably) "I'll Save the Last Dance for You." Skeeter Davis had the funniest answer song to Hank Locklin's "Please Help Me I'm Falling," she replied "I Can't Help You, I'm Falling Too." Even Elvis received the honor of an answer song. While in the Army, he recorded "Are You Lonesome Tonight?" and his smoldering voice made the most of the spoken narration. During the answer songs fad, the question offered an obvious temptation, and both Thelma Carter and Dodie Stevens gave the obvious answer, "Yes, I'm Lonesome Tonight." As these names suggest, answer songs were usually one-hit flukes by unknown singers whose lack of identity did not detract from the success of the record since only the song, and not the performer, mattered.

The East Coast thus presents a fascinating instance of ethnic continuity in that gifted Italians sang, and gifted Jews wrote songs. This had happened before in the history of American popular music, but the new generation which came out of the ethnic neighborhoods had no need of Hollywood or even Broadway, because it had its own media—45 rpm singles and television. But this new generation came not only after Tin Pan Alley but also after Elvis and the other greats from the fifties. As a result Northern music lacked the intensity of the early Southern music; by this very fact, however, it gave the audience a new sense of sharing and participating in the music. It was a time of amateurish or even anonymous celebrities, and it was thus a time when men who had limited musical talent but unlimited determination and vision could create musical empires. One such man, Don Kirshner, did just that in New York, and another did it in Detroit. His name was Berry Gordy, Jr.

Notes

¹On these Italian groups see Edward R. Engel,, *White and Still All Right* (New York: Crackerjack Press, 1977).

²Greg Shaw, "Brill Building Pop," in *The Rolling Stone Illustrated History of Rock and Roll*, Jim Miller, ed. (New York: Random/Rolling Stone, 1980), p. 122.

³Simon Frith, *Sound Effects* (New York: Pantheon, 1981), p. 33.

⁴*Life*, 24 November 1961, p. 75.

⁵Quoted in Marshall and Jean Stearns, *Jazz Dance. The Story of American Vernacular Dance.* (New York: Macmillan, 1968), p. 4.

⁶*Ibid.*, p. 1.

⁷*Ibid.*, p. 4.

Chapter 8:
Detroit Rises for the First Time

Emerson once said that "An institution is the lengthened shadow of one man," and Motown Records is clearly the lengthened shadow of Berry Gordy, Jr. Gordy's life is the stuff of American myth, a Horatio Alger story of a poor kid who made good. Gordy's career divides neatly into two parts; first came a phenomenal decade in Detroit (from 1961, when "Shop Around" by the Miracles went gold, to 1972), and another phenomenal decade or so since 1972 in Hollywood. The two parts of Gordy's career give us a way of understanding him, and the rise of Motown, by analogy with two other entrepreneurs whose lives are also the stuff of American myth, and who also got rich by giving the American public what it wanted.

Any successful entrepreneur in Detroit calls to mind a comparison with Henry Ford, of course, and Ford served as a perhaps unconscious, but nevertheless, formative model for Gordy, even though the two men lived at different times, belonged to different races, and manufactured different products. When Gordy moved Motown to Hollywood in 1972, over half a century had passed since Samuel Goldwyn moved his production company to Culver City in 1918. Nevertheless, these two men have more in common than any other two entertainment executives I know of. Unlike Ford, both men were outsiders (Goldwyn was a Polish Jew, Gordy a black), yet both prospered by creating entertainment which the WASP society around them adored. Gordy's similarities to Ford and Goldwyn suggest that certain thematic patterns recur again and again in American success stories, and thus in American society itself.

In the best American tradition of innocence, Ford, Goldwyn and Gordy were untutored geniuses. Like Frank Sinatra, they could have taken "My Way" as their theme song. What I like to call the Daniel Boone syndrome—the need to move as soon as you can see the smoke from your neighbor's chimney—operates in their lives. That is to say, these strong men had a need to act autonomously, without social restrictions. But people who embody the Daniel Boone syndrome in the twentieth century face a quandary: on one hand, they must be independent and do it their way, but on the other hand, doing it their way (making cars, movies, and records) is predicated on pleasing others. This quandary pervades the lives of many American businessmen, of whom Howard Hughes represents the most extreme example.

Gordy once said that he wanted to set up Motown as a "factory-type operation,"[1] and in Detroit that meant modeling your operations on a car factory. If you are an entrepreneur in Detroit, that means modeling your work after that of Henry Ford. The typically American vacillation between democracy and elitism appears in Ford's career, and thus in Gordy's as well.

If we consider Ford's career only through the early twenties, he is the ultimate democratic capitalist. He revolutionized the automobile industry by building the Model T, the car for the common man, as opposed to earlier cars, which were often toys for the rich. And on January 5, 1914, Ford's board of directors "gave the press an announcement that the company was reducing the work day to eight hours, converting the factory to three shifts instead of two, and instituting the five-dollar wage."[2] This startling new labor policy earned Ford the enmity of his fellow capitalists, and headlines all over the world. In addition to sharing the profits of the company with the workers (a move which had the effect of stabilizing the work force), Ford opened free schools for his workers. Many of them were first-generation (non-Jewish) immigrants from Eastern Europe who spoke English poorly, if at all. Obviously, such workers could not take orders on the assembly line, much less become American citizens. Moreover, since no one learns a language in isolation, Ford's schools taught more than English; they taught the American way of life, and were in fact referred to as Americanization schools.

It is difficult to believe that Gordy did not know about Ford's Americanization schools and that he did not use them as the model for what can only be called his finishing school for Motown performers. The school was located in a house near the studio, and "One floor was for choreography, another for musical arrangements, and a third for wardrobe design. The training began with grooming, etiquette, diction, elocution, table manners, and personal hygiene."[3] Maurice King, one of the teachers, has given this account of the pressure cooker atmosphere of the school:

"We heated the performers until they cracked, then we heated them up again. There were times when they couldn't hardly stand the strain because of the pressure, when they could hardly remember anything because they were so exhausted, crying and disgusted with themselves because they couldn't get it perfect."[4]

Two things seem significant here. First, Gordy *owned* the performers, as the movie studios owned performers in the thirties, and he treated them as MGM treated Judy Garland, for instance. Second, he was determined to make everything about them white except the color of their skin. Their etiquette and hygiene lessons made them acceptable to the middle-class whites who have always constituted the principal audience in America. (At the same time, Martin Luther King, Jr. was presenting himself to middle-class whites as a well-dressed, well-spoken man whom they had no reason to fear.)

Ford's assembly line depended on standardization; as his famous quip had it, "You can have a Ford in any color you want, as long as it is black." Gordy's corporation depended on standardization, too. He had a phenomenally high percentage of hits to releases, and to achieve this he minimized product differentiation, to use a marketing phrase. The Motown Sound was recognizably the same from one record to another. Motown's standardization appeared most obviously, though, in the elaborately choreographed routines for which the Temptations and other groups became famous. Since no major white groups ever worked up comparable routines, we may ask: Why not? (Surely there were some white singers who could dance!). One answer is that the standardization of clothing, mores, and what have you, has been a predominant feature of middle-class American life, and as such, it had great prestige for upwardly mobile blacks. So Gordy standardized his dancers' movements on the stage just as Ford standardized his workers' language in the Americanization schools and his workers' movements on the assembly line.

One man, Cholly Atkins, links Motown to the past of black performers and also shows what was new about Motown's mix of dancing and singing at live concerts. Cholly was a veteran of the great days of dancing in Harlem in the thirties, when the Savoy Ballroom and the Cotton Club had weekly dance contests. But in the thirties, the dancers were improvising to live music by great bands such as those of Count Basie and Duke Ellington, and the musicians were improvising, too. The dancers and musicians created a fantastic synergistic excitement. By the sixties, though, records had standardized the expectations of the audience, which came to Motown's road shows to hear hits, not improvization. As a result, the dancing was standardized, too. Thus, we have a technological as well as a social explanation for the famous Motown performance style.

In training the performers to dance and dress well even before their songs made the charts, Gordy was reversing the usual professional development of most black groups (and of most white groups, for that matter). Usually, groups would start out performing live at whatever gigs they could get, and did well just to keep their instruments in tune—never mind dancing. If they were lucky, the groups would impress an agent or a producer and get a recording contract and then maybe a hit record. But since they knew only a few songs, and had no stage routines, they often had short careers. But at Motown, Gordy himself put the groups together from local auditions and his own staff (Florence Ballard and Diana Ross of the Supremes worked as secretaries there). Since Gordy had his own songwriters and arrangers, the groups recorded before they ever performed live. Yet Gordy assumed that concerts and television appearances would follow the hit records, so he planned for them from the beginning. As a result, they had more diversity and their careers lasted longer.

The diversity which characterized the performers characterized Motown as a whole. From the beginning, the company did not have to rely on a single performer or a single group for hits. In the period 1961-1964, the Miracles, the Marvelettes, Mary Wells, Martha and the Vandellas, Marvin Gaye, and the Supremes all had at least three Top Twenty hits. This balance continued in the late sixties as well.

As Ford's workers and Gordy's performers began to prosper from their hits, their bosses gave them the same piece of advice: buy a house. In both cases, it was a profoundly American, and thus a profoundly middle-class, piece of advice. The bosses wanted their outsiders (Ford's Eastern Europeans, Gordy's blacks) to internalize the American ideal, and then externalize it in the classic symbol of bourgeois prosperity.

Classic American entrepreneurs like Ford and Gordy need to say "I Did It My Way" because they are intuitive geniuses. They guess what will work; they follow their hunches, which they often can't explain and which often seem absurd to those around them. As a result, they have to make others do it their way, too. This exercise of power entails authoritarian, and thus elitist, attitudes. This operation of the Daniel Boone syndrome in Ford's career appears ;most clearly in his obsessive distrust of bankers (a major cause of his notorious anti-Semitism). In making himself independent of New York bankers, he began the decline of finance capitalism which is a major factor in the evolution of twentieth-century corporations.

Related to Ford's need to free himself from dependence on bankers was his vertical integration of his operations. Eventually, miners dug ore in Ford-owned mines, shipped it in Ford-owned ships to Ford-owned smelting plants which shipped the steel to Ford-owned plants, and so forth. Here, too, Ford offers an obvious analogy with Gordy, who also brought vertical integration of his operations. Motown artists recorded in Motown studios, and paid Gordy for the recording costs; they signed their publishing rights over to Jobete Publishing, which Gordy owned. They also signed management contracts with International Talent Management, Inc., which Gordy owned. As Peter Benjaminson points out, the recording contracts and the management contracts often created a conflict of interest, since the performers made more money from recording than from performing.

This financial conflict of interest exemplifies the way the democratic and elitist principles began to conflict in Gordy's career as they had conflicted in Ford's career before him. Both men wanted to keep on doing what had worked for them in the past. After all, who can argue with popular success in America? So Ford refused to change the design of the Model T despite advances in manufacturing techniques, and in the winter of 1921-22 purged his top executives, who had argued for change (his intransigence led to the rise of General Motors in the twenties). In the thirties, Ford turned into a strike-breaker and union buster; he hired vicious gangs of thugs to enforce company discipline.

Ford's biographer comments on his erratic qualities, and saying "It was another of Ford's disabilities that as the years passed he more and more separated himself from other men."[5] Gordy changed in the same way. As Benjaminson says, "The man who built the Motown Machine changed a great deal as his company changed. He became increasingly less accessible to his own employees, the press, and the general public over the years—to the point of paranoia."[6] His sister Esther Edwards gave him an oil painting of himself dressed as another short outsider who made good, Napoleon, and he hung it in his house. If Ford's authoritarianism alienated his key executives, Gordy's authoritarianism alienated his key performers and writers. Mary Wells left, and

She was followed by Brenda Holloway, Kim Weston, the Jackson Five, Gladys Knight and the Pips, the Spinners, Barrett Strong, the Temptations, the Isley Brothers, Jimmy Ruffin, and the Miracles. Several songwriters left, including Holland-Dozier-Holland, Ashford and Simpson, and Gordy's brother-in-law Harvey Fuqua. This departure led in turn to the exodus of the Four Tops and Edwin Starr because these performers felt they could no longer count on a steady stream of hit material.[7]

No record company can lose this phenomenal array of talent with impunity, and Motown began to slip on the charts, as a later essay will show.

Gordy's need for control hurt him in other ways as well. He could have greatly increased his personal wealth and Motown's operating capital by turning the company into a publicly-owned corporation, and selling shares. In fact, lawyers once prepared the papers, but he refused at the last minute, presumably realizing that as head of a corporation he would have had to release sales figures and deal with a board of directors. The Daniel Boone syndrome really had a hold on him.

It was partially as a response to the difficulties with recording artists that Gordy moved Motown to Hollywood in 1972, and here the analogies between Gordy and Samuel Goldwyn come into play. Goldwyn "was the *only* independent producer in Hollywood to make it and sustain it—and on his own terms,"[8] and Gordy was the only independent record producer to make it and sustain it on his own terms. As outsiders, a Polish Jew and a black, the two men have a good deal in common. The key to their management strategies is personal control. Like Gordy, Goldwyn was the sole stock holder in his corporation, and thus "was under no obligation to make his profit and loss figures public."[9] To this day, some doubt remains as to whether "Shop Around" really went gold because no one outside the Motown organization can check the sales figures.

The phrase "your personal touch" occurs in the lyrics of the Temptations' classic "(I Know) I'm Losing You," and it describes the way Goldwyn and Gordy operated. Entertainment is a much more volatile industry than automobiles, yet they had produced spectacular successes by trusting their intuitions even more than Ford did. As a result, they often couldn't tell people what was wrong with the rushes of a scene or a master of a record, but insisted on having it done over again anyhow. Sometimes the re-make resulted in a better take or master, sometimes it didn't. Both loved to exert their power by firing people and then re-hiring them. Goldwyn once fired Nat Deveridge, an agent, and then called him up to play bridge that same night! Compare that incident with the following scenario from a former Motown employee whom Benjaminson does not name: "He'd fire me and I'd stay off work for three or four days. Then he'd call me and say "Come back to work or you're fired.""[10] "Come back to work or you're fired" is a Goldwynism worthy of the man who said, "Anybody who would go to see a psychiatrist ought to have his head examined."

Although Goldwyn and Berry have certainly provided entertainment history with memorable anecdotes, they also resemble less colorful entrepreneurs. In 1962, when Goldwyn's career was over and Berry's was just beginning, a social scientist named Everett Hagen published a book in which he suggested that successful entrepreneurs in Third World countries often came from "status deprived" groups.[11] Unfortunately, he didn't consider that this principle of status deprivation as a motivating force explains the success of Jews in the high risk entertainment business. The same principle also helps to explain Gordy's success, which coincided with the civil rights movement, and thus occurred at a time when a black man could sell black music to the white market by sweetening it.

And that is the final intriguing paradox about Goldwyn and Berry, these two outsiders got rich by pleasing a WASP audience to which they had never belonged. They both ran afoul of the civil rights movement. Goldwyn's troubles came with the filming of *Porgy and Bess*. In 1957, he signed Sidney Poitier to play the lead, but civil rights leaders criticized the actor for agreeing to appear in a "condenscending, insulting relic from the past."[12] Poitier withdrew from the project, but Goldwyn put immense pressure on him and he capitulated. Poitier felt uneasy about the project then, and for a long time afterwards. For one thing, he felt that the dialect in the book and in the lyrics made blacks sound ignorant (it never occurred to Goldwyn to bring a black writer to work on the much-revised screenplay—as the black press pointed out). "So during rehearsal without consulting (director Otto) Preminger, Poitier's accent gradually shifted from Catfish Row to that of an English gentlemen—and the rest of the cast followed his lead."[13] Similar compromises which pleased no one were made, and the film opened in June of 1959 to unanimously bad reviews.

Gordy's problems with the black community were similar, but more diffuse. Motown music did not exactly raise black consciousness any more than *Porgy and Bess* did. The company, with its success and money, found itself increasingly alienated from the blacks of Detroit, and during the riots of 1967, it received many threatening telephone calls from them. Bomb threats from soul brothers are not conducive to making commercially viable music, and people generally believe that they, in addition to Gordy's other problems, had a lot to do with his decision to move to white Hollywood. But only the first part of Gordy's career, the time when he was creating the Motown Sound, concerns us here, and it is to the Motown Sound that we now turn.

The Motown Sound did not spring full-blown from the mind of Berry Gordy. Rather, it evolved from the black music of the fifties, and the Miracles may serve as a case in point. Believe it or not, they started out as a doo-wop group. Their first record, "Got a Job," appeared during the answer songs fad of 1960 as a response to the Coasters' classic "Get a Job," and they covered the Coasters' humorous style very adeptly. Their other early records, such as "(I Need Some) Money," sound very much like the Coasters and the Drifters. But Gordy wanted a white style with mass appeal, so as the Motown Sound developed, it came to resemble the Platters' secularized gospel sound, only with a beat and fewer strings. Whereas the Platters' sound consisted of just the lead tenor, the "oohs" of the rest of the group singing backup, and those lush strings which mark it as coming from the fifties, the Miracles' sound has fewer strings, relying on Smokey Robinson's sweet tenor, the backup, and the beat of drums and tambourines. This sound first appears on what Gordy said was Motown's first gold record, "Shop Around"; it is thinner and less complex than the Platters' work.

The beat sustains the Motown Sound, of course. It creates the internal consistency of Motown records; light but insistent, it works well with the expressive, readily identifiable voices of Smokey Robinson, Diana Ross, and the others. In fact, the sax break on "Shop Around," now seems a little disruptive, a holdover from fifties rhythm and blues. By contrast, a plunking piano is virtually the only audible instrument on the Supremes' "Baby Love" from 1964. It was as though the Motown Sound split into swinging ballads by the vocal groups and instrumental numbers by Junior Walker and the All Stars. By 1966, on "You Can't Hurry Love," Diana Ross has emerged as a soloist, so that almost the entire record consists of her voice (once accurately described as "mosquito thin") against an insistent, but muted drum with tambourines and a murmuring bass. Elaborate arrangements, such as the one on "Dancing in the Street" by Martha and the Vandellas were a rarity.

Given the abundance of Detroit talent which Gordy found and trained, the determining factor which made the Motown Sound successful in its day, and readily identifiable now, was the meshing of transistors and tambourines. This statement requires some explanation, so let's begin with the transistors.

In 1961, Freddie Cannon had a hit with "Transistor Sister." The song refers to the way Japan's post-war recovery made its first penetration into the American market with cheap, portable transistor radios which rapidly caught on among teenagers. David Morse, who was the first to understand Motown's success on this new medium, explains how it worked:

There is an intriguing parallelism between the rise of Motown and the tremendous expansion in the market for small transistor radios in the 60's. Spector's own records had too much reverberation for them to be really effective in this medium. Moreover, Motown's light, unfussy, evenly stressed beat, its continuous loop melodies were the ideal accompaniment for driving.[14]

But kids had been listening to rock ' n' roll in their cars for some time before Motown; now they could listen to it at the beach, the swimming pool, or virtually anywhere. Naturally, these little radios had very low-fi speakers, and no bass to speak of. They couldn't handle the heavy drums sound of fifties rhythm and blues, which in any case would have overpowered the voices of the Supremes, for instance. But the music needed the beat for dancing, and for snapping your fingers to. What to do? Without giving the matter much conscious thought, Motown's arrangers turned to an instrument which they had grown up with, the tambourine.

Poor blacks in the South used the tambourine as an accompaniment when they sang hymns because they couldn't afford a piano; then, too, it fit in well with the percussive traditions of African music. When blacks went North, they took their tambourines with them into their storefront churches:

After all, many Motown performers—Stevie Wonder, Marvin Gaye, Diana Ross—had grown up singing in church choirs and many others were children or grandchildren of ministers. The tambourines that Florence Ballard and Mary Wilson tapped delicately against their hips while Diana Ross sang were gentle reminders of Motown's gospel roots.[15]

In a way, then, that no one planned or anticipated, the tambourine, taken from its gospel context, proved to be an ideal percussion instrument for secular music which people listened to on transistor radios. Here, too, the social and the technological explanations merge.

Generally, though, Motown music has very little of a gospel quality, except for some of Marvin Gaye's early work. He was a singer of considerable versatility, and one can hear the influence of three other black singers in his voice. Marvin had been listening to Brook Benton before he recorded "Pride and Joy," but no matter who got the songwriting credits, the song is modelled—to put it delicately—on Ray Charles' version of Sy Oliver's "Yes Indeed." "Pride and Joy" has the same chords as "Yes Indeed," Marvin sounds just like Ray. In addition, his call and response interchanges with his backup singers, who sound like the Raelettes, have the same dynamics as Ray's interchanges with the Raelettes.

But the most remarkable example of secularization in the Motown canon is "Can I Get A Witness," which offers an intriguing comparision with Ray's "Hallelujah I Love Her So." If Ray's song features gospel chords and presents religious emotion as secular emotion, "Can I Get A Witness" presents a complete religious environment put to the service of a secular emotion.

"Can I Get A Witness" has such importance in the ongoing process of the secularization of black music that it deserves a separate discussion. On this song, Motown's great songwriting team of Holland-Dozier-Holland casts Marvin as a preacher. The song secularizes a standard feature of black church services, the preacher's call for someone to witness for the Lord. Sociologist Arthur Paris, who studied black church services, tells us that a witness usually includes, "A recounting of the instances of the Lord's blessing for which the person is thankful (deliverance from personal and financial problems, ill health, spiritual and emotional trials, and so on)."[16] Witnessing for the Lord is an adaptation to Protestant theology of the group participation which appears in African rituals. Paris even comments that:

The performance of the sermon is a collaboration between the messenger and the congregation. They support and encourage the messenger, offer affirmation and comment; he is the mouthpiece of their consensus and the medium by which the Word of the Almighty is mediated to the faithful...When the preacher is really preaching, when he is "in gear," "making it right," and the congregation is right with him with encouragement and affirmation, the chemistry of the situation leads to a meeting of God and man in history (*kairos*) through the agency of the Word. Again, there is a close analogy to jazz: When the interplay among the musicians is "right," and the soloists are "really into it," the bounds of technique are transformed, the moment transcended, and the musicians and the audience transported.[17]

The chemistry of this interaction between preacher and congregation not only resembles jazz in its ensemble feeling, it specifically resembles the chemistry of the interaction between jazz bands and dancers in the thirties.

Holland-Dozier-Holland take this interaction, the classic call and response situation of black church services in which they had grown up, and do two things with it. First, they secularize it, since Marvin is singing about his woman, not the Lord. Second, and more radically, they reverse the preacher's message. Whereas preachers preach about God's justice, Marvin sings about the way his woman is doing him wrong—she is "never home" and treats him "so unkind." So, when Marvin pleads "Can I Get A Witness," he is asking the congregation to affirm that this is not the way things should be. He believes, not in the Lord, but that "a woman is a man's best friend."

The record has other unusual features. Holland-Dozier-Holland wrote very long lines which rarely scan, and which have awkward, approximate rhymes such as week/be and mind/cryin'. To give the effect of a sermon, Marvin sings throughout the whole record; there is no instrumental break as such, although the horns come in on the first chorus.

"Can I Get A Witness" is such an important record thematically that we may pause here to ask: Of the three principal groups of outsiders who have created American popular music, Italians, Eastern European Jews, and blacks, why is it that only blacks (and Southern whites) have secularized their religion? The Italian singers and Jewish songwriters have hardly ever secularized elements of their own religion. One answer is that both Catholicism and Judaism make a sharp distinction between clerics and the layity. Whereas Catholic and Jewish men undergo extensive training and make lifelong commitments before they can officiate at services, they do not in Protestant churches—especially Southern Protestant services. Thus, both Jerry Lee Lewis and Little Richard have preached. In Southern Protestant churches (and their counterparts in Northern ghettos), a "calling" is all that is required, so that a teenager "on fire for the Lord," as the formula has it, can preach and even serve as a minister (The President of the Student Body during my senior year in high school was in fact a minister at a church out in the county).

The emphasis on youth as opposed to maturity, on feeling as opposed to training, makes for an obvious link between Protestantism and popular culture. Moreover, salvation in Protestant churches is a matter of grace, not works, as in Catholicism. Protestants accept Christ as their "personal savior." When the tempo of secularization increased in the fifties, the lover tended to replace Christ, and happiness tended to replace salvation.

After "Can I Get A Witness," the tension between the sacred and the profane ceased to exist in Motown music, as the contrast between that song and another Holland-Dozier-Holland classic, the Supremes' "Baby Love," shows clearly. David Morse makes this important point about the lyrics of Motown songs:

> It is also characteristic of Motown music that it gives the chorus or refrain a more important position in the structure of a song. Rather than following a 32-bar pattern, repeated over and over with different words, the song is cleanly divided into separate section of verse and chorus, each verse serving as a bridge between repetitions of the chorus. Such songs appear to move not in a straight line but in a circle. Usually they do not come to a definite conclusion but fade out over a chorus which is freer and more improvised than anything which has preceded it.[18]

That is to say, Motown songs offer a continuous experience, appropriate for sampling from time to time in the casual situation of listening to a transistor radio.

Motown songs do not contain narratives, and the music does not build to a climax. Rather, they have lyrics which state a principle ("Shop Around," "You Can't Hurry Love") or use extended comparisons ("It's Growing"). Three famous Motown songs employ a verbal twist which takes a public situation and transforms it into a private situation—the Miracles' "Shop Around", and "I Second That Emotion", and the Supremes' "Stop! In the Name of Love." These songs follow in the tradition of Perry Como's hit from 1954, "Wanted," which coyly states the desire for a love as a want ad in the employment section of the classifieds. These Motown songs do the same thing, but change a principle of good consumerism, an application of Robert's Rule of Order, and a policeman's traditional cry into emotional statements.

And who advises the young lover to shop around? Well, Mama does, that's who. She is the cost-conscious head of a black household, and her prominence, an innovative feature of Motown lyrics, expresses the situation of many black households where there is an absent father. It's also Mama who says, "You Can't Hurry Love," which seems like an adaptation of advice about frying chicken. Mama's prominence in Motown lyrics marks these songs as distinctively black, even if they aren't funky, for white lyricists simply don't write about Mama's worldly wisdom and her advice in the ways of the world, in this way.

More than any other style, Motown music illustrates the principle that rock 'n' roll is both an art and a business. As the first record company created by and for rock 'n' roll, Motown Records shows that even when innovations occur in the organization and style of American popular music, they occur in ways which make sense in terms of other innovations in American society. Of course, Motown continued to evolve and grow, and in the late sixties, its strengths proved to be weaknesses as well, but to say this is to get ahead of the story. For now, we continue our journey westward.

Notes

[1]Quoted in Stanley H. Brown, "The Motown Sound of Money," *Fortune*, September 12, 1967, p. 104.

[2]Allan Nevins, *Ford: the Times, the Man, the Company*, I (New York: Charles Scribner's Sons, 1954), p. 533.

[3]Peter Benjaminson, *The Story of Motown* (New York: Grove Press, 1979), p. 38.

[4]*Ibid.*, p. 39.

[5]Nevins, *Ford*, p. 582.

[6]Benjaminson, *The Story of Motown*, p. 582.

[7]*Ibid.*, p. 151.

[8]Carol Easton, *The Search for Sam Goldwyn* (New York: William Morrow and Company, 1976), p. 289.

[9]*Ibid.*, p. 146.

[10]Benjaminson, *The Story of Motown*, p. 113.

[11]See Everett E. Hagen, *On the Theory of Social Change* (Homewood, IL: The Dorsey Press, 1962).

[12]Easton, *The Search for Sam Goldwyn*, p. 275.

[13]*Ibid.*, p. 280.

[14]David Morse, *Motown and the Arrival of Black Music* (New York: Macmillan, 1971), p. 23.

[15]Benjaminson, *The Story of Motown*, p. 31.

[16]Arthur E. Paris, *Black Pentecostalism. Southern Religion in an Urban World* (Amherst: U. of Massachusetts Press, 1982), p. 58.

[17]*Ibid.*, pp. 76-77.

[18]Morse, *Motown and the Arrival of Black Music*, p. 40.

Chapter 9:
California Rises for the
First Time, Too

As those well-known connoisseurs of rock, Ronald and Nancy Reagan, have attested, the Beach Boys are an American institution. They are the only group from the early sixties which remains intact and can still draw large crowds for its concerts. We now understand that they are more than the nostalgia act we thought them to be in the early seventies. So much like an institution are they, in fact, that with only a few changes Alan Gowans' comments about another Los Angeles institution apply very well to them:

Not the least interesting aspect of Forest Lawn, objectively considered, is its fly-in-amber preservation of the outlook and values of the white Protestant Anglo-Saxon America on the eve of World War I, when its predominance in American culture still seemed assured by Nature and Nature's God.[1]

By analogy, we can say that the Beach Boys represent the outlook and values of white Protestant Anglo-Saxon teenagers in the early sixties. Having said that, we immediately realize that they must mean much more than this. Their stability, their staying power, and their ability to attract new fans prove as much.

The Beach Boys' attitude toward their first concert, in Sacramento, in 1963, suggests what is to be explained about them. Although "Surfin' Safari" had broken big in Los Angeles on Candix, a local label, they worried about whether surf music would appeal to an audience as far inland as Sacramento. The answer came very soon, and soon afterwards they were appealing to kids in such non-surfing areas as Iowa and Vermont. "Surfin' U.S.A." became what we now call an anthem, whereas "High School U. S. A." became a mere historical curiosity. Why?

The answer lies, I believe, not in the Beach Boys' collective talent, which was considerable, and not in Brian Wilson's genius, which was unquestionable, but in the way their music plugged into one of the most potent of all American myths—the myth of the frontier. I believe that this statement holds, even though the Beach Boys never thought about it in this way and were as surprised as anybody else when they made it big.

Our understanding of our myth of the frontier comes from Frederick Jackson Turner's famous 1893 essay, "The Significance of the Frontier in American Life," in which Turner distinguishes American from European institutions in the following way:

101

The peculiarity of American institutions is the fact that they have been compelled to adapt themselves to the changes of an expanding people—to the changes in crossing a continent, in winning a wilderness, and in developing at each area of this progress out of the primitive conditions of the frontier into the complexity of city life.[2]

Turner explains that adaptation to frontier conditions brought about the democratization of European settlers, and mentions a number of dates and sources for this. But Turner's essay has to do only occasionally with historical description; like "Surfin' U.S.A." it mostly has to do with mythology, and we sense the presence of mythology in passages such as this one: "American social development has been continually beginning over again on the frontier. This perennial rebirth, this fluidity of American life, this expansion westward with its new opportunities, its continuous touch with the simplicity of primitive society, furnish the forces dominating American character."[3]

Only when Turner is talking specifically about geography can we think of him as a historian. But the Puritans' "errand into the wilderness," the first version of the opposition of innocence and experience, of democracy and elitism which Turner proposes, was not purely geographical. The Puritans were seeking the City of God, which has no coordinates on a map. Similarly, Turner's frontier, which promises "perennial rebirth," and thereby creates the "fluidity of American life," only seems to appear on a map. In fact, it represents the promise of America: That American society is never fixed, that opportunities abound, because America is, and always must be, in the process of becoming. Turner localized, then, the promises of American life in the frontier. He was thus talking, not about places, but about symbols; he was analyzing, not history, but mythology. If America is the frontier, and America is the promised land of the Puritans, then what is more poignant than the loss of the frontier? Turner's essay begins with a quotation from the 1890 Census to the effect that the frontier has closed, and this fact gives what he says an elegaic quality.

But if the frontier has a mythical quality, so does the closing of the frontier. The closing of the frontier is an archetypal event in American consciousness, something like the Fall of Adam and Eve, and it keeps happening again and again. Turner's "perennial rebirth" also implies a perennial death. One historian says that it happened before the Civil War, while others say that America's entrance into World War I surely closed the frontier. Another way of thinking about the frontier is to say that television closed the frontier yet again in the fifties when the networks created a national culture. There were no frontiers in the global village of teenagers which *Bandstand* was helping to create, and the growth of national corporations seemed to limit the promise of individualism in American life—Berry Gordy notwithstanding.

Since Americans associated the frontier with the West, three great Western movies which dealt with the closing of the frontier appeared in the sixties. Just as the Beach Boys were getting started in 1962, John Ford released his last great film, *The Man Who Shot Liberty Valance*. And two major films from 1969 provide a possible answer to the question—Is tragedy possible in

America? The deaths at the end of Sam Packinpah's *The Wild Bunch* and George Roy Hill's *Butch Cassidy and the Sundance Kid* suggest that, yes, something like tragedy occurs when the frontier closes (When our heroes die in these two movies, they die south of the border, where they have gone in search of the place where the frontier hasn't closed). After all, if the frontier has formed American character, and if the frontier closes, you can't light out for the territory, in Huck Finn's classic phrase, and only death remains.

The closing of the frontier has a special pathos in Los Angeles, where you only have to stand on the beach at Malibu and look toward Hawaii to convince yourself that no further expansion is possible. The climate and the economic opportunities of Southern California made it seem to promise more than it could deliver—just like America herself. So Nathaniel West's *The Day of the Locust's* and, of course, Raymond Chandler's *The Big Sleep* made Southern California a place of decadence, a city of mean streets. Hence, the ironies of Humphrey Bogart, as the lone man of honor who could walk the mean streets in *The Big Sleep* (1946), very much as Gary Cooper did when he had to deal with the effects of the closing of the frontier in *High Noon* (1952).

But the individualistic response to the closing of the frontier, as in *The Big Sleep* and *High Noon*, requires unique men, men who are no less heroic for being tragic, and great American popular art generally eschews tragedy, decadence, and despair by providing reassurance. It reassures people that their worst fears, fears which they do not and cannot fully articulate, will not come to pass. In the case of the Beach Boys, their music satisfied the profoundly American desire to believe that, despite all the evidence to the contrary, the frontier had not closed, and never would close. To paraphrase the title of a great surfing movie, the Beach Boys transformed the beach from the end of the frontier to the endless frontier. Their music lets us believe, if only briefly, that if endless expansion isn't possible, that doesn't matter, because endless fun is possible: just catch a wave. What Turner himself said about America's westward expansion certainly applies to the Beach Boys, even if he didn't have them in mind when he said: "In this advance, the frontier is the outer edge of the wave."[1] If the waves at Malibu *are* the frontier, then the frontier can never close, and the possibility of trauma is averted. To put it another way, if Berry Gordy represented the Daniel Boone syndrome in entrepreneurship, the Beach Boys represent the Daniel Boone syndrome set to music.

The Beach Boys thus created a regional music with national significance, much to their surprise. Significantly, it was the first major style which California had ever created, the first major style which grew out of the California experience. To be sure, Bing got his start in Hollywood, but he sang with jazz bands which had come from the East Coast, as the great Tin Pan Alley songwriters did after the advent of the talkies. In the fifties, Chet Baker had a certain success, but only among cool jazz fans. So the Beach Boys established a musical identity for Southern California, as opposed to Hollywood. It was essential to the way they made it so big, so fast that there had never been a South California tradition of popular music as such, and very few show biz greats have ever enjoyed such an advantage.

The Beach Boys broke at about the same time as Motown, so there is a natural comparison between them. If Motown whitened up fifties rhythm and blues, the Beach Boys whitened up rock 'n' roll in general (The influence of rhythm and blues appears only once in their music—in Mike Love's *shtick* as a circus barker on "Amusement Parks U.S.A." which comes from the Coasters' "Little Egypt"). I emphasize the point because surf music did not have to sound as white as they, and Jan and Dean, made it. We can hear another possibility in the surf music of Dick Dale, who was very big on the Coast in the early sixties. He made very black surf music, music which shows that he had been listening to Little Walter and Jimmy Reed, among others. His funky "Night Owl" and his cover of Buster Brown's 1959 rhythm and blues hit, "Fanny Maye" are cases in point. Then, too, he gets a rawer sound out of his Fender guitar than anything on a Beach Boys record—an indication that he had also been listening to Duane Eddy.

The role of the frontier in American mythology explains why the Beach Boys go on a "Surfin' Safari," and why they're "on safari to stay." There's more to this than alliteration. A safari is a hunting trip, a secular version of the Puritans' errand into the wilderness, a search for excitement instead of holiness. A safari creates its own frontier, and a permanent safari, like an endless frontier, is a contradiction in terms but it is no less satisfying an image for that. It is this promise that keeps their music fresh when other forms of popular culture from that time which relied on Southern California as a setting, such as *77 Sunset Strip* (and its imitator, the appropriately named *Surfside Six*) have become badly dated. (The same applies to Annette and Frankie's beach movies such as *Beach Blanket Bingo* (1966).

And what was it about surfing that fascinated people in Sacramento and points east? Unlike such obviously strenuous sports as football, surfing seems effortless. Indeed, in "Catch a Wave," the Beach Boys say that anybody can do it, just as Carole King says that anybody can do "The Loco-Motion." Moreover, when you surf, you are riding the wave, and thus exhibiting a harmony with nature which Americans often long for, and rarely achieve. In surfing, we have Manifest Destiny as fun in the sun.

Like Motown, the Beach Boys did away with the saxophone breaks and the heavily accented bass of rhythm and blues; like Motown, the Beach Boys combine a rhythm section with the vocals, so that we often hear the instruments only during the breaks (And there is an occasional similarity in the lyrics; "Surfin' Safari" and "Surfin' U.S.A." name places where you can surf). But whereas Motown used tambourines and light drums, the Beach Boys used drums plus a heavy bass (although you can hear tambourines on "Help Me Rhonda" and "Then I Kissed Her"). In fact, the bass, drums, and overdubbed tenor vocals virtually define surf music. Perhaps the bass reminds us of the sound of booming waves.

If the Beach Boys didn't take anything from rhythm and blues, they took a lot from Chuck Berry, and in the relationship between Chuck and the Beach Boys, rock 'n' roll history, as opposed to the careers of individual performers, begins. "Surfin' U.S.A." uses the music of "Sweet Little Sixteen," of course, and "Fun, Fun, Fun" begins with the classic guitar run from "Johnny B. Goods." There is also a Chuck Berry guitar break on "Surfin' Safari."

But after the guitar run on "Fun, Fun, Fun," the Beach Boys lapse into their standard vocals-and-bass style. No call and response relationship between the vocals and accompaniment ever appears in their work, as it does in much of Chuck's work, because the vocals are so much more important. There is still a bluesy quality in his music which is absent in the Beach Boys'. The difference between them has a lot to do with the difference between rock 'n' roll's first five years and its second five years. Few of the major innovators had grown up in a culture in which rhythm and blues, blues, or country music dominated. It is understandable, then, that their music had a lot in common with the mainstream American pop tradition.

To generalize, the Beach Boys take what Chuck gave them (and all of us), and take its various features to the limit. At one extreme, they simplify the lyrics by eliminating narrative (another similarity to Motown) and metaphor. At the other extreme, they complexify (if that's a word) the vocals. After all, Chuck didn't have their voices. It is not coincidental that one of the rare songs by a black group which the Beach Boys covered was Frankie Lymon and the Teenagers' "Why Do Fools Fall in Love," for Frankie's falsetto anticipates their own. Their complex harmonies don't seem forbidding or arty because their voices often threaten to break in a charming, amateurish way, although of course they never do.

For Chuck, the studio was passive; for Brian, as for Phil Spector, it was another instrument, and not just on "Good Vibrations." Overdubbing was foreign to Chuck's musical genius and his musical heritage; it was essential to Brian's. Here is what he said about it: " 'Sing it once, sing it again over that, so both sounds are perfectly synchronized. This makes it much brighter and gives it a rather shrill magical sound without using echo chambers. It makes it sound spectacular, so much power.' "[5]

The Beach Boys' lyrics are both more specific and more general than Chuck's. On one hand, the Beach Boys deal, not with the generalities of "high school" or "rock 'n' roll music," but with a specific sport, surfing, and specific places where you can surf. And "Little Deuce Coupe" has more of the specifics of hot rod jargon than anyone had ever heard before in American popular music. Counter-balancing these specifics, though, is the series of adolescent fantasies which the lyrics present. As Chuck's lyrics never do, the Beach Boys' lyrics define away social restrictions and mundane limitations, as in "Wouldn't It Be Nice."

Contrast, for example, "Fun, Fun, Fun" and "Sweet Little Sixteen," Although the lyrics of both songs deal with a fun-loving teenaged girl, Chuck puts his girl in a social situation and keeps her there. After her fun, she will be "back in class again." The Beach Boys, on the other hand, put their girl in what seems to be a social situation, but which turns out to be a fantasy. They seem to create a crisis when their girl's father takes away the keys to her Thunderbird—but the crisis turns out not to be a crisis at all when the singer offers her more fun, fun, fun. Similarly, in the contest between the Ford and the Cadillac in Chuck's "Maybellene," he has a tough rival, and only the intervention of a rainstorm saves the day. But no class distinctions exist in the Beach Boys' fantasies, and nobody has ever beaten the Little Deuce Coupe, and to hear them tell it, no one has ever come close. The Beach Boys don't have to chase after unfaithful girls, as Chuck does in "Maybellene," because there are "two girls for every boy" (Alternately, when the girl is unfaithful, the Beach Boys either pine, as in "Wendy," or seek consolation with someone else, as in "Help Me Rhonda"). Fun thus becomes the New Frontier, to use a political phrase of the day; it defines away social restrictions, as the frontier does. Endless fun is as much of a fantasy, and just as reassuring, as an endless frontier.

Incidentally, the significance of fantasy in the Beach Boys' lyrics explains something they don't do. They never refer to television, movies, or even rock 'n' roll itself. Such references would have contradicted the fantasy by situating their teenagers too definitely in the mundane, recognizable world.

We might describe the Beach Boys' sound as "Chuck Berry meets the Four Freshmen in Southern California," for the Beach Boys are one of the many groups in American popular music whose style consisted of an amalgam of disparate elements. Brian listened to the Four Freshmen a lot when he was in junior high school and high school, and it's easy to understand why. For one thing, Brian had good taste—the Four Freshmen won *Down-beat's* poll as "Best Vocal Group" for four years, 1953-56. For another, they were as WASP-ish a group as ever made it big in jazz; although they recorded in LA, they were originally from Indiana. Then, too, their repertoire must have appealed to Brian. They didn't play sterile, cool jazz or inaccesible bebop; rather, they liked romantic ballads which let them show off their lush harmonies and orchestrations, as on their album *Voices in Love.*

From the Four Freshmen, Brian learned to let the vocals dominate everything else by suppressing the instruments to avoid interfering with the Bach-like harmonies. Two songs seem especially reminiscent of the Four Freshmen, the slow scat singing on "Surfer Girl" recalls the Four Freshmen's "Tuxedo Junction," where they sing nothing but "oohs" and "aahs" for the whole song. And the effective use of bass vocals on "Little Deuce Coupe" may owe something to the way Ken Albers sang bass for the Four Freshmen.

From these comments it becomes obvious that if Brian admired Chuck, he assimilated the Four Freshmen. Brian and the other Beach Boys were too white and too suburban, to cover fifties rock 'n' roll, as the Beatles were doing at the same time. Their genius lay in their ability to create a unified group sound, and they couldn't learn anything about that from Chuck. Still, assimilation requires great creativity, and they didn't just imitate the Four

Freshmen. They took the Four Freshmen's music, which has no identifiable roots in a particular place or time and re-defined it in terms of their situation. They added the electric guitar and organ and did away with their horns.

Like Forest Lawn, the Beach Boys have become an American institution because they offer us immensely appealing fantasies. We know that their songs represent fantasies, but we sing along with them anyhow, because the Beach Boys are, more than any other group treated in this book, what Brian called a song which he and Mike Love wrote for the *Little Deuce Coupe* album, "The Spirit of America."

Notes

[1]Alan Gowans, *Learning to See. Historical Perspectives on Modern Popular/Commercial Arts* (Bowling Green: Bowling Green U. Popular Press, 1981), pp.93-4.

[2]Frederick Jackson Turner, "The Significance of the Frontier in American History," in *The Turner Thesis*, George Rogers Taylor, ed. (Boston: D. C. Heath and Company, 1956), p. 1.

[3] *Ibid.*, pp. 1-2.

[4] *Ibid.*, p. 2.

[5]Quoted in David Leaf, *The Beach Boys and the California Sound* (New York: Grosset and Dunlap, 1978), p. 44.

SECTION III
1964-1974

Chapter 10:
What Happened in the Sixties, Anyway?

After serving as president of Students for a Democratic Society in 1963-64, Todd Gitlin later became a sociologist, and wrote a book about media treatment of SDS, *The Whole World is Watching*. While working on it, he realized that, "What happened was not what I thought was happening at the time it happened."[1] What he says applies to many of us who have lived through the sixties. We all knew that something important was happening, but more of us were like Dylan's Mr. Jones than we wanted to admit. We were confused and often frightened during the sixties, though we did our best to deny it. The sixties still confuse and frighten, even embarrass, us. Like the characters in Lawrence Kasdan's *The Big Chill* (1983), we sit around and wonder what happened to us during that period when we could feel ecstasy at the latest Beatles record during the day, agony while watching the evening news (as compiled in the litany of horrors on Simon and Garfunkel's "7 O'Clock News/Silent Night", and feel both as we watched *Easy Rider* (1969) that night.

There's so much about the sixties that we don't know, and may never know. It's not just that we don't know the truth about the assassination of President Kennedy, although that uncertainty continues to haunt us. There may have been other conspiracies, and we may never know the truth about them, either. Is it true, as Phillip Norman suggests in *Shout!*, that Brian Epstein was murdered? We don't know. Is it true that Jimi Hendrix was once kidnapped by some renegade Mafiosi? Jerry Hopkins tells the story in *Hit and Run*, his biography of Jimi. If Hopkins doesn't quite believe it after checking the stories, what should we think?

Between what we didn't understand at the time, and what we may never know, the sixties remain an enigma not just for those who love the music, but for everybody who wants to understand American society. Since we need to understand the interrelationships among all those horrendous events, this section begins with an essay which treats the music only incidentally. This general essay examines some of the recurring themes and images in American culture, in the belief that they form the context in which statements and events from the sixties become meaningful and coherent.

To begin with, we need to set time limits on the sixties. In his book on the Beach Boys, David Leaf says of 1964, "It was also the year that the decade called 'The Sixties' finally began in California."[2] Because we cannot think of the sixties without the Beatles, and since the Beatles did not get to America until February 7, 1964, let us say that the sixties began in early 1964, in the aftermath of the assassination of President Kennedy. As for the end of the sixties, it came with a shocking abruptness on December 7, 1969. At the Rolling Stones' free concert at Altamont, California a Hell's Angel killed a black man while Mick Jagger was singing "Under My Thumb." (The Maysles' film *Gimme Shelter* (1970) documents this moment). We are talking about five years, a period of innovation in music comparable to the period from 1954 to 1959, but which was much more complex.

We can best make sense of these five years, when so much happened so fast, by grouping the period's events into a four category matrix.

The Space Program	The War
Sex, Drugs, and Rock 'n' Roll	The Movement

We can read this matrix both across and down. For instance, to go across, the government instigated the space program and the war. It suppressed, with varying degrees of success, sex, drugs, and rock 'n' roll; and the movement. But we can read the matrix down as well. If the space ships helped us explore outer space, the sex, drugs, and rock 'n' roll helped us explore inner space— "the canyons of your mind." Ominously, the war and the movement kept us on the ground. The government caused violence not just in the war, but also in its suppression of the movement. By contrast, the movement usually succeeded in remaining non-violent. Finally, the space program and the war and sex, drugs, and rock 'n' roll and the movement; all represent at unprecedented intensity, two of the great mythological themes of American history: the frontier and the covenant.

Both the space program and the war had essentially the same impetus: the American need for an endless, fluid frontier, which served as a symbol for social mobility and the promise of democracy. Although it took President Kennedy some time to commit America to putting a man on the moon, we now think of the association between the New Frontier and the space program as an obvious one. As early as 1960, a Kennedy campaign statement in the trade journal *Missiles and Rockets* stated that "This is the age of exploration; space is our great New Frontier."[3] The success of the first Soviet manned space flight on April 12, 1961, and the failure of the American-backed invasion of Cuba at the Bay of Pigs a week later, gave the President a sense of urgency about the space program as a means of restoring American prestige. Soon, on May 25, 1961, he delivered the famous speech "Urgent National Needs," before Congress in which he said "I believe that this Nation should commit itself to achieving the goal, before this decade is out, of landing a man on the moon and returning him safely to earth."[4]

Since hardly anyone grasped the symbolic import of the space program in 1961, the President was surprised at the ease with which he was able to get the enormous appropriations from Congress, and the astronauts were surprised at the way they became heroes. (Tom Wolfe documents this in merciless detail in *The Right Stuff*.) Just over eight years after this speech, on July 20, 1969, Neil Armstrong did in fact land on the moon.

This dramatic event, which the whole world watched on television, symbolically enclosed the earth; it gave us a sense of the earth not as the measure of the known and the knowable, but as one stop on a round trip. For Americans, the moon landing definitively closed the frontier in a literal sense. In doing so, it gave us a sense of intimacy and closeness, and that sense defined much of the personal style of the sixties.

However, British novelist C.P. Snow's gloomy prediction did not immediately come true: "It will give us the feeling, and the perfectly justified feeling, that our world has finally closed in. This is forever the end of the mortal frontier."[5] Snow failed to understand the capacity of popular culture to act as symbolic compensation, however; and this capacity made *Star Trek* (1966-69) into a cult. Producer Gene Rodenberry gave us an essential hint for understanding *Star Trek* when he once described it as *"Wagon Train* to the stars." Captain Kirk, Mr. Spock, and the other characters in the program were exploring a world in which the frontier did not and could not close.

After President Kennedy committed American money and prestige to putting a man on the moon, he assigned special responsibility for the space program to his Vice-President, Lyndon Johnson, who had been advocating it since 1958. Johnson was a complex, possibly even a tragic, man. If his domestic programs expressed his continuing commitment to the New Deal which first brought him to Washington, his new commitment to the space program expressed his Texan's sensitivity to the need to keep the frontier open. Because the same obsessed Texan promoted both the space program and the war, and because both policies initially evoked automatic, widespread support from the American people, can we say that the space program and the war were both expressions of the American need to keep open the frontier?

Historian William Appleman Williams would say so. In a provocative essay called "The Frontier Thesis and American Foreign Policy," Williams makes the point that, "[Frederick] Turner gave Americans a nationalistic world view that eased their doubts. settled their confusions, and justified their aggressiveness.... Expansion a la Turner was good for business and at the same time extended white Protestant democracy."[6] Williams analyzes Turner's influence, and that of Brooks Adams, a man with similar attitudes on Secretary of State John Foster Dulles and the Cold War: "And Dulles might well claim that his plan to liberate all people not ruled according to the precepts of individualistic democracy was the definitive statement of the [frontier] thesis."[7]

When we consider the meaning of the frontier in this sobering way, we realize that Turner suppressed both halves of the self/other opposition. He shows no awareness of the destruction of the cultures of native Americans, the others; he says nothing of treaties which we broke in the process of pushing back the frontier. Nor does Turner deal with the businessmen who opened the frontier, the railroad magnates and land speculators whose greed supplied a prime motivation for the expansion of the frontier. So what seemed to him the source of America's democratic spirit in the nineteenth century subsequently turned into a justification for military intervention in foreign countries in the twentieth century.

President Johnson had inherited, then, a belief in the use of force abroad as an implicit assumption of the political system in which he had had so much success. No wonder he became increasingly paranoid about critics of the war, and that his representatives could not give any coherent defense of the war unless they were preaching to the converted. So, when Secretary of State Dean Rusk testified before the Senate Foreign Relations Committee on February 18, 1965, he:

> ...Never pointed to anything concrete as a justification of the war; he never implied there was any economic or geographic reason why it made any difference who controlled Vietnam. His arguments referred solely to intangibles: the United States was fighting in Vietnam to prevent the "other side" from starting other wars elsewhere.[8]

That is to say, Rusk could neither give a persuasive defense of the war nor articulate the implicit assumptions about the frontier in which he and the other supporters of the war believed. Since neither side could articulate its assumptions, mounting frustration resulted.

Michael Arlen has aptly called the war in Vietnam "the living room war," because we watched it on television. Many of the tensions of the sixties derived from television's new dominance as America's news medium. (CBS expanded its evening news to a half hour on September 2, 1963; The *Huntley-Brinkley Report* did the same thing a week later.) As McLuhan said in *Understanding Media*, television is a cool, involving medium; another way to make the same point is to say that television meant that we got our news primarily from visual images, not from print. John Chancellor of NBC News seems to have been the first to understand the effect of TV on the public in the sixties.

> Older people, ones who grew up on newspapers and magazines, were used to being their own editors, you see; in print, you can read stories which please you—my Dad, for example, would read sports and business pieces in the *Chicago Tribune* but then skip articles on gossip and rape. My point is this—in television you can't do that. You could watch a thirty-minute newscast, but to do so you had to watch the whole thing. And so some Americans—the guys Agnew really appealed to—were furious at us for blasting them with the bad news they weren't accustomed to as well as the good news—and there kept being less of it every year—they *were* used to watching.[9]

But it wasn't just middle-aged white men who had grown up reading newspapers and who now watched television who felt upset by the news in the sixties. Sometimes even newspaper stories upset people as subtle as novelist Joan Didion, who, one day in the sixties, read

> ...The story of Betty Lansdown Fouquet, a 26-year-old woman with faded blond hair who put her five-year-old daughter out to die on the center divide of Interstate 5 some miles south of the last Bakersfield exit.... Certain of these images did not fit into any narrative I knew.[10]

It is obvious why Didion, as a novelist, would want images to fit into a narrative. What is less obvious, but much more important, is that we all carried narratives in our heads during the sixties, and that we kept trying to make the media images which we experienced correspond to those narratives.

By itself, no analysis of the events, statements, and ideas of a a given time can ever explain that time in a satisfactory way, for it does not account for the expectations which people bring to their experience. Those expectations determine people's perceptions of themselves, and of the world around them as well. These expectations thus have effects which are all the more insidious because they come from the unconscious. In twentieth-century America, those expectations come from popular culture, especially sports and the mass entertainment media, such as movies and television.

A major style of American popular culture, in which the performers wear familiar clothing and perform in familiar situations, is called "realism." We perceive works which obey the conventions of realism as referring unambiguously to an external reality, and we therefore come to expect that our experience will correspond to our media experiences. We love to say of a media experience, "It's just like real life," and interviewers love to ask movie stars if they're like the characters they play in movies. We internalize popular culture as a collective dream which we experience personally, and having a dream and trying to make it come true is as American as apple pie.

Let us consider television news in this connection. The war in Vietnam was "the living room war," because we watched it on television. Arlen observed, "For TV the news worthiness of daily events is still so restrictively determined by visual criteria."[11] What made good television was battle footage—the kind of stuff we were used to seeing in movies and newsreels about World War II. The reporters and editors sensed that battle footage would make a perplexing war in a distant, obscure country seem more familiar by meeting the viewers' expectations. So we got lots of three-minute segments of combat, such as our boys blowing up an ammo dump.

In all too many cases, though, what the blowing up of the ammo dump says is that when you blow up an ammo dump it goes boom-boom and there is a lot of smoke, and that is about it. Daily journalism in general seems to e virtually rooted in its traditional single-minded way of presenting the actuality of daily life, as if some invisible sacred bond existed between the conventional structures of daily journalism and the conventional attitudes of so many of the people whom daily journalism serves...It is now especially evident, and damaging, in Vietnam, where, for the most part, American journalism has practically surrendered itself to a consecutive, activist, piecemeal, the-next-day-the-First-Army-forged-onward-toward-Aachen approach to a war that even the journalists covering it know to be nonconsecutive, non-activist, a war of silences, strange motions, where a bang on the table gets you nothing and an inadvertent blink causes things to happen in rooms you haven't looked into yet, where there is no Aachen, and "onward" is a word that does not seem to translate very well in the local languages.[12]

Aachen was the first important German city which fell into the hands of the Allies during World War II, and Arlen's reference to it here implies an awareness that people perceived those three-minute newsclips as snippets of war movies. Thus, the American love of immediate sensation for its own sake created immense frustration because there never seemed to be a narrative in the news about Vietnam. There was lots of action, and thus good television, but not much sense. As Arlen also implies, the war was not a visual story, but the journalists had to tell it on a medium which re-defined news as visual information.

During a press conference, Robert Kennedy once commented that, "Nothing prepares a man for life like war and football." Very few people ever grow up in America without hearing some version of a similar connection between popular culture and adult experience, such as "Football builds character." With the inauguration of President Kennedy, this connection took on even greater importance in the sixties.

It is appropriate that President Kennedy's father, Joseph Kennedy, had been in the movie business, among other things, for President Kennedy's success in the televised debates with Nixon made him a media star of the first order. President Kennedy understood the importance of image building. He accepted a Publitzer Prize in 1957 for *Profiles in Courage,* a book he hadn't written. He greatly augmented the accounts of his heroics when his PT boat was sunk during World War II. When Hollywood decided to make a movie about his PT experience he maintained script control, and picked Warren Beatty to play the lead. (Beatty was unavailable, so Kennedy settled for Cliff Robertson.) So *PT-109* (1963) turned into yet another war movie which we took as the truth about war.

President Kennedy's father had served as ambassador to England, and had brought up his sons to think of themselves as British aristocrats. The President had a special susceptibility to the panache of James Bond's derring-do, as in the movie *Dr. No* (1962). The Bond mystique surely had something to do with the Green Berets, which the President created over the protests of the Army. This enables us to establish a connection between two American media heroes named John—John Kennedy created the Green Berets, and John Wayne glorified them.

The Duke's legend played a hitherto unsuspected role in the sixties, and deserves consideration. The hundreds of movies which he made fall into three general categories: westerns, war movies, and sports movies. Taken together, he played out an allegory of the Turner thesis on the silver screen. Wayne's narratives often depict the encounter of self and other, of Americans and foreigners, of whites and non-whites; and in that encounter whites win, as in *The Sands of Iwo Jima* (1949). In *Red River* (1948), for instance, he announces a moral justification for American expansion when he moves south into Mexican territory and says, "It's not right for one man to have that much land." *Red River* led directly to the movie which meant the most to him, *The Alamo* (1960). He put a great deal of his own money into the saga of Davy Crockett and the American defense against Santa Ana; he also produced and directed it.

Even more relevant here, and more controversial, was *The Green Berets* (1968); Wayne believed so much in this defense of the war that he put up his own money when no one in Hollywood would back such a controversial project. The audience liked it, and it brought in $9,000,000 during its first year, which made it the tenth-highest grossing movie for 1968.[13] At least partially because John Wayne played so convincingly what we wanted to believe, Americans from President Johnson down to the men in the jungles believed that the war in Vietnam would play itself out according to the familiar movie narrative of the endless, ever-receding frontier.

The Duke thought of himself as a conservative. Yet it might prove useful to re-define "conservative" and "liberal" in terms of attitudes about the frontier. In the sixties, conservatives believed that with enough determination they could keep the frontier open; liberals believed that the frontier had closed and accepted the consequences of that fact.

In order to understand the pervasive quality of what I have been calling the frontier/John Wayne narrative, we need to rid ourselves of a misconception about the sixties, the misconception that young people opposed the war. In fact, if President Nixon's infamous phrase "the silent majority" has any validity at all, it refers to the silent majority among the young. As political scientist Seymour Martin Lipset put it in 1971:

The fact that the Vietnam war is a horror, a blunder, whatever words one wants to call it, was recognized earlier and most continually by people over fifty than by younger age groups. Every poll taken from 1965 to the most recent one..in May 1971, which reported on answers to whether the Vietnam war is a mistake or not, correlated by age group, shows the younger the group, the fewer who say it is a mistake.[14]

Lipset continues, "In 1968, the younger people were more likely to have voted for George Wallace."[15]

These facts sound odd to us because they do not correspond to the media image of the sixties. Because there were so many more young people than ever before, and because so many more of them were in college, it was big news when even a small percentage protested war and racism. Like the shots of soldiers blowing up ammo dumps, it was good television. The fact is, protest in the sixties was a function of something Americans don't like to talk about— class. The vociferous minority of students who protested the war came from relatively affluent families. The working class kids who actually fought the war constituted a majority, and they consistently believed in John Wayne and supported American policy until President Nixon's invasion of Cambodia.

One such working class kid was Ron Kovic. He grew up in an ethnic community on Long Island, and loved John Wayne: "Like Mickey Mantle and the fabulous New York Yankees, John Wayne in *The Sands of Two Jima* became one of my heroes.[16] Naturally, then, when he met the Marine recruiters who came to his high school, he couldn't see them for what they were: "I couldn't help but feel I was shaking hands with John Wayne and Audie Murphy."[17] So he joined up as soon as he could and served a tour of duty in Vietnam. Upon returning from it, he was "enraged with the people who were demonstrating in the streets against the war," and re-enlisted. During his second tour he accidentally killed one of his own men.

I can't describe the pain. It was incredible, tragic. I felt like my whole being had been torn out. For those seconds, I felt like I was going to faint. My heart was racing. They were doing everything they could to save him. I couldn't look over to where they were talking and trying to bandage him.
Then somebody yelled in my direction, "He's dead." I rode back in the amtrack with him right by my foot, and he was dead.
It wasn't like a John Wayne movie at all; the good guys weren't supposed to kill the good guys.[18]

Indeed, the war wasn't at all like the John Wayne movie that kept playing in the soldiers' heads, and soldier after soldier made the same agonizing discovery which Ron Kovic made. As Charles Anderson soberly puts it in his book *The Grunts*, "The grunts—newbys, short-timers, and lifers alike—could see now that what happens to human beings in mechanized warfare has absolutely no poetic or theatrical possibilities."[19]

Nowhere in his moving and passionate book *Born on the Fourth of July* does Kovic conceptualize his very representative, very American dilemma as Joan Didion does, but she certainly speaks for him when she says:

I was supposed to have a script, and had mislaid it. I was supposed to hear cues, and no longer did. I was meant to know the plot, but all I knew was what I saw: flash pictures in a variable sequence, images with no "meaning" beyond their temporary arrangement, not a movie but a cutting-room experience. In what would probably be the middle of my life I wanted still to believe in the narrative and in the narrative's intelligibility, but to know that one could change the sense with every cut was to begin to perceive one's experience as rather more electrical than ethical.[20]

Arbitrarily ordered images, images arranged in such a way as to deny narrative coherence, frustrate us. In our optimistic American way we believe that we, or somebody, can arrange those images in a more satisfying way, so that things will turn out all right in the end. But in the sixties no one could.

In Francis Ford Coppola's *Apocalypse Now* (1979), there occurs a bizarre scene which ties together the John Wayne/frontier narrative, American popular music, and the Presidency. Just after the AirCav takes the Viet Cong village, to the thunderous accompaniment of Wagner's "Ride of the Valkyries," Robert Duval as Captain Kilgore instructs a corporal to get out his surfboard and try the waves, even before the last shots have died out. Kilgore will not take no for an answer, and finally the shocked, frightened kid starts taking off his clothes. It so happens that the kid is named Lance Johnson, and that he was a champion surfer in California. Why would such a major artist as Coppola turn Lyndon Johnson into a surfer, and what did LBJ and the Beach Boys have in common?

There is a loose but suggestive association between the careers of President Johnson and the Beach Boys in that both embodied an implicit belief in the frontier as the unending hegemony of white Protestant democracy. It would be simplistic and inexcusable to blame the Beach Boys for Vietnam, or to resort to the name-calling which Marxists like so much, and say that they play imperialistic music. The world is more complicated than that, and the interrelations among its constituent parts more subtle than such namecalling would allow. It makes more sense to explain the Beach Boys' appeal in areas where no one has ever seen a beach by reference to the appeal of the frontier in American history. Having noticed that, we can also notice the relationship between the popularity of the Beach Boys and the popularity of the war.

After the Beach Boys failed to appear at the one brief, shining moment of the counterculture, Monterey Pop (17-18 June, 1967), their popularity started to decline. "Good Vibrations" was their last major hit, and they went through some hard times until *Rolling Stone* rehabilitated them with a cover story in 1971.

In Vietnam, the number of American troops went over one half million in 1967, and protests against our presence there increased. Then, in January of 1968, the Tet offensive gave the lie to government propaganda about the progress of the war. First Eugene McCarthy, and then Robert Kennedy, entered the race against Johnson. Finally Johnson announced on March 31, 1968, "I shall not seek, and I will not accept, the nomination of my party for another term as your President..."[21] And although the war had not ended in 1971, it was winding down.

Another narrative form, football, caused lasting frustration during the sixties by providing us with another set of unconscious expectations. The sixties were, after all, the heyday of the Green Bay Packers, who won the NFL title in 1965-66, and the first two Super Bowls, in 1967 and 1968. Who can forget Bart Starr, Paul Hornung, and Jim Taylor? The Packers' coach was Vince Lombardi, after whom the Super Bowl trophy is named, and who summed up his philosophy of life in the line, "Winning isn't the most important thing— it's the only thing."

Just consider the satisfying things about sports in general, and football in particular. In football, you always know who the good guys are, and who the bad guys are—they wear different uniforms. You know whose territory is whose, and it's always good to invade the enemy's territory. You know how things come out in the end.

Like John Wayne movies, football is supposed to prepare you for life. In his superb documentary *Hearts and Minds* (1974), Peter Davis intercuts between war scenes and football scenes, to show the similarity. The film also includes scenes from the official welcome home rally in Linden, New Jersey, for returned POW George Cocker. Cocker repeats in his speech the slogans which he learned while playing high school football, and which sustained him in his captivity: "When the going gets tough, the tough get going," and "Quitters never win, and winners never quit."

Because we had been taught to make a connection between football and life we kept on expecting the war to be like a football game, and it kept on frustrating our expectations. As Lt. Calley insisted while on trial for his role in the My Lai Massacre, in Vietnam you couldn't tell the good guys from the bad guys—they all looked alike. Since no one could tell the friendlies from the unfriendlies, the safe thing to do was to shoot them all. In the same way, no one could draw a map which showed which territory belonged to the friendlies, and which territory belonged to the unfriendlies, because everything kept shifting around. In terms of general strategy, the tenaciously held belief that winners never quit created strong resistance to stopping the bombing and withdrawing the troops. After all, we expected that there would be a clear sign that we had won, just like in a football game.

Let us not forget that the implicit analogy between the war and sports animated the opponents of the war as well as its supporters. In rooting for Uncle Ho and NLF ("Ho, Ho, Ho, Chi Minh; NLF is gonna win."), the marchers were doing something which sports fans had been doing for years: siding with the underdog.

One obvious analogy with anti-war marchers during the sixties was the phenomenon of the Mets fan. Mets fans were much discussed at the time because they didn't seem to care whether their team won or lost. They rooted for the Mets simply because they weren't the Yankees. Because protesters were cheering on the underdog in much the same way, they adapted sports cheers in their marches. In her book on Dylan, Betsy Bowden recalls marching in demonstrations and chanting, "Two, Four, Six, Eight: Organize and Smash the State." We recognize here a variant of a chant which marchers had repeated at their high school football games when someone got hurt: "Two, Four, Six, Eight; Who Do We Appreciate?"

But there is another narrative which subsumes both the John Wayne narrative and the football narrative, and which incorporates just about everything of importance that happened in the sixties. It is an incomplete narrative of sufficient complexity to incorporate conflict, and it gives America its identity as nothing else does. This narrative is even older than America itself. Beginning on the good ship *Arbella* in 1630, when John Winthrop delivered a sermon, "A Model of Christian Charity," to the future founders of America. Winthrop promised them:

We shall find that the God of Israel is among us, when ten of us shall be able to resist a thousand of our enemies, when He shall make a praise and glory, that men shall say of succeeding plantations: "The Lord make it like that of New England." For we must consider that we shall be as a city upon a hill, the eyes of all peoples are upon us. So that if we shall deal falsely with our God in this work we have undertaken, and so cause Him to withdraw His present help from us, we shall be made a story and a by-word through the world: we shall open the mouths of enemies to speak evil of the ways of God and all professors for God's sake....[22]

Winthrop's "Model of Christian Charity" is probably the most important single document in American culture, for it defines the promise and obligations of our society. Winthrop told his fellow Puritans, as so many people have told their fellow Americans, that a great deal is riding on what we do. What we do matters because we have a covenant with God; we are settling not just a New England but a New Israel as well.

From those to whom much is given, much is asked. If the Puritans were to provide a model of Christian charity which would light up decadent Europe, then they had a triple obligation: to God, to their community, and to themselves. The Puritans needed to subject themselves to relentless self-examination because they believed in salvation through grace, not works; no one could be sure who was saved, and who would burn in hell forever. But there were certain signs which indicated God's favor, and prosperity was one of them. Gradually, as the apocalyptic fervor of the settlers faded, covenant theology began to define the transcendent meaning of America, rather than Christianity. America is neither a church state, nor a completely secular one; it has, not a state religion, but a civil religion.

This civil religion, as sociologist Robert Bellah has called it, has both social and personal implications. In social terms, the covenant means that we believe that America is a special and specially blessed country. The covenant takes on special significance during times of crisis, such as wars; hence, Abraham Lincoln used religious imagery about the Civil War dead in referring to the field of battle as "this hallowed ground" in the Gettysburg Address. Therefore, Americans tend to think of their wars as crusades, so that ministers during World War I depicted our troops as led by "Christ in Khaki." In personal terms, civil religion justified a concern with self which was often difficult to distinguish from self-aggrandizement and greed; hence, Andrew Carnegie could call his book about philanthropy *The Gospel of Wealth* (1900).

Bellah says in his book *The Broken Covenant* that the covenant of which Winthrop spoke so ringingly and eloquently was soon broken by the arrival of slaves in America.[23] No one was ever able to explain how we could keep a covenant with God, while allowing such an abomination to exist. This is how, as Greil Marcus has put it so well, America became too much to live up to, and too much to ignore.

The tension of American history, then, has been the tension of a narrative of an incomplete covenant. Each generation of Americans feels that it must supply the happy ending to the narrative to build the city upon a hill; eventually it realizes that it, too, forms a part of a historical process, like the generation before it and the generation after it. (The ubiquitous happy endings of American popular narratives supply surrogates for the happy endings which we cannot realize in history.)

Just as the football narrative supported both the government's decision to escalate the war and the protestors' demonstrations against those decisions, so the implicit belief in the covenant supported both the war and the movement which opposed it. The belief that America has God on its side is complemented by the belief that America is especially corrupt, racist, or militaristic. In their fundamental agreement on America's special mission, both the defenders and attackers of the status quo are in essential agreement about the existence of the covenant.

We can now understand Turner's frontier thesis as a specific instance of covenant theology. Implicit in Turner's essay is the belief that Americans had a right to push the frontier ever westward, thereby displacing the native Americans by the thousands, a belief justified by the covenant. Because America has a covenant with God, it has a manifest destiny to push back the frontier, or so people believed. If this process defined Americanization, as Turner argued, then we could not let it cease with the closing of the real frontier. In the twentieth century, the frontier dynamic was exported under the guise of making the world safe for democracy, and incidentally, of opening new markets for American products.

The major public figures of a society have no immunity from its conditioning, and in fact often occupy the positions they do because they represent its expectations in a pure form. We now understand that it was not just Dr. King who had a dream in the sixties. Lyndon Johnson, Robert McNamara, and J. Edgar Hoover also had dreams, and they exerted their very considerable capacities to make those dreams come true.

In the sixties the historical dynamics of convent theology destroyed the Presidency of Lyndon Johnson, who was as paradoxical a man as Richard Nixon. On the one hand, President Johnson gave us a Civil Rights Bill in 1965 that President Kennedy could not have pushed through. On the other hand, his obsession with the war caused great suffering, and eventually turned even his closest supporters such as Bill Moyers against him.

Johnson's support for civil rights at home, and his belief in the war abroad, both derive their justification from the covenant. President Johnson argued for the Civil Rights Bill because segregation was an abomination, just as slavery had been. It broke the covenant, and therefore had to be abolished. If it was our duty to abolish segregation, which was a moral issue, it was also our duty—again, imposed by the covenant—to help the people in Vietnam because they had asked us to help. Once committed to the war, we had a duty to see it through because the covenant imposed on us a special responsibility toward other countries. Politicans who told us—as many of them did—that "Our will is being tested in Vietnam" were drawing on covenant theology to make an analogy between military decisions and moral fortitude.

Robert McNamara, Secretary of Defense under both Kennedy and Johnson, seems out of place in any discussion of covenant theology. We think of him as Mr. Rationalism, a hard-driving businessman, disciplined, totally secular. But as David Harlberstam shows in his book *The Best and the Brightest*, he is a more complex and traditional than we thought at the time. Indeed, Halberstam says that, "In business philosophy as well as personal life, McNamara was a puritan..."[24] and that "the total belief in what he was doing" made him so effective.

Secretary McNamara was a puritan and a believer; he believed in the secular authority of numbers the way John Winthrop believed in the divine authority of God. McNamara believed that numbers always refer to something that exists, just as Ron Kovic believed that John Wayne movies refer to war in some direct, unambiguous way. Since McNamara believed that numbers do not lie, the war turned into a matter of body counts and kill ratios, not people. (Television news directors liked this, because they could show the numbers as charts and graphs on the evening news.) He turned into a prisoner of the military who gave him the numbers; he did not have it in him to doubt those numbers, as the reporters on the scene in Vietnam doubted them. As long as he was using reliable numbers he was brilliant, but he so confused quantification and rationalism that he started to resemble the cartoon character Mr. Magoo, who never understands that he is deluded. So Halberstam reluctantly but justly concludes, "He was, there is no kinder or gentler word for it, a fool."[25]

The covenant lived on with a vengeance in the South, where it was as important in the politics of the sixties as it was in the music of the fifties. Indeed, we may understand the social upheavals in the South during the sixties as a further development of the process which produced the great rockers of the fifties.

Any metaphor as rich as the covenant lends itself to varying interpretations. The South defended first slavery, and then segregation by saying that it had a covenant within a covenant, so to speak. If America was unique and thus different from England—so went the implicit argument—the South was unique, and thus different from the rest of America. So the South defended slavery as a "peculiar institution," and segregation as justified by "states' rights." In the sixties, support for the war and a belief in white supremacy had a transcendent meaning for Southerners, and they clung tenaciously to that meaning. Although their actions seemed paradoxical to Northerners—Southerners seemed to be supporting the government and resisting it at the same time—an implicitly covenantal belief informed both attitudes.

Elvis supported the war and despised demonstrators. So did his fellow Mississippian John Stennis, who chaired the Select Committee on Standards and Conduct in 1968, and who served on the Armed Forces Committee. Richard Russell, senior senator from Georgia, chaired that committee, and Stennis and Russell believed the generals who told them that the bombing would work. The most important of those generals was William Westmoreland from South Carolina, who served as commander of the U.S. Military Command in Vietnam, 1964-68. And Dean Rusk, from Georgia, served as Secretary of State, 1961-68.

Certainly no account of prominent Southerners in the sixties can leave unmentioned Billy Graham from North Carolina. As a devout admirer of the Puritans, Graham stood for the evangelical Protestantism in which so many

Americans believed because he himself believed it so completely. Graham's biographer Marshall Frady said, "He constitutes finally the apotheosis of the American Innocence itself—that plain, cheerful, rigorous, ferociously wholesome innocence which, to some, as one Egyptian editor put it during the days of Vietnam, 'has made you nice Americans the most dangerous people on the face of the earth.' "[26] As a true believer, Graham appealed deeply to Johnson, and in turn he thought Johnson was a believer as well. Johnson sorely needed believers during his Presidency, and constantly beseeched Graham to stay at the White House as often as possible. Each man profited from associating with the other.

But a belief in the covenant also includes a belief in one's right to denounce America as sinful, and two Southerners in the sixties did so. One was William Fullbright of Arkansas, who chaired the Senate Foreign Relations Committee. The other, of course, was Dr. Martin Luther King, Jr.

Dr. King was a Southern Baptist preacher, and thus he formed a curious pair with his alter ego Billy Graham, who was also his only serious rival as a public speaker. Both of them used a language informed by the richness of Biblical metaphor, yet they differed on the most disputed point of their common evangelical heritage—the relationship between individual morality and social morality. For Graham, as a white man who believed in the Southern version of the covenant, no relationship between the two existed, for morality consisted of "getting right with God," as the Southern formula has it. (Since he did not believe in a social morality outside the individual's relationship with God, he never took a public position on the war.) In this sense, Graham remained a traditional Puritan.

As a black man educated in the North, however, Dr. King insisted that a relationship between individual and social morality did exist. Then he moved outside the church to involve himself in secular activity, in politics. He and his dream of an egalitarian, multi-racial society represented covenant theology in the process of secularization, at a stage when it still retained much of its religious force and religious rhetoric.[27]

It is not surprising, then, to find that the battle hymn of the movement, "We Shall Overcome," is a secularized hymn. Dr. King often referred to it as a spiritual. Its opening and closing phrases come from an old spiritual, *No More Auction Block For Me*, and its lyrics come from Charles Findley's gospel song of transcendence, *I'll Overcome Some Day*.

Most whites probably heard "We Shall Overcome" for the first time on television, which had a lot to do with evoking widespread middle-class support for civil rights. By covering Dr. King's protests in Birmingham, Alabama, in 1963, television brought what had formerly been a regional experience into people's living rooms everywhere. In making Bull Conners, Birmingham's Commissioner for Public Safety, a part of national experience, television created a sense, not so much that segregation was wrong, but that the people who were doing the segregating offended middle-class sensibilities.

Television coverage of the civil rights movement also provided a striking and satisfying contrast to the news clips from Vietnam. In Alabama, we could tell the good guys from the bad guys, and you rarely could in Vietnam. Television coverage from Selma provided images which held the promise that good would triumph over obvious and identifiable evil. But a covenant is a promise, and a promise unfulfilled created frustration. In August of 1965, the Watts riot erupted; this began the increasing violence which characterized the late sixties.

Television made Dr. King a certified celebrity. But by any standards, he was a remarkable man, and was able to use his celebrity status for the good of the cause. Others, lacking his character and experience, had less grace under pressure. Television coverage essentially destroyed SDS when it made that small group of idealistic people a part of the national experience. This did not happen as part of a plot, but because the leadership of the organization was not prepared to deal with national exposure. Television coverage also imposed crises of conscience for sincere idealists like Tom Hayden. Although these idealists had a genuine commitment to democratic principles, they soon sensed that they could take their programs to the American public only if the media, i.e. television, certified them with celebrity labels such as "antiwar leader," and the like.

By 1968, television coverage of riots and demonstrations had become a repeated closed tape loop. In May, the serious uprisings at Columbia University in New York City which eventually closed that institution were undertaken in deliberate imitation of the riots at the Sorbonne in Paris in April, which the kids at Columbia had been able to watch on television via the new statellite transmissions. The framing and editing of such images gave them great power, and created the need in viewers to act them out, thereby becoming celebrities at second hand. When they saw themselves on television they became real celebrities. It is most appropriate that when a Columbia student, James Kunen, wrote a book about his experiences there, it was made into a movie: *The Strawberry Statement* (1970).

The most serious riot of 1968, for the nation as a whole, was the police riot at the Democratic Convention in Chicago in August. One group of demonstrators there let themselves be filmed while practicing a snake dance. They had seen some Japanese students doing it on television, so they adopted it without realizing it would do no good on Chicago's wide streets. Mayor Daley saw the news clip on the local evening news, and seized the occasion to send in his riot police. I cannot describe the results better than Todd Gitlin:

Across Michigan Avenue from the Conrad Hilton Hotel, as floodlit demonstrators took up the rousing chant, "The whole world is watching! The whole world is watching!" in front of the cameras, police clubs swung, blood flowed, cameras ground, image became reality, reality was doubled back as image, and accusation became self-fulfilling prophecy. It was this cycle that the Nixon Administration eventually seized upon and furthered to justify repression—including repression of the press itself for amplifying the bad news—and its own paranoia.[28]

What Gitlin doesn't mention is that America had finally become what John Winthrop had anticipated—a city upon a hill. His now famous image gives prominence to America because of geography; he could not have imagined that twentieth-century technology would give America world-wide prominence, and that that prominence would not come from a display of virtue, as he had hoped, but from a display of the failure to keep the covenant.

A final quote in connection with the political meaning of the covenant in the sixties: "All we need is faith...The truly revolutionary force of history is not material power but the spirit of religion."[29] We might think that these words came from Dr. King, but in fact they came from his most implacable enemy, a man who did more harm to the civil rights movement than George Wallace. This man held more power for longer than any other man in American history, yet—like Dr. King—he never held elected office. His name was J. Edgar Hoover.

An FBI agent testified, "We were operating an intensive vendetta against Dr. King in an effort to destroy him."[30] FBI agents were notoriously slow to help civil rights workers in the South, and left them to the dubious mercy of the local authorities. How did it happen, then, that Hoover acquired such power, and that he kept it so long?

We know now that Hoover could blackmail high government officials without presidential intervention because he was a product of the media, "another John Wayne, a celebrity presumed to possess in real life the heroic qualities he displayed on the screen."[31] Like John Wayne, Hoover became a celebrity in a movie, *G-Men* (1935). Although Hoover did not appear in *G-Men*, it created his role; by presenting the director of the FBI as the solution to the problem of organized crime in America it made Hoover into a legend.

We also know now that although no crime wave erupted during the thirties, the newspapers told a different story. Lurid headlines about gangland murders distracted people from their troubles, and sold newspapers. After the newspapers created an imaginary crime wave, the movies created an imaginary G-Man to deal with it. Between them, these two media enclosed Hoover in an enchanted mythological circle. Thus, "Hoover's power had its sources in the hopes, fears, and needs of the American public, drives that are openly expressed only in American popular entertainment."[32] In this way, Hoover had thrust upon him a role as a defender of the unity of white, All-American culture against the gangsters who were usually Italian (Al Capone), Irish (Dion O'Banion), or Jewish (Meyer Lansky).

Covenant theology causes Americans to think of the struggle between the authorities and the criminals as an allegorical struggle between good and evil for the soul of America. Because Americans believe that their popular culture refers unambiguously to an external reality, they believed the movies, the comic strips, and the TV shows which showed FBI agents as the good guys.

Like all the public figures discussed here, Hoover believed in his image as a good guy fighting the forces of evil. In this, he reminds us of President Kennedy. Just as President Kennedy had retained control over the movie *PT-*

109, so Hoover retained control over the scripts, casting, and sponsorship of the television series *The F.B.I.* (1965-1974). Like his fellow Americans, he could not distinguish between the images and the reality of the FBI. Predictably, then, he started choosing agents who resembled Efrem Zimbalist, Jr., the star of the show—agents who had the "Zimmy look," as he called it.

As long as circumstances allowed Hoover to play the role of the mythological good guy tracking down the bad guys, he had the freedom to do anything he wanted—and he exercised that freedom. But...

In the sixties Hoover began to encounter a new type of enemy who had rebelled against the law out of conscience—Daniel Berrigan, Martin Luther King, civil rights workers, anti-war activists, and sometimes, it seemed the whole student population. These new "fugitives" who populated the FBI's Most Wanted List couldn't easily be passed off as formula villains. Hoover's implausible attempts to explain the unrest of the sixties in formula terms made the whole G-Man concept seem irrelevant.[33]

Still, only after Watergate cracked widespread belief in the moral probity of the government, did the general public give credence to the abuses by the FBI and by Hoover himself—abuses which had been documented for years. Hoover's failure to perform his mythological role in the allegory of the covenant is still a major source of the enduring bitterness about the sixties.

In "A Model of Christian Charity," John Winthrop tells his fellow Puritans that, "We must be knit together in this work as one man."[34] The Puritans believed deeply in maintaining a close-knit community, and not just for protection against the native Americans. They also believed in the necessity of maintaining the community's virtue as a whole, so as to realize the goal of creating the city upon a hill. As the secularization of covenant theology progressed, however, "the ethical responsibility of each sect member to scrutinize his brother's conduct was generalized into an informal pattern of busybody-type nosiness."[35] That is to say, when parents wished to have their children internalize community standards of conduct, they asked them, "What would the neighbors think?"

The Puritans had emphasized the relationship between the self and God; in the secular second half of the twentieth century, we re-defined that emphasis as a concern with the self for its own sake. But neither the affirmation of the covenant nor its denial was ever complete; hence the general ambiguity of young people in the sixties about political involvement, and hence the attraction of the rationale that you were engaged in political activity if you wore your hair long.

Mick Jagger understands this very well, as an interview with Chet Flippo printed in *Rolling Stone* in 1980 makes clear.

Chet Flippo: Mick, did it ever seem to you that ten or eleven years ago rock & roll was a powerful social force, and that since then it's been slowly defanged or coopted?
Mick Jagger: (He shook his head) No. That was obviously a false notion.
Chet Flippo: But, for example, "Street Fighting Man" *was* a rallying point, politically.

Mick Jagger (shrugged). Yeah, but that was during that radical Vietnam time. It was merely *then*. You've always got to have good tunes if you're marching. But the tunes *don't make the march*. Basically, rock & roll isn't protest, and never was. It's *not* political.... The whole rebellion in rock & roll was about not being able to make noise at night and not being able to play that rock & roll so loud and boogie-woogie and not being able to use the car and all that.[36]

Rock 'n' roll was revolutionary in that it re-distributed the emphasis of the covenant from community standards to personal standards, from relative asceticism to relative hedonism. In the sixties, rock 'n' roll as rebellion meant a 4/4 beat you could dance to and electric guitars; its celebration of sex, drugs, and music in the lyrics derived from black music as distinctly as its 12-bar blues structure did. This discovery of hedonism by the young, immensely facilitated as it was by the Pill and general prosperity of the times, constituted a form of social change, but not a call to coordinated political action. As Mick says, the music was *not* political, and thus it was not revolutionary in the sense that ascetics like Lenin or Mao or Che would ever have recognized.

The mistaken association of music with political agitation simply because the establishment disliked both of them has another form, the mistaken belief that protest songs were popular in the sixties. People usually cite "Blowin' in the Wind" in this regard, and Peter, Paul, and Mary's version did get to #2 in the popular music charts in June of 1963, but that song is in no way typical. Like its author, it is unique. Clearly, some groups did sing protest songs, such as "Fixin' to Die Rag," by Country Joe and the Fish, and "Volunteers" by the Jefferson Airplane, but none of these songs enjoyed the popularity of the #1 single of 1966, "The Ballad of the Green Berets," by Staff Sargeant Berry Sadler. Both the single and the album of the same name were certified gold soon after their release.

Music did not proclaim political revolution, but redefined the meaning of the covenant. How did it do that? We can begin with two of the most important and most intellectual songwriters of the sixties, Bob Dylan and Paul Simon.

Two of Dylan's early songs are important here: "With God on Our Side," and "Maggie's Farm." "With God on Our Side" recapitulates American history in terms of the covenant's divine justification for expansion and war—all treated with bitter irony, of course. If "With God on Our Side," is very general, "Maggie's Farm" is very personal. When we hear Bob snarl, "I ain't gonna work on Maggie's farm no more," and hear the angry electric guitar, the sense of rebellion as denial of the covenant seems obvious.

Paul Simon's "Fifty-ninth Street Bridge Song (Feelin' Groovy)," has a very different sound, and an intriguing history. "That's a great dope song," somebody said to me about it once during the sixties, and its easy, dreamy tone made it the ideal accompaniment to a joint. The crux of the song occurs in the couplet:

I've got no deeds to do, no promises to keep
I'm dappled and drowsy and ready to sleep.

Simon had been an English major at Queens College and knew American poetry well. The singer might be familiar with Robert Frost's famous, much-anthologized poem, "Stopping by Woods on a Snowy Evening," whose final quatrain goes as follows:

> The woods are lovely, dark and deep,
> But I have promises to keep,
> And miles to go before I sleep,
> And miles to go before I sleep.[37]

As a consummate New England Protestant, Frost has internalized the obligations of the covenant, which have all the more force for being unspecified, and is expressing here the effect of those obligations. The poet feels anxious and restless; the repetition of the last line suggests the obsessive quality of his striving to keep an already broken covenant.

If we compare "Stopping by Woods on a Snowy Evening" with the lyrics of "Feelin' Groovy," we realize that Paul has rewritten and reversed Frost's poem. If Frost's poet—like so many Americans—has some hard travelling to do before he sleeps, Paul's is ready to sleep now. *He* did not ask for, or make, a covenant, so he can do whatever he wants. He has cut himself off from those who did make one, and thus from history. Like Jim Morrison in "When the Music's Over," he has cancelled his subscription to the resurrection. The lyrics of these songs, then, deny covenantal obligation in favor of hedonism, as do the lyrics of Otis Redding's "Sitting' on the Dock of the Bay", the Young Rascals' "Groovin' ", the Grass Roots' "Let's Live for Today", and the Strawberry Alarm Clock's "Incense and Peppermints." But as a writer for the *LA Free Press* said in 1967, "Being free is full of obligations."[38] By the sixties, covenant theology had survived much since 1630, and it survived the appeal of hedonism in rock 'n' roll by turning hedonism into an obligation.

Consider the Beach Boys' homage to the recording studio, "Good Vibrations." Through the overdubbing and the echo effects, we can clearly hear Mike Love sing, "Gotta keep those lovely vibrations happening with her." But if rock was all about the denial of obligations, and about being free, what is that word "gotta" doing in there? Doesn't "gotta" imply obligation? It states an obligation to the self, an obligation to have good times. Similarly, on the Jefferson Airplane's "Somebody to Love," Grace Slick sings, "You better find somebody to love," which sounds like a threat: you'd better pair off with someone, or run the risk of being left out. Thus the covenant re-appeared in sixties rock 'n' roll as a secularized version of the Puritan obligation to self-examination: a hip covenant. Now, of course, the obligation involved sex, drugs, rock 'n' roll, and doing your own thing, not soul-searching. But in these and other statements of the obligation to do these things, the strength and continuity of the covenant clearly manifest themselves.

Other versions of the covenant, and thus of the continuity of rock 'n' roll history with the American past, appeared in the sixties. For instance, "I'm A Believer," by the Monkees went to #1 in December of 1966; they followed the song up with "Daydream Believer," which did very well in 1967. Both of these songs continued the tradition of Frankie Laine's big hit from 1953, "I Believe." Whereas "I Believe" proclaims a belief in the natural order of things, "I'm A Believer" recounts a narrative of conversion. Formerly, Mike Nesmith tells us, he doubted, but "Then I saw her face/Now I'm a believer." He has a personal belief—he doesn't tell us *what* he believes in, but it doesn't seem to have anything to do with a just society. It is important to understand the significance of the great success of "I'm A Believer" in the context of the sixties, since belief signals belief in some version or other of the covenant, as in the Lovin' Spoonful's "Do You Believe in Magic?"

Finally, two recordings respond to the covenant in different ways. During the summer of 1968, whose horrors included the Republican Convention in Miami, and the Democratic Convention in Chicago, the Rascals had a big hit with "People Got To Be Free." Here, "free" refers to something like a social imperative. A very different, non-verbal response is Jimi Hendrix's unforgettable arrangement of "The Star-Spangled Banner." By the time Jimi runs the familiar melody, which we associate with football and baseball, through his delays and reverb on his guitar he creates an unsettling, disturbing, and thought-provoking experience. The raw, strained, metallic sound expresses better than anything I know the American sense that the covenant with God is broken. Its dissonance does not let us rest, and it's certainly not something you can dance to. But the very decision to play the national anthem at Woodstock is an affirmation that we are Americans in the process of defining what it means to be an American, or re-defining our relationship to the past.

It remains only to answer for the period 1964-1974 the four questions of McLuhan's tetrad wheel, and to specify the dominant medium for the music, and the sociology of the groups. I do so here only in the most general terms, as a way of defining the themes of the following essays.

In April of 1964, the Beatles had the first five songs on the Top 40 charts; "Can't Buy Me Love"; "Twist and Shout"; "She Loves You"; "I Want to Hold Your Hand"; and "Please Please Me." It takes no great imagination to figure out that this unprecedented feat marked the beginning of a new era. Just as rock began in 1954 as (in part) a reaction to the Army-McCarthy hearings on television, so Beatlemania arose (in part) as a reaction to the assassination of President Kennedy, the televised funeral, and the televised murder of Lee Harvey Oswald by Jack Ruby. The following winter was the winter of America's discontent, when people wondered then, as they wonder now, how these things could happen in America. It was the immense good fortune of the Beatles to release us from our grief. They let us feel good again. Five years later, Altamont meant the end of flower power, and peace and love, and it therefore changed the style of the music.

After the extraordinary period of musical innovation, 1964-69, there followed a period of assimilation set from 1969 to 1974. During this period, rock tended to split into the simple, direct style of albums on which acoustic guitars and pianos dominated, like Carol King's *Tapestry* and James Taylor's *Sweet Baby James,* and the heavy metal sound of Grand Funk Railroad, Led Zeppelin, T. Rex, and the others.

The diffusion of technological change is often determined by institutions, as in the way the record companies marketed the 45 and 33 1/3 rpm records during the fifties. In the period 1964-69, a government decision had a profound effect on the music. This was the FCC's decision in 1965 to force radio stations which had both an AM and FM frequency to broadcast different programming on each. Just as the rise of television in the fifties freed a great deal of air time for popular music, so the FCC's decision freed a great deal of air time in the sixties. This decision led to the underground FM stations of the sixties. Among other things, it created a national audience for Bob Dylan, who simply was not a Top 40 radio performer. (The media situation was a little different in England, as will be shown later.)

Popular music changed in various ways during the sixties, but one way few have noticed concerns the sociology of the performers. For the first time in the history of American popular music, major innovators were coming in significant numbers from middle-class WASP families. For once, location was not especially important, except negatively: there were no new white performers from the South. Virtually all the important groups, both American and British, came from middle-class, and even upper middle-class, white families. To take the most extreme examples, Jim Morrison's father was an admiral in the Navy, and Grace Slick's father was an investment banker listed in *Who's Who.*

We can conveniently take the first two of McLuhan's questions in the tetrad wheel together: "What does it enhance?" and "What does it obsolesce?" Both of these questions have to do with the way technology re-structured popular music during 1964-69. The period enhanced editing, most obviously on *Sargeant Pepper* by the Beatles, but elsewhere as well. Making an album began to resemble the cumbersome, laborious process of making a film, rather than just going into the studio and playing songs. Here the analogy with film seems useful and informative. If Elvis, like his fellow Southerner D. W. Griffith, created a new intensity in rock 'n' roll, then the Beatles, like Sergei Eisenstein, demonstrated that the tape recorder/camera did not function to preserve and recreate the immediate experience of performance. Rather, the creativity that produced the final record/film appeared in the editing, not exclusively or even primarily in the performance.

The new importance of editing obsolesced live concerts. This statement does not mean that no one went to concerts, of course, for concerts made more money than ever. It means, rather, that editing—and that really means the recording studio—re-defined the concert. For one thing, it limited what groups could play at concerts, since they obviously could not bring the studio to the concert hall or stadium with them. Moreover, the audience came to the concerts generally knowing what it would hear. Eventually, the performers met those expectations by bringing the editing process to the concert hall itself. They gave up their control over the sound to an editor who sat at a control board and mixed the sound as it was coming through the loudspeakers.

It seems odd to say that rock retrieved intimacy as a listening experience, since we think of the sixties in connection with major public events such as Monterey Pop, the Human Be-In in San Francisco (January 9, 1967), and Woodstock. But if Top 40 radio was suited for listening in the car or at the beach, underground FM radio was not. The aural complexity of the Beatles' white album, and the imagistic density of Dylan's *Blond on Blonde* made for frustrating listening in a car. Stoplights, street signs, and exit ramps distracted one's attention from the intense involvement which the music demanded. Thus, rock was best suited for home listening—preferably on headphones. The archetypal implied listeners on a classic late sixties album like the Doors' *Strange Days* would be a group of friends sitting on the floor in a candlelit room passing around a joint. This experience of music in an intimate environment retrieved the setting, if not exactly the ambience, in which people listened to the radio in the 1920s.

The fact that people listened to rock in private space is related to the sense of closeness, in both the senses of communality and enclosedness, which the space program created by closing the frontier. And to stress this implied listener in private space implies an answer to McLuhan's final question: "What does it reverse into?" By reversing the listeners' environment from private space to public space, rock reversed into disco.

Notes

[1]Todd Gitlin, *The Whole World is Watching. Mass Media in the Making and Unmaking of the New Left* (Berkeley: U. of California Press, 1980), p. 295.

[2]Leaf, *The Beach Boys and the California Myth*, p. 49.

[3]John M. Logsdon, *The Decision to Go to the Moon: Project Apollo and the National Interest* (Cambridge: The MIT Press, 1970), p. 66.

[4] *Ibid.*, p. 129.

[5] *Ibid.*, p. 2.

[6]William Appleman Williams, "The Frontier Thesis and American Foreign Policy," in *History as a Way of Learning* (New York: New Viewpoints, 1973), p. 142.

[7] *Ibid.*, p. 153.

[8]Thomas Powers, *The War at Home. Vietnam and the American People, 1964-1968* (New York: Grossman Publishers, 1973), p. 113.

[9]Quoted in Curt Smith, *Long Time Gone, The Years of Turmoil Remembered* (South Bend: Icarus Press, 1982), p. 156.

[10]Joan Didion, *The White Album* (New York: Simon and Schuster, 1979), p. 13.

[11]Michael J. Arlen, *Living-Room War* (New York: The Viking Press, 1969), p. 113.

[12] *Ibid.*, p. 114.

[13]John Boswell and Jay David, *Duke, The John Wayne Album* (New York: Ballantine Books, 1979), p. 126.

[14]Seymour Martin Lipset, Symposium Statement in *Technology, Power, and Social Change*, Charles A. Thrall, ed., (Toronto: Lexington Books, 1972), p. 83.

[15] *Ibid.*

[16]Ron Kovic, *Born on the Fourth of July* (New York: McGraw-Hill, 1976), p. 43.

[17] *Ibid.*, p. 61.

[18]Quoted in *The Sixties*, Linda Obst, ed. (New York: Random House/Rolling Stone, 1977), p. 224. Compare Kovic's statement to a comment by one of the participants in the My Lai massacre of 1968: "Maybe this was the way wars really were. Maybe what we saw in the movies and on TV wasn't so, that war was running around and shooting civilians and doing this kind of thing." (Michael Bernhardt, quoted in Seymour M. Hersh, *My Lai 4. A Report on the Massacre and Its Aftermath* (New York: Random House, 1970), p. 186.

[19]Charles Anderson, *The Grunts* (San Raphael, CA: Presidio Press, 1976), p. 145.

[20]Didion, p. 12.

[21]Quoted in Powers, p. 314.

[22]*The American Puritans. Their Prose and Poetry*, Perry Miller, ed. (Garden City, NY: Anchor Books, 1956), p. 82. In this very brief treatment of covenant theology, I am not giving the topic the space it deserves. I am relying on Perry Miller's work on the enduring significance of the Puritans for American culture as a whole; see especially his *Errand into the Wilderness* (Cambridge, MA: The Belknap Press, 1956).

[23]See Robert Bellah, *The Broken Covenant. American Civil Religion in Time of Trial* (New York: The Seabury Press, 1975).

[24]David Halberstam, *The Best and the Brightest* (New York: Random House, 1972), p. 233.

[25] *Ibid.*, p. 250.

[26]Marshall Frady, *Billy Graham, A Parable of American Righteousness* (Boston: Little, Brown, 1979), p. 15.

[27]On the movement as expressing covenant theology, see Roger G. Betsworth, *The Radical Movement of the 1960's* (Metuchen, NJ: The Scarecrow Press, 1980).

[28]Gitlin, p. 187.

[29]J. Edgar Hoover's *Master of Deceit* (1958), quoted in Richard Gid Powers, *G-Men. Hoover's FBI in American Popular Culture* (Carbondale, IL: Southern Illinois University Press, 1983), p. 235.

[30]Quoted in Harris Wofford, *Of Kennedys and Kings. Making Sense of the Sixties* (New York: Farrar, Straus, Giroux, 1980), p. 205. Hoover was able to maintain his vendetta against Dr. King because he had some incriminating tape which he had made in 1943 while the young Jack Kennedy was having an affair with a woman accused of being a Nazi spy. These tapes explain why President Kennedy re-appointed Hoover, and why Attorney General Robert Kennedy did not attempt to curb Hoover's abuses of power.

[31]Powers, p. xviii. My comments on Hoover here derive from Powers' brilliant and important book.

[32] *Ibid.*, p. xii.

[33] *Ibid.*, p, xix.

[34] *The Puritans. Their Prose and Poetry*, p. 83.

[35]Michael Hughey, *Civil Religion and Moral Order. Theoretical and Historical Dimensions* (Westport, CT: Greenwood Press, 1983), p. 90.

[36] *Rolling Stone*, August 21, 1980, p. 41.

[37] *Complete Poems of Robert Frost* (New York: Holt, Rinehart and Winston, 1965), p. 275.

[38]Liza Williams, "Which Way to the Exit"; quoted in *The Hippie Papers*, Jerry Hopkins, ed. (New York: Signet Books, 1968), p. 19.

Chapter 11:
On Beatlemania

"Until late in their careers, the Beatles simply had no idea what was happening to them."[1] In this, the Beatles were like many of us in the sixties. But mostly they were not like most of us, because in addition to everything else they had phenomenal luck. It takes nothing away from their talent and achievement to notice that they had better luck with management than any other act before or since. They had a manager who was literally infatuated with them, especially with John Lennon, and who was ready to do anything for them. Although Brian Epstein made some serious mistakes in managing the Beatles because of his insecurity and lack of street smarts, no one could ever question his devotion to them. They had a sophisticated producer who gave them a chance when no one else would, and who devoted himself tirelessly and selflessly to their music. George Martin richly deserves his present reputation and the respect which he presently enjoys. Finally, they had a music publisher who was a rarity among men in his line of work—he was both honest and hardworking. The Beatles made Dick James of Northern Songs a rich man, but by pushing their songs he helped to turn them from a popular group into a phenomenon.

That phenomenon took on the name Beatlemania. Among the many things we didn't understand then was that Beatlemania occurred in two versions—first a British one, and then an American one. Of course, all successful acts "come along at the right time," as the cliche has it. But the elements which made up that "right time" in England were not quite the same as the elements which made up that "right time" in America, although some similar patterns did occur.

Beatlemania started in England. Most Americans do know that the Beatles started out by listening to Elvis, and then covering songs by Chuck Berry and Motown groups such as the Marvelettes. American rock 'n' roll meant something quite different in England than it did in America, and people heard it in very different ways.

A crucial difference between England and America has to do with class. In America, we like to believe that we have no classes (although it isn't true), whereas in England, everybody recognizes that classes exist. This essential fact about British social history has numerous ramifications.

World War I, or the Great War, as the British call it, showed the aristocracy as inept, and thus lacking in a justification for its privileges and continued concentration of wealth. As a defense mechanism, its spokespersons began to decry the democratization which they found characteristic of the modern world.

Modernization and democratization amounted to two aspects of the same thing in America, so America became an easy and obvious target for condemnation by the British establishment, especially after World War II. As Dick Hebdige writes, "Increasingly, as the fifties wore on, this negative consensus which united cultural critics of all persuasions began to settle around a single term: Americanisation."[2] Hebdige particularly notes the disdain which English novelist Evelyn Waugh held for everything which he perceived as identifiably American, such as streamlining of cars and domestic appliances and jazz.

Thus, when the Beatles were listening to Elvis and the other fifties rockers, they were doing something which had class significance. If the English Establishment disliked the brash vigor of American culture, the English working class embraced it eagerly. This attitude suggests that class in England forms a rough analogy with that of race in America. Lacking the opportunities afforded to whites, American blacks produced a music which celebrated the pleasures of the moment, which was all they had. The English working classes have also lacked opportunities for social mobility, so John Lennon, Paul McCartney, George Harrison, and Ringo Starr responded to black American music, and its celebration of the moment.

The great fifties rockers came from the South, and the Beatles, as the whole world knows, came from Liverpool, in northern England. But through a quirk of cultural history, the North in England turns out to have the same meaning as the South in America. In the fifties, the South was the provinces, far from New York and Los Angeles; in media terms, it was the provinces because it had a higher residual oral tradition than the North. Similarly, in the early sixties in England, the North was the provinces, far from London. Like the South, it had a higher residual oral tradition if only because the English working classes had little opportunity and/or incentive to go to school.

But if the English North and the American South were similar in these respects, the meaning of performance differed in an important way between the two regions. As we know, Southern rock expressed the ongoing process of secularization, and this process caused extreme tension in the lives of some Southern performers:witness the difficulties of Little Richard and Jerry Lee Lewis. No such stresses affected the Beatles, for they grew up amid various performance traditions. There was, of course, the centuries-old tradition of the English folk song, but more relevant to their lives and class situation was the music hall, a late Victorian institution which brought sentimental song and slapstick comedy to the common folk.

In various interviews, the Beatles have mentioned the advantages of growing up in a sea port, one of which was that sailors often brought home the latest American records. But there's something omitted here: why were records so important? Why didn't they just listen to the radio?

To an American, the obvious question is, why didn't they listen to the local Top 40 station? The answer is there was no such thing in England: "Despite the relaxation in the tone and style of BBC broadcasting allegedly affected by the advent of commercial television in 1954, rock 'n' roll was deliberately ignored and resisted by the BBC radio networks."[3] Thus, an essential and far-reaching difference between the media histories of England and America appears. In America, it has primarily been outsiders who controlled the media; in England, it was the Establishment.

Without the intense synergy produced by Top 40 radio as it interacted with the record industry, the British record industry remained a small, backward business before Beatlemania. The industry produced primarily classical music and traditional jazz (British for "Dixieland") on LPs for the middle and upper class market. Working-class kids, who often could not afford to buy records, went to clubs such as the Cavern Club in Liverpool, even over their lunch hour. This media deprivation resulted in the following startling statistic: in 1963 there were said to be some 20,000 rock groups operating in Britain (400 in Liverpool alone).[4] As someone said, the British are a nation of amateurs. Be that as it may, since "pop music" meant primarily "live music" it took a relatively small number of record sales to send "Please Please Me" to #1 on March 2, 1963.

The question is, "What did they have to start with, and what did they do with it?" Wilfrid Mellers described the uniquely British sources of their musical sensibility, which they blended with what they got from American records. Mellers mentions, for instance, that:

One can scarcely disentangle traditional folk sources from music-hall ditties tipsily bellowed in pubs or from dance-music blown and scraped by the Celebrated Working Men's Band. The fiddle, accordion and cornet, sometimes with string bass as support, sometimes with tin whistle as chirpy obligato, created a sonority almost as relevant to Beatle music as blues guitar and country harmonica.
Nor, in Liverpool's working-class society, were older, even rural, folk traditions entirely submerged. In Lancashire mining areas austere, old-style model tunes surprisingly survived..[5]

It is this blend between English and American music which created the Beatles' sound.

If the blues was the music of American adults, Beatles music was the music of British working-class teenagers. To quote Mellers again, "The Beatles' music is more open, whiter, fresher, tenderer than the age-old black blues, for its Anglo-Irish affiliations lead it toward innocence rather than blueness."[6] Yet these different elements remain suspended in balance, most obviously in "It Won't Be Long." This song uses a call and response, or what Mellers calls "quasi-African homophony," in the relationship between John's vocal and George and Paul's backup, and indeed between John's vocal and George's guitar. But just as George's guitar has no bluesy vibrato, as Chuck Berry's often did, the lyrics do not deal with infidelity and breaking up, as blues lyrics often do, but with joyous anticipation.

Mellers notices that their early music often has an ambivalence about key. "She Loves You" uses E flat chords, yet the melody suggests that C is the root. Similarly, "A Hard Day's Night," for instance, vacillates between C and

B flat. Chords from both keys balance the opposition of the daily grind of the world outside as distinct from what the lyrics say happens "when I get home to you." But what sounds a lot like an American rock song presents a British reality, that of a married working-class couple.

The innocent melodic inventiveness of early Beatles music comes across wonderfully in "I Saw Her Standing There," which "teeters between C and B flat."[7] Its melody uses only four tones, and thus matches the innocence of the opening couplet: "Well she was just seventeen/You know what I mean?" This couplet would have been impossible as a musical and cultural signal without Berry's "Sweet Little Sixteen" and the rest of teen music of the fifties. So in addition to the opposition of America and England, we have further oppositions, such as the pristine folk melodies versus occasional blue notes and blues energy; found love versus lost love ("I Saw Her Standing There"; "It Won't Be Long"; "A Hard Day's Night" versus "Misery"; "You Can't Do That" and "Yesterday"). And, the lyrics work variations on the age-old opposition of man and woman.

In some but not all of these glorious songs, man addresses woman, as in "A Hard Day's Night". On "You're Going to Lose That Girl" and "She Loves You," man is addressing man; or, more properly, a Liverpudlian is addressing his mate. John is addressing Paul, perhaps. This realization makes the ambivalence of the key signatures, combined with the lack of chord resolution, seem like a completeness, an unsullied inclusiveness, "For their most erotic songs do not so much desire and yearn for fulfilment (as does tonal harmony) as enjoy themselves where they are."[8]

This realization in turn helps us understand what they took from America. In fact, they did not learn a lot from the giants, Elvis and Chuck, but they had roots in Motown and girl groups. (Thus they covered the Marvelettes' "Please Mister Postman," as well as "Boys" and "Baby It's You," by the Shirelles.) The lack of clear musical resolution, of coming to a definitive climax, and the absence of narrative in the lyrics (at least until "Norwegian Wood") relate early Beatles music to Motown.

More important, though, is the connection with the girl groups. If the Beatles sometimes talked man-to man, then they may have gotten the idea from the girl groups who sometimes talked girl-to-girl. On the Crystals' "He's a Rebel" and the Shangri-Las' "The Leader of the Pack," we are overhearing girls talking to each other, perhaps between giggles at a pajama party. We can imagine them saying "Do You Want to Know a Secret?" If the line "You know what I mean" suggests adolescent inarticulateness, then so does the Ronettes' "Da Doo Ron Ron," where the nonsense syllables wonderfully convey the inexpressibility of the feeling, as carried through in the exuberant vocals and the driving beat. (The same holds for the Shirelles' very similar song, "I Met Him on a Sunday.") Once we start thinking about these early Beatles songs in connection with the girl groups, we think of connections with specific songs. Paul's "Tell Me What you See" recalls the Chantels' "Look In My Eyes," and although the Drifters were not a girl group their Goffin/King classic, "Up on the Roof" resembles John's "There's a Place."

But of course these songs by the Chantels, the Crystals, and the other groups have a very different *sound* than that of the early Beatles songs. "He's a Rebel" has the Latin bayon rhythm which Phil Spector liked so much, and employs handclaps and a saxophone for accent. Such sound textures didn't correspond to the Beatles' genius, and they didn't use them. Rather, the Beatles' early music represents not so much the style of the girl groups' music as its essence, its innocence and exuberance. (Hence the appeal of Buddy Holly, whose music also has these features.) We might even say that the Beatles improve on this style in some cases. On the Crystals' "Then He Kissed Me" the wall of sound seems overwhelming and seems to work against the innocence of the lyrics and the cheerful vocals. The Beatles had no such studio resources at their disposal, and in fact made an asset of their direct, yet melodically sophisticated sound.

This completeness which frees them to talk man-to-man, contains the germ of their later development as well. "She Loves You," reversed and generalized, becomes "Nowhere Man" and "For No One." Having other thematic interests than the man/woman opposition, the Beatles could readily generalize them to the human condition. Significantly, "Tomorrow Never Knows" is addressed to everyone, both men and women.

It was one thing for the Beatles to build up a following at the Cavern Club in Liverpool with such imaginative songs; it was something else for them to inspire Beatlemania. Beatlemania, both in its English and in its American versions, was the result of a synergistic interaction between them and their larger social context. This interaction reached a critical mass and exploded, astounding everyone.

Although Beatlemania has some common societal elements in England and America such as general prosperity, British boys didn't have the recurrent fear of American boys—the draft—because the government had abolished National Service in 1960. The other uniquely British factor in creating the energy system we now call Beatlemania was the popular press.

On Fleet Street in London, the British have a number of scurrilous dailies such as the *Daily Mail*, which John mentions in the lyrics to "Paperback Writer," for which the *New York Daily News* is the only American equivalent. These sensational dailies compensate for the staidness of BBC radio, as it were. In the summer of 1963, these papers had a field day with the Profumo scandal, when the Conservative Secretary of State for War was revealed to have the same mistress as the Russian naval attache. Revelation followed steamy revelation until even the *Daily Mail* and its ilk sensed that the public had had enough. "Finally, by the end of September, every editor on Fleet Street was longing for a diversion from this incessant heavy news—something light, something unconnected with the aristocratic classes; something harmless, blameless, and, above all, cheerful."[9] That something was, of course, the top British group for 1963 in *Melody Maker's* poll.

The press needed the Beatles as much as the Beatles needed the press. Their soon-to-be-famous wit and charm made for good copy, but there was more to it than that. Phillip Norman, their biographer, slyly notes how the British press played fast and loose with the facts about their popularity. They performed on TV's *Saturday Night at the London Palladium*, on October 13, 1963—England's equivalent of the *Ed Sullivan Show*.

Next morning, every mass-circulation British newspaper carried a front-page picture and story of "riots" by Beatle fans outside the London Palladium.

This official outbreak of Beatlemania in Britain has certain puzzling aspects. In every case, the published photograph of that "1,000 squealing teenagers" was cropped in so close that only three or could be seen. The *Daily Mail* alone published a wide-angle shot—Paul McCartney and Neil Aspinall emerging from the Palladium, watched by one policeman and two girls.[10]

Thus the press added hype to the already potent combination of sympathetic management, personal charm, and extraordinary talent. No one disputes that the Beatles gave the girls something to scream about; but now the girls read that teenagers were rioting over the Beatles, so they came to concerts ready to riot. And they did.

Girls had screamed for pop stars before, but never, never—as they did at the Beatles' ABC Cambridge concert—hunched into a fetal position, alternatively punching their sides, covering their eyes and stuffing handkerchiefs and fists into their mouths. Later, when the curtain had fallen and the last dazed girl had been led through the exits, a further difference from the scream that greeted Valentino was manifested. Hundreds of the cinema seats were wringing wet. Many had puddles of urine visible beneath them.[11]

The cover of their first album, *Please Please Me* showed them on a balcony in a block of what the English call Council Flats—working-class turf. The cover of their second album, *With the Beatles*, showed them in their Beatle haircuts and black turtlenecks. That cover made elegant esthetes of them, and helped to generalize the appeal of pop music to the Establishment. By generalizing their appeal in this way, at Brian's urging, they did something like what Elvis had done, only in a British context. Just as Elvis had made what was originally a regional style acceptable to many American whites in the fifties, so the Beatles made what was originally a working-class sound acceptable to the British middle and upper classes. Only when this generalizing happens does popularity become a phenomenon.

Still, England remained a highly tradition-conscious society, Beatlemania or no Beatlemania, and the BBC was not amused. The BBC continued to ignore pop music. British teenagers still couldn't listen to their fave raves on the radio, so someone else filled this need. On Easter Sunday, March 29, 1964, Radio Caroline—named after President Kennedy's daughter—went on the air as the first of the pirate radio stations in England. Radio Atlanta, another so-called pirate, went on the air on May 9. (The two merged later that summer.) A

Gallup poll revealed the astonishing fact that "In its first three weeks Radio Caroline gained nearly seven million listeners. This figure did not include listeners under the age of seventeen and that total was from a potential audience of only twenty million people."[12] The financial implications of such ratings were not lost on other entrepreneurs, and a number of other pirate radio stations appeared, such as Radio Scotland, King Radio (an easy listening station) and Radio London. Of all of them, Radio London, with its recorded station breaks and jingles, most resembled an American Top 40 station. It sounded so exotic to British ears that it inspired the Who's album *The Who Sell Out*.

If the BBC ignored teenagers, the popular press never forgot them. It had had a field day with the Teddy boys in the fifties, to mention one case in point. These were working-class kids who adopted the Edwardian clothing as a means of symbolic class mobility, since the social structure precluded real class mobility. Their self-assertion in the form of narcissism was contemporary with, and analogous to, the narcissism of Elvis' "Blue Suede Shoes." Although the press exaggerated their number and their threat to the social order, it had no dramatic prototypes with which it could label them, and they soon lost their news value.

By 1964, however, the situation had changed. The respectable couples who had formerly taken their holidays at East Coast resorts like Brighton now went to Costa Brava, and their absence made the working-class kids who went there as day-trippers on Bank Holidays all the more prominent. And just as the press turned the Beatles' popularity into Beatlemania, it turned these kids into Mods and Rockers.

The first Mods and Rockers event took place at the East Coast resort of Clacton on Easter weekend, 1964. It was a cold, wet Sunday, and the kids who had gone there found little to do. They milled around, and broke some windows. There was some uneasiness, but no more than that. On the whole, it was a dull weekend, and dullness does not sell newspapers.

"On the Monday morning following the initial incidents at Clacton, every national newspaper, with the exception of *The Times*. . .carried a leading report on the subject. The headlines are self-descriptive."[13] Some of those headlines read: "DAY OF TERROR BY SCOOTER GROUPS" (*Daily Telegraph*); and "YOUNGSTERS BEAT UP TOWN—97 LEATHER JACKET ARRESTS." (*Daily Express*) Reading these headlines, we would think that this is yet another example of media hype, and that the press managed to sell papers by making a story out of a non-story. We would also think that in England (as in America) throughout the sixties, the media created a closed tape loop whereby they produced self-fulfilling prophecies of teenage violence. There was no more violence at Clacton at Easter, 1964, than there was a crime wave in America in the thirties, but when people read the newspaper reports of both, they believed in them.

The newspapers thus imposed coherence on chaos, and made everyone into a performer. Stanley Cohen summarizes this now familiar story:

The media created some sort of diversionary sideshow in which all would seek their appropriate parts. The young people on the beaches knew very well that they had been typecast as folk devils and they saw themselves as targets for abuse. When the audiences, TV cameras and police started lining themselves up, the metaphor of role playing becomes no longer a metaphor, but the real thing.[15]

The papers, then, assigned the kids roles as Mods, who wore neo-Edwardian suits and rode motor scooters (a rough British equivalent for American kids' hot rods), and Rockers, who wore leather jackets and rode motor bikes (motorcycles, in American English).

Cohen mentions an incident which suggests why these stories sold so well. At a time when the *Daily Mail* said that each Beatle was making 5,000 pounds a week, the papers reported that one kid who was arrested at Margate offered to pay his 75 pound fine with a check. As late as four years later, the story was still circulating within the British Establishment as typical of teenage affluence and self-indulgence. What hardly any papers reported was that this offer was sheer teenage bravado: the kid was quite poor, and didn't even *have* a checking account. Clearly, stories about teenage rampages sold well because their elders who vividly remembered the deprivations of the war years, envied the kids, youth and salaries, which were marginally better than they had been in the past. The solid citizenry wanted to believe that the new consumerism would lead to no good, and wanted to read stories which confirmed their belief. And the popular dailies gladly obliged them.

But this is only a partial account of the rise of the Mods and Rockers, for—just as in America in the sixties—all the stories relied on an implicit narrative. This narrative involved the encounter between British tradition and American popular culture which produced the Beatles.

The phrasing of certain headlines reveal what was actually going on. The Belgian papers just across the Channel from Clacton pronounced, "West Side Story on East Coast." What happened was that the movie version of *West Side Story* had just been released, (1961), and provided a set of expectations about teenage behavior. The implicit, mostly unconscious, process of reasoning seems to have gone as follows: British working-class kids are listening to, imitating, and learning from, rock 'n' roll, which is the music of American teenagers. American teenagers organize themselves into gangs, like the Jets and the Sharks in *West Side Story*. When the Jets and the Sharks met, they fought over territory and girls. Therefore, this must have been what happened at Clacton, Margate, Brighton, and at the other resorts. And as a result of the power of media to create reality where none had existed before, the Mods and Rockers did organize themselves. In doing so, they closed the tape loop, thereby paradoxically confirming everyone's belief in the accuracy of the media.

The *Daily Mirror* conveniently identified for us the other American prototype for the Mods and Rockers story when it headlined its story about Clacton, "WILD ONES INVADE SEASHORE—97 ARRESTED." The image of kids listening to raucous music and riding into a resort on their motorcycles evoked memories of Marlon Brando in *The Wild One,* and because this image was a lot more titillating than the reality, which was that most of the kids hitchhiked, the *Daily Mirror* drew on it. One success deserves another on Fleet Street, so the *Daily Mirror* later ran a story whose headline sounds like the title of a Roger Corman movie, THE GIRLS WHO FOLLOW THE WILD ONES. That people readily accepted *The Wild One* as an appropriate prototype is indicated by a headline in the Brighton *Evening News* after Whitsun, 1964: THOSE WILD ONES ARE TO BLAME AGAIN. Notice that it reads, not "the" wild ones, but "those" wild ones—the ones that everybody knows about. They have done it again, just as we knew they would. In times of confusion, it is very satisfying to everyone when self-fulfilling prophecies fulfill themselves. It proves that some order, at least, is left in the world.

The key word "wild" may serve here as an indicator of the irrelevance of the distinction between news reporting and popular entertainment in the sixties. After the success of *The Wild One,* American movies used "wild" as a code word to lure people, and the newspapers were just imitating them. Elvis' *Wild in the Country* (1961) is probably the most immediately relevant of these movies, but there were also:

> *The Wild and the Innocent*   (1959)
> *Wild Guitar*   (1962)
> *The Wild Seed*   (1965)
> *The Wild Angels*   (1966)
> *Wild in the Streets*   (1968)

The English movie industry knew a good thing when it saw one, and cashed in on the trend with *The Wild and the Willing* (1962).

The American media also played an important part when the Beatles invaded Kennedy Airport on the seventh of February, 1964. Through the legendary telecast of the *Ed Sullivan Show* on the ninth and the Carnegie Hall concerts on the twelfth, American Beatlemania was typically American, i.e., typically outlandish. David Newman, who co-wrote the screenplay for *Bonnie and Clyde* (1968), managed to get a ticket for one of the Carnegie Hall Concerts, and remembers, "Then the Beatles came out. Then the screaming really started. It sounded like nothing I had ever heard in my life. It was like, well, a tape loop. Even a police siren runs out before it revs up again. This was a nonstop siren that lasted the entire concert."[15] By April, they had the top *five* songs on the charts—something that no act—not even Elvis—had ever done. I predict that no act will ever do that again. And so it went, through the filming of *A Hard Day's Night* (1964), and the frenzied world tour which followed. Cities and countries blurred for the Beatles, and the screaming never let up. "It was a fame now divorced from their music and personalities."[16] Clearly, the social context and the needs of the fans played an even greater role in American Beatlemania than in English Beatlemania.

Because this was America, there was much hype. On the day the Beatles arrived, WINS and WNEW radio stations repeated every fifteen minutes a promise that every kid who went out to the Kennedy Airport would get a free T-shirt. Murray the K promoted the Beatles tirelessly over WINS, and in the best American tradition of hype, while promoting the Beatles he was promoting himself as the fifth Beatle.

Rick Sklar, program director of WABC-AM in New York, did the same thing. As he tells the story in his autobiography *Rocking America,* when he left his box at the Beatles' Carnegie Hall concert, he had decided on a new promotion; he had decided to introduce every Beatles song with a jingle identifying the station as "W A Beatle C." Sklar ran Beatle look-alike campaigns and stole pressings of new Beatles records even before they were released. When he aired them, he put in a "W A Beatle C" jingle every fifteen seconds to prevent off-air dubbing by rival stations. All this was happening on a station which often had as much as a 25 share in the New York market, and whose nighttime audience covered half of America. Sklar admits that this station rode the Beatles' coattails, but rightly points out that the Beatles rode his coattails, too. The whole episode represents one of the clearest examples of media synergy in the history of broadcasting.

But no amount of hype alone could have produced American Beatlemania. Phillip Norman has summarized the historical context:

It was a moment when the potential existed for a madness which nothing indigenously American could unleash. It was a moment when all America's deep envy of Europe, and the eccentricity permitted to older-established nations, crystalized in four figures whose hair and clothes, to American eyes, placed them somewhere near Shakespeare's *Hamlet.* It was a moment simultaneously gratifying America's need for a new idol, a new toy, a painkilling drug and a laugh.[17]

Among other things, Norman is referring here to the understanding that the Beatles served as a catharsis after the assassination of President Kennedy, very much as Elvis had served as a catharsis after McCarthyism. An American act which came on as brash and cocky, as they did, would have been perceived as lacking in respect for our fallen hero and for the sensibilities of the country at large. But they were British—emphatically and visibly so. They had no obligation to mourn, so they could toss off jokes and sing joyous love songs. Better still, we could laugh at them and clap our hands to the beat. Because they were British, they reassured us that it was okay to be happy again.

The Beatles were linked to President Kennedy in odd ways. By a freak of history, *With the Beatles* was released in England on November 22, 1963, and after that fateful day they had the effect of replacing him in our affections, which sorely needed an outlet. Like him, they were young, handsome, witty, poised, self-assured (or so it seemed), and—above all—successful. While President Kennedy was alive, journalists had repeatedly proclaimed that he was "having fun" as President. It helped that his privileged life had accustomed him to the trappings of fame and to projecting this image. While none of the Beatles had had privileged lives, they had been performing together for almost four years, and had had to rely on their ready wit to get out of tense situations in Hamburg and in those gritty working-class towns in Northern England. Such experiences had given them a stage presence, and nothing seemed to faze them. Fame, fortune, and reporters did not keep them from having fun, just as they had not kept President Kennedy from having fun.

If the Beatles resembled and possibly replaced the idol, President Kennedy, they did so more completely because they formed a contrast to all those gawky Teen Idols. Fabian and Frankie Avalon now seemed like slicked-up, ethnic versions of the Boy Next Door. In contrast to the Teen Idols, the Beatles had a slightly exotic, aristocratic quality, and that quality made the difference between the sporadic frenzy which the Teen Idols evoked and the mass hysteria which the Beatles evoked.

Like President Kennedy, the Beatles had an accent which marked them as different. We couldn't tell they had working-class accents, as their British audience could. For us, all British accents sounded the same, and they all meant elegance and sophistication. As a result, the Beatles didn't help to create a youth culture in America as they had in England. Rather, they represented a recycling, at a different level, of the youth culture in America which had originally inspired their music.

The Beatles appealed to the rising tide of baby boomers. In 1964, there were a million more 18-year-olds than the year before, and this trend continued throughout the sixties. Demographically, the net result was to lower the median age (it got down to 27.2). Then, as the baby boomers went through college, they kept listening to the Beatles, and lots of younger kids did, too. The youth cohort, as demographers call it, increased in absolute size and spending power. No wonder, then, that the Beatles' best-selling album was *Abbey Road*, which came out at a time (1968) when the majority of the baby boomers were at a receptive age.

If in England the Beatles broadened the appeal of the previously much dreaded Americanisms, in America they did something like this with music and hair style. Everybody talked about their hair, which seemed outrageous in comparison to American boys' crewcuts. Because we didn't perceive them as working-class kids, they legitimized long hair for us. Before the Beatles, only intellectuals and greasers wore long hair; now it was okay for middle-class kids, too. If, in McLuhan's terms, the Beatles obsolesced the crewcut, they also obsolesced folk music. Before Beatlemania, such major figures of the sixties as Stephen Stills, Larry McGuin, Bob Dylan, and Janis Joplin were still singing-folk music, and accompanying themselves on acoustic guitars. After Beatlemania, they all started to rock.

Notes

1Philip Norman, *Shout! The Beatles in Their Generation* (New York: Fireside, 1981),

p. 5.

[2]Dick Hebdige, "Towards a Cartography of Popular Taste 1935-1962," in *Popular Culture Past and Present*, Bernard Waites *et al.*, eds. (London: Croom Helm, 1982), p. 199.

[3]*Ibid.*, p. 202.

[4]Dave Harker, *One for the Money. Politics and Popular Song* (London: Hutchinson, 1980), p. 79.

[5]Wilfrid Mellers, *The Music of the Beatles, Twilight of the Gods* (New York: Schirmer Books, 1973), p. 31.

[6] *Ibid.*, p. 42.

[7] *Ibid.*, p. 34.

[8]Richard Middleton, *Pop Music and the Blues* (London: Victor Gollancz, 1972), p. 172.

[9]Norman, *Shout!* p. 186.

[10] *Ibid.*, p. 188.

[11] *Ibid.*, p. 191.

[12]Paul Harris, *Broadcasting from the High Seas. The History of Offshore Radio in Europe 1958-1976* (Edinburgh: Paul Harris Publishing, 1977), p. 21. All the dates in this paragraph come from Harris' informative book.

[13]Stanley Cohen, *Folk Devils and Moral Panics. The Creation of the Mods and Rockers* (London: MacGibbon and Kee, 1972), p. 30. The newspaper headlines and other information in this section also come from Cohen's perceptive book.

[14]Quoted in *Rolling Stone*, February 16, 1984, p. 42.

[15]Norman, *Shout!*, p. 235.

[16] *Ibid.*, p. 225.

Chapter 12:
Dylan's Words in Freedom

"I'm a trapeze artist," Dylan announced to a couple of astonished interviewers in 1965.[1] This is the kind of thing that he often said during the sixties when he was defending his work. Like his songs, his conversation was interesting but hard to understand. Dylan wasn't saying anything new however, for modern artists had been comparing themselves to circus performers for a long time. The German philosopher Friedrich Nietzsche, to whom Dylan refers in the liner notes to *Highway 61 Revisited,* once compared the artist to "a tightrope walker," and a major figure in the Dada movement, Tristan Tzara, proclaimed in 1915 that, "We are circus ringmasters."[2] Virtually every major European artist of the first half of the twentieth century was interested in circus performers as metaphors for the artistic life outside normal society. What was surprising was not the comparison itself, but that a songwriter with hits on the charts would use it.

Dylan's use of the trapeze artist image and his references to Nietzsche suggest that it may prove useful to understand the artists of the early twentieth century, who provide some precedents for Dylan's work. For instance, some statements in the "Manifesto of Futurist Musicians 1910" by Balilla Pratella anticipates Dylan's "Ballad of a Thin Man' and "The Times They Are A-Changin." Dylan could easily have said, as Pratella did half a century before him:

I appeal to the *young*. Only they listen and only they can understand what I have to say. Some people are born old, slobbering spectres of the past, cryptograms swollen with poison. To them no words or ideas, but a single injunction: *the end.*[3]

Similarly, Pratella's fellow Italian Futurist, Francesco Marinetti, seems to be predicting Dylan's evolution when he says the following about the artist of the future in his essay, "Destruction of Syntax—Imagination Without Strings—Words-in-Freedom 1913": "He will begin by brutally destroying the syntax of his speech...Breathlessly he will assault your nerves with visual, auditory, olfactory sensations, just as they come to him."[4] Certainly many people, and not just adults, thought that Dylan was assaulting their nerves with his raw, snarling voice. Dylan certainly seemed, in the middle sixties, to be "brutally destroying the syntax of his speech." And his imagination could certainly do what Marinetti said that the poet's imagination must do, namely, "weave together distant things *with no connecting strings,* by means of essential *free* words."[5] Dylan's songs, then, fulfill the promise of Marinetti's "words in freedom."

Of all the modern artists, Dylan most resembles Picasso. Both of them dominated their peers as no other single person did; both of them went through one period of startling stylistic innovation after another. Just as no one can understand the history of modern art without a knowledge of Picasso, so no one can understand the history of popular music after 1964 without a knowledge of Dylan.

After all, Dylan has substantial connections with painting. His girlfriend at the time was an art student. In his glorious long poem "Joan Baez in Concert, Part II" Dylan, says that he first understood what beauty meant when he heard Baez sing "in a painter's house" at Woodstock. And, Dylan took up painting and did the album covers for The Band's *Music From Big Pink* and his own *Self-Portrait.* Although he presumably began drawing by imitating Woody Gutherie, who had illustrated *Bound for Glory,* some of Dylan's drawings in *Writings and Drawings by Bob Dylan* have a distinctly cubist look. And the final poem in *Writings and Drawings* is titled "When I Paint My Masterpiece."

Dylan and Picasso share one final similarity, they both are assimilative artists. Dylan once wrote, "Yes, I am a thief of thoughts."[6] Both take the images and styles around them, and imaginatively transform them, thereby creating works which are both distinctly their own and traditional at the same time. Their works often came about as a reaction to the works of other artists, and evolved in analogous ways.

The first three phases of Dylan's career correspond remarkably well to the first three phases of Picasso's career. In the first phase, called his Blue and Rose Periods, Picasso used the colors and images of Post-Impressionism to create paintings about the alienation of modern life, often using circus performers as his subjects. If we omit Dylan's first album as having mostly historical interest today, his first phase consists of two albums, *The Free-Wheelin' Bob Dylan* (1963) and *The Times They Are A-Changin'* (1964). Dylan performs the songs on the albums in the style which he took from Woody Guthrie. He sings in his untrained voice and accompanies himself on guitar and harmonica.

In 1906, Picasso more or less singlehandedly created Cubism with his painting "Les Demoiselles d'Avignon," which shocked even his fellow painters. This work merged non-representational color with the harsh angularity of the African masks which Picasso admired so much. The painting marked a major break with the representational esthetics which had dominated Western art since the Renaissance.

Dylan's second, or Cubist, period consists of four albums: the transitional *Another Side of Bob Dylan* (1964), and the three albums which made him a legend or a demigod in his own time: *Bringing It All Back Home* (1965); *Highway 61 Revisited* (1965); and *Blonde on Blonde* (1966). Like Picasso in his second phase, Dylan shocked even his admirers when he rejected explicit social commentary for a startling new style. Just as Picasso assimilated Post-Impressionist color to the harsh angularity of African masks, so Dylan assimilated surrealistic lyrics to the harsh rhythms of the electric guitar. Dylan himself may have had some awareness of these analogies. (for the line "In the museum infinity goes up on trial," from "Visions of Johanna" on *Blonde on Blonde*), clearly refers to the demise of linear perspective in Cubism.

In the twenties, Picasso continued to paint in the Cubist style, but in some works he also radically simplified his style, doing away with color and complex composition in favor of line alone. This classical period (so called because some of his works have Greek subjects) corresponds to the period of Dylan's last two albums of the sixties, *John Wesley Harding* (1967) and *Nashville Skyline* (1969). Like Picasso in the twenties, Dylan radically simplified his style in these two albums. He did away with the surrealistic lyrics, complex metaphors, and electric guitars of his previous three albums.

In each of these three phases, Dylan was creating new musical forms and styles by reacting against the world around him, but not in simple or obvious ways. Considering Dylan's overwhelming importance in the sixties, each phase deserves a separate discussion.

We can begin by asking about Dylan what we asked about the Beatles, "What did he begin with, and what did he do with it?" When he was growing up in Hibbing, Dylan listened to AM radio and discovered Hank Williams, his "first idol," as he later called him. But he was also listening to rhythm and blues on clear channel stations, and this music prepared him for Elvis and for Little Richard. People who knew him in Greenwich Village in the early sixties said that he wanted to be "bigger than Presley," and even as late as 1970 he still spoke in awe of Elvis. "I liked Elvis Presley. Elvis Presley recorded a song of mine. That's the one recording I treasure the most..."[7] Dylan in fact met Elvis in Las Vegas, and wrote a song, "Went to Meet the Gypsy" about the experience. But, as he told an interviewer for *Sing Out!*, "I always wanted to be 'Little Richard'."[8] In fact, his high school yearbook records his ambition as "to join Little Richard." Many of his great songs draw on the music he heard, as well as the movies he saw, in Hibbing.

Still, his creative evolution did not begin until he discovered Woody Guthrie, and Woody's *Bound for Glory*. As most people know, Dylan's first phase derives, in one way or another, from Woody. The use of the acoustic guitar and harmonica, the populism and the social protest in the lyrics—all of these are Woody's trademarks. All the Greenwich Village folkies knew that Dylan idolized Woody, and he never tried to conceal it. But interviewers often annoy performers when they ask about influences because performers sense that the general concept of influence implies nothing more than a mechanical transfer of styles.

As a case in point, we can consider "I Shall Be Free," from *The Freewheelin' Bob Dylan*, which is derived from Woody's "We Shall Be Free." Woody's song is not a protest song, as the title might suggest, it is an odd combination of wacky lyrics and the promise of religious salvation: "We shall be free when the good lord sets you free." Woody sets the verses of the song in someone else's henhouse. He tries to steal a goose (it rhymes with "loose"), a preacher has a fight with a rooster, and so forth.

In "I Shall Be Free," Dylan retains the melody of Woody's version as well as Woody's phrasing and guitar style. While he keeps the wacky sense of humor which plays on incongruities of various kinds, and the *aabb* stanza form, he reworks the lyrics into a contemporary, urban setting. In the song President Kennedy calls him up, and Dylan says that Brigitte Bardot will made the country grow, he watches television and mocks a Brylcream commercial. He throws in the word "chitlins," which seems out of place, from Woody's song, and takes the phrase "a little lady right by my side" from another, similar, song, Woody's "Talkin' Fish Blues." This woman is a "maneater," a metaphorical use of a term which Woody had applied, in its literal meaning, to a shark. In "Talkin' Fish Blues," Woody rides a 100-pound catfish into town. Although nothing like this happens in "I Shall Be Free," Dylan adapts Woody's surrealism for his own purposes.

To put it simply, Woody's "We Shall Be Free" is a rural folk song performed by an older man, and Dylan's "I Shall Be Free" is a hip, urban song performed by a highly individualistic young man (Dylan's change of the pronoun from "We" to "I" is indicative of his individualism.) Dylan takes the song at a faster tempo than Woody does, and plays and sings with great exuberance. As a matter of fact, Dylan is so full of himself that he can hardly sing for giggling.

Dylan's wonderful sense of humor comes through again and again during his first period, despite the contrary instance of "Masters of War." Again and again he sets up an absurd situation, only to undercut it with a deliberately inappropriate cliche. My favorite example comes from "Talkin' World War III Blues." After Dylan dreamed of the atomic holocaust he says,

> I lit a cigarette on a parking meter
> And walked on down the road.

While we are still mentally digesting the implications of lighting a cigarette on a parking meter, Dylan ends the stanza with the devastating line, "It was a normal day." And he uses a completely deadpan delivery for this line, knowing that any inflection will detract from its impact. Similarly, when he drives off in an unoccupied Cadillac, he delivers the line, that a Cadillac is "a good car to drive." He pauses to make us wonder why he, of all people, would say such a thing—ends with "after a war."

Dylan may have acquired the knack for putting together such incongruities not as much from Woody's songs as from Woody's *Bound for Glory*. One of the many wonderful things about Woody's book, in addition to its honesty and lack of self-pity, is its humor. From time to time, Woody sets up expectations in two lines, and then undercuts them in a deadpan third line, very much as Dylan does in "I Shall Be Free." Thus, Woody says of a hypocritical man in Okeemah, "He had studied to be a preacher, read most of the books on the subject, and was bootlegging liquor in his eating place."[9] This same syntactical sequence occurs when Woody describes a job he had in a cheap hotel for transient workers: "It was my job to show folks to their rooms and show the rooms to the people, and try to convince them that they was really rooms."[10]

Even the minor detail that the holocaust in "I Shall Be Free" begins at three o'clock seems to come from Woody. It happens to have been the time when Woody left home for good: "This is a right nice day for hittin' the road.'Bout three o'clock in the afternoon."[11]

But Dylan was never just a Woody Guthrie clone, and even "Talkin' World War III Blues" has another source. It seems likely that he took the situation of survival after a nuclear war from the film *On the Beach* (1959), although after the Cuban missile crisis, nuclear war was certainly on people's minds. In addition, he refers to Ray Charles' "What'd I Say," not to poke fun at Ray, of course, but at the whites ("Rock-A-Day Johnny"—Johnny Holliday?) who covered and profited from black Rhythm and Blues.

Dylan himself indicated an important source for the early work. In the same interview in which he said he was a trapeze artist, he also said:

I don't read much. Usually I read what people put into my hands. But I do read Hemingway. He didn't have to use adjectives. He didn't really have to define what he was saying. He just said it. I can't do that yet, but that's what I want to do.[12]

Dylan's choice of Hemingway bespeaks an affinity. Like Dylan, Hemingway had left the north country to seek his fame and fortune. Like Dylan, Hemingway was interested in painting, and his adjective-free prose, which so attracted Dylan, came out of his desire to produce an effect comparable to the direct effect of painting. Although Dylan talks about Hemmingway's style, Hemingway also seems to have provided him with an enduring image—the rain.

It rains all through Hemingway's breakthrough novel about World War I, *A Farewell To Arms* (1927), and it rains in the famous last adjective-free sentence. "After a while I went out and left the hospital and walked back to the hotel in the rain."[13] In context, that simple sentence has a devastating impact. Frederic Henry, the speaker, is walking back to the hotel in Switzerland from the hospital where his love, Catherine Barkley, has died in childbirth. Frederic Henry, a tight-lipped American hero, does not express his grief. He does not need to, for we feel it. We feel it with particular intensity because it is raining on him, and the rain has come to symbolize the horrors which World War I visited on people.

As a generalized, environmental image, rain does not lend itself to simplistic ideological interpretations. Dylan apparently sensed this, for surely "A Hard Rain's A-Gonna Fall" derives from *A Farewell to Arms* because it suggests, not so much the single explosion of The Bomb, but the murderous fallout from which we can't escape—as Frederic Henry couldn't escape. When Dylan images fallout as rain, he makes it more familiar, and therefore, more frightening. Among other things, The Bomb is a symbol of technological change, which is why Dylan implicitly compares social change and rain in "The Times They Are A-Changin' "; he warns parents that "the waters/around you have grown."

We find a different but related, use of metaphorical rain in the ominous "Ballad of Hollis Brown," when Dylan tells Hollis that his wife's screams are "stabbing" him "Like the dirty drivin' rain."

Hemingway once said that he liked to describe "what the weather was like," and Dylan's imagery of the wind is related to the rain imagery as a symbol for social change, as in "Blowin' in the Wind." Like the rain, the wind which often accompanies it brings adversity, as in "Girl of the North Country," who lives in a region where "the winds hit heavy." (Similarly, the rain "rattles heavily" in the poem "Walls of Red Wing"). The absence of wind, then, has a positive significance, and in Dylan's utopian poem "When the Ship Comes In," we learn that "the winds will stop."

To judge from the evidence of the endpapers of *Writings and Drawings*, Dylan literally wrote his songs on the typewriter, as Woody had done. In this he differed from virtually all the other major figures of the sixties, who composed by trying out chord combinations on the guitar or piano, often with a tape recorder running. Nevertheless, he was a performer, not a poet; the songs were meant to be heard, not read. As a result, he relied on the traditional song devices of repetition, whether repetition of initial sounds (alliteration), of initial words in a line (anaphora), or of final sound (rhyme).

The early songs often have striking alliteration, as in "where the winds hit heavy" and "her hair hangs" from "Girl of the North Country"; and "build the big bombs" and "unborn and unnamed" from "Master of War." If the density of these lines marks them as Dylan's, his use of anaphora was not so unique. He took over anaphora from folk songs, but he used it much more extensively than his models. In "A Hard Rain's A Gonna Fall", the tension builds and builds, as he begins seven lines in the second stanza with "I saw" and seven lines in the fourth stanza with "I met." This song exemplifies his adaptation of folk sources, because it derives from "Lord Randall," and thus promises a narrative. But the anaphora of the surrealistic images which follow one another without connection denies this promise of narrative.

Dylan is also unique among his contemporaries in his use of the stanza form. With only a few exceptions, his songs adhere to a consistent stanza form, as in "Don't Think Twice, It's All Right", which consists of four eight-line stanzas, with an *ababccdd* rhyme scheme. The very complex "A Hard Rain's A-Gonna Fall", however, has five stanzas, which he organizes by syntax rather than by rhyme. Each stanza begins with a question addressed to "my blue-eyed son" and repeated with a minor variation in the second line. Then there follows the series of first-person statements in the past tense which produce the anaphora, and then the stanza ends with the two-line refrain which repeats the work "hard" five times, perhaps to match the anaphora of the preceeding lines.

The point is that there is a balance in the songs on Dylan's early records. Dylan accompanies himself on acoustic guitar and harmonica, playing very simple melody lines, with frequent repetitions. Such repetitions, and the repetitions of the stanzaic forms, make it easier to understand what Dylan is saying in his rough voice, and the flights of fantasy and humor in the lyrics.

In contrast to the complexity of "A Hard Rain's A-Gonna Fall", "Oxford Town" has a provocative simplicity. This song has four-line stanzas with an odd rhyme scheme—*aaaa*. It is very difficult, even for an experienced writer, to sustain such a demanding stanzaic form, and Dylan cheats a little in the third stanza when he rhymes son/bomb/come/from. Still, the aural and syntactic repetitions of these two songs create tensions which call for a resolution. But that resolution never comes, and thus transmits a tension to the listeners which can move them to do something about the situation to which the songs refers.

True folk singers work within an established tradition. Dylan was never a true folk singer, but he did draw on traditional folk forms, most obviously the three-line, 12-bar, down home blues. Although he never sounded like Robert Johnson, Dylan retained this stanzaic form, which consists of one line repeated twice, and then a third rhyming line which resolves or completes the situation of the first line. "Ballad of Hollis Brown", "Corrina Corrina" and "Down the Highway" all have this blues stanza for which his harmonica serves as an appropriate complement. Dylan even imitates a Southern accent on "Down the Highway."

The consistency of Dylan's stanzas has an analogy in a more general pattern of oppositions which pervade his songs. While this pattern does not appear in every song or explain every song, it holds true often enough to show that Dylan's work has the consistency which we would expect in a major creative force. His songs in the first phase of his career sort themselves out according to the following set of oppositions:

Anger/Compassion
Social/Personal
Outside/Inside

It is possible to understand how this pattern conforms to his work simply by listing the major songs from his first phase by classification:

Anger Songs
"Masters of War"
"Oxford Town"
"The Times They Are A-Changin'"
"Ballad of Hollis Brown"
"With God on Our Side"
"The Lonesome Death of Hattie Carroll"

Compassion Songs:
"Girl of the North Country"
"Don't Think Twice, It's All Right"
"One Too Many Mornings"
"Only a Pawn in Their Game"

The first thing to notice here is that each left-hand term of the oppositions is related to the other left-hand terms. The anger songs deal with social issues, like war, racism, and poverty, as they affect outsiders like James Meredith, Hollis Brown, and Hattie Carroll. If no outsiders figure in the song, Dylan presents himself as an outsider singing them, as in "Masters of War" and "With God on Our Side." Dylan *sounds* angry on these songs and the ostinato of his repeated guitar chords builds up a great deal of tension.

The songs which express anger at an external situation deal, in one way or another, with America's covenant with God. The most obvious example is "With God on Our Side," where Dylan's savage irony undercuts the covenant as a justification for American expansionism. Oddly enough Dylan, poses as a Jeremiah, a castigator of America, i.e., (the Establishment for its shortcomings).

Another irony about these songs is that Dylan insists that it doesn't matter who he is, as in the beginning of "With God on Our Side." This insistence on anonymity was consistent with Dylan's persona of being an orphan at this time. To deny one's own past, to create one's self as one goes along is a profoundly American attitude; Marlon Brando does the same when he allegorically represents America to Maria Schneider's Europe in *Last Tango in Paris* (1972). (In *American Gigolo* (1982), Richard Gere refuses to tell Lauren Hutton anything about his past, saying, "You can learn everything there is to know about me by making love to me"). In his early days in Greenwich Village, Dylan told a lot of lies about himself—that he had run away from home a lot, that he had travelled about in the West, that he used to play honky-tonk piano, and so forth. Part of this came from a love of putting people on as a way of performing, but a more serious part came from his deeply felt lack of identity. He was a midwesterner, a kid from the provinces in the big city, a Jew amid goyim folksingers. So he made the best of it, and drew on the symbolism of the outsider in American folklore until he had enough money and power to disappear behind his professional achievements.

In contrast to the anger songs, the compassion songs are personal, and on them Dylan picks out arpeggios on his guitar to create an appropriately gentler sound. The contrast in the guitar styles between, "Ballad of Hollis Brown" and "Girl of the North Country" makes this clear. But not all of the compassion songs are personal. "Only a Pawn in Their Game", dealing with the murder of Medgar Evers in Mississippi, ought to be an anger song, but it is not. Dylan gives it the most compassionate reading of any of his early songs. Where we would expect anger at a vicious racist, we have only understanding. When an anomaly like this occurs in a general pattern, it usually gets worked out somehow at a later date. This is just what happened with "Only a Pawn in Their Game."

Just as the best-known period of Picasso's long and varied career is his Cubist period, so the best-known period in Dylan's ongoing and varied career is what is called his second, or electric, phase. Despite the storm of protest which his songs created, history has vindicated them.

The scandal erupted during Dylan's infamous performance at the 1965 Newport Folk Festival, when he showed up with Mike Bloomfield on electric guitar, and Al Kooper on organ. Most accounts say that people booed Dylan's new sound, but Al Kooper swears in *Backstage Passes* that it didn't happen like that. What we *do* know for sure is that the reviews said that people booed. As a result, the usual tape loop occurred. When Dylan played Forest Hills a little later, the audience had read that people booed his electric sound at Newport, so they felt obliged to boo him, and they did. Major innovations such as this never occur for just one reason, so we can best understand the significance of Dylan's decision to go electric by investigating his context in 1964-65, when Beatlemania was raging, and changing popular music for good.

Dylan had various personas during his first phase, but his favorite was that of the innocent, the country boy who has come to the big city and who sees the truth about it. This persona was not so much false as it was incomplete; if Dylan was a hayseed, he was a hayseed who was soaking up European culture as fast as he could. The following story about Dylan, by folksinger Dave Van Ronk, illustrates the point.

"Being a hayseed, that was part of his image, or what he considered his image at the time. Like, once I asked him, 'Do you know the French Symbolists?' And he said, 'Huh?'—the stupidest 'huh' you can imagine—and later, when he had a place of his own, I went up there, and on the bookshelf was a volume of the French poets from Nerval to almost the present. I think it ended at Apollonaire, and it included Rimbaud, and it was all well-thumbed, with passages underlined and notes in the margins. The man wanted to be a primitive, a natural kind of genius. He never talked about somebody like Rimbaud. But he *knew* Rimbaud, all right. You see that in the later songs."

The French Symbolists and Surrealists profoundly affected Dylan's work in his second phase. As Van Ronk says, Arthur Rimbaud, to whom he refers in the brief liner notes to *Desire,* served as a model. Rimbaud's experimentation with homosexuality and with drugs made him an archetypal modern artist, even without his writing. His work itself with its profusion of bizarre images and denial of narrative, has a deliberate disorienting effect, as in the first stanza of "The Drunken Boat":

> As I was going down impassive Rivers,
> I suddenly felt I was no longer guided by my haulers:
> Screaming Redskins had taken them for targets,
> Nailing them naked to colored poles.[15]

It is not coincidental that it was Rimbaud who coined the term, so applicable to so much of the sixties, "the derangement of all the senses." The discovery of Rimbaud and the other modern French poets expanded Dylan's work, creating the long lines and surrealistic images which characterize his second period.

As usual in Dylan's work, the key is the way he combined different things. He took the obscure and baffling imagery of the Symbolists and balanced it against the sound of electric guitars. The sound led you to expect readily accessible lyrics like the Beatles' "She Loves You," so you kept on thinking that the next time, or the next time after that, the lyrics would make perfect sense. They never quite make sense, but by then you were hooked.

Contemporary American artists were also affecting Dylan at this time. They lived in his neighborhood on the Lower East Side, and came to prominence at about the same time he did. Given Dylan's openness to the world around him and his interest in painting, it is impossible to imagine that he did not know the work of the painters who created what we now call Pop Art—Jim Dine, Tom Wesselman, Andy Warhol, Roy Lichtenstein, Robert Rauschenberg, and Claes Oldenburg. Like Dylan, they came from somewhere else (Oldenburg from Chicago), made names for themselves by shocking the establishment and overwhelming it with the audacity of their work. By the seventies, they were no less audacious and talented, but they had grown wealthy, and had turned into the establishment—just as Dylan had.

Just as Dylan accepted the electric guitar with all its commercial implications, so the Pop Artists accepted such popular graphic forms as advertising and cartoons with all their commercial implications. If Dylan Americanized French Symbolism in his songs, Roy Lichtenstein did something similar in his witty versions of Picasso, which recreated well-known Picassos in the style of cartoons, as in his *Woman with Flowered Hat* (1963). Andy Warhol accepted American popular culture in another way—as a valid subject for art; he did *Marilyn Monroe* (1962); and *Elvis I and II* (1964). Pop Artists often practiced juxtaposition in the form of assemblages, which were works in mixed media, such as Jim Dine's *Summer Tools* (1962), which juxtaposed gardening tools to a painted surface. It was a time when artists sat around and discussed what was real and what was not.

We can see what Dylan made of all this by looking at the cover of *Bringing It All Back Home*, which states Dylan's new esthetic credo of assemblage as musical eclecticism. Photographed through an iris lens, which distances the images, Dylan is in the foreground and the elegant Sally Grossman (wife of his manager Albert Grossman) sits on a sofa in front of a white neo-classical fireplace (How can it be that no one has asked him where this was shot?). Dylan holds a copy of a movie magazine which features a cover story on Jean Harlow by Louella Parsons, and a gray cat. Between him and Sally the following albums lie on the sofa: *The Folk Blues of Eric Andersen, Lotte Lenya, Robert Johnson, King of the Delta Blues,* and *The Impressions*. Behind Sally, stands a half hidden copy of the album which began his second period, *Another Side of Bob Dylan*. On a white table to her side we notice, among other things, a harmonica and a copy of the issue of *Time* which named Lyndon Johnson as Man of the Year.

This carefully composed cover is an assemblage very much in the spirit of mid-sixties Pop Art in New York. Like the Pop Artists, Dylan is telling us what sources are important to him, and that he takes them all equally seriously. Less obvious is the odd photograph on the inside of *Blonde on Blonde*, in which Dylan is holding a pair of pliers in one hand and what looks to be a photograph of his great-grandmother in the other; it seems to come straight from one of Jim Dine's mixed-media works of the period.

Pop Art also affected the titles of the songs as well as the graphics for the album covers, most obviously, "I Shall Be Free No. 10." This use of a number in a title is taken from the artists' practice of indicating one of a number of different treatments of a major theme, as in Tom Wesselman's *Great American Nude No. 10* from 1961. On *Blonde on Blonde* Dylan acquired a habit of using nonsensical adverbs in song titles, such as "Queen Jane Approximately," a habit which probably comes from similar nonsensical titles which the Surrealists gave to their works, such as Marcel Duchamp's "The Bride Stripped Bare by Her Bachelors, Even." Finally, the odd title of *Blonde on Blonde* seems to be Dylan's wordplay on the painting of Ad Reinhardt, an artist who had a major show at the Jewish Museum in 1965, and who specialized in black on black abstract paintings at the time. Reinhardt's *Abstract Painting, Black* from 1960-61 is an example.

It appears that another major factor in Dylan's second phase was his discovery of the most influential book of the sixties, Marshall McLuhan's *Understanding Media,* which appeared in 1964. Here are the aspects of his book which seem most relevant to Dylan.

McLuhan argued that technology does not simply exist "out there," and that it does not simply serve us; but rather, through technology we extend our organs and senses with important psychic consequences which we ignore at our peril. Just as he argued that there exists a relationship between technology and the body, so he also argued that there exists a relationship between technology and the artist. Unlike most previous critics who had lamented the alienation of the artist from the technological world, McLuhan asserted that:

In the history of human culture there is no example of a conscious adjustment of the various factors of personal and social life to new extensions except in the puny and peripheral efforts of artists. The artist picks up the message of cultural and technological challenge decades before its transforming impact occurs.[16]

Or, in the words of the writer Wyndham Lewis, whom McLuhan liked to quote, "The artist is continually engaged in writing a history of the future because he is the only one who understands the nature of the present."[17]

And it was the nature of the present, McLuhan argued, that the world was undergoing a profound change as a result of electric technology which was starting to replace literacy. That is, "The ultimate conflict between sight and sound, between written and oral kinds of perception and organization is upon us."[18] For McLuhan, the sounds of radios, telephones, record players and the like were changing our perceptions. He conceptualized this change as the replacement of the eye, the organ which we use for reading, by the ear, the organ we use for hearing. McLuhan says of Western man that "His own electric technology now begins to translate the visual or eye man back into the tribal and oral pattern with its seamless web of kinship and interdependence."[19] Moreover, in a sentence that must have pleased Dylan, McLuhan concluded, "Radio and gramophone gave us back the poet's voice as an important dimension of the poetic experience."[20] Finally, very much in the spirit of the times, McLuhan provocatively associated high culture and popular culture as equally valid and equally interesting in passages such as this: "The advent of electric media released art from this strait jacket [of literacy] at once, creating the world of Paul Klee, Picasso, Braque, Eisenstein, the Marx Brothers, and James Joyce."[21]

Although Dylan does not refer to McLuhan by name, and might even deny that he read him, either he read *Understanding Media,* and applied it to his work, or his albums from the mid-sixties constitute a startling empirical confirmation of McLuhan's theories. The first of these seems more likely. How else than by reference to McLuhan are we to make any sense at all of Dylan's comments on the eye and the mouth in the liner notes to *Highway 61 Revisited:*

I cannot say the word eye anymore...when I speak this word eye, it is as if I am speaking of somebody's eye that I faintly remember...there is no eye—there is only a series of mouths—long live the mouths.[22]

As usual, Dylan personalizes what McLuhan wrote, both here and on the liner notes to *Bringing It All Back Home.* In it he juxtaposes high culture and popular culture more in the spirit of McLuhan than of Pop Art, in order to set us up for a deadpan putdown: "i would not want to be bach, mozart, tolstoy, joe hill, gertrude stein or james dean/they are all dead."[23] (During this period he adopted e.e. cummings' mode of refusing to use capitals, and writing "t" instead of "to").

But it is always the songs themselves which matter to us, and a number of Dylan's major songs are informed by McLuhan's opposition of the eye and the ear. We can begin with "My Back Pages," with its curious assertion, "I was so much older then." This song derives from the attitude expressed in "Joan Baez in Concert. Part II"; entranced by the beauty of her voice, he confesses:

Oh how feeble foolish small an' sad
'F me t' think that beauty was
Only ugliness an' muck[24]

Essentially, in "My Back Pages," Dylan is repenting his literacy. He images his past as pages from a book, of course, but more importantly, he also understands what McLuhan meant when he said that literacy fixes ideas in space like letters on a page and dichotomizes them. Dylan said he believed in ideas as maps, and in "lies that life is black and white." Literacy refers to the past, from whose straitjacket (as McLuhan put it) the new oral age has released him, with the result that he feels a resurgence of wholeness and youth. Hence, the paradox that he's younger than he was.

The way print fixes words into place on the page suggests that those words refer to something equally external; the visible and always present sequence of those words suggests that logic and rational thought exhibit comparable continuity with a beginning, middle, and an end. Like most other modern artists, Dylan will have none of this, and begins the song with the aggressively surrealistic line "Crimson flames tied through my ears." That line cannot refer to anything tangible in the external world and it was the problematic issue of reference that ultimately proved crucial in his break with the folkies and protest songs. In order to comment on, and change, a situation in the external world, a protest song has to refer to it in ways which the listeners can identify. But in the sixties it was just this problem of reference which the media made so difficult, and therefore Dylan sensed the inadequacies of protest songs without being able to explain the problem to anyone. After all, it was in the difficulty of explanations that the problem arose.

Four of Dylan's major songs work variations on the eye/ear opposition of *Understanding Media.* In "Ballad of a Thin Man," Dylan has Mr. Jones, the American Everyman, walk into the room "with a pencil," which means that he represents literacy and the repression of the vital instincts which literacy implies for McLuhan. Dylan tells him that he "should be made to wear earphones," not only for the sake of the rhyme and not only as a punishment, but as therapy. Greater attention to sound will balance his over-emphasis on literacy, and thus, sight. Dylan both jeers at him and expresses concern when he keeps repeating that Mr. Jones doesn't know what is happening. Dylan does know, not just because he is young, but because he is an artist, one of the few who understand the nature of the present.

The visionary masterpieces from *Blonde on Blonde,* "Visions of Johanna." "Desolation Row," and "Sad-Eyed Lady of the Lowlands," all contain images of eyes and visual values. In "Visions of Johanna" Dylan takes jewels and binoculars as symbols of conspicuous consumption for display and a device for extending vision, and places them in an incongruous position, on the head of a mule (The cover of the Rolling Stones' *Get Yer Ya-Yas Out* shows how ridiculous this looks, and is their homage to Dylan). From his vantage point on Desolation Row Dylan says he can't "read too good." And of course the singer in "Sad-Eyed Lady of the Lowlands" has both "warehouse"—cheap and devalued—"eyes" and "Arabian drums." The drums represent the new orality, but Arabian may imply that the new oral world is still not here.

Dylan put out the albums of his second period during the course of a little over three years; therefore, he must have written these masterpieces in rapid succession. We don't know anything about their chronological order and he didn't group them in any obvious way on the albums. Nevertheless, some of the songs do seem to fit together in thematic groupings, often in pairs.

For instance, two songs from *Another Side of Bob Dylan* indicate the struggle he went through during the transition to his second phase: "Chimes of Freedom" and "I Shall Be Free No. 10," both of which refer to and play off against his recent past. "I Shall Be Free No. 10" refers to his earlier "I Shall Be Free," which in turn derived from Woody, "Chimes of Freedom" is a synthesis of a folk standard which was exquisitely recorded later by Judy Collins, "Bells of Rhymney" and—unlikely as it may seem— Allen Ginsburg's poem "Howl."

As Judy sings it, "The Bells of Rhymney" names the bells of various villages in England and hints at religious feeling without developing or evoking it. But what "Bells of Rhymney" hints at, "Chimes of Freedom" presents with an awesome fusion of passion and technical skill. In Dylan's evolution this song generalizes the compassion songs which were addressed to women. The word "tolling" occurs no less than nine times in the lyrics, and raises the question whether Hemingway's *For Whom the Bell Tolls* had anything to do with the creation of the song. It amounts to a modern equivalent of John Donne's "Send not to ask for whom the bell tolls; the bell tolls for thee."

"Chimes of Freedom" teems with densely alliterated phrases such as "bells of bolts" and "mistreated mateless mother." Both of these devices have their stylistic origins in a phrase from "Only a Pawn in Their Game": "from the poverty shacks through the cracks to the tracks." "Poverty shacks" anticipates the phrase "cathedral evening" from "Bells of Rhymney" in that both phrases combine two nouns rather than an adjective and a noun, as we would expect. Furthermore, the repetition of shacks/cracks/tracks thickens the sound of the line, drawing our attention to, and away from, the crime it decries.

We can understand why the compassion songs begin with "Only a Pawn in Their Game" by noticing the importance of a related song, "Stuck in Inside of Mobile (With the Memphis Blues Again)." This is a nice song to listen to, and Dylan gives it a spirited performance which seems appropriate for a song which we can only take as a verbal joke. But it is not a masterpiece, because in it Dylan is still caught in autobiographical references no less than in "Spanish Harlem Incident." He uses "Mobile" and "Memphis" here not just because they are both Southern towns which begin with M. Mobile was the birthplace of Hank Williams, and Memphis was where Elvis lived. Thus, the song expresses a creative block, a fear that he will not be able to make the evolution from acoustic guitar (Hank) to electric guitar (Elvis). This song, so different in obvious ways from "Only a Pawn In Their Game," is nevertheless related to it. Dylan could not indulge in the self-righteous castigation of Southern rednecks as the folkies did, because he respected the work of Southern rednecks like Hank and Elvis too much to reduce them to stereotypes. He surely sensed the pain in Hank's rendition of "Your Cheatin' Heart," for instance.

To return to "Chimes of Freedom," it begins with Dylan's true words about freedom in its incomplete sentences and baffling syntax. Each of the six stanzas ends with the phrase "the chimes of freedom flashing." To use the technical term, Dylan is using synesthesia, the representation of one sense by another. Synesthesia flaunts the unverifiability of poetry, because we do not usually see the sound of chimes or of anything else. The fifth and sixth lines of each stanza begin with a gerund—flashing, tolling, striking—and the anaphora thus achieved creates a sense of wonder that there are so many forms of human misery.

"Chimes of Freedom" begins when some kids, an unidentified "we," duck inside a doorway, presumably on the Lower East Side during a thunderstorm, and ends by extending its sympathy to the "whole wide universe." This universal compassion provides the source for almost everything else that Dylan did during the sixties.

Because of this, and because Dylan's importance partially stems from his capacity to synthesize popular culture and high culture into something unprecedented, we need to realize that in "Chimes of Freedom" Dylan is replying to the most famous poem by a fellow Jewish poet, Allen Ginsberg's "Howl." Written in 1955, "Howl" begins, "I saw the best minds of my generation..." and then lists the people who seek sensation of any kind, such as drugs and homosexual activity, in compensation for the alienation which they feel. Ginsberg writes long lines in free verse and a series of them begin with "who...who...who." This may have suggested to Dylan the way he could use anaphora in a similar way by enumerating all the people for whom the chimes toll in compassion. Dylan's song has the same rush of surrealistic, narrative-free imagery, and the same compassion for society's misfits. Dylan took from "Howl" the device of combining two nouns into a phrase, rather than an adjective and a noun, as we would expect. Ginsberg's "negro streets" and "madman bum" thus become Dylan's "cathedral evening" (Dylan even extended this to the unforgettable "motorcycle black madonna/Two-wheeled gypsy queen" in "Gates of Eden"). But Ginsberg's "Howl" is a purely secular poem which creates its effects by presenting pure sensation as valid for its own sake. In response to this nihilism, Dylan affirms what Ginsberg says that his "angelheaded hipsters" burn for: "the ancient heavenly connection to the stars, dynamic in the machinery of night." Dylan's vision brings heaven and earth together, just as it brings together all the people in "the whole wide universe."

A great artist can create the new only by coming to terms with the old, and Dylan does this in "I Shall Be Free No. 10." Its title refers us to his own "I Shall Be Free." "I Shall Be Free No. 10" forms a complete pair with "Chimes of Freedom" because Dylan gives the songs different readings. He sings "Chimes of Freedom" with all the gravity his cracked voice can muster, but you can practically see him grinning on "I Shall Be Free No. 10."—begins with an affirmation of his averageness and commonness. This denies the expectations of his fans as "It Ain't Me Babe" denies the expectations of a girl. When Dylan sings that he "ain't different from anyone" he seems to be referring to a very moving passage from Woody's *Bound for Glory* in which Woody talks about some faith healing he did in Oklahoma and about the stereotypes which people wanted to impose on him.

They thought I was a mind reader. I didn't claim to be, so some of them called me a fortune teller and a healer. But I never claimed to be different from you or anybody else. Does the truth help to heal you when you hear it? Does a clear mind make a sick body well? Sometimes.

But this homage to Woody is also Dylan's declaration of independence from him. This song consists of one nonsensical stanza after another, and ends with a giggle, a guitar strum, and a reference to what he learned "over in England"— the lesson of Beatlemania—that electric guitars and fun are part of life, too.

The freedom from Woody meant freedom from external, social concerns (although that is not all there is in Woody), and finds its first expression in the internal exploration of the song which the Byrds electrified so wonderfully, "Mr. Tambourine Man." This classic, possibly intended as a tribute to the tambourines of Motown, is unique in Dylan's work because of its celebration of dancing for the sheer joy of it. Dylan did not abandon Woody, as all the folkies thought, he generalized and modernized him. His commitment to his listeners remains intact, and he re-affirms this commitment in "Pledging My Time" and "Queen Jane Approximately."

"Pledging My Time" plays itself off against Johnny Ace's soul classic which went to #1 in 1955, "Pledging My Love." But Dylan is not singing "forever, my darling" to a girl, as Johnny did; he's hoping the audience will come through for him by matching its commitment to his. In "Pledging My Love" the "poison headache" and the "stuffy room" represent the literate states of mind which the new oral art will purge. These states of mind also appear in "Queen Jane Approximately," another song which entices an audience, not a girl. But the audience must do its part; it must tire of disdainful family members and advisers with plastic. Dylan is offering himself to those in distress, just as Woody had before him. He refused to keep re-writing "Blowin' in the Wind" because he sensed that the true issues of his day were general ones, such as the phenomenon of the closed tape loop, which prevented people from experiencing their own lives first-hand; the dichotomy between high culture and popular culture; and the perversions of the covenant. Dylan dealt with those issues as directly and as forcefully as Woody had dealt with the issues of the thirties.

We can now understand the great importance of "Chimes of Freedom" by understanding that as it merges nature and society it anticipates the way Dylan will merge other oppositions as well. In his second period, this generalization applies to the distinction between social songs and personal songs, which disappears for all practical purposes (The few purely personal songs, such as "Positively Fourth Street" are not masterpieces). As a case in point we might take "It Ain't Me Babe," which sounds like a personal song. But in "It Ain't Me Babe," with its refrain of "no no no" Dylan is replying to Beatlemania, and specifically to the refrain of "She Loves You,"—"yeah yeah yeah," to the stereotypes of romantic love.[27] The song thus has to do with social attitudes, not memories.

The opposition between anger songs and compassion songs remains, however, as this list shows:

Anger Songs:
"Maggie's Farm"
"Gates of Eden"
"Like a Rolling Stone"
"Ballad of a Thin Man"
"Positively Fourth Street"

Compassion Songs:
"All I Really Want To Do"
"Chimes of Freedom"
"To Ramona"
"Subterranean Homesick Blues"
"It"s Alright Ma (I'm Only Bleeding)"
"Queen Jane Approximately"
"Rainy Day Women #12 and 35"
"Sad-Eyed Lady of the Lowlands"
"Tombstone Blues"
"Just Like A Woman"

Yet much has changed, even in these oppositions. One has only to look at the lists to realize that the compassion songs now greatly outnumber the anger songs. Moreover, the opposition itself becomes less distinct. Whereas Dylan had nothing but scorn for William Zanzinger in "The Lonesome Death of Hattie Carroll," he has both scorn and compassion for the more general figure of Mr. Jones.

As Betsy Bowden has said, this ambiguity between anger and compassion appears clearly in "Like A Rolling Stone." She has shown that every word and every sound counts. For instance, "We see that the phrase 'rolling stone' contains two of the vowels and two of the consonant sounds most often repeated throughout the song: long *o*, short *i, 1,* and terminal *m/n/g i* is "time," in the phrase "Once upon a time," a phrase which seems very incongruous after the drum crash followed by guitar and organ chords which begin the song. Yet this is the point: Dylan reacts to her outmoded expectations by denying that "they lived happily ever after." Miss Lonely is living unhappily, and that is what the song is about. The sounds which recur in one word after another take on a meaning of their own, as when the long *i* of "time" links Miss Lonely's Latin-based diction of compromise/realize/alibis/eyes to the fairy tale time. Sounds associate her with literacy, from which the street and the mystery tramp—surrogates for the singer himself—will purge her. Unlike Miss Lonely, the singer uses Anglo-Saxon words and street slang like "scrounging" and "hanging out."

He is jeering at her, taunting her, as he taunts Mr. Jones. If the singer wished to diminish Mr. Jones' literacy with headphones, he is dealing with the fact that Miss Lonely has lost her literacy—she has no visual qualities because she is now invisible. Two words which begin with "d," "diplomat" and "diamond," associate her with the upper class. She is now invisible because she belongs to the less literate lower classes, out on the street.

"Like a Rolling Stone" thus deals with a traditional American motif—the democratization of a snobbish woman by a populist man. This motif recurs throughout American films, in such as classics as *It Happened One Night* (1934), and—more relevant to Dylan— *Singin' in the Rain* (1952). Speaking of movies, Bowden mentions such fifties movies as *The King and I* (1956) as the source for the mystery tramp. Indeed *The Lady and the Tramp* sets up the same opposition between the snobbish lady and the populist man, but more relevant to "Like a Rolling Stone" is one of the most powerful films of the fifties, *A Streetcar Named Desire* (1951). *Streetcar* opposes Brando's animal physicality to Vivien Leigh's neurotic snobbism. Brando, as Stanley Kowalski, attacks her verbally, as Dylan attacks Miss Lonely but is drawn to her despite himself. Dylan says that Miss Lonely's got "no secrets to conceal," which is essentially what Brando says to Leigh when he finds out about her past.

The song has other oppositions as well, such as that between the "rolling stone" and the "diamond ring" and the "Napoleon in rags" and the "finest clothes" which Miss Lonely used to wear. They are consistent with this opposition between democracy and elitism. But the opposition is not an absolute one, for Dylan breaks the song into two halves with a harmonica break before the third verse. In the third verse, as Bowden says, "He combines her fairy-tale meter with his street-world diction; the Anglo-Saxon but also polysyllabic 'understood' mediates between the two kinds of language."[29] Dylan names, and thus humanizes, Miss Lonely in the second verse, and therefore "By the end of the third stanza Miss Lonely has become a victim, albeit one who asked for it, instead of a haughty bitch."[30] In the repetitions of "How does it feel?" he is jeering at her, but he also wants her to feel for her own sake.

"Like a Rolling Stone" is the other half of "Subterranean Homesick Blues." In both songs Dylan describes a situation and gives advice about dealing with it. Yet, if Miss Lonely's problem comes from her elitism and gentility, the kid's problem in "Subterranean Homesick Blues" comes from outside, which in turn relates that song to "Rainy Day Women #12 and 35." Dylan takes "Subterranean Homesick Blues" at such a fast tempo that this complex song remains baffling even after repeated listenings. Because the song exists only on record in any real way, an interesting problem arises in connection with Dylan's advice:

Don't follow leaders
Watch the parking meters

As Bowden says, these lines have various possible meanings, all of which confuse more than provoke. This song hardly belongs to Dylan (except in a legalistic sense) any more than "God Bless America" belongs to Irving Berlin—that song belongs to *us*—I suggest that the way I heard these lines for years makes more sense than the version in the printed text.

Don't follow leaders
(They're) walkin' parkin' meters

"Walkin' parkin'" is like what Bowden calls the rocking horse rhyme "drinking thinking" of "Like a Rolling Stone," and in this version the second line strengthens and explains the first line. "Walkin' parkin' meters" is a typical Dylan line—a surrealistic image which conveys both uniformity and graft, economically and forcefully.

If the opposition between anger and compassion becomes ever more tenuous, the opposition between inside and outside does not, although the two oppositions are related.

Inside Songs
"It Ain't Me Babe"
"Desolation Row"
"Visions of Johanna"
"Stuck Inside of Mobile (With the Memphis Blues Again)"
"Sad-Eyed Lady of the Lowlands"

Outside Songs
"Highway 61 Revisited"
"Just Like Tom Thumbs's Blues"
"Temporary Like Achilles"

In a way, the difference between inside and outside is the difference between Dylan's first and second periods, On the cover of *The Freewheelin' Bob Dylan*, Dylan and Suze are striding down Fourth Street; on the cover of *Bringing It All Back Home*, Dylan is also with an attractive woman, but is now inside and comfortable. Beatlemania created a youth culture which made him into an insider. Similarly, he is inside with a woman in "It Ain't Me Babe" and "Desolation Row." And in both "Chimes of Freedom" and "Visions of Johanna" he is part of an unidentified "we"—people who are inside a doorway and a loft respectively.

As usual in Dylan, the outside is threatening, In "Love Minus Zero/No Limit" on a rainy night the wind "howls like a hammer." The singer stands "inside the rain" on "Just Like a Woman," and the person addressed in "Just Like Tom Thumb's Blues" is lost in the rain at a time when he or she should be saved—at Easter. But the song also offers refuge inside Melinda's room and in New York.

The outside takes on more than meterological symbolism, however, as Miss Lonely and the kid know. For them, the outside represents an unfamiliar and potentially dangerous situation to which they must adapt. This treatment of the outside helps to explain something which seems a little odd—Dylan's reversal of highway imagery in "Highway 61 Revisited." In the early, acoustic period the road and the highway often mean freedom and liberation. But in the age of four-lane interstates with air-conditioned cars whizzing along them at seventy miles per hour, the cameraderie, and the adventure of the road which Woody had experienced in the thirties, did not exist. So Dylan treated the highway as a place where Abraham would kill his son at the order of a vengeful God (a startlingly effective, and very Jewish, incongruity), and a showbiz venue for World War III—of which someone will no doubt sell postcards.

Dylan relies on the distinction between inside and outside in three of the great songs of his career—"Gates of Eden," "Desolation Row," and "Sad-Eyed Lady of the Lowlands." All of them deal with the covenant—by which Dylan means the broken covenant. "Gates of Eden" has nine stanzas, all sung in essentially the same way, with the same phrasing and the same instrumentation. The absence of variation creates the same tension as his early anger songs, but here it is the tension of the broken covenant, not of specific historic acts. The last line of each stanza makes a statement about the gates of Eden which mark the boundary between inside and outside. The name of the song refers to the well-known trope for America as a garden, and specifically as the Garden of Eden, a refuge of purity. If, in "Masters of War", Dylan attacked the history textbooks which justified American militarism, in "Gates of Eden" he evokes a totalitarian Eden primarily by making negative statements about it. The Gates of Eden, we learn, emit no sound, and there are no kings or sins inside them. What's real and what's not doesn't matter inside; therefore, there are no trials or truths outside. Clearly, believing makes it so inside the Gates of Eden.

If Dylan only evokes a frightening Eden, he populates "Desolation Row." He gives the song a frame by stating that he and his Lady are on Desolation Row in the first stanza, and by telling us in the last stanza that we should write to him only from Desolation Row. In between the first and last stanzas, he tells us who lives inside Desolation Row and who lives outside. Inside are Cinderella, Cain and Abel, the hunchback of Notre Dame, the Good Samaritan, and Einstein. Outside are Ophelia, Dr. Filth, the agents and the "superhuman crew," and Ezra Pound and T.S. Eliot. Two figures are out of place—Casanova, who is being punished for trying to escape to Desolation Row, and Romeo, who is inside and should be outside.

What are we to make of all this? We might begin by recalling that various people have said that "Desolation Row" is Dylan's version of Eliot's "The Wasteland." Both works have startling images of modern urban life and rely on the reader's, or listener's, knowledge of cultural allusions, rather than on a sequential narrative. Like "The Wasteland," "Desolation Row" gives new meaning to myths by placing them in a contemporary urban setting. In this sense "Desolation Row" represents the culmination of songs such as "Bob Dylan's 115th Dream", which rely on anachronisms and allusions for their effect.

If Eliot refers to Chaucer, the English Metaphysical Poets, Wagner, and many others, Dylan refers to historical characters like Einstein, Casanova, and Ezra Pound and T.S. Eliot; to fairy tale figures like Cinderella ; and to literary characters like Ophelia, Romeo, and the hunchback of Notre Dame. Just as we must catch Eliot's references to understand "The Wasteland," so we must understand Dylan's references to understand "Desolation Row." Apparently, Dylan knew this, so he puts Pound and Eliot, as representatives of high culture, in a captain's tower, an opposition of high culture and popular culture paradoxically made possible only at a time when popular music had more receptivity to high culture than ever before. Probably as compensation for his approximation to high culture, Dylan's guitar begins "Desolation Row" with an introduction which seems to derive from yet another memory from Hibbing days—the chorus of Marty Robbins' #1 hit from 1959, "El Paso." These Mexican chords have an exotic sound, and the reference clues us to the fact that Dylan's song, like Marty's, is about a place. It also has the additional function of telling us that what we are hearing belongs to and with the culture of all the people.

Dylan had good reason to feel uneasy about the similarity to Eliot, for he shared the rejection of Romanticism which characterized Eliot's generation. Thus, he puts Ophelia outside Desolation Row; her lifelessness, her sexlessness (she wears an iron vest), and her belief in the rainbow (shades of Dorothy in *The Wizard of Oz*) give her the literate, abstract attitudes of which Dylan repented in "My Back Pages." But as with Miss Lonely, not all is lost, because she peeks into Desolation Row.

Even this much has great significance, for Desolation Row is a place which represents a state of mind. The people who live there are generally outcasts, like Cinderella and the hunchback of Notre Dame, or they are people who care, like the Good Samaritan. So Einstein seems out of place on Desolation Row, but he fits right in once we remember that Dylan has absorbed his McLuhan well. In *Understanding Media*, McLuhan makes Einstein a key figure in the change which he is celebrating: "Einstein pronounced the doom of continuous or 'rational' space, and the way was made clear for Picasso and the Marx brothers and *MAD*."[31] Here and elsewhere, McLuhan associates Einstein with the orality of the new electric world. Very much in this spirit, Dylan makes Einstein do something that seems out of character with what we know of the historical man, but appropriate for his significance—he was famous long ago for playing electric violin on Desolation Row. He creates sound with an electrical instrument; the change which he symbolizes makes literacy obsolete, so he makes it ridiculous by reciting the alphabet.

The instrumental introduction has as important a function for "Sad-Eyed Lady of the Lowlands" as it does for "Desolation Row." Organ and drums, an unusual combination, begin the performance, for four 6/8 measures. They set up the opposition between the sacred—the quiet, churchlike organ—and the profane—the rhythmic drums of rock 'n' roll. This opposition engenders other, comparable oppositions—none of which is ever resolved. After Dylan plays his harmonica for four measures, he begins to sing, and the first line of the lyrics contains four words with *m*-sounds: "mercury mouth" and "missionary times." In the reverent atmosphere which the organ creates, these *m*-sounds suggest to us, if only unconsciously, "Mary" and "Madonna." So Dylan continues to evoke associations in this masterpiece, rather than state generalizations; here he evokes a profoundly religious sadness which can make listening to this song an essential experience.

The opposition of inside and outside more or less corresponds to the opposition between the sacred and the profane. He is outside her gate, something which houses don't have, but which temples and estates usually do have. He repeatedly addresses her, but she never replies, as Christ never replies to the Grand Inquisitor in *The Brothers Karamazov* by Dostoyevsky, an author whom Dylan mentioned several times in interviews during the sixties. But if he is outside, he claims to appreciate her, as the unnamed "they" do not. This claim makes him a relative insider, and this ambivalence has its own analogy, in the symbols of literacy and orality, the "warehouse eyes" and "Arabian drums" which he offers her.

The Sad-Eyed Lady is independent of him and complete in herself. She is complete in the way she combines opposing entities, such as the sun and the moon, Spanish manners and her mother's drugs (more *m*-sounds!). She combines the mechanical and the organic, as when she places her "streetcar visions" on the grass. She repeatedly combines profane attributes with sacred ones: mouth/missionary times; eyes/prayers; and songs/hymns. These unresolved oppositions give us to understand that, while she has a transcendent quality, she nevertheless participates in history. She herself has a past: she has memories of Steinbeck's Cannery Row, which suggests humble beginnings, and she has a "magazine husband" who left her. Because she did not conform to the stereotypes which glossy advertisements had led him to expect? But because she is both a person and a symbol, she has a history which is more than personal. When we learn that the sea is at her feet, we realize that she is also the Statue of Liberty, which Dylan saw and pondered during his rides on the Staten Island ferry. This association with the Statue of Liberty means she represents the promise of the covenant, which has given American history a sacred as well as a profane meaning. Both these meanings are combined in what Robert Bellah has called "civic religion."

Once we understand her association with the covenant, we also understand who "they" are. They are, among other things, the Masters of War. They are all the people over the years who have broken America's covenant with God. The singer tells her that "they" have attempted to bury her by abolishing the covenant, and they intend to carry her as acolytes carry an icon in a religious procession. The fourth and eighth lines of each stanza contain other verbs which imply the profane rather than the sacred associations of these verbs in the first stanza: outguess/ impress/ just kiss/ resist/ mistake/ persuade/ employ; and, finally, destroy you.

Only one of these profanations has come to pass; in the fourth stanza which associates her with the Statue of Liberty, Dylan uses the past tense to describe what they have done. This stanza enumerates what the movers and shakers of American history have done to the covenant. They showed her "dead angels," the kind you would expect to find inside the silent gates of Eden, as symbols of their profanation of native American gods, perhaps, and mistook her as a justification for militarism. They wanted her to "accept the blame for the farm," that is, to resort to the covenant exculpate the nation from the shame of slavery.

The Lady has survived all this, but at a cost. She is "sad-eyed," an attribute which makes us think of Mary in a *Pieta*, grieving over the broken body of her crucified Son. But she is not doing this alone because there is a third character in the song, the prophet. Like the Lady, the prophet is "sad-eyed" because "no man comes." The Lady does not grieve for her son, but rather because she has no son. Has God turned His face from America because of her sins? Should we wait for deliverance in the future?

We listen to an unusually long, 32-bar coda of harmonica and organ which invites us to ponder the imponderables which we have just heard, and to balance the contradictions of our American identity. More than anything else in rock 'n' roll, "Sad-Eyed Lady of the Lowlands" intensifies our sense of America as a country which, to repeat Greil Marcus' words, is too much to live up to and too much to ignore.

Clearly, Dylan's work makes great demands on the listener. That these demands do not become unreasonable and merely create frustration instead of fascination derives from Dylan's continued use of consistent stanza forms. We realize that they constitute as much of an innovation as his imagery when we recall that, ever since the thirties, the relationship between the verse and the chorus had been changing in popular song. The emergence of such stars as Frank Sinatra and Bing Crosby had produced an emphasis on the chorus at the expense of the verse. As in so many other ways, Dylan reverses this trend. Only occasionally, as in "Rainy Day Women #12 and 35," does he write a song with a catchy chorus which people go around singing to themselves. Usually, his songs have a chorus only insofar as the last line of each stanza contains, or refers to, the title. He invented a number of different stanza forms without definite models, although we can find some similarities in the work of the nineteenth century British poet, Robert Browning.

Michael Gray noticed that the rhymes sandals/vandals/handles in "Subterranean Homesick Blues" come from Browning's "Up in the Villa— Down in the City," a poem which exhibits various stanza forms.[32] The eighth stanza, for instance, rhymer *aabbcc*, which happens to be the rhyme scheme for "Highway 61 Revisited." The tenth stanza of the same poem rhymes *aabbcccdd* which is very close to the rhyme scheme of "Visions of Johanna," which is *aaabbbcc*. He seems to have learned one particular kind of rhyme from Browning, which is called a "mosaic rhyme." A mosaic rhyme consists of one word rhymed with a two-word phrase. Browning uses a number of mosaic rhymes in his virtuoso piece "Christmas-Eve and Easter-Day." such as "between us/genus," "appetite/clap it tight," and "affirm...any/Germany." Whether or not he got the idea from Browning, Dylan liked mosaic rhymes so much that he incorporated them into the stanza form of "Absolutely Sweet Marie." This song has a five-line stanza which rhymes *ababb*, where the *a* rhymes are consistently mosaic rhymes. Thus, in the first stanza Dylan rhymes "jump it/trumpet" and in the second stanza "half sick/traffic." To be sure, Tin Pan Alley songsmiths had sometimes used mosaic rhymes, such as "apartment/heart meant" in Cole Porter's "These Foolish Things," but hardly anyone else in the sixties had Dylan's discipline and verbal mastery to create such stable structures for his startling imagery. The tensions between his surrealistic, unpredictable images and his traditional, predictable stanzaic forms produces the extraordinary effects to which we responded so intensely.

But there's an odd fact about Dylan in the sixties. While no one disputes his preeminence, he had very few hits, as this chart shows:

Dylan's Top Ten Hits in the Sixties:

Song	Highest Position	Date
"Like a Rolling Stone"	7	7/24/65
"Positively 4th Street"	7	10/2/65
"Rainy Day Women #12 and #35 "	2	4/16/66
"Lay Lady Lay"	7	7/12/79

That's it. Two #2's and two #7's. Several dozen acts such as Sonny and Cher, the Rolling Stones and the Beatles, did better than this. So how did Dylan get to be such a big deal with so few hits?

The answer lies in the changed media situation. In 1965, the FCC decreed that radio stations which had both AM and FM must, in the future, broadcast different programming on each. Just as the advent of television had produced a great deal of air time when the comedy and variety shows moved from radio to television, so in the sixties this ruling produced a great deal of air time. Moreover, this air time was on FM frequencies, which could be used for broadcasting in stereo, so that listeners could appreciate the full effects on radio of the albums they liked. It was this ruling which produced the underground FM stations which played the best, and most innovative, rock in a serious context. These stations first put their format on the air in San Francisco, where they usually shared time with ethnic programming such as the Portugese Hour. As they spread to the other major market areas, they created a national audience for Dylan which Top 40 radio would never have given him. For one thing, his songs were too long to fit in between commercials. For another, they were too complicated. It was not especially pleasant to listen to "Visions of Johanna" while you were driving, because you couldn't puzzle out the imagery while also paying attention to stop lights, exit signs, and highway advertisements. In McLuhan's terms, these difficulties meant that underground FM stations, and the music which they played, obsolesced the implied situation of Top 40 listeners: the car. Underground FM stations, which played album cuts in stereo, created a new implied situation for listeners. Like Dylan in so many of his songs of the times, these implicit listeners were inside, in a crash pad, or a dorm room. Many listeners sat around and passed joints and bottles of wine; they were absorbed in themselves and in their separateness.

So it was not Dylan's fate to have the popular, and populist, appeal of Elvis and the Supremes. He never wrote any good boogie music: "Louie Louie" is more danceable and better body music than any of his masterpieces. No matter how much he wanted to be a populist, he had an elitist appeal which made up in its intensity what it lacked in numbers. It *was* his fate, however, to be recording at a time when a media complex was coming into being which could deliver his music to its proper audience.

The most striking fact about the two albums of Dylan's third period, *John Wesley Harding* and *Nashville Skyline*, is the way the opposition between anger and compassion songs, attenuated in his second period, disappears. All the songs on *John Wesley Harding* are compassion songs. This change means that, of the three oppositions with which he began, anger/compassion, social/ personal, and inside/outside, only inside/outside remains. Much else disappears as well, for Dylan seems to be obeying the dictum of the architect Mies van der Rohe, "Less is more." We can say, then, that his innovations continue, only less obviously.

The long lines, complicated stanza forms, and ingenious rhymes disappear. The allusions to movie stars and musicians disappear, as do the surrealistic images, electric guitars, and the mythological places such as "Desolation Row." Dylan no longer makes positive, startling connections; his flow of surrealistic imagery ceases after *Blonde on Blonde* and he replaces it with relationships. Dylan now starts by negating; every song on *John Wesley Harding* has one or more negative phrases, of which the following is only a partial list: "never known"; "no reason"; "without restraint"; "I don't call it anything"; "nothing is revealed"; "don't put a price"; "don't dismiss"; "without family or friends"; and so forth. In this minimalist esthetic, names which do not have external connections such as Tom Paine and St. Augustine generally disappear, to be replaced by roles: "drifter"; "judge"; "hobo"; "immigrant." These roles imply situations, not places. The deliberately truncated style of the lyrics makes every word count. In such stylized rhetoric the archaic diction of folk songs reappears in phrases like "the fairest damsel."

We can think of these changes as a resolution of the contradiction which pervades Dylan's second period. On one hand, Dylan proclaimed that he wasn't different from anyone, that he was not a leader of a movement; on the other hand, he often gave people advice about how to live their lives, such as the famous "Don't Follow leaders" from "Subterranean Homesick Blues," The issue was, "By what authority do you, Bob Dylan, tell people to question authority—or to do anything else?" In the context of the late sixties, he couldn't give a meaningful answer to this question, so he stopped giving advice and stopped creating mythological places. In his third period, he gives advice in only two songs. "The Ballad of Frankie Lee and Judas Priest" and "I Threw It All Away," but the advice is so general that no one could seriously argue with it.

Dylan is still asking however, us to contrast his songs with other songs. "I Dreamed I Saw St. Augustine" provocatively contrasts with the protest song which Joan Baez was performing a lot, "Joe Hill," which begins "I dreamed I Saw Joe Hill." By playing off the martyred and potentially sanctified union organizer against the father of the church, Dylan calls our attention again to the interrelationships between the sacred and the profane.

Another opposition which has been implicit all along breaks down—the opposition between society and the singer. If the society has sinned, the singer cannot deny his own participation in that sin, and thus cannot unambiguously condemn that sin ("I Dreamed I Saw St. Augustine"). A tension grows between this participation in a sinful world and the negations of the songs, as we realize that the theme of the album is the relationship between society and the individual. Hence, Dylan needs only one symbolic woman, such as Johanna or the Sad-Eyed Lady, and she has no name. This music, incidentally, has the effect of obsolescing such oppositions in society as rock/country and western, and hippie/redneck. Dylan specifically negates these oppositions by having Johnny Cash join in with him on "Girl from the North Country" on *Nashville Skyline*. Dylan had always known that there was no reason to turn off the country music stations.

As an album with a coherent theme, the relationship between the society and the individual, *John Wesley Harding* is a concept album, and as such has a definite progression. It begins with historical individuals who are outside, with the threat which outside always implies in Dylan, and thus involved in society and history. It then moves inside, to personal relationships which deny society and history. The album begins with the title cut. "John Wesley Harding," a song which exaggerates and undercuts, the frontier/John Wayne/ *High Noon* myth by giving our hero a gun "in ev'ry hand." Despite all this artillery, the song does not enumerate any positive accomplishments. When he leaves, the situation is "all but straightened out"—he has no commitment to see things through. All we know for sure is that no one has filed charges against him, and that no one knows of a foolish move on his part.

Another historical figure who represents social commitment, Tom Paine, appears in "As I Went Out One Morning." We might think of this song as narrated by Harding himself. The tension in it derives from the opposition between Tom Paine, who is named no less than three times, and the mysterious fair damsel in chains. She may represent the dark side of the Sad-Eyed Lady who can harm the hero by chaining him to something external. As a deist, Tom Paine represents purely secular commitment, of the kind that Joe Hill had, and apologizes "for what she's done." He does the right thing for the wrong reason.

The remaining ten songs on the album resolve themselves into pairs as well, although not all of them follow each other. If the first two songs deal with the meaning of social commitment, "I Dreamed I Saw St. Augustine" and "I Pity the Poor Immigrant" confront the meaning of participation in a sinful world. St. Augustine is known for his docrine of original sin, which had great influence on Martin Luther, and therefore on Protestantism in general. Yet the impetus for the founding of America was to escape from sin, and thus to kill St. Augustine. The song concludes when the singer realizes the futility of what he has done. The song paired with it, "I Pity the Poor Immigrant," is Dylan's most general statement of compassion for Americans, for we are all immigrants, except for the native Americans whom we killed, and the blacks whom we enslaved. This man, alienated from life as well as death, with his unsatisfiable needs, symbolizes the American on the make, and he most of all deserves our compassion when his dreams come true. For then he realizes that neither fortune nor fame ought to be what they claim.

In addition to these songs on social commitment and sin, the other paired songs on the album include songs on financial success ("Dear Landlord" and "Ballad of Frankie Lee and Judas Priest"); justice ("Drifter's Escape" and "I Am a Lonesome Hobo"), and honesty ("All Along the Watchtower" and "The Wicked Messenger"). "The Wicked Messenger" is particularly interesting because it is Dylan's last song about art. The messenger is presumably a performer of some kind, he makes his bed "behind the assembly hall." He is caught between his audience and his conscience. His audience wants only good news, that is, the comforting happy endings which predominate in American popular culture. But the messenger says that the soles of his feet are burning; in order to meet this demand, he cannot draw his strength from the land on which he lives. As Frost wrote in an unforgettable line, "The land was ours before we were the land's." *John Wesley Harding* does have a happy ending, but like the happy endings of Frank Capra's films, it is an earned happy ending. The final pair of songs celebrate love, first outside in a social context ("Down Along the Cove"), and then inside with a denial of the external world, the past, and the future ("I'll Be Your Baby Tonight"). Significantly, it is only on these two songs that we hear Pete Drake's steel guitar, with all the sentimental associations which it conveys in country and western music.

Just as the Beatles interpolate a chorus of "She Loves You" into "All You Need Is Love," so Dylan begins *Nashville Skyline* with a re-recording of "Girl from the North Country," to show the contrast between the past and the present. He can sing it as a throwaway duet with Johnny Cash because he has worked through the complex series of oppositions which growing up in America imposes on us all. Only now can he celebrate the traditional American joys of being inside and being in love. There remains, however, the need to confess past misdeeds ("I Threw It All Away"), and the problem of mistrust ("Tell Me That It Isn't True"), and these discordant notes remind us that the problems of personal identity in America are not like math problems—they do not just get solved and go away. They keep recurring, so Dylan keeps confronting them.

Only at the beginning did Dylan tell his admirers what they wanted to hear. They wanted simple answers to simplistic problems and they imposed those simple answers on the enigmatic "Blowin' in the Wind." The truth is, American audiences are as diverse as American music, and no one can please all of those audiences all the time. So Dylan, as the dominant force in American music in the sixties, proceeded to alienate one or more parts of his audience with everything he did. He admired Hank Williams, but he alienated the Southerners who also admired Hank Williams by writing protest songs like "Oxford Town." The folkies didn't know Hank Williams very well, but he alienated them by playing electric guitar, like the Beatles. He alienated many Beatles fans by writing songs which no one would play on Top 40 radio. At the end of the sixties, he alienated the hippies who were into acid rock by recording a mellow country and western album. So it went, and so it goes.

What Dylan's fans wanted from him, more than anything, else was the reassurance that they didn't need to change. He understood, in ways which he couldn't articulate, that to believe that media experiences in the modern world unambiguously referred to something in the external world was to live in the past. He further understood that it is dangerous, both personally and socially, to live in the past. (The danger of living in the past is a favorite theme in the films of both Alfred Hitchcock and Orson Welles.) When he matured as an artist, he broadened his social commitment to include putting people through changes which would get their heads together—as we would have said at the time. But his audiences had to earn those changes, and any explanations of his songs would have dissipated their power to create them.

These considerations made the A.J. Weberman phenomenon understandable and symbolic. A.J. Weberman proclaimed himself a Dylanologist, by which he meant that he devoted himself to castrating Dylan's songs by reducing them to biographical references. This was nothing more than old-fashioned romantic reductionism, which people had been practicing for over a century. But Weberman in his trivialization of Dylan's work struck a responsive chord in many people. Like Dostoyevsky's Grand Inquisitor, Weberman acquired a popular following because he relieved people of the responsibility for their lives. After all, if Dylan's songs are nothing more than diary entries, they don't have anything to do with us, and with the always threatening changes which we need to make.

Notes

[1]Quoted in Bob Dylan, A Retrospective, Craig McGregor, ed. (New York: William Morrow, 1972), p. 84.

[2]Tristan Tzara, Seven Dada Manifestos and Lampisteries, Barbara Wright, trans. (London: John Calder, 1977), p. 1.

[3]Quoted in *Futurist Manifestos,* Umbrio Apollonio, ed.; R.W. Flint et al. trans. (New York: The Viking Press, 1973), p. 31.

[4] *Ibid.,* p. 74.

[5] *Ibid.,* p. 98.

[6] *Writings and Drawings of Bob Dylan* (New York: Alfred E. Knopf, 1974), p. 106.

[7]Quoted in *Bob Dylan. A Retrospective,* p. 84.

[8] *Ibid.,* p. 308.

[9]Woody Guthrie, *Bound for Glory* (New York: E.P. Dutton, 1968), p. 217.

[10] *Ibid.,* p. 218.

[11] *Ibid.,* p. 249.

[12]Quoted in *Bob Dylan, A Retrospective,* p. 59.

[13] Ernest Hemingway, *A Farewell to Arms* (New York: Charles Scribner's Sons, n.d., p. 314.

[14]Anthony Scaduto, *Bob Dylan* (New York: Grosset and Dunlap, 1971), p. 82.

[15] *French Symbolist Poetry,* John Porter Houston and Mona Tobin Houston, trans. (Bloomington: Indiana U. Press, 1980), p. 75.

[16]Marshall McLuhan, *Understanding Media: The Extensions of Man* (New York: McGraw-Hill, 1964), p. 64.

[17]Quoted in *Ibid.* p. 65.

[18]*Ibid.,* p. 16.

[19]*Ibid.,* p. 50.

[20]*Ibid.,* p. 53.

[21]*Ibid.,* p. 54.

[22]*Writings and Drawings by Bob Dylan,* p. 182.

[23]*Ibid.,* p. 158.

[24]*Ibid.,* p. 80.

[25]There's an informative analogy between Hemingway's and Dylan's relationship to leftist society. When Hemingway remained true to his art by refusing to treat the Spanish Civil War in a partisan spirit in *For Whom the Bell Tolls,* it caused him to fall from favor with Greenwich Village leftists such as Max Eastman. In the sixties, "Mississippi is this generation's Spain," as an article in The Times put it, and in the sixties Dylan remained true to *his* art by refusing to treat the Movement as a truth in black and white. Not surprisingly, he fell from favor with the heirs of Max Eastman, who still lived in Greenwich Village and who still hadn't learned anything about art.

[26]Guthrie, *Bound for Glory,* p. 238.

[27]Betsy Bowden was the first to notice this. See her *Performed Literature* (Bloomington: Indiana U. Press, 1982), p. 107.

[28]*Ibid.,* p. 80.

[29]*Ibid.,* p. 89.

[30]*Ibid.,* p. 90.

[31]McLuhan, *Understanding Media,* p. 163.

[32]Michael Gray, *Song and Dance Man. The Art of Bob Dylan* (New York: St. Martin's Press, 1981), p. 68.

Chapter 13:
High Culture as Popular Culture

Dylan as Picasso? Paul Simon as Robert Frost? Don't such comparisons just make pretentious claims for rock 'n' roll? It's only rock 'n' roll, right? Not in the sixties, it wasn't. It makes no sense to debate the association between high culture and popular culture as an abstract truth; what does make sense is to consider what we know about the formative experiences of both the audience and the performers in the sixties. These experiences differed in America and in England, so it seems best to take each country in turn.

Landon Jones says in his book *Great Expectations:*

What we would later call the generation gap was at first an education gap. Eighty-five percent of the baby boomers born from 1947 to 1951 completed high school, compared to only 38 percent of their parents. More than half of them had gone to college, a proportion unthinkable in their parents' era. The baby boom will always seem different from other generations if only because no generation, before it or after it, produced so many college graduates.[1]

Jones cites overwhelming statistics to show how higher education formed the sensibility of the baby boomers. In the years from 1964 to 1970, from Beatlemania until just after Altamont, more than 20 million kids entered the period between the ages of 18 and 24.

The result was a $100-million boom in higher education. In the decade from 1963 to 1973, total enrollment at all institutions of higher learning doubled from 4.7 million to 9.6 million—five times as many students as were enrolled in 1940. The annual growth rate of college rose from 2 percent to nearly 9 percent.[2]

The day had passed when America reserved a college education for its elite. The American kids who were going to college in such huge numbers didn't necessarily learn to love Beethoven, yet no matter how much they griped about the lack of relevance of their classes, they lost some of their defensiveness about high culture. After all, it was the very demand for relevance that made people open alternative universities where courses in Dylan were taught. And after all, it was these kids who made up the sellout crowd in New York's Metropolitan Opera House when The Who performed *Tommy* there on March 7, 1970. This performance of the first rock opera at a prestigious opera house represented a culmination of five years of unprecedented association between popular culture and high culture. Never before had the performers and the audience shared so much interest in, and awareness of, high culture.

173

This interest and awareness appears in, among other things, the names which groups chose for themselves. Here as elsewhere the sixties marked a break with the past. Group names indicate how the performers want to present themselves to their audience, and names have undergone an evolution of their own.

If we begin with black groups in the fifties, we notice that they often had code names which marked them as black. This tendency begins at least as early as the Inkspots, but the Ravens, the Crows, the Penguins and even Hank Ballard and the Midnighters come to mind. Then came bird groups such as the Orioles and the Flamingos. By contrast, the Crew-cuts were clean-cut white kids, and the Four Freshmen appealed to college audiences. It is fair to say that most groups in the fifties had names which identified them in some way.

It was girl groups such as the Shangri-Las and the Dixie Cups that created the first major break with descriptive names which referred to the performers, although it was not a complete one. The Beatles played what the British called Beat Music, and the Rolling Stones paid homage to Muddy Waters in their name, so that you knew they were a blues-based group. Later American groups, especially on the West Coast had deliberately silly, non-referential names, of which The Chocolate Watch Band and The Peanut Butter Conspiracy are two of my favorites.

But the truly startling change came when major groups gave themselves names which didn't describe them or their music; rather, they took their names from something which they shared with their audience—high culture. No one had ever done this before, but it made sense in the sixties, as the following table shows.

Sixties Groups Whose Names Have Literary Sources

Group Name	Source
Big Brother	George Orwell's *1984* (1948)
The Doors	Aldous Huxley's *The Doors of Perception* (1955)
Steppenwolf	Herman Hesse's *Steppenwolf* (1927)
Blood Sweat and Tears	Winston Churchill, Speech before the House of Commons, 13 May 1940: "I have nothing to offer but blood, toil, tears and sweat."
The Ides of March	William Shakespeare's *Julius Caesar* I, ii, 18 "Beware the ides of March."

Notice that Blood Sweat and Tears and the Ides of March have names which come at the end of a quotation, so that to get it you have to know the first part as well. Since almost all American kids have to read *Julius Caesar* in high school, that Shakespearian tag is especially indicative. Furthermore, these names as well as that of Big Brother promise something threatening. Music was so loud and so heavy that it did have an agressive quality—so that it is no surprise that in 1969 a group formed which called itself War.

This use of high culture came from the fact that a new socio-ethnic group entered popular music in the years 1964-69: middle-class white kids who had gone to good suburban high schools as well as college. Aside from the Motown groups, Sly and the Family Stone, Jimi Hendrix, Otis Redding, and a few others, the major rock acts were white. Let's take the personnel of the following sixties bands: Buffalo Springfield, The Byrds, The Doors, Iron Butterfly, Jefferson Airplane, the Lovin' Spoonful, and the Mamas and the Papas. In the specific case of the Buffalo Springfield, the group consisted of: Neil Young, Stephen Stills, Richie Furay, Dewey Martin, and Bruce Palmer. No ethnic names there at all. In fact, there are only three ethnic names in all of these groups put together: Zal Yankowski of the Lovin' Spoonful (Jewish); Ray Manzarek of The Doors (Czech); and Jorma Kaukonen of the Jefferson Airplane (Finnish).

Most of these WASP kids had not only gone to good high schools, they had also gotten into good colleges, where they dropped out after listening to the Beatles. Janis Joplin dropped out of the University of Texas, as Grace Slick had dropped out of Manhattanville College, where she had taken classes with Tricia Nixon. Jim Morrison dropped out of two schools, Florida State and UCLA, and, remarkable as it may seem, John Phillips of The Mamas and the Papas, had dropped out of West Point! While people often said that these kids were rebelling against American society, they were in fact too much a part of it to rebel in any consistent way. They just wanted to re-define it a little, and they did.

The question of what Jewish musicians did for rock in the sixties is an interesting one. While Bob Dylan, Paul Simon, and Art Garfunkel are clearly of major importance, they didn't make mainstream rock, music you could dance to, and after them, there's only two short-lived groups, the Paul Butterfield Blues Band, and the Blues Project, also known as the Jewish Beatles. On the other hand, the role of Jews in entrepreneurial roles increased. More than any other non-performer, Bill Graham made San Francisco what it was in the late sixties. Clive Davis as president of Columbia Records signed up Big Brother and other West Coast acts after Monterey Pop. Jerry Wexler produced Aretha Franklin's legendary sessions at Atlantic and Lou Adler managed the Mamas and the Papas. Meanwhile, a group of articulate writers, most of whom worked for *Rolling Stone,* were creating the new genre of rock criticism. They included Jonathan Eisen, Jon Landau, Greil Marcus, and Robert Cristgau.

Simon and Garfunkel represent one way of merging high culture and popular culture; they were very much New York Jewish intellectuals, yet their music came from the same milieu as Dylan's—the Greenwich Village folk clubs, most notably Gerde's Folk City. The Doors represent another way of doing the same thing. Although Jim Morris grew up in Florida, The Doors were as much a LA group as Simon and Garfunkel were a New York group. If Simon and Garfunkel sang sweetly, The Doors came at you with their loud, driving music.

Art Garfunkel published, as liner notes on *Wednesday Morning 3 AM*, a letter which he wrote to Paul Simon. In it he says, "There may or may not be a market for intellectuality." As it turned out, there was a market for intellectuality plus Everly Brothers harmonies, once Tom Wilson had dubbed an electric guitar and drums onto their acoustic version of "The Sounds of Silence." Art just didn't realize what the baby boom had done to college enrollments. But the fact that Art would wonder about it so self-consciously and so publicly reminds us of how alienated the folkies were from Brill Building Pop and Motown. In fact, there were a number of affinities between the audience for Beethoven in New York, and the audience for folk music in New York, between Gerde's Folk City downtown, and the newly opened Lincoln Center uptown. Both of these seemingly different venues attracted relatively small audiences. Both audiences had great disdain for music which attracted large audiences and both audiences believed in the purity of the music which they liked, and in the superiority of New York to the rest of America. More important, both audiences devoted themselves to the music of a culture which was not their own. The people who went to Lincoln Center to hear Beethoven were paying homage to a foreign culture; the people who went to Gerde's Folk City to hear Mance Lipscomb were also paying homage to a foreign culture. It was these affinities that caused the best of the folkies to break with acoustic music, and it was these affinities taken as a group which constitute the much-disputed "it" in *Bringing It All Back Home*.

When major acts of the sixties merged high culture and popular culture, usually what happened is that the lyrics came from high culture and the music and instrumentation came from popular culture. Paul Simon conceded to a reporter from *The New Yorker* (an appropriate magazine for him) that "Maybe it's English major stuff."[3] But he needn't have felt so defensive about his lyrics, since there were plenty of English majors listening to him. They could pick up on the oxymorons of "The Sounds of Silence," since they themselves had found similar passages in the English metaphysical poets who had inspired Paul. They appreciated the association of high culture and popular culture in the phrase "From Tolstoy to Tinker Bell" in "Cloudy." They had read Edward Arlington Robinson's poem "Richard Cory," which Paul set to music with an insistent drum beat. These youngsters perceived themselves and their environment in esthetic terms, so that when the singer describes his situation as "a still-life water color" on "The Dangling Conversation," it made sense to them. And even if they didn't realize that "For Emily, Wherever I May Find Her" referred to Emily Dickinson, they could certainly appreciate Art's exquisite voice.

It is a cliche to say that in the twentieth century art and love replaced religion, as when Catherine Barkley tells Frederic, "You are my religion," in *A Farewell to Arms*. Paul's version of this occurs in "Kathy's Song": "The only truth I know is you." Affected by the same loss of sanctity in the world which affected Dylan, Paul appropriated the Christ imagery of high culture in "Sparrow" and "Blessed." At other times, nothing remains but a Sartrean sense of individual existence, as on "Patterns" where the bongo drums give an aural equivalent of the repetitiveness of existence suggested in the lyrics. Only rarely do his lyrics and his jazz-influenced guitar lines deny the covenant in favor of hedonism, as in "Fifty-Ninth Street Bridge Song (Feelin' Groovy)."

My dictionary defines "Phillippic," as in Paul's "A Simple Desultory Phillippic," as "any discourse or speech of bitter denunciation," and while it doesn't exactly denounce Dylan, it certainly pokes fun at him. The nonsensical lyrics of the first verse make one reference after another to figures from high culture, as Dylan was doing at the time, and on the second verse, Paul parodies Dylan's drawl and harmonica. To make sure everybody gets the point, Paul drawls, "It's All right ma, everybody must get stoned." At the end, he mumbles, "I lost my harmonica, Albert," which all the insiders knew to be a reference to Dylan's relationship with Albert Grossman. This song is the first recorded reaction to Dylan as the major force in American music, but it is not the only one in Simon and Garfunkel. The lyrics of "Flowers Never Bend With the Rainfall" has a Dylanesque use of rain and the tambourine gives it a Dylanesque sound.

Dylan affected all the folkies in one way or another, and we can take an album by Judy Collins, *Wildflowers*, as a case in point. After recording a number of Dylan's songs on earlier albums, Collins showed that she had fully assimilated his surrealistic, evocative imagery in her wonderful song "Albatross." The eclecticism of this album shows how artistically a folkie could blend high culture and popular culture. It contains two songs by her West Coast counterpart, Joni Mitchell, three songs by the poet Leonard Cohen, and one song—sung in French—by Jacques Brel. The music for *Wildflowers* was arranged and conducted by Joshua Rifkin, who had studied at Princeton and the Juilliard School of Music. Rifkin's principal areas of interest are Renaissance and Baroque music, which probably accounts for the presence on the album of a ballad—sung in Italian—by the blind Italian composer Francesco Landini (ca. 1325-1397). The variety of musical styles on *Wildflowers* is as typical of the sixties as is the album's title.

Things were different on the West Coast. If Simon and Garfunkel created a sound in Greenwich Village, The Doors created a sound at UCLA film school. For Simon and Garfunkel's estheticism, The Doors offered theatricality. For Simon and Garfunkel's sincerity, The Doors—which is to say Jim Morrison— offered sexuality.

Although Jim didn't know it, while "Light My Fire" was #1, his father was promoted to admiral in the U.S. Navy. So it wasn't just his fame and money that made him different. As his biographers say, "Jim's education, intelligence, and background further separated him from many of his fans.... Whether he liked it or not, he was the obvious product of a Southern upper-middle-class family: charming, goal-oriented, and in many ways politically conservative."[4]

Like Dylan, Morrison claimed that he was an orphan (his own brother Andy didn't know that Jim was singing on "Light My Fire" until he recognized him on the album cover), and astonished interviewers by paraphrasing the precepts of modern art. Richard Goldstein reported about Jim that "He suggests you read Nietzsche on the nature of tragedy to understand where he is really at. His eyes glow as he launches into a discussion of the Apollonian-Dionysian struggle for control of the life force."[5] Jim was thinking here of Friedrich Nietzsche's *The Birth of Tragedy from the Spirit of Music* (1872), which has had a great impact on modern artists. In it Nietzsche audaciously reversed the usual reverence for Socrates by saying that Socrates began the split between mind and body, roughly between the Apollonian and Dionysian, by intellectualizing. However, says Nietzsche, there is hope because Wagner's music is reuniting mind and body, as well as philosophy and myth. These arguments had as much appeal for Jim as they had had for T.S. Eliot and Marshall McLuhan, who had also drawn on them. But Jim was a singer, and he could think of his performances as living embodiments of Nietzsche's ideas. In particular, "When the Music's Over" has a strongly Nietzschean quality, in its association of the power of music to make you "dance on fire," and in its affirmation that the alternative is death.

Jim also found inspiration in the writings of the French playwright and theorist Antonin Artaud. Much taken with Nietzsche, Artaud wanted to abolish the opposition between high culture and popular culture, by which he meant what McLuhan later called oral culture. Artaud took Mayan hieroglyphics and Balinese dance as models for his "theater of cruelty"—a theater experience which would transfigure its audience. He denounced the constrictions of written texts and stage sets. It was not as far from UCLA, where Jim read Artaud, to the Whiskey A Go Go, where The Doors got their first big break, as it may have seemed.

To read Artaud's essays is to feel oneself at the source of the Doors' performances. Their song "Break On Through," for instance, is surely a gloss on Artaud's statement, "To break through language in order to touch life is to create or recreate the theater."[6] On the same page, Artaud says that "This leads to the rejection of the usual limitations of man and man's powers, and infinitely extends the frontiers of what is called reality."[7], which in turn led Jim to tell interviewers that he was testing the limits of reality.

Thinking of the unifying role of myth in oral societies such as that of Bali, Artaud wrote. "The true purpose of the theater is to create Myths."[8] Other modern artists such as T.S. Eliot and Igor Stravinsky had the same thought. Stravinsky wrote an oratorio, *Oedipus Rex*, with a text by the French poet Jean Cocteau. But the singers just stood there and sang, and they sang in Latin at that. Artaud hated it: "And if, for example, a contemporary public does not understand *Oedipus Rex,* I shall made bold to say that it is the fault of *Oedipus Rex* and not of the public."[9] Artaud's insistence on the need for intense emotional contact between performer and audience makes him sound like a populist here, and makes him the probable source for Morrison's version of the Oedipus myth in "The End." Thanks to the presence of FM underground stations and an audience which sensed a need to exorcise (a favorite word of Artaud's) its literacy, Jim could create a performance piece which made the myth real and immediate.

In "The End," Jim mentions neither Sophocles or Oedipus by name. He didn't have to because most of his audience had read Sophocles or Freud, or both. So his protagonist takes "a face from the ancient gallery," and that suffices. "The End" begins with brooding guitar arpeggios with some echo; even the tambourines sound ominous. When Jim begins to sing we notice an atmospheric echo to his voice. We don't exactly know what the "blue bus" is but then we don't need to.

Jim serves as both narrator and protagonist. He refers to the "killer" who is not yet a killer, of course, and that he "paid a visit" to the brother's and sister's room, thus situating the action in a familiar suburban house. In the confrontation with his parents Jim becomes Oedipus: "Father, I want to kill you." Because of the censorship, he couldn't tell his mother what he wanted to do to her, at least not clearly, so he screams over the crashing cymbals and throbbing guitar chords. He was in effect proving Artaud wrong when Artaud said, "No one in Europe knows how to scream anymore."[10] In his use of the Oedipus myth in "The End," Jim was in effect showing that there was no meaningful difference between the education gap and the generation gap.

Artaud thought that theater should involve "the exteriorization of a kind of essential drama."[11] Consistent with this, and with everything that Artaud meant by the Theater of Cruelty, Jim sings, "it hurts to set you free." The "you" is the Oedipus complex itself, which is also a part of the performer. As a result, we don't know whether this simply takes place in his head, or what. The point, though, is that we don't need to know, since the power of the "The End" lies in its effect as ritual exorcism, and that power had an immediacy which no one in the late sixties could deny.

In England people don't think of high culture and popular culture in the same way as we Americans do. The following story about Gene Vincent by Jack Good, who brought rock 'n' roll to BBC Television, illustrates the point.

"Fortunately, Vincent suffered from a bad leg—having fallen off a motorbike—and wore leg irons. This gave me the clue. As he limped, I saw that he must become a Richard III figure, dressed entirely in black, including black gloves. He must hunch his shoulders and lurch in sinister fashion toward the camera before singing. I arranged on his first television appearance for him to walk down several flights of stairs so that his limp would be emphasized. I even gave him a medallion to wear around his neck to make him look more Shakespearean. When I saw him gingerly trying to negotiate the steps, I had to run round the back of the set and shout, 'Limp, you bugger, limp.' "[12]

Try to imagine Dick Clark presenting Gene Vincent as Richard III, and you will immediately understand something important about the social context of British rock. Because the Old Boys dominate the media, the role played by Jewish entrepreneurs in America is played in England by graduates of Oxford and Cambridge. Thus, Kit Lambert, a graduate of Trinity College, Oxford, who managed the Who in the sixties, is the brother of composer Constance Lambert.

British rockers drew more on classical music than their American counterparts. Jeff Beck based his "Beck's Bolero" on Ravel's "Bolero," and Procol Harum based their ravishing "A Whiter Shade of Pale" on the Bach Cantata "Sleepers Awake." (The lyrics come from an Old English poem of the same name.) The Beatles' "Because" is based on Beethoven's "Moonlight Sonata" played backwards, and Paul McCartney got the idea of using the B flat trumpet on "Penny Lane" at a performance of Bach's Brandenburg Concertos. Rather more startling, because of its juxtaposition with Mick Jagger's lascivious voice, is the Rolling Stones' use of a harpsichord on "Lady Jane." And Pete Townshend says that the chords for "I'm a Boy" and "Pinball Wizard" come from the seventeenth-century British composer Henry Purcell.[14]

In the sixties England sent a smaller percentage of its young people to college than any other European country with the exception of Turkey. As a result, where did the youth pick up its awareness of art and culture? As Simon Frith has observed, the answer is art school, a British institution which has no American equivalent.

One of the most obvious sociological characteristics of British rock musicians, particularly of those who emerged in the classic 1960s period, is an art-school background. (John Lennon, Keith Richard, Ray Davies, Peter Townshend, Eric Clapton, Jimmy Page, David Bowie—this list of the most famous only hints at the extent to which art school is a normal part of the rock career.)[15]

To Frith's list we need to add the names of Ron Wood, Ian Drury, and Bryan Ferry. Clearly, something was happening here at a place which turned out the leaders of the Rolling Stones, the Beatles, the Who, the Kinks, and Led Zeppelin.

The art school in England is an institution designed to prepare kids to go into advertising and the like. But in the early sixties it was more than a mere vocational school; it was a lively place tolerant of nonconformity where Pop Artists such as Peter Blake taught. (Blake designed the cover for *Sargeant Pepper*). It was at least in part because of his art school background that John Lennon was so receptive to Yoko's dada and minimalist ideas. But the British rocker on whom art school had the greatest impact was Pete Townshend, who went to Ealing Art College.

At Ealing Pete heard lectures by such artists as Jasper Johns and Larry Rivers, and learned that the old distinction between high culture and popular culture no longer made any sense. Ealing helped prepare him to write the first rock opera. But he was able to write *Tommy* only because an odd combination of personal and social factors gave him the attitudes of an alienated modern artist.

Townshend grew up thinking that he was ugly because he had such a big nose. He was also influenced by the Mod movement which the music of the Who expressed. To understand the meaning of The Who you have to understand Mod.

Mod was the response of working-class youth in the London area during the early sixties to a contradiction. On the one hand, when they left school at 15 and went to work, they could begin to enjoy the new consumer culture. On the other hand, as Tom Wolfe so trenchantly put it in his essay on Mod, "There is hardly a kid in all of England who harbors any sincere hope of advancing himself in any very striking way by success at work."[16] In this situation, the Mods resorted to a democratization of the Beau Brummel syndrome. About the only thing in their lives which they could control was their clothing, so that they became obsessed with clothing. Let's listen to Peter Meaden, the Who's first manager, on the meaning of clothing for a Mod.

"You see, when you're a Mod you need things tailor made. The jacket has to be tailor made, the shoes have to just right—you do understand that? The detail is like custom built, b-i-l-t-custom built—and you shoot a man if his shoulders are wrong, you know? You just don't go back. You just look at him and you feel ill, you know?[17]

As Beau Brummel had compensated for his loss of status by narcissistic self-involvement, so the Mods 150 years later compensated for their denial of status by narcissistic self-involvement. It seems remarkable to me that no one has noticed the similarity between the Mods and early Elvis, the "hillbilly cat." Surely "Blue Suede Shoes" was the first Mod song. Memphis rednecks and London working-class kids hated being outcasts and responded to their situation in essentially the same way—through their clothing.

Mod clothing was an end in itself; "the point is not making it with girls...the point is simply immersing yourself for one hour in The Life, every lunch hour,"[18] as Tom Wolfe put it. This overwhelming importance of appearance explains some essential things about The Who. For one thing, it explains why their audiences at the gritty Goldhawk Club in Shepherd's Bush, where they started out, was almost all male.

For another, the Mod obsession with appearance combined with the British dramatic tradition to create a strongly theatrical quality to The Who's performances. They used Marshall amps to play louder than anyone else. And then there's the matter of Pete's stage mannerisms. He would strum his guitar in great windmill-like arcs of his right arm, do splits in in the air, and then destroy his guitars and the amps. Inspired by Pete, Keith would kick over his drum kit. In his book on The Who, Dave Marsh says that Pete got the idea from a lecture by the Austrian artist Gustav Metzke when Metzke exhibited paintings which he had dipped in acid. The various stages of erosion were supposedly a new form of beauty. Be that as it may, Pete's awareness of auto-destruction doesn't explain why the audience liked it when Pete smashed his guitars. His audience didn't respond to what Pete did because Pete was simply acting out his own self-hatred and frustration; the audience responded to it because it meant something to them in that particular setting.

As a spectacle, rock concerts create a disparity between the effort which the musicians exert and the volume which they create. Very little effort generates very great volume—given enough Marshall amps. This disparity gives a sense of incompleteness and unease, so the musicians compensate, rather as Elvis had compensated when electricity cleared the stage in the fifties. Pete's electric Rickenbacker gave him the freedom to strum his chords in a spectacular manner. It's noteworthy that acoustic guitarists never used such histrionics or banged up their instruments, and that this performance style began with one of the earliest electric guitarists, T-Bone Walker. But the technology had a demonic quality, too, for it produced a volume of noise which engulfed the Mods rather as the surrounding society engulfed them. So to use the guitars and amps and then smash them was to create a sound environment and then destroy it—an act which gave a cartharsis to the Mod need for power and the Mod frustration. One consequence of their extraordinary theatricality was that for years The Who were primarily a live act, and despite the success of "My Generation," had recurring difficulties in making the record charts, especially in America.

The narcissism and frustration of the Mods also explains something which makes the music of The Who unique for its time—the lack of love songs. With the exception of "Substitute," they don't address any of their major songs, such as "My Generation" or "I Can't Explain" or "I'm Free" or "Pinball Wizard" to girls. They don't even treat girls as sex objects. The only theme that matters to Townshend in the sixties is achieving identity by overcoming the isolation of the Mod style.

The theatricality of The Who's performance style, which depended on volume, and their lack of love songs may have something to do with an unusual feature of their music. While "My Generation" has something of the call-and-response feel of the talking blues on which it is based, as do "Can't Explain" and "The Magic Bus," their music is primarily a music of minimal differences. It is intervals of only a tone or a halftone that create what melody there is in "I Don't Know Myself" and "I'm Free." Pete is known for his use of suspended, or sus, chords, which diverge by a tone or a halftone from the tonic; seven of the fifteen chords in the introduction to "Pinball Wizard" are sus chords. Sus chords lend themselves to being played at 100-120 decibels with lots of sustain, for no one can play or sing unusual melodies at that volume. Since there are no lyrics about love in The Who's music, there is also nothing like the one-octave release in the chorus of "I Want to Hold Your Hand."

I can sum up what all this has to do with high culture by saying that the one line for which The Who will always be remembered, "Hope I die before I get old," amounts to a reworking of Oscar Wilde's "The Picture of Dorian Gray." In Wilde's story, the picture ages but Dorian himself does not. Thus it makes sense to say that the Mods also had historical ties to turn-of-the century gays like Wilde. Both groups felt a similar alienation from the British Establishment. Gays have played a major role in modern art, since its basic theme is alienation of one kind or another.

Pete acted out the role of the modern artist in creating *Tommy* and found sympathy with his ideas in Kit Lambert. Lambert's Oxford background left him indifferent to rock as such (he first sought out The Who because he hoped to use them in a film), and he urged Pete to develop rock into an operatic form. This seemed both attractive and desirable to Pete, but when he started working on *Tommy,* he found himself yet again in another version of the bind which had created the Mod movement in the first place. This time the bind was more cultural than social, although the two aspects were related. The issue was rebellion, and its different meanings in high culture and popular culture in England. As Dave Marsh explains,

Within the century-old conventions of music hall tradition, rebellion was not a concept, much less an issue. Within the context of high art, rebellion was not only a possibility—in modernist terms, it was a necessity. But high art rebellion was the province of avant-gardism, which was in theory and in practice innately hostile to the mass culture of which rock was perhaps the most articulate (and certainly the angriest and least apologetic) part.[19]

But the rebellion of such essential avant-garde works as Picasso's "Les Demoiselles d'Avignon" and Stravinsky's *The Rites of Spring* caused such furors, even among other artists, that they had to be explained. The twentieth century became a century of theories and manifestoes and explanations as no other previous century had been. Tom Wolfe put it this way, "In short, the new order of things in the art world was: first you get the word, and then you can see."[20] In the sixties, first you had to understand "what the artist was trying to do," and then you could understand the work. When he was working on *Tommy,* Pete got into the act by giving interviews in which he explained what he wanted to do.

Dave Marsh, who read them all, says that there are literally hundreds of these interviews in both the British and American press. In them Pete did what Dylan and Jim Morrison were doing at the same time: he paraphrased avant-grade theorists like Artaud on self-hatred and the like, with similar effects. The journalists were mesmerized, so mesmerized that they failed to see the proverbial forest for the trees. They failed to understand that for the first time a work of popular culture would depend for its meaning not on its immediate impact and appeal but on "the theory behind it." We can now enjoy the irony: the guy who wrote "Can't Explain" is doing his best to explain his music to anyone with a press card. Pete's attempts to explain what can't be explained finally led him to Meher Baba and a sense of the ineffable in the universe.

As it turned out, *Tommy* didn't need Pete's explanations, for its Mod theme of overcoming isolation in the modern world found a resonance in non-Mods as well. Although the motivation for his trauma remains unclear on the record, if not in the movie, Tommy is a deaf, dumb, and blind kid. What better way to image the isolation of the Mod from the world than to deny him the use of his senses? Unlike "The End," *Tommy* was conceived as a studio piece, and recorded before it was performed live. It is something like a monodrama in that it really has only one singing part, Tommy, who makes contact with the world in magical ways. Only by magic can a deaf, dumb, and blind kid become a pinball wizard. If he cannot make contact with people, then he will make contact with technology—and he does. Probably what most people remember about Tommy, though, is "See Me Feel Me."

Since this song expresses the need to overcome isolation, the quintessential Mod theme, it's interesting to notice what Pete does with the music. As Tommy, Roger sings the line "See me, feel me, touch me, heal me" (an indicative progression) in straightforward G Major. But when Tommy stops singing about himself, and addresses his fans in the verse, which begins, "List'ning to you" the key changes. It has so many sus chords and flatted thirds and sevenths that it sometimes sounds like C major. The ambivalence of reaching out to others is carried through, then, in the music as well as in the lyrics.

Paul Simon, Jim Morrison and Pete Townshend all had different experiences with higher education. Paul actually went so far as to graduate from Queens College; Jim didn't graduate from either Florida Sate or UCLA, but when he felt like it, he could wow his teachers with his wide reading and quick intuition. Pete didn't graduate from Ealing Art College, but while there he discovered marijuana, Bob Dylan, and American rhythm and blues, auto-destruction and Peter Blake. The experience of college had a decisive effect, then, on each of these three major figures from the sixties. In their different ways, they were able to grasp the meaning of high culture, and to re-interpret it to create a synthesis which had immediate meaning for their audiences, whose own educational background made them receptive to such a synthesis. This problematic relationship between high culture and popular culture, like the problematic relationship between live and recorded performance, was one of the hallmarks of the sixties.

Notes

[1]Landon Y. Jones, *Great Expectations. America and the Baby Boom Generation* (New York: Coward, McCann and Geoghegan, 1980), p. 87.

[2]*Ibid.*, pp. 82-3.

[3]Quoted in *The New Yorker*, September 2, 1967, p. 26. *The New Yorker* was an especially appropriate magazine for Simon and Garfunekl, and not only because its gentility and good taste corresponded to the gentility and good taste of their music.

Paul Simon's lyrics had a good deal in common with the poetry of L.E. Sissman, a man who worked in advertising and who wrote for *The New Yorker*. The striking phrase "hello darkness" in "The Sounds of Silence" seems to come from *Hello Darkness*, the title of a collection of Sissman's poems from the sixties.

[4]Jerry Hopkins and Danny Sugarman, *No One Here Gets Out Alive* (New York: Warner Books, 1980), p. 153.

[5]Richard Goldstein, *Goldstein's Greatest Hits* (Englewood Cliffs, NJ: Prentice-Hall, 1970), p. 94.

[6]Antonin Artaud, *The Theater and Its Double*, Mary Caroline Richards, trans. (New York: Grove Press, 1958), p. 13.

[7]*Ibid.*

[8]*Ibid.* p. 113.

[9]*Ibid.*, p. 74

[10]*Ibid.*, p. 141.

[11]*Ibid., p. 50.*

[12]Tony Palmer, *Love Is All You Need* (New York: Grossman Publishing, 1976), p. 224.

[13]See *The Book of Rock Lists*, Dave Marsh and Kevin Stein, eds. (New York: Dell/ Rolling Stone, 1981), p. 160.

[14]Steve Clark, ed. *The Who In Their Own Words* (New York/London: Quick Fox, 1979), p. 70.

[15]Simon Frith, *I The Sociology of Rock* (New York: Pantheon, 79), p. 168.

[16]Tom Wolfe, *The Pump House Gang* (New York: Farrar Straus and Giroux, 1968), p. 104.

[17]Ted Dicks, ed. *A Decade of The Who* (London: Fabulous Music, 1977), p. 25.

[18]Wolfe, *The Pump House Gang*, p. 102.

[19]Dave Marsh, *Before I Get Old. The Story of The Who* (New York: St. Martin's Press, 1983), pp. 212-3.

[20]Tom Wolfe, *The Painted Word* (New York: Farrar Straus and Giroux, 1975), p. 62.

Chapter 14:
Sargeant Pepper
An Electric Performance

At the beginning of *The Man With a Movie Camera* (1928), a film by the Russian moviemaker Dziga Vertov, preparations are being made for a theatrical performance. The audience files in, and oddly enough in a silent film, the musicians begin to play. Then we have a shot from a performer's point of view, facing the audience from stage center. Then the audience disappears and rows of seats go up and down by themselves. As the film progresses, Vertov uses variable camera speeds, dissolves, and split screen effects, in which one half of the image revolves clockwise and the other half revolves counterclockwise. As film historians have said, *The Man with A Movie Camera* has more to do with the process of film making than anything else. Hence, the beginning in the theater makes perfect sense, for the meaning of the film is that film is obsolescing what was then called "the legitimate theater," which is to say, performances by live actors. That is why the audience disappears.

It is helpful to keep *The Man With A Movie Camera* in mind when listening to the Beatles' phenomenally important album *Sargeant Pepper's Lonely Hearts Club Band,* for just as Vertov's film obsolesces live stage performances, so the Beatles' album obsolesces live musical performances. This statement doesn't mean, of course, that rock 'n' roll groups—except for the Beatles themselves— stopped giving live concerts. On the contrary, live concerts were more important than ever. But after *Sargeant Pepper* the creation of sound in the studio, not in the concert hall or arena, produced the important innovations in music. *Sargeant Pepper* exists only as a record to be played. The fact that no one could perform it means that after it the studio mediated in an essential way between the performers and the audience, and that the subsequent history of rock 'n' roll makes no sense without an understanding of the role of the studio as an active agent in creating the music.

Innovations such as *Sargeant Pepper* never take place in a cultural vacuum. In this album the studio obsolesces a particular kind of live performance, the kind of live performance which the Beatles had grown up with, and which their parents had enjoyed when they were young—the music hall. Indeed, Paul McCartney once told Tony Palmer, "My dad used to work the lights in the local music halls."[1] and that he wanted to put a statue of music hall star Bud Flanagan, of the team of Flanagan and Allen, on top of every fire hydrant in London.[2] It was Paul who suggested to George Martin the concept of Sargeant Pepper's Lonely Hearts Club Band as a unifying device for the album, so his attachment to the music hall tradition takes on real importance. Since the music hall contributed so much to the form and texture of the album, we need to know something about this very British institution.

Charles Morton opened the first music hall in London in 1861 as an outgrowth of musical performances in taverns and tea gardens, but the music hall rapidly spread into the northern provinces and established itself as the single most important institution of working-class people. Colin Macinnes calls it "an art of working-class self-assertion."[3] Since the music avoided anything overtly obscene women as well as men could enjoy themselves there on a Saturday night. Anything smacking of formal organization had an upper-class association, and so "Music hall was, essentially, a performance made up of single acts with no kind of continuity as in musical comedy or revue."[4]

The music hall flourished in the working-class North of England; at one time there were no less than 22 music halls in Liverpool alone. It was here that Charlie Chaplin got his start. As one afficianado said, "Come to think of it, all the really big names in Music Hall came from the North Country."[5] The two greatest music hall stars of the twentieth century came from the North: George Formby and Gracie Fields. In particular George Formby, with his toothy grin and ukelele, symbolized the working-class hero long before Lennon wrote a song with that name. Formby's simple, catchy melodies and populist appeal make him comparable in importance to Hank Williams in American country music.

But radio, records, and film obsolesced the music hall in England, as they obsolesced vaudeville in America. As music hall merged with variety theater after World War I, talent continued to come from the North, though. Such comedians as Billy Bennett, Ken Dodd, Tommy Handley, and Albert Modley— all household names when the Beatles were growing up—came from Liverpool; the Beatles came by the clever repartee with which they charmed the press quite naturally.

The music hall made itself felt in British pop music as late as the fifties and sixties. An example is Lonnie Donegan, who scored big with the pseudo-folk hit, "The Rock Island Line."

Lonnie Donegan soon revealed a closer descent from George Formby than from Leadbelly, and reflected it in songs like "My Old Man's a Dustman" and "Does Your Chewing Gum Lose Its Flavor (On the Bedpost Overnight)" And just as the musicians themselves moved easily into rock and roll, music-hall influences permeated early indigenous rock music in England. The early idols, Tommy Steele and Cliff Richard, tended to be scruffy rather than menacing or sensual... Steele's later career makes it seem that he is basically a popular entertainer in a long London tradition who made use of the available style in the late fifties.[6]

Tommy Steele's ties to the music hall mark him as a transitional figure.

Many people, even some in England, don't realize that the Beatles started out in what was left of the music halls. They and the hundreds of other beat groups needed the music hall.

The only outlet for these new sounds was through the old music hall circuit. For the booker, rock and roll was merely the latest novelty, which, if it managed to arouse sufficient interest, would bring new people into the halls. The rest of the evening's entertainment was unchanged: stand-up comics, jugglers, animal acts, dancers, singers, and a pit band. The pit bands, incidentally, were offended when asked not to play for rock and roll acts. The idea of a man coming on stage with his *own* band was thought very odd.[7]

After the Beatles made provincial origins and a working-class accent fashionable, Herman's Hermits (from Manchester) capitalized on their working-class roots by recording Murray and Weston's cheeky song about proletarian identity, "I'm Henry the Eighth, I Am." They had written this song in 1911, and music hall great Harry Champion had made it into a standard, only he sang the verses, not just the chorus, as Herman did.

The cover of *Sargeant Pepper* includes both American and British celebrities, so we need to consider here the only major contemporary American musician the Beatles put on it: Bob Dylan. Since the Beatles had such a great effect on him, it's easy to forget that he had a great effect on them, too. Phillip Norman says in *Shout!* that after the Beatles stopped touring, John would sit around the house for days listening to Dylan. He picked up some things, too, for the phrase "my head in my hand" migrated from Dylan's "Honey, Just Allow Me One More Chance" to the Beatles' "You've Got to Hide Your Love Away," which even features a tambourine. "Ballad of a Thin Man" may have suggested "Nowhere Man" to John and Paul, and they may have generalized Dylan's desire to make Mr. Jones wear headphones into the much-discussed refrain of *Sargeant Pepper*, "I'd love to turn you on." Finally, the Beatles may have noticed Dylan's use of the opposition of inside and outside, for it is this opposition which informs *Sargeant Pepper* from beginning to end.

If Dylan's opposition of inside and outside did indeed have something to do with the organization of *Sgt. Pepper,* it was not simply because Dylan was a great songwriter and performer. More to the point, this opposition had immediate relevance to the Beatles' own situation. Like music hall performers before them, they had made it by performing outside, in public places such as the Cavern Club, and then, later, literally outside in Shea Stadium. Now, however, they had gone inside, to the legendary Abbey Road studios, where only the privileged few were allowed. If they were obsolescing live performances, they were in effect obsolescing performances outside. But, more generally, people in the sixties had a very strong sense of the difference between inside and outside; they talked a lot about "getting your head together"; and "where's your head at"; and "the canyons of your mind." There was a matching of various components of the Beatles' musical heritage, their personal situation, and their influences, with the general cultural situation of the times.

The album begins with audience noise, a brass band introduction, and a reference to the fact that the band began "twenty years ago today." Paul acts as compere, complimenting the audience and introducing Billy Shears, who is the opening turn at a music hall. But it is all a fake. There is no such group as Sargeant Pepper's Lonely Hearts Club Band; it's the Beatles in the studio; we're not an audience in a theater, either. We are not listening to a live performance in public space, but to a recorded performance in private space which presents itself as a live performance in public space. So the opposition inside/outside corresponds to the opposition present/past.

The Beatles invite us to think about the opposition between the present and the past on the cover of the album when they pose in their late sixties finery while to their left stand their wax statues from Madame Tussaud's. If an evening at a music hall had consisted of a series of unrelated turns, so had *Meet the Beatles* consisted of a series of unrelated songs. *Sargeant Pepper* also seems to have a series of unrelated songs in different styles but, fact, it has a unity, and not just because of the presence of the theme song on both sides. The album has a unity because of the way it keeps ringing changes on the opposition between inside and outside, with all the reverberations which that opposition had then—and still has today.

More specifically, the Beatles could stay inside the studio because of the four-track tape recorders which allowed George Martin to dub in the ambience noise, for instance. And here we find another way in which the Beatles are linked to the girl groups, for the Shangri-Las' "The Leader of the Pack" was among the first records to use taped sound effects (a motorcycle, in this case) to create a fictive setting.

The album begins outside, in public space, but immediately goes inside, where the audience noises fade away, to leave Ringo alone in the studio singing about his isolation. On "With A Little Help from My Friends," there occurs the first of many instances of balance between inside and outside; Ringo is clearly alone and inside, but he reaches out to others. More specifically, he responds to their questions so that we have a dramatic vignette of the kind we might expect in a theater rather than on an album.

We go inside in a different sense on the acid song, "Lucy in the Sky with Diamonds," which is the Beatles' version of "Mr. Tambourine Man." (There's surely more than a hint of Dylan in the alliteration of "plasticine porters." Did Dylan's phrase "diamond sky" become "the sky with diamonds"?) There is some echo on John's performance of the surrealistic verse, which is a slow waltz. But, the refrain changes to the familiar 4/4 of rock 'n' roll. It has repeated notes, and John's vocal needs no echo here. So there's no answer to the question, Is "the girl at the turnstile" someone he saw in the underground, or a figment of his imagination? Is she outside in the world, or inside, in his head?

"Getting Better" harks back to "With a Little Help from My Friends" in that the lyrics of both songs present someone reaching out. Mellers calls it a "raggy music-hall song, evoking school rebel and angry young man."[8] But here George's repeated guitar figure and the mocking chorus form a counterpoint to the cheerful tone of the lyrics. If the song questions in "With A Little Help From My Friends" expressed concern, the guitar here has the opposite effect; it undercuts the optimism and the music-hall ambience as well.

As he sings the first line of "Fixing A Hole," Paul presents himself as doing a household chore, fixing the roof; but the second line takes us from outside to inside, because it turns out that the rain gets into his mind. To take "the time for a number of things" is to express the way drugs make it necessary to slow down one's actions. On "Fixing a Hole" the Beatles make the correspondence between the internalization of awareness through drugs and the internalization of music through the studio more concrete than anywhere else on the album.

This brings us to the finale of Act I of our evening at the Abbey Road Music Hall, "She's Leaving Home." Fittingly, this song takes the form of a vignette, as "With a Little Help From My Friends" and "Getting Better" did. On "The Times They Are-A Changin' " Dylan had warned parents that their children were "beyond their control." "She's Leaving Home" works out the implications of that situation, but does so as a compassion song. Neither in the gentle strings nor in the vocals is there any more irony than there is in "Sad-Eyed Lady of the Lowlands."

It's clear that the Beatles were talented enough to adapt their talents to the live performance, for "She's Leaving Home" is the first Beatles song which we can imagine on the stage. It is easy to imagine the girl might act out her part in pantomime while Paul sings the narrative, and John and George sing the parents' part in falsetto. Like so much modern art, though, "She's Leaving Home" is an incomplete narrative; what it does not say is as significant as what it does say.

"She's Leaving Home" does not have the usual verse-and-chorus structure of earlier Beatles songs, and Mellers has some good things to say about the implications of that.

The arching cello tune is as beautiful as it is comic; and the irregular structure enacts the comic story, conveying not merely the fact of the girl's departure but all the muddled hope, apprehension and fear in the girl's heart, the fuddled incomprehension of the parents.[9]

And so "She's leaving home bye bye." Paul sings the words slowly and there are chords between each word which echo the parents confusion. At the end, a harp arpeggio begins on the root of A, goes up to E, and ends at C. The song ends on a subdominant major triad. The root A thus represents home, where it all begin, and where it all will probably end. This wonderful sequence represents a new, and higher, version of the completeness of the songs which gave rise to Beatlemania.

Side one concludes with "Being for the Benefit of Mr. Kite," a song which returns us to the performance setting of "Sargeant Pepper's Lonely Hearts Club Band." "Being" has such archaic language, (i.e. the word "hogshead,") that it must be set in the nineteenth century. Yet nothing is ever quite that simple on this great album, for the writing has a complexity which is very much of the twentieth century. In the middle section John consistently rhymes an end word with a word in the middle of the next line. The sound is very much of the twentieth century and was in no meaningful sense produced by musicians. George Martin got the basic hurdy-gurdy effect by playing an organ duet with John: "What we'll do is to slow the whole thing down by a half. You play the tune twice as slow and an octave down, and I'll do my runs as fast as I can, but an octave down as well. Then, when we double the tape speed, it'll come out all nice and smooth and very swirly."[10] Notice that the crucial thing here is the final effect which comes through the loudspeakers, not the performance. What he calls the "wash," the background to "Being for the Benefit of Mr. Kite," was produced by taping some albums of Victorian steam organs, cutting up the tape into little bits, throwing them up in the air, and splicing them together. The result was thus at several removes from anything that could be called a performance; but it was not—as had been the case in the past—several generations removed in terms of sound. The sound remained as full as they wanted it to be, so "Being for the Benefit of Mr. Kite" holds its oppositions of inner and outer, of studio sound and lyrics which refer to live performance in as fine a balance as anything Dylan ever did.

Thus, the album which began in a social setting of the external world concludes side one in a personal version of the external world, with some alternations between inner and outer along the way. These vacillations become more pronounced on side two, which begins with the radical contrast between the song which puns on the album's theme, "Within You, Without You," and "When I'm Sixty-Four."

Like "Fixing a Hole," "Within You Without You," denies that the distinction between inside and outside is really a distinction at all. In technical terms, both songs resolve the dichotomy of inside and outside into a binary pair. If "Fixing a Hole" assimilates the inside of your head to the inside of a roof, then "Within You Without You" assimilates each individual to everyone else: "we're all one." On the first cut on side two, the drug-free side, George plays the sitar. Although he gets more melody out of it than his teacher Ravi Shankar would have, it still has an exotic sound and its associations with Oriental thought deny that East and West are so different after all; the drone, with its lack of consistent time signatures, suggest a state of being "beyond yourself."

"When I'm Sixty Four" has marked and deliberate contrasts to "Within You Without You." George's song denies time, Paul's accentuates it. George's song uses a sitar, Paul's has an archaic music-hall sound which reminds Mellers of George Formby.[12] George's song affirms the possibility of transcendence, Paul's denies it: "Who could ask for more." Together, the two songs balance the East and the West, inside and outside. Moreover, "When I'm Sixty Four" associates the past and the present in a way which relates to side one.

The phrase "twenty years ago today" fixes the beginnings of Sargeant Pepper's Lonely Hearts Club Band in 1947. The Beatles bring the past and the present together by taking on the collective persona of Sargeant Pepper's Lonely Hearts Club Band, and they bring the generations together.

The next two songs, "Lovely Rita" and "Good Morning Good Morning" are also opposed in some ways. "Lovely Rita," with the wittiest lyrics John ever wrote, constantly sets up expectations and then denies them, just as the young man has frustrated expectations about Rita and the other girls he meets. "Good Morning Good Morning," though, presents the thoughts of an older, married man who also has hopes about the girls he meets. There are few obvious studio effects on "Lovely Rita." "Good Morning Good Morning" begins with taped barnyard sounds and ends with a fox hunt which goes from right to left, and then barnyard sounds again. This rural ambience undercuts the suburban vignettes of the lyrics.

After the reprise of "Sargeant Pepper's Lonely Hearts Club Band," "A Day in the Life" concludes the album. The title of the song seems to be a truncated version of *A Day in the Life of Ivan Denisovich,* the novella by Russian novelist Alexander Solzhenitsyn. Unlike Solzhenitsyn's novella, which deals with one day in the life of one prisoner in one of Stalin's many concentration camps, the Beatles' song has a more general effect—a day in the life of everyman.

"A Day in the Life" begins with a strummed acoustic guitar and strong piano chords and builds its effects slowly. The song begins on the outside, as it were, when John sings about what he has read in the papers, and seen at the pictures. He has read about a man who died in a car crash, and seen a war movie. If the English army "has just won the war," then this places the action in 1946 or 1947, just as the opening cut of the album did. The studio effects also distance us from the first two verses of "A Day in the Life," as when George Martin puts a half-second delay in the rhyme "laugh/photograph" which sounds like "la-augh'/"photogra-aph."

After a cacophonous crescendo, Paul returns us to the everyday world, with an alarm clock, and an internal, first-person narration of a morning in the life. After this contrast, a heavily echoed "Ahhh" and another crescendo lead us into the finale. Here we have the final assimilation of outside to inside, when John associates those famous 4,000 holes in Blackburn, Lancashire (outside, in the north of England), to the Albert Hall (inside, in London). To quote Mellers for one last time, "A Day in the Life" ends by "leading into another and wilder electronic trip that seems to be also an atomic explosion, obliterating both public revelry and private love."[13]

That final E major chord may threaten to obliterate, but does not in fact do so because it lasts so long—24 bars, to be precise. George instructed the 42 classical musicians hired for the occasion to slide up from the lowest note their instruments would play to the highest notes each instrument could reach that was near a chord of E major. He took that sound and dubbed onto it a piano chord artificially lengthened by having it recorded with the volume control way down, and then moving it up as the sound died away.[14] In this way the studio gave the piano the sustain of an electric guitar. The very long chord forces us to slow down and assimilate what we have heard, rather as the very long coda at the end of "Sad-Eyed Lady of the Lowlands" does.

When *Sargeant Pepper* came out it rapidly went platinum, and re-defined rock as music produced in a studio. This new definition of rock had many effects—some direct, some indirect. Take the names of albums and album covers, for instance. After *Sargeant Pepper*, the Beatles put out a double album which they called *The Beatles*. But no one else called it that. It had an all-white cover, with The Beatles in embossed letters on the front. It seems to have been the first rock album in history without a picture or a drawing on the cover. It didn't need one, because sound which couldn't be produced by performers commanded everyone's attention.

It was because of the studio that the Beatles were able to do something unheard of in popular music. For almost four years they continued to put songs on the charts and put out million-selling albums without a single live concert. They even named one of their final albums after their studio: *Abbey Road*. (Similarly, The Band named its first album after its home recording studio, *Music from Big Pink*.) And for *Let It Be*, their last album, they hired the man who had pioneered the use of the recording studio as an instrument in itself, Phil Spector.

The new importance of the studio also intensified the need for a concert to sound just like an album. Of course, fans had been going to concerts in expectation of hearing a group's hits for a long time, but the new importance of the studio intensified this expectation. By the time people got to a concert in the last sixties, they had heard the group's latest album on FM radio, and on their own stereos (and often on headphones, at that). As a result, groups took the studio into the concert hall, in the form of a mixing board.

We can speculate that the predominance of the technology which mediated between the performers and the audience had something to do with the demise of matching outfits. In the past, matching outfits had marked the performers as belonging together and as being set apart from the audience. In the sixties, what set the performers apart from the audience was their command of the technology, so they started wearing the same tie-dyed T-shirts and patched blue jeans as everybody else. In short, they looked about as anonymous as the cover of the white album.

Others were not so lucky. Part of the reason it took Pete Townshend so long to make *Tommy* is that The Who recorded it before they performed it— something they weren't used to doing. In LA, Brian Wilson was having one problem after another. He wanted to stay in the studio and create avant-garde music, but the other Beach Boys as well as Capitol Records wanted him to keep re-writing "Help Help Me Rhonda." He was emotionally unsuited to deal with these pressures, and so what might have been a great masterpiece, *Smile*, was aborted.

The Doors were putting songs on the charts, and they didn't suffer from internal dissension, but they were having trouble keeping Jim Morrison sober. Morrison was self-indulgent and self-destructive. According to Mark Amatin, Living Theater employee, by 1969 Jim was saying that "His work had been a religious experience, but it had become entertainment, and he was extremely dissatisfied."[15] It devastated Jim, good student of Artaud that he was, to realize that the fans reacted to a poor performance very much as they reacted to a great one. He couldn't accept an essential fact of the late sixties, namely that the fans were reacting to the sounds inside their heads as much as they were to what was coming through the loudspeakers. This meant that the fans were turning him into a record, a thing; this dehumanization was just the opposite of the intense performer/audience interaction which meant so much to him. Deprived of it, he went to Paris, where Artaud had made his name, and died. McLuhan once commented that television killed Marilyn Monroe; if so, the recording studio surely killed Jim Morrison.

Notes

[1]Tony Palmer, *All You Need Is Love*, p. 235.

[2]*Ibid.*, p. 89.

[3]Colin Macinnes, *Sweet Saturday Night* (London: MacGibbon and Kee, 1967), p. 14.

[4]*Ibid.*, p. 23.

[5]G.J. Mellor, *The Northern Music Hall* (Newcastle: Frank Graham, 1970), p. 14.

[6]Dave Laing, *The Sound of Our Time* (London: Sheed and Ward, 1969), p. 107.

[7]Palmer, *All You Need Is Love*, p. 222.

[8]Wilfrid Mellers, *Twilight of the Gods*, p. 89.

[9] *Ibid.*, p. 93.

[10]George Martin with Jeremy Hornsby, *All You Need Is Ears* (New York: St. Martin's Press, 9179), p. 204.

[11]See *ibid.* pp. 204-5.

[12]Mellers, *The Twilight of the Gods*, p. 94.

[13]*Ibid.*, p. 100.

[14]See Martin, *All You Need Is Ears*, pp. 211-212.

[15]Quoted in Jerry Hopkins and Danny Sugarman, *No One Here Gets Out Alive*, p. 221.

Chapter 15:
Anxious Beatles

So there they were, isolated in the studio. They didn't want to tour, and they didn't have to. But without the immediate contact with an audience they found themselves—even more than Pete Townshend—in the situation of a paragon of high culture like Marcel Proust. Proust was famous for, among other things, having his study lined with cork to keep out disturbing noises. Proust needed to cut himself off from the world in this way because of his sensitivity to its nuances. In the same way, the Beatles used their money and power to cut themselves off from a world to whose nuances they had such sensitivity. They wound up, then, in the studio, whose acoustically treated walls bore more than a passing resemblance to the walls of Proust's study.

Alone in his study, Proust could contemplate his past; alone in the studio, the Beatles could contemplate *their* past. And when they contemplated their past, what they realized was that they owed their careers to America. For all their roots in the British music hall tradition, their musical inspiration had come from America, and it was in America that they became, not just pop stars but Legends. They had been awestruck when "I Want to Hold Your Hand" went to #1 in America, and Dylan had made far more of an impact on their music than any of their British contemporaries. In effect, they had to ask themselves, "What would we be without America?"

This question produced the white album, which is as much of a concept album as *Sargeant Pepper*. It has a unifying theme, the encounter with America, which is stated in the first cut, as the first cut of *Sargeant Pepper* creates the fictive music hall. Just as the Beatles wish the audience good night on the reprise of "Sargeant Pepper's Lonely Hearts Club Band," so they wish everyone good night at the end of the white album. On *Sargeant Pepper*, they defined themselves with regard to British music. On the white album the dynamic which informs and unifies the music is the Beatles' need to define themselves with regard to American music. And since sixties rock came out of the interchange between British and American performers, in doing this, they were in effect creating the sound of their time.

Fortunately, we have a very useful way of understanding the Beatles' situation, which has many precedents in high culture. When an artist is suffering from an acute awareness of a debt to the past, critic Harold Bloom says that that artist is suffering from the anxiety of influence. Bloom has read Freud on father-son relationships, and has suggested that we can take the Oedipal complex as a model for the relationship between the artist and a major figure from the past. The figure from the past—Elvis, for example—functions as a

195

father who dominates the son, who must in turn prove himself against the father in order to become a man. Bloom calls the father figure a "precursor," and the son figure an "ephebe," from the Greek word for student. In Bloom's scheme, the ephebe suffers from the anxiety of influence when he fears that the precursor has created so much that he has nothing left to say. In Freudian terminology, the ephebe can only work through the anxiety of influence, and thereby become a mature artist, by creating work which will match the work of the precursor. Thus it happens that "The covert subject of most poetry for the last three centuries has been the anxiety of influence."[1]

Bloom's ideas have a far wider applicability than he knows. They apply not just to poetry, and not just to high culture, but to all forms of creativity in the modern world—including rock 'n' roll. Dylan, for instance, was certainly what Bloom would call a strong artist, but he began by suffering from the anxiety of influence as a result of having Woody Guthrie as a precursor. He achieved his independence from Woody in "Chimes of Freedom" and "I Shall Be Free No. 10," and in his second period he became a precursor for others, threatening them as Woody had threatened him. Thus, Paul Simon expressed his anxiety of influence from Dylan in "A Simple Desultory Phillipic."

Bloom has proposed six "revisionary ratios," or relationships in which ephebes work through their anxiety of influence from their precursors. The one which interests us here is "apophrades." Bloom took this word, which refers to the ancient Greek belief that there were certain days when the dead returned to inhabit their former houses, to describe what happens when as ephebe overcomes a precursor. Apophrades is:

The triumph of having so stationed the precursor, in one's own work, that particular passages in *his* work seem to be not presages of one's own advent, but rather to be indebted to one's own achievement, and even (necessarily) to be lessened by one's greater splendor.[2]

Thus, what happens in apophrades is that a ephebe takes on a precursor in such a way that he makes us remember the works of both together. Indeed, if the ephebe has sufficient strength, he may make us think of him instead of the ephebe when we listen to the precursor's work. Since Bloom loves paradoxes, he defies chronology by saying that in apophrades, the ephebe influences the precursor.

It seems to me that Bloom's ideas apply to popular culture, but only if we can give up our sentimental ideas of popular performers as happy-to-lucky kids having a good time. They may be that, but sustained popularity creates many of the same stresses as creativity in high culture. For these reasons, I believe that apophrades makes sense as a way of understanding the meaning of the white album. As Mellers says, "Julia" is the only song on the whole album which has no irony, and irony in evoking the work of other artists usually signals the presence of the anxiety of influence.[3] So we can say that in the white album the Beatles work out their anxiety of influence from American performers, and bring about an apophrades. That is to say, they so cleverly rework the songs of their precursors that we may well think of the Beatles even when we listen to the precursors. Moreover, as the album progresses, the Beatles draw on other forms of American popular entertainment in addition to music.

The first cut on a concept album has particular importance, since it must state the theme in such a way that the listener knows what to expect on subsequent cuts. This explains why "Back in the U.S.S.R." sets up three sets of interrelated oppositions. First, it opposes the two military superpowers, the U.S.A. and the U.S.S.R., in such a way as to suggest that they have similarities as well differences. Second, the style evokes the fifties, so that we have the opposition of the sixties and the fifties. Third, the Beatles are British musicians who are paying homage to/working out their anxiety of influence from/American musicians, so we have the opposition of England and America.

The title "Back in the U.S.S.R." plays itself off against Chuck Berry's "Back in the U.S.A." Just as Chuck has "Touched ground on an international runway," so the Beatles "flew in." Both Chuck and Paul (who sings it for the Beatles) are glad to be home, but we can't take Paul's patriotism seriously, and thus it undercuts the patriotism of Chuck's song. More generally, though, the refrain states the theme of the album: "Back in the U.S., back in the U.S., back in the U.S.S.R." (Although it doesn't show up on the lyrics sheet, at the end of "Cry Baby Cry" Paul sings a variation of this theme over a catchy riff, "Can you take me back to where I came from?"

There's more though, because in the second verse the Beatles shift to a Beach Boys falsetto, to sing the glories of "Ukraine girls" and "Moscow girls," making the connection to the Beach Boys' "California Girls." Brian Wilson's Northern girls "who keep their boyfriends warm at night" get refracted through the Beatles' imagination to become a plea to "keep your comrade warm." Hardly anything in this remarkable song has a single meaning, so "Georgia's always on my mind," refers to an autonomous republic in the Southern part of the Soviet Union and to Hoagy Carmichael's classic. "Georgia On My Mind" was known to the Beatles, of course, in Ray Charles' version.

People have often said that these and the other musical references on the white album are parodies, but I think there's more to it than that. If they are parodies, are the Beatles poking fun at Chuck Berry and the Beach Boys? Why would they want to do that? But people have decided that anything in rock which refers to another song or another artist is parody, and they let it go at that. I don't think that the Beatles were merely being petty, malicious or vindictive; I do think that they were working out their anxiety about the influence of American music on them and that to do that they chose the sound of the most influential American performer of the fifties, and the sound of the most emphatically American group of their time. In evoking, and simultaneously re-working, Chuck Berry and the Beach Boys, the Beatles were also defining some of the differences between the Beatles era and the pre-Beatles era. Furthermore, they were proclaiming themselves a group which had no one recognizable sound. If the eclecticism of *Sargeant Pepper* fit in well with the conceit of the music hall, so here their eclecticism shows their mastery of many styles.

It's worth noting that hardly anyone in the sixties had the skill and confidence to adopt someone else's singing style in this way. The only other example I know of is "I Dig Rock 'N' Roll Music," by Peter, Paul, and Mary. The song, which might be subtitled "The Folkies' Revenge on Rock 'N' Roll," parodies the Mamas and the Papas in the first verse, Donovan in the second, and The Beatles in the third verse. The song is cleverly done but shallow, and I hear little more in it than professional jealousy and a purer-than-thou snobbism.

Nine other songs on the white album have verbal and/or stylistic references to American popular music. At the end of "Happiness Is A Warm Gun" John sings with the stridency of a soul singer while Paul and George sing doo-wop harmony behind him, which is very much like their "shooby-doowah" backup singing on "Revolution 1." "I'm So Tired" has repeated rhymes, which are extremely rare in Beatles songs, and which must have come from Dylan. (There's also a reference to tobacco, which came to England from America.)

"Rocky Raccoon" is one of the key songs on the album, and makes a series of complicated references. Paul begins it with a Dylanesque drawl, but reverts to his Liverpool accent occasionally. He thus juxtaposes England and America, as well as past and present, when in this tale of the wild West Rocky finds a Gideon's bible in his hotel room, a clue to the origin of the title.

During Beatlemania the Beatles couldn't stir from their hotel rooms without risking life and limb. Whatever they learned about American culture they learned from their hotel rooms. They must have been startled to find a Gideon's Bible in every hotel room and they put that in the song. Since they couldn't go out, they watched TV. One program they saw was The Bullwinkle Show, a cartoon which was shown on Saturday mornings in 1964. Bullwinkle's best friend in the cartoon is Rocky Squirrel, who for the sake of alliteration became Rocky Raccoon in the song. Paul gives the song a cheerful reading, and the bouncy music belies the violence of the narrative, so that it sounds like an aural version of a cartoon which has violence that no one takes seriously. The cartoon-like quality of "Rocky Racoon" fits in well with the fairy-tale-like quality of some of the other songs.

The lyrics of "Rocky Raccoon" re-work "The Shooting of Dan McGrew," a well-known poem by Robert W. Service (1874-1958). Service spent some time as a young man in the gold rush country of Alaska and British Columbia, and he wrote several poems about miners. Service sometimes sounds like Dylan, as in the opening lines of "The Shooting of Dan McGrew":

A bunch of the boys were whooping it up in the Malamute saloon;
The kid that handles the music-box was hitting a jag-time tune;
Back of the bar, in a solo game, sat Dangerous Dan McGrew,
And watching his luck was his light-o'-love, the lady that's known as Lou.[4]

Then a stranger bursts upon the scene, plays piano for a bit, and shoots Dan McGrew.

The Beatles took Service's poem and made from it the scenario for a Western. The "lady that's known as Lou" became the lady who "called herself Lil," and the Beatles take away Dan McGrew's last name, but they let him win the gunfight in their ironic reversal of the happy ending we expect. The Beatles also add a stock character, the alcoholic doctor (suggested by Doc in *Gun-Smoke*?).

"Yer Blues" is the Beatles' only blues, and it has the traditional aab 12-bar structure. John sings it in a Southern accent and it is here that he mentions Dylan by name. On "Helter Skelter" John does a manic Little Richard vocal (he had earlier recorded "Long Tall Sally") for the Beatles' version of acid rock.

"Honey Pie" and "Good Night" are remarkable stylistic exercises, even for the Beatles. The lyrics of "Honey Pie" give yet another version of the encounter between England and America, when a girl from "north of England way" (Cilla Black?) goes to America, and makes it big in Hollywood. The chiche "legend of the silver screen" creates an ironic distance, a distance which is also established by the music, which recalls 30s show biz movies. They even further distance the song by putting in record hiss on one line; a voice filter occasionally makes Paul sound like Rudy Vallee. "Good Night" refers to more recent American musicals. It has shimmering strings in the best *Sound of Music* tradition, and makes peace with the past, although yet again our knowledge of the Beatles' other music makes us aware that they do this song with ironic affection.

Popular music grows out of, and expresses, a culture. The various American styles in the songs on the white album cannot be separated from the commentaries on American culture which the songs make. American popular culture primarily means cowboy movies to Europeans, and the back of *Rubber Soul* has a picture of George in a cowboy outfit. Cowboy movies fascinate us all because they are set in an Eden-like wilderness of the frontier. The Beatles construct fairy tale settings and bouncy music while singing narratives of frontier violence. After all, it has been said that the essential American imperative is to seek the great good place, a place where everything is okay. In fact, the Beatles themselves wrote songs about this search, both before the white album ("Yellow Submarine") and after it ("In An Octopus's Garden").

The first of the fairy tale songs is "Ob-La-Di, Ob-La-Da," a fairy tale about capitalism. In it, Molly and Desmond live happily ever after in the market place. Not only do the lyrics exploit the anachronistic quality of a fairy tale about capitalism, there is also the hint of sexual ambiguity when Paul tells us that Desmond "does his pretty face." Despite its British setting, "Ob-La-Di, Ob-La-Da" prepares us for three ironic songs about the propensity to violence in American life which became so obvious during the sixties.

The mere title of "The Continuing Story of Bungalow Bill" tells us a lot. A "continuing story" is a soap opera, with all the sappy sentimentalism which that implies. Yet everybody understands that "Bungalow Bill" is a play on Buffalo Bill, the symbol of the whites who slaughtered the buffalo and the Indians who were dependent on them as the course of Empire made its way westward. Yet in the sixties such heroism was a fantasy for a Walter Mitty-like man who lives in a bungalow.

In the sixties hippies called themselves "flower children" and opposed the war. In this song the children mock Bungalow Bill by asking him "What did you kill?" And after the line "All the children sing" all the Beatles join in, so they are associating themselves with the children. There's a bit of buffoonery in the delivery of some of the lyrics, so the Beatles distance themselves from the song by clapping at the end.

After "While My Guitar Gently Weeps" "The Continuing Story of Bungalow Bill" leads to "Happiness Is A Warm Gun," with which it forms a pair, like some of the pairs on *Sargeant Pepper*. "The Continuing Story" deals with violence ironically and externally, while "happiness" deals with it internally. We have no fairy tale setting this time, for the song shows how gentleness can mask violence. The song has a complementary stylistic instability. John begins it in a warm, intimate manner, but ends it in a strident shouting style. One of the finest touches on the album occurs when Paul and George sing "bang bang shoot shoot" in a doo-wop style. It is the first time we have ever heard doo-wop backup singing used for anything other than a love song; like the sly line "when I feel my finger on your trigger" it makes us aware of the connection between sex and violence in a manner which we cannot readily forget. Guns and shooting also appear in "Rocky Raccoon," which presents the traditional Western as a fairy tale. If anything, it intensifies the irony with its bouncy music and Paul's irrepressibly cheerful vocal.

"Revolution 1" concludes this series of songs about violence, and does so by bringing it all back home. Like "Happiness Is A Warm Gun," it has doo-wop backup singing, but hardly any other ironic qualities. Rather, the easy, lazy rhythms and and singable melodies contrast with the complicated ironies of previous songs. In this relaxed atmosphere, their denunciation of "minds that hate" sounds convincing.

"Revolution 1" forms an obvious pair with "Revolution 9." The first song denounces political revolution as false and the complex tape collage shows the true revolution, the revolution of sensibility. In this case, the revolution of sensibility, or "where your head is at," as we said in the sixties, is carried out by the technology of the studio, as when the sound swirls from left to right and back again. The Beatles are using studio effects for their own sake, without the frame of the music hall performance. There is some glorious music on "Revolution 9" with an angelic chorus. But as soon as we start to listen to the music as such the tape stops, to remind us that this is not a performance.

The spoken words relate to the encounter between England and America as well. A man with a strong British accent mentions the American dance crazes at the time the Beatles were starting out when he says, "The Watusi; the Twist." Someone else says, "Take this, brother; may it serve you well." which has a Shakespearean ring. A little later we have American popular culture: the taped sounds of a crowd at a football game roaring "Hold that line" and "Block that kick."

If anything, the white album is more revolutionary than *Sargeant Pepper,* for it presents popular music which has acquired historical consciousness. You have to understand the past in order to understand the juxtapositions between the past and the present which the Beatles are making. As with Pete's explanations of *Tommy,* the immediate experience of the music will not suffice. The expression of historical consciousness resembles nothing so much as T.S. Eliot's *The Wasteland,* which was also written in London. The Beatles refer to, and rework, Chuck Berry in the first line, just as Eliot refers to, and reworks Chaucer in his first line. In both cases the artists assume that we know the originals, and that we understand that they are making conscious references to them.

But the revolutions of the white album did not mean that allusions to the past would continue indefinitely in the Beatles' music. Having come to terms with the past of British popular music in *Sargeant Pepper,* and with the past of American popular music in the white album, they had freed themselves to write their own music. And this they did, gloriously, in *Abbey Road,* where Paul's lyricism and John's surrealism play off against each other to produce continual delight. No wonder it's the biggest-selling Beatles album.

Notes

[1]Harold Bloom, *The Anxiety of Influence* (New York: Oxford U. Press, 1973), p. 148.

[2]*Ibid.,* p. 141. Roy Lichtenstein's cartoon-style versions of Picasso's portraits represent another way of working through the anxiety of influence. The anxiety of influence also appears in American architecture of the sixties; see Vincent Scully, *The Shingle Style Today; Or, the Historian's Revenge* (New York: George Braziller, 1979).

[3]Mellers, *Twilight of the Gods,* p. 131.

[4]Robert W. Service, *The Complete Poems of Robert Service* (New York: Dodd, Mead and Company, 1940), p. 29.

Chapter 16:
Mid-Atlantic Stones

The Rolling Stones are the world's greatest rock 'n' roll band. They have the #1 singles, the platinum albums, and the concert receipts to prove it. No group has ever played so much rock 'n' roll so well for so long. But they may not be *England's* greatest rock 'n' roll band. They came from the London suburbs so they didn't have anything like the roots in British folk music or British popular entertainment which the Beatles had. Nor did they come out of an indigenous British social movement, as The Who came out of Mod. (Although the Stones resemble The Who in that both groups started out with a phenomenally talented yet self-destructive musician, and the Stones did attract some Mod followers.) The Stones created themselves by re-working the music they listened to on Chess, Motown, and Atlantic records, and it was for this reason that all of their first five albums contained cover versions of other people's songs. In fact, Mick and Keith started writing songs themselves only because Andrew Loog Oldham, their first manager, urged them to. Writing did not come naturally to them, as it did to John and Paul in their school days at Liverpool. If the Beatles were inspired by American music and things American in general, the Stones were overwhelmed and inhibited by them. (Keith's first idol was Roy Rogers.)

So we can use Tom Wolfe's term for Englishmen like the Stones: They are "Mid-Atlantic men."

They are Englishmen who have reversed the usual process and...gone American.
The most obvious example of the Mid-Atlantic Man is the young English show-business figure, a singer, a musician, manager, producer, impresario, who goes American in a big way. A singer, for example, sings American rhythm and blues songs, in an American accent, becomes a... *pal* of American entertainers, studs his conversation with American slang...[1]

(If Mick, and that is clearly who Wolfe has in mind, is a Mid-Atlantic Man, it is quite appropriate that in 1971 he compared himself to the consummate Mid-Atlantic Man who was born Archibald Leach in England: "In the end, I'm probably going to be like Cary Grant with a lot of old ladies writing letters to me.")[2] As Wolfe makes clear in his sardonic essay, the problem with being a Mid-Atlantic man is that you tend to lose your identity.

To put it in artistic terms, the early Stones were suffering from the anxiety of influence. They had lost themselves in the blues. Their precursors were the likes of Muddy Waters, Sonny Boy Williamson, and Jimmy Reed, so naturally they felt intimidated. How could they ever play like that? They weren't black—

they weren't even American! As artists usually do, they dealt with their anxiety of influence by creating an ironic distance between themselves and their precursors. Thus, their anxiety of influence from the American blues masters is the source of the irony and ambiguity which has characterized their music for so long.

Needless to say, they responded to the music of the sixties as well as to the music of black men born long before in Mississippi. Whatever else it is, the history of rock 'n' roll in the sixties is the history of the interaction of the Beatles, Dylan, and the Stones, and it is convenient to describe that interaction here.

The Beatles blew everything open with Beatlemania, and in doing so they paradoxically helped Oldham to understand why the Stones would make it. He once explained why he signed them up the very next day after seeing them for the first time: "Music. Sex. The fact that in just a few months the country would need an opposite to what the Beatles were doing."[3] That is to say, given the Beatles, England would soon need a complement to them. This was a very shrewd understanding—especially for a nineteen-year-old hustler—of what promotions people call "positioning." And indeed, in 1964, at the height of Beatlemania in America, *The Rolling Stones* went to #1 in England.

The Stones' career was bound up with that of the Beatles in other ways as well. John and Paul wrote the Stones' first hit, "I Wanna Be Your Man," and the Stones recorded *Their Satanic Majesties Request* as a response to *Sargeant Pepper*. Meanwhile, the Beatles had convinced Dylan to take up the electric guitar, and he soon started to affect their music. He also affected the Stones' music, as *Between the Buttons* and *Let It Bleed* attest.

Thus, the Stones did not affect Dylan or the Beatles in any apparent way during the sixties, although they affected the Stones. This situation did not come about because of a lack of talent or originality on the part of the Stones, but because the Stones had what we may call a permeable sensibility. They are comparable only to Dylan in the way their music plays itself off against other people's music in remarkably creative, and remarkably diverse, ways. (Just compare Eddie Cochran's "Nervous Breakdown" with the Stones' "Nineteenth Nervous Breakdown.") The paradox of their identity is that they acquired it by taking on, and rearranging, the identity of other people's music. I am not being perverse about this; it's just that there's no resolution to this paradox, just as there is often no resolution in their songs. With these general considerations in mind, let's follow the Stones through the sixties, noting the importance of three key songs, "Not Fade Away"; "Satisfaction"; and "You Can't Always Get What You Want."

I have said that the Stones used irony to create a distance between themselves and their precursors. But that irony was not always there—they had to acquire it. When they first started playing with Alexis Korner, they were suffering from an early symptom of the anxiety of influence—the belief in purity. Like Greenwich Village folkies at just the same time, they expressed nothing but disdain for commercial music.[4] Robert Palmer cites a quotation from Mick

Jagger from 1962 to the effect that, "I hope they don't think we're a rock and roll outfit."[5]

As it turned out, though, the early Stones were closet rockers. Mick later confessed, "We were blues purists who liked ever so commercial things but never did them on stage because we were so horrible and so aware of being blues purists."[6] This schizophrenia didn't last, primarily because of Keith. You could say that his decadence saved the Stones. Where blues purists were concerned, Keith was decadent even before he started taking heroin because he was doing something about as bad—he was listening to Chuck Berry. He once recalled that during the early days, "On one hand I was playing all that folk stuff on guitar. The other half of me was listenin' to all that rock and roll, Chuck Berry, and saying yeah, yeah."[7] Ultimately, "all that rock and roll" won out, but not right away. It is true that the Stones were too talented to remain purists, but it is also true that the composition of the group precluded an extended period of imitation. The blues greats from Charley Patton and Robert Johnson to Muddy Waters and B.B. King, as well as Chuck himself, were singer-songwriter-guitarists. The trouble was, the Stones didn't have anybody who could do it all like that.

Instead of one star, the Stones had, in addition to a rock solid rhythm section, a hot singer and a hot guitarist, and one guy who could play anything from a guitar to a harmonica. Brian's phenomenal talent, and his ability to play any instrument he picked up help to explain the diversity of sound textures on the records which the Stones made while he was alive. As Tom Wheeler has explained,

The band is built around a two-guitar sound, itself an extension of Richards' own uniqueness. He helped blur forever the line between lead and rhythm guitar, substituting a riffing technique in which melodic embellishments are grafted onto a vigorous rhythmic treatment of chords, partial chords, and low-register lines.[8]

This two-guitar sound, or guitar-and-whatever-Brian-was-playing sound evolved in fascinating ways, but at least in the sixties it was not an identifiably Chuck Berry sound, no matter how important he was for the Stones.

Because of this distribution of talent in the band, the Stones covered only a few blues classics—not nearly as many as you would expect—such as Muddy's "I Just Want to Make Love to You" and "I Wanna Be Loved"; and Willie Dixon's "Little Red Rooster" and "I'm a King Bee," which Muddy had recorded. When they played these songs they took them at faster tempos and higher volumes than the originals. They had to because they were playing to a different audience. The easy tempos of many of Muddy's records, his way of repeating phrases, and his interchanges with his sidemen, are predicated on an audience with whom he shared a consensus about the world, a consensus which grew out of shared experience. That shared experience fostered an empathy with the music, a readiness to take it as it came. The Stones' audiences lacked that consensus and that shared experience. They needed to be blown away. So (if the cover versions give any indication of the live versions) the Stones speeded up the tempos, smoothed out the rhythms, and went out and blew them away.

Mick did not have the voice or stage presence of a blues master, but he took on the voice and stage presence of a rhythm and blues singer of the late fifties and early sixties—thereby becoming Mick Jagger. As the following partial list shows, neither Chuck Berry nor Muddy Waters provided anything like as much material as rhythm and blues acts did.

Rhythm and Blues Songs Covered by the Stones in the Sixties

Song	Singer
"Everybody Needs Somebody to Love"	Solomon Burke
"If You Need Me"	Solomon Burke
"Good Times"	Jerry Butler
"Under the Boardwalk"	The Drifters
"Can I Get a Witness"	Marvin Gaye
"Hitch Hike"	Marvin Gaye
"I've Been Loving You Too Long (To Stop Now)"	Otis Redding
"Pain in My Heart"	Otis Redding
"That's How Strong My Love Is"	Otis Redding
"It's All Over"	Bobby Womack

No other major group covered so many songs, and this fact suggests that a real affinity existed between the early Stones and rhythm and blues. And the fact that both Otis and Aretha later covered "Satisfaction" tends to confirm this.

It's no more paradoxical than anything else about the Stones' evolution that the first Stones song was "Not Fade Away," by Buddy Holly. Of course, it doesn't sound like a Buddy Holly song, but that was the point. Their creativity manifested itself not in writing the song, but in making it new for us. They married Buddy Holly to Bo Diddley, whose "Mona" they had covered. The full sound of the two electric guitars, with that catchy, unmistakable Bo Diddley rhythm—dat dat dat dat dat-dat dat—practically obscured the lyrics, which were odd and elliptical enough anyway. The result was a new song.

Although Mick and Keith did not write "Not Fade Away," they did write "Heart of Stone." But even when they did write a song, it came out as an amalgam of black music—specifically, an amalgam of a doo-wop classic, "Hearts of Stone" by the Charms, and Muddy's "I'm Ready." In "I'm Ready," as in a number of Muddy's songs, he presents himself in the lyrics as a stud, and the Stones clearly picked up on this. If Muddy is ready to make love to a woman all night, then Mick says that he is hard, not just sexually but emotionally as well—she will never break his heart of stone.

It's worth noting here that Mick did *not* pick up on a recurring theme in both downhome and Chicago blues—the lament about a woman's infidelity. For people who grew up in the Delta, images of infidelity came readily to mind. One of my favorites is "somebody's been pickin' potatoes in my field." In "Long Distance Call," Muddy says "another mule's been kickin' in yo' stall." Neither infidelity nor rural imagery ever appear in Mick's lyrics—his urban, teenage audience would not have known what to make of them. Once again, a difference in the social setting of the music, and thus in the audience, produces a difference in the music.

The relationship between "Heart of Stone" and "Hearts of Stone" is even more complicated. There was no one for Mick to sing doo-wop harmonies with, so he discarded that part of the Charms' arrangement. The clearest link between the two songs is the repetition of key words. In the Charms' song, "please," "no," and "never" are often repeated, so Mick repeats phrases like "never break." What's especially interesting is that "Hearts of Stone" derives from a Dr. Watts hymn, "Hearts Of Stone, Relent, Relent." In his version, the hearts of stone belong to sinners. The Charms secularized the hymn by transferring the image from sinners to women, but Mick says that he himself has the heart of stone. Even though Mick probably didn't know Dr. Watts' hymn, "Heart of Stone" represents the beginning of the Stones' flirtation with Satanism.

"Back Street Girls" is not satanic, but it does have threatening, domineering quality. "Back Street Girl" is what happens when Muddy meets the Everly Brothers in a London suburb. The predominant feature of Muddy's lyrics on "I Just Want to Make Love to You" is anaphora, the repetition of "I don't want to..." at the beginning of several lines in each verse. Mick darkens the spirit of the song by reworking these lines as negative commands, also repeated throughout the verse. But of course "Back Street Girl" doesn't sound anything like a blues song because Mick croons it to the accompaniment of an acoustic guitar and an accordion, and no one but Clifton Chenier can play the blues on an accordion. Actually, "Back Street Girl" belongs to a group of songs in which the lyrics and the instrumentation work against each other to produce a dramatic tension. This group includes "Play With Fire"; "Paint It Black"; and "Lady Jane."

On "Play With Fire," Mick threatens the woman, yet sings gently to her. "Back Street Girl" backs up its description of a degrading relationship with a schmaltzy accordion. An unusual feature of "Paint It Black" is the echo on Mick's vocal, which is backed up by Keith's acoustic guitar and Brian's nearly buried sitar. On "Lady Jane," Brian plays arpeggios on a harpsichord to match the arpeggios on Keith's acoustic guitar. The anachronistic sound of the harpsichord is matched by the anachronisms in the lyrics such as "on bended knees" and "I pledge my troth."

None of these songs remind us of "Bye Bye Love, or "Bird Dog," but they bespeak the enduring presence of the Everly Brothers in the Stones' music. With their country harmonies and their twin guitars, the Everlies affected the

Stones as no other white act ever did. They gave the Stones an appreciation for what the acoustic guitar could do for musical understatement. Given their ironic sensibility, though, the Stones did with these principles just the opposite of what the Everlies did with them. Where the Everlies put guitars and voices in sync to put across teenage mawkishness, as in "Wake Up Little Susie," the Stones put guitar and voice out of sync to dramatize despair and exploitation.

"Satisfaction" is the first anthem of the sixties. It defined the mid-sixties, just as "Blowin' in the Wind" defined the early sixties, and "Light My Fire" defined the late sixties. It has such trademarks of the Stones'songs as a complex genealogy and a lack of resolution. "Satisfaction" is also a consummate Mid-Atlantic song in that the artists from whose work it derives—Muddy Waters, Chuck Berry, and Bob Dylan—are all American. The first verse of "Satisfaction" begins, "When I'm riding in my car..." This is of course a homage to Chuck Berry songs about riding in your car and listening to Top 40 radio, as in "No Particular Place to Go" and "You Can't Catch Me." But it was a fantasy situation for British kids, who didn't have cars. (After the Stones broke big, Keith bought a car before he had a drivers' license.) Mick takes this situation, and works Muddy's "I Can't Be Satisfied" into it—with a twist. The point of Muddy's lyrics is that he can't be satisfied in the sense that he can go on forever; Mick turns insatiability into dissatisfaction, and does so with Dylan's help. In the first verse he talks back to a radio commercial for an unnamed product; in the second, he talks back to a TV commercial for a detergent. (The third verse, with its infamous reference to menstruation, has no source other than Mick's decadence.) Both of these verses seem to derive from "Bob Dylan's 110th Dream," where he jeers at a Brylcreem commercial, and asks "Mr. football man" what he's going to do about African drummer Olatungi.

It is on "Satisfaction" that Keith's riffing style comes into its own. The unforgettable "Satisfaction" riff is the first thing we hear on the record, and it recurs throughout the song like a Wagnerian leitmotif of dissatisfaction. The "Satisfaction" riff is as memorable as anything ever recorded, largely because Keith used a fuzz tone for it. The fuzz tone fuzzes the sound, making it less clearcut and less distinct, making progression and resolution ambiguous. "Satisfaction" has, among other things, a wonderful fit between lyrics and instrumentation.

"Going Home" is at once a consolidation and a breakthrough; as such, it has greater importance for the Stones' evolution even than "Satisfaction." It's a breakthrough in that it's by far the longest thing they've ever done, at 11:35, and thus allows the band to stretch out, jam, and work variations on the theme. Mick jams, too, in his own way. The length of the piece allows him to try, one after another, various accents and styles of black singers. You can hear how he has assimilated the aspiration of Otis Redding, for example, which is probably a carryover from African languages, in the way Mick sings "ha" and "got ta, got ta." He also does something very unusual (for him, at least); he sings in a falsetto. On "Going Home" Mick works through his anxiety of influence from black singers; at the same time he was mastering the performance style which he had put together from watching James Brown and Tina Turner.

In January of 1967 the Stones released a very unusual album, *Between the Buttons*. It has only one hard rocker, "Please Go Home," and a lot of eclectic music with vibraphones, organs, and trombones. When something this odd happens to a group with as strong a musical personality as the Stones, we may justifiably look for an outside influence. In the case of *Between the Buttons*, the influence was named Bob Dylan. You don't hear Dylan's influence on every cut on the album, but he's there on a number of them. "My Obsession," doesn't sound like Dylan at all—it's very frantic—but it has his repeated rhymes, as do "Please Go Home" and "Complicated." "Who's Been Sleeping here?" has a harmonica which is not Brian's Little Walter imitation of the earlier bluesy songs, but Dylan's folk harmonica, and Mick uses Dylan's phrasing, only with a fuller backup sound.

"She Smiled Sweetly" is the Stones' version of "Sad-Eyed Lady of the Lowlands." Like "Lady," it begins with a dirge-like organ—the only song by the Stones which does-and presents the woman as an image of reassurance. Here, too, Mick uses Dylan's slow, careful phrasing, as when he sings, "Where-does-she-hide." "She Smiled Sweetly" is much shorter and simpler than "Sad-Eyed Lady of the Lowlands"—What rock song isn't?—but it's a tribute to the Stones' courage and capacity for continued growth that they would create something in a vein so foreign to them.

The album ends with the very ambitious "Something Happened to Me Yesterday," which takes Dylanesque enigmas in the lyrics, and plays them off against startling instrumentation. It begins with a brass band, yet; there's some trad jazz in it, and at one point there's a duet between Keith's acoustic guitar and...a tuba! The cut gives the impression of balancing Dylan's far-out lyrics with an old-fashioned sound, especially since it has a campy ending in which Mick recreates the ending of a thirties radio show, and gives his fans a secular benediction: "So if you're out tonight on your bike—wear white. Evening, all." The creation of a fictional performance setting makes for a transition between the Stones' earlier work and the watershed in their career, *Their Satanic Majesties Request*.

It is more difficult for us to appreciate *Their Satanic Majesties Request* than anything else in the Stones' catalog. The album lacks the irony and the gutsy, hard-driving rock that the Stones do well. We expect these things from the Stones, and when they don't provide them, we decide that the album isn't very good. In fact, though, the Stones were taking chances, as usual. (In an interview with MTV VJ J.J. Jackson, Mick said that it was the biggest risk that they had ever taken.) The one thing which didn't change was the lack of resolution in their music; without the other qualities which usually accompany it, it seemed then, and seems now, harder to take.

The thing is, though, the Stones were taking care of important business: Having assimilated black music, and having learned from Dylan, they were coming to terms with the Beatles by overcoming their anxiety of influence from the world's most famous pop group, and the songwriters who had helped them get their start. As the Stones' only concept album, *Majesties* is clearly a response to *Sargeant Pepper,* which had come out in June of 1967; *Majesties* came out in November of that year, but the Stones had been to some of the *Sargeant Pepper* sessions, so they knew what the Beatles were doing.

The two albums resemble each other in a number of ways. The Beatles use ambience noise to create the fiction of a performance setting on "Sargeant Pepper's Lonely Hearts Club Band." Ambience noise creates a carnival setting for "She's A Rainbow," and a cabaret setting for "On With the Show." The lyrics of "Sing This All Together" (but certainly not the instrumentation) recall the lyrics to "With A Little Help From My Friends." Then, too, there's the matter of drugs, as in "Lucy in the Sky with Diamonds." The name of the Stones' album is a pun on the legend on the cover of their passports, Her Britannic Majesty Requests. If the album is like a passport, then the Stones are taking us on a trip. Furthermore, the tape loops and reverb effects on the album created a sound which was generally associated with drugs at the time.

The picture on the cover of *Majesties* is of a child's toy which shows a different picture from different angles. From one angle, the Stones are looking straight ahead; from another, Keith and Charlie are looking at each other, as are Brian and Bill. The music is like that, too—it consists of disparate elements. Take "Sing This All Together," for example. The song has an unusually memorable melody for a Jagger-Richard number, and the Stones sing it in a good-timey, amateurish way. Yet both this song and its reprise on what the Stones insisted on calling the "front side" (they had adopted Dylan's conceit of avoiding capital letters) are awash with the unusual sound textures which can only be produced in the studio. The Stones could never perform the song on stage, yet we associate them with dynamite live performances. A Stones concert is an intense drama with larger than life figures, yet the theme of the song is your basic sixties trip of togetherness and common origins. Similarly, on Bill Wyman's "In Another Land" (a characteristic sixties title; cf. *Stranger in a Strange Land*), his voice is double-tracked; one track has a tape delay, and the other does not. And so it goes throughout the album. When does a lack of resolution turn into chaos? It is characteristic of great innovative periods in music that they baffle our attempts to answer this question.

We can group four songs on the album under the common heading of "In Another Time." "Citadel" and "the lantern" are set in the past (deriving, perhaps, from "Lady Jane"), and "2000 man" and "2000 light years from home" are set in the future. The latter two may derive from the Stones' fantasy of making a movie of *A Clockwork Orange;* they never had the rights to the property, but they talked themselves into believing that they did. "2000 man" projects the generation gap into the future, as when Mick sings that his name is a number, and that he is alienated from his son. More ambitious is "2000 light years from home," which seems like a space version of "She's Leaving Home." But the Stones' song is cosmic, rather than domestic. It's aurally more complex, too. While the strings of "She's Leaving Home" are in the background,

Keith's fuzztone guitar is in the foreground on "2000 light years..." and is balanced against Mick's heavily echoed voice. As if all this were not enough, tape noise throughout creates something like a wall of sound.

The last cut, "on with the show" is the most accessible. "Ah," we may think, "This is what they should have been doing all along." A barker announces "Big live show—they're naked and dance!" and "Continuous show!" A tape filter changes Mick's voice when he greets us, "Good evening one and all." One has the impression that the Stones are defining themselves against the Beatles by placing this cut last, as opposed to "Sargeant Pepper's Lonely Hearts Club Band," the first cut on *Sargeant Pepper*. As opposed to the Beatles' cheerfulness in a music hall, the Stones offer decadence in a cabaret. But it is not quite the Stones, either, for Mick promises such Tin Pan Alley standards as "Moon River" and "Stormy Weather."

In effect, with *Majesties,* the Stones said to the Beatles, "We can do that stuff, too." But there's much more to it than that, for the Stones were also responding to their times, as the Beatles had done, and they were assimilating the potential of the studio—something which every major group had to do in one way or another in the late sixties. The Stones had now come to terms with white music as well as black music; they could now do anything they wanted to do.

What they did was to create two of the supreme albums in rock 'n' roll history, *Beggars' Banquet* and *Let It Bleed*. Taken together the two albums have a unity, and the songs fall together into groups. Like the songs on the white album, they show an opposition between the past and the present. It's both the Stones' past and their present, and—because they were who they were— it's the past and the present of rock 'n' roll as well. Their confidence and mastery enabled them to realize more fully the dramatic tendencies which had been implicit in their music all along.

The songs which have stylistic references to the past usually come from the Southern tradition. Now that they had assimilated Muddy Waters and the Everly Brothers, they reach beyond them to the general tradition which produced their music. So the Southern songs split into black songs and white songs.

Black Songs	White Songs
"Love In Vain"	"You Got the Silver"
"No Expectations"	"Country Honk"
"Parachute Woman"	"Dear Doctor"
"Prodigal Son"	"Factory Girl"

"Love In Vain," the Robert Johnson song, is the first downhome blues the Stones covered. Unlike their earlier covers of Chicago blues numbers, the song goes at the slow, deliberate pace at which Johnson recorded it in 1937, and Mick gets the accent so right that he rhymes "vain" and "hand" ("hain"), the way Delta blacks do. But they cannot suppress who they are, and we cannot forget it, so they put in a mandolin break (played by Ry Cooder). It's hard to think of a stringed instrument more inappropriate for the downhome blues than the mandolin, so its tinkling sound reminds us that this is the late sixties, not the late thirties.

"No Expectations" is the Stones' reworking of "Love In Vain." They take the situation of the lyrics of "Love In Vain"—going to meet a train—and redo it with some differences. In Johnson's song, the woman leaves; in their song, the man leaves; Johnson uses the usual *aab* stanza form of the blues; the Stones use couplets. Since this is their song, there's no need for a mandolin, and we hear a strummed acoustic guitar and a slide guitar. Similarly, "Prodigal Son" is sung in a semi-authentic drone.

For the first time the Stones were able to draw on the white version of the Southern tradition; they even felt enough confidence to use American place names in "Country Honk" and "Dear Doctor." Dylan probably gave them the impetus to do this, for he had assimilated country and western music, which was practically as foreign to him as it was to them. Like Dylan, they appreciated the fine guitar work as well as the naive surrealism of the metaphors of country and western music. They had the musical talent, and they turned the surrealism into a slyness and self-consciousness which country music had always lacked, and whose absence had often constituted a major attraction of the music. The Stones' decadence has various meanings, and one of them is that what they admire, they subvert.

Take "Country Honk" (aka "Honky Tonk Woman"), for instance; the album version begins and ends with an aural pun—the sounds of a honking car horn. Into the middle of this spirited country rock number, Mick comes on as a tease with one of his cleverest lines: "She blew my nose, and then she blew my mind." And then there's the very hokey "Dear Doctor" in which Mick's overdone Southern accent goes well with the odd situation—the *man* is afraid to get married, and presumably afraid of the woman herself, so that his mother has to comfort him, and he has to drink "bourbon so sour." His dilemma is resolved only when he gets a note from her—whose contents he narrates in a wonderful falsetto—in which she says that she's run off to Virginia with his cousin Luke. By this time, Mick had such a strong image as a macho man that it affected the meaning of everything he did. By taking on the mask of a Southern redneck, he could work against that image, and sing about a woman who left him—thereby reversing the situation of "Please Go Home," for example.

The one American song set in the present is "Midnight Rambler," which may well be Mick's response to the Doors' "The End." Like "The End," it is narrated by a murderer. In the late sixties and early seventies, Mick took on the mask of the Boston Strangler and turned the song into a performance piece. Sara Davidson reported that during the 1970 European tour,

During "Midnight Rambler," Mick took of his shoes and twirled them in the air, shed his hat and scarf, and then took off his metal-studded belt, raised it high, and, his face a snarl, whacked the belt on the ground. Dust flew. The crowd screamed.[9]

Just as there's ambiguity in "The End"—is it all taking place in Jim's mind or not?—so there's ambiguity in Mick's performance of "Midnight Rambler." While he lashes out at a victim, he symbolically undresses, too, and his sexual ambiguity suggests that he is simultaneously the victim and the murderer.

The songs on *Beggars' Banquet* and *Let It Bleed* which are set in the present also fall into two groups. One group of songs comments on Western society in the late sixties, while in the second group the Stones play on their image.

Social Songs	*Self-Conscious Songs*
"Sympathy for the Devil"	"Live With Me"
"Street Fighting Man"	"Stray Cat Blues"
"Salt of the Earth"	"Jig-Saw Puzzle"
"You Can't Always Get What you Want"	

On "Live With Me," Mick announces that he has "nasty habits"—because he "takes tea at three." Things get more decadent as the song goes along, but that's the kind of witty play on their image, and on the audience's expectations which that image created. On "Stray Cat Blues," Mick talks to an underage groupie, but the most important thing about the song is the best Stones jam since "Going Home." The most complex of their self-conscious songs, though, is "Jig-Saw Puzzle"—an aptly named song, since their musical heritage is a jig saw puzzle. The song has some echoes of Dylan, especially in the first verse, where the opposition of the tramp and the bishop's daughter may owe something to "Like a Rolling Stone." Like the gangster in the second verse, she has been an outcast "all her life." This sounds like Dylan, too, but then in the third verse Mick does something that Dylan would never have done: He characterizes each member of the band in a separate line, and concludes that the guitar players have been outcasts all their lives.

The easy way to explain the first of the Stones' great social songs, "Sympathy for the Devil," is to say that it's Mick in his Lucifer mask. There's more to it than that, though, for the lyrics correspond suggestively to the way the Devil presents himself to Ivan Karamazov in Dostoyevsky's *The Brothers Karamazov*. Like Mick's, Dostoyevsky's Lucifer is witty and self-conscious. Both of them speak to people who have denied the existence of evil—what puzzles them is the nature of his game—and who have thereby denied themselves any way of dealing with it. Notably, Mick's Lucifer transcends ideology as well as time— he had something to do with both the Russian Revolution and Nazi Germany.

Corresponding to this verbal historicism is the stylistic historicism of "You Can't Always Get What You Want." The lyrics have Dylanesque enigmas, such as the "footloose man" at the woman's feet and the use of the last word in a line to explode its meaning, as when he goes to the demonstration to "get my fair share of...abuse." Nevertheless, the song has a juxtaposition of opposites unthinkable in Dylan—rock 'n' roll and the London Bach Chorus. The chorus sings a cappella, and then gives way to another odd juxtaposition— Keith's acoustic guitar and Al Kooper's French horn.

After all this, the lyrics cannot "make a statement," as the political types kept wanting the great performers to do. Like the Beatles' "Revolution 1," it denies the validity of demonstrations; or, to take the obvious analogy, "You Can't Always Get What You Want" estheticizes the revolution just as "Street Fighting Man" does. If "there's nothing for a poor boy to do but to sing in a rock 'n' roll band," then if the demonstrators don't vent their frustration, they'll "blow a 50-amp fuse." Here Mick directs the irony and ambiguity of the self-conscious songs toward his contemporaries. The beliefs that "we can change the world," and that nothing matters but the here and now can only evoke irony from performers with the historical consciousness which the Beatles and the Stones put to such imaginative use in the late sixties.

The statement that limitations to desire exist, and that wants and needs do not always coincide was far more subversive than any overt political statement which the Stones could have made. The fact that the Stones put "You Can't Always Get What You Want" as the last cut on their last album in the sixties suggests two conclusions. First, it suggests that some of the intensity of the adulation which rock stars received in the sixties came not so much from the fact that they served as fantasy projections (although that was part of it) as because the great ones created and maintained a distance between themselves and their fans. Second, if the Stones, who had it all, could say "You Can't Always Get What You Want," then the utopian dreams of the sixties were fading. It was time to start sucking in the seventies.

Notes

[1]Tom Wolfe, "The Mid-Atlantic Man," in *The Pump House Gang* (New York: Farrar, Straus and Giroux, 1968), pp. 46-7.

[2]Quoted in S.K. Oberbeck, "Mick Jagger and the Future of Rock," *Newsweek*, January 4, 1971, p. 48.

[3]Quoted in Jeremy Pascal, *The Rolling Stones* (Seacaucus, NJ: Chartwell Books, 1977), p. 22.

[4]Apparently, only the Southern tradition in American music can inspire its admirers with a belief in purity. No one has ever been a purist about the music of Irving Berlin.

[5]Quoted in Robert Palmer, *The Rolling Stones* (Garden City, NJ: Doubleday, 1977), p. 38.

[6]Quoted in Tim Dowley, *The Rolling Stones* (New York: Hippocrene Books, 1983), p. 33.

[7]Robert Greenfield, "Keith Richard: The Rolling Stone Interview," *Rolling Stone*, August 19, 1971, p. 25.

[8]Tom Wolfe, "Keith Richard," *Guitar Player*, April, 1983, p. 68.

[9]Sara Davidson, "Mick Jagger Shoots Birds," *Atlantic Monthly*, May, 1971, p. 98.

Chapter 17:
Yes, But What About AM Radio?

It's a funny thing about AM radio in the sixties. Since FM underground stations had obsolesced Top 40, people tended to think of AM as something they had listened to as kids, as something not to be taken seriously. AM radio tended to lose the college kids, but it held the junior high school kids, who kept discovering it. A survey conducted in Florida in 1967 showed that:

The teenager most likely to be listening to the radio is a thirteen-year-old girl with a transistor radio. She is most apt to be of low intelligence and to make low grades in school. Her favorite type of music is rock and roll, and she is relaxing while she listens most of the time.[1]

This girl, and the junior high school kids she represents, was not listening to The Who or The Grateful Dead; she was listening to Sonny and Cher, Paul Revere and the Raiders, the Monkees, the Turtles, and the Association. The opposition of FM and AM radio stations involved both an age difference and a media difference.

What had happened by 1967 was that another generation gap had formed in addition to the much-ballyhooed one between people who were under 30 and those who were over 30. This was a mini-generation gap, but a no less real one for that. This gap existed between the kids born at the beginning of the baby boom in 1947-48, and those kids who were born in the middle of it, in 1953-54. The first group was 20 in 1967; it had experienced the ecstasy of Beatlemania, and then matured as the Beatles matured. The second group was 14 in 1967, and this meant that it entered adolescence at a time of wrenching change which baffled even adults. Unsure of themselves as fourteen-year-olds notoriously are, and even more unsure of the world around them, they wanted music which acknowledged the times, as in Sonny and Cher's "The Beat Goes On," and the Monkees' social commentary song "Pleasant Valley Sunday," but which did not frighten or disorient them. Everybody but the kids who liked it called it bubblegum music. Nobody seems to have noticed that a media difference corresponded to this demographic difference.

The primary record for Sonny and Cher and the other Top 40 acts was still the 45 rpm single; FM underground stations, on the other hand, were playing cuts from the albums which their listeners were buying. This opposition never became an absolute one, and most major groups were played on both AM and FM stations. Still, a certain segmentation of groups with regard to production values and, especially, the length of cuts occurred. Thus, the Doors put out "Light My Fire" both in the album version, played on FM, and the shorter version, played on AM. (In the late sixties, CBS acknowledged this segmentation by appointing Mike Klenfer as director of FM promotion.)[2]

In effect, FM underground and Top 40 stations made another distinction as well, although it was not a conscious one, and became apparent only later. As it worked out, the acts which had broken before Beatlemania, and did not evolve as later acts did, did not get played on FM underground stations. Elvis may have been the King of Rock 'N' Roll, but I never heard anything by him in the two years I listened to KSAN and KPIX in San Francisco. The same distinction applies to girl groups, the Beach Boys, and to Motown acts. The case of Motown, in particular, offers some revealing considerations.

Motown was riding high on the charts; it posted 5 #1 songs in 1965, 3 in 1966, and 2 each in 1967, 1968, and 1969. In each of these years there were numerous 2's, 6's, and 10's. So the Motown machine hummed along, turning out songs which we now think of as sixties classics, such as the Supremes' "You Can't Hurry Love," and the Four Tops' "Walk Away Renee."   Yet, oddly enough, Motown was not what was happening. What was happening was screaming guitars, sexy lead singers, and elaborate studio productions. It was not just that Motown acts did not cut any songs of protest, or even of social awareness of any kind, until Edwin Starr's "War" in the fall of 1970, although that played a role. Rather, it was more that Motown music revealed the iron hand of Berry Gordy in its precision and professionalism. At a time when college kids wanted ecstasy, Motown offered them entertainment. At a time when the world was threatening to go out of control, the college kids who constituted the prime audience for rock 'n' roll wanted music and performers which also threatened to go out of control—to "test the limits of reality," as Jim Morrison put it. The trouble was, none of them believed that Smokey Robinson or Diana Ross would test the limits of reality. Some white performers like Jim and Janis Joplin would; some black performers like the Chambers Brothers and Jimi Hendrix certainly did. But no one from Motown did.

So who kept Motown on the charts for all those years? One answer is that teeny-boppers did. The solid harmonies of the Four Tops made them the best teeny-bopper group of the sixties; their records, like "Reach Out" and "Bernadette" sounded good in the sixties, and they still sound good today. They offered romance, not sex; fantasy, not "danger at the edge of town." Pre-Beatlemania performers and pre-Beatlemania entrepreneurs could not adapt to the changing demands of the recording studio, so they stayed on AM radio. As they got older, their audiences got younger.

It wasn't just teeny-boppers who were listening to Motown, though. For what is probably the only time in the history of American popular music, a major record company made huge profits while mostly ignoring the college kids. Motown was making music for a split audience—for junior high school kids and for their parents. A caption to a picture in the *Fortune* story on Motown explains the marketing strategy by which Gordy accomplished this demographic miracle: "Motown's biggest moneymakers, the Supremes, are penetrating deeper into the mass popular-music market with Rodgers and Hart songs and personal appearance at Miami Beach and Las Vegas."[13] When all else fails, when the Southern tradition can no longer provide the inspiration for innovation, American performers can always rely on the New York-Hollywood tradition, with its tried and true songs which pull large, affluent adult audiences in ritzy venues. It is significant that two of the biggest money-making acts of all times, Elvis and the Supremes, did not write their own material, did not make concept albums, and wound up wowing audiences in Las Vegas.

Although Motown was the most visible expression of black music in the sixties, it wasn't everything. On the contrary, the sixties was a great age of individual performers of soul music, which is to say that secularization continued apace. The usual pattern was for an unusually gifted singer to start out with a gospel group, and then turn into a solo act. Since these singers did not usually write their own material, they often interpreted, not to say transformed, other people's material. As with Motown acts, the principal interest on their records was the vocal style, so they did well on AM radio, too.

Lou Rawls, who started out with a gospel group called the Pilgrim Travellers, and started singing secular music in about 1958 when he toured with Sam Cooke, whose career went through a very similar evolution. Dionne Warwick was the daughter of Lee Warwick of The Drinkard Singers, another gospel group; she herself sang with the group, as did her sister Dee Dee. When gospel-trained singers from Southern families turned to secular music, their momentum sometimes carried them all the way to white pop music. Thus, Dionne Warwick had her greatest success with material such as "Do You Know the Way to San Jose" by Burt Bacharach and Hal David, a songwriting team squarely in the New York-Hollywood tradition.

The master of gospel-derived soul in the sixties, though, was Wilson Pickett. He formed a gospel group, the Violinaires, in Detroit in the fifties, but went secular when he wrote and sang lead on the Falcons' "I Found A Love," which could just as easily have come out, "I Found the Lord." After Pickett signed with Atlantic in 1964, Jerry Wexler took him to Memphis, where he cut "In the Midnight Hour," a variation of the black gospel standard by the same name, with Booker T. and the MG's. Melisma, the vocal embellishment of the virtuoso black gospel singer remained essential for Wilson; just listen to "In the Midnight Hour," or "Mustang Sally," and you'll notice that he hates to sing one note where five or six will do. But it wasn't just Wilson who was doing this; two of the great soul classics of the sixties, Percy Sledge's "Your Love Is Taking Me Higher," and Jackie Wilson's "Ninety-Nine and a Half (Won't Do)" are also derived from hymns.[4]

And then there was Aretha Franklin, the most obvious example of secularization in black music in the sixties. She was the daughter of a great preacher and a great gospel singer in his own right, C.L. Franklin of Detroit's New Bethel Baptist Church, We might think of Aretha as the female Elvis; like Elvis, she begins with gospel but does so much more. Like Elvis, she has such talent that she can dominate any material, and thus can have a very eclectic repertoire. At one extreme, she covers "Satisfaction," imitating Mick's phrasing at the ending, and then cutting loose with whoops and hollers against the brass. Although she keeps the gospel backup in the persons of the Sweet Inspirations, the sharp brass section (often led by King Curtis) forms a secular counterpoint. It is appropriate that the song on which her gospel training most clearly comes through is "Son of a Preacher Man." It begins with gospel chords on the piano, and the piano dominates throughout, as you would expect on a hymn. Aretha uses a lot of melisma, as when she sings "wa-a-as," and she sings "hallelujah" a lot. In fact, "Son of a Preacher Man" is a good reply to Ray Charles' "Hallelujah I Love Her So." As the sixties ended, it was easy for her to cover such hymn-like hits by white composers as "Let It Be" and "Bridge Over Troubled Water."

Aretha broke soul music for the mass white audience, and her only rival in terms of pure talent, Otis Redding, benefited from what she did. He is unique among the soul singers of the sixties in that gospel singing meant very little to him, even though he was literally the son of a preacher. He shared Aretha's eclecticism; she covered his "Respect," and they both covered "Satisfaction" as well as "Try A Little Tenderness." If Aretha was the female Elvis, Otis was the black Elvis. He could sing sweet and he could sing hot. His premature death was the greatest loss of the sixties.

The success which Aretha and Otis had in making both the pop and the R&B charts brings up the question of the relation of blacks and whites in music. Many blacks at the time would have been surprised to learn that white musicians were playing on Motown and Stax/Volt records. Racial crossover often bothered the gatekeepers more than the audiences, though. It's been said that Otis' "Satisfaction" would have done better if white DJ's had pushed it more. By the same token, black DJ's wouldn't play the Righteous Brothers, despite the fact that they did well on the R&B charts. Bill Medley once complained to an interviewer, "A lot of rhythm & blues stations won't play Righteous Brothers records. They used to, but the records got yanked, once we went around to visit the stations and they found out we were white...that was it, man, that was it."[5]

Much Top 40 music was clearly and undeniably white; sometimes it owed something to black music, sometimes it did not. In connection with Motown's continued popularity, we should remember that The Mamas and the Papas had a successful, if short, career by adapting their original folky style as the Mugwumps to the Motown Sound. They had such features of the Motown Sound as the importance of vocals (they were a male/female group like the original Miracles), consequent suppression of instrumentation, and a lack of narrative in the lyrics. Most indicative of all, perhaps, were the tambourines, as in "California Dreamin'."

Top 40 stations played new acts, too. The Monkees had one song after another in the top 10 during the mid sixties, as the following table shows.

The Monkees' Top 10 Hits

Song	Highest Position	Date
"Last Train in Clarksville"	#1	9/10/66
"I'm a Believer"	#1	12/10/66
"A Little Bit Me, A Little Bit You"	#2	3/25/67
"Pleasant Valley Sunday"	#3	7/22/67
"Daydream Believer"	#1	11/18/67

During a period of about two years the Monkees had no less than three #1 songs, one #2, and two #3's. And they did this, mind you, against the toughest competition imaginable, for Dylan, the Beatles, the Rolling Stones, and all the other major groups from the sixties were at the height of their powers. As if this record of hits were not enough, they also had their sitcom, *The Monkees*, which ran from September, 1966 through August of 1968. They also made a little-known movie, *Head* (1969).

The Monkees were not one-hit wonders and their success was not a fluke. Any pro in the record business will agree that there is not enough hype in the known universe to create three #1's in two years. There must have been something in the grooves which made those records sell. So the Monkees offer a test case for one's allegiance to democracy or elitism. In the sixties, a lot of critics showed their nascent elitism by giving the Monkees a lot of abuse; they said that MCA had had to hire studio musicians because the Monkees themselves couldn't play, and so forth. As usual, such criticism misses the point, and expresses the same elitism and snobbishness which characterizes those people who won't listen to anything but Beethoven. The crucial point is that no one bribed all those kids who bought Monkees' records, and gave them their three #1's. Yes, it's true that the Monkees were a manufactured group, but they were a very *popular* manufactured group. Why did they, and the other bubblegum groups like the 1910 Fruit Gum Company, succeed when they did?

We can get an answer from the man who manufactured the Monkees, Don Kirshner. As an entrepreneur who had scored his first big successes at about the same time as Berry Gordy had, he—like Gordy—never made the transition to acid rock and concept albums. Rather, he reacted to the growing complexity of the Beatles' music just as Andrew Loog Oldham had reacted to their initial success. Just as Oldham had sensed in 1963 that the Beatles were creating a need, not for an imitation, but for an opposite, so Kirshner sensed in 1966 that rock was making demands of emotional maturity and cultural sophistication which the 14-year-olds who listened to Top 40 could not meet. He later told an interviewer:

When I did the Monkees, the Beatles were getting married, they weren't touchable to the public any more; they had lost their innocence. I knew that if a group like the Monkees came on TV, it would take all the marbles.[6]

Having identified the mini-generation gap before anyone else, he proceeded to fill it with the Monkees.

It is indicative that Kirshner thought of the Monkees as a television group. By positioning them in this way he continued the association between Top 40 radio and television which had begun with *Bandstand*. In fact, network television had a lot of trouble with rock 'n' roll during the late sixties, since it was an lp/FM radio form. In September of 1964, ABC responded to Beatlemania by putting *Shindig* on the air; the show's principal discovery was Bobby Sherman, and Sonny and Cher often appeared on it. But the talent did not consist exclusively of lightweights, for both the Beatles and the Rolling Stones did the show. As a matter of fact, *Shindig* demonstrated the media power of the youth movement very dramatically; the network daringly put it against the #1 show in the country at the time, *The Beverly Hillbillies*, which then dropped to #18.[7] NBC did not fail to notice this fact, and put on *Hullabaloo* the following January. The Beatles did the show once, in January of 1966, but hosts included pre-Beatlemania favorites such as Frankie and Annette as well as those television reliables, Sonny and Cher. Finally, Dick Clark himself got into the act by putting on a most unusual thing, an afternoon music show sponsored by a network. This was *Where the Action Is*, on Clark's network, ABC, which was a regular spot for Paul Revere and the Raiders.

However, none of the these shows lasted past the spring of 1967, when *Where the Action Is* went off the air. The limitations of network television, demographic as well as technical, doomed all attempts to make music shows viable. The rock 'n' roll feeling came across better on the two great comedy shows of the late sixties, *The Smothers Brothers Comedy Hour*, and *Laugh-In*.

Since elitist critics despise television as a commercial medium ruled by the all-mighty dollar, a few words on rock 'n' roll and commercials can conclude this chapter. After Beatlemania, Ellie Greenwich, one of Don Kirshner's stable of songwriters (she wrote "Da Doo Ron Ron" and "The Leader of the Pack"), turned to commercials. After Donovan had a hit with "Wear Your Love Like Heaven," he sold the rights to a cosmetics company which introduced a new line aimed at the teenage market, and called—what else?—"Love."[8] But remember that the key band in the San Francisco counter-culture, self-conscious revolutionaries that they were, the Jefferson Airplane, made radio commercials for the San Francisco-based blue jeans manufacturers Levi-Strauss. The Airplane's commercials had a parodistic quality, complete with sound distortion, so that they gave the impression of making fun of commercials. But they were still selling a product none the less.

To sum up, we can say that in the sixties AM radio and television continued their close association, but now with the difference that the principal innovations were occurring on albums played on FM stations. As a result, the innovators perceived the media complex which had created rock 'n' roll as...impure. The controversy over bubblegum music merely recycled the controversy among the folkies over Dylan's electric phase. To hippies in 1967, the Monkees smacked too much of commercialism, just as Dylan's electric phase had smacked too much of commercialism to folkies in 1965. The search for purity never lies dormant for long; its recurrence attests to the phoenix-like nature of the dialectic between democracy and elitism in America. It's a good thing that elitism never wins.

Notes

[1]George Arlen Booker, *The Disc Jockey and His Impact On Teenage Musical Taste As Reflected Through A Study in Three North Florida Cities,* unpublished dissertation, Florida State University, 1968,p. 89.

[2]See Spitz, *The Making of Superstars,* p. 242.

[3]Caption, "The Motown Sound of Money," *Fortune,* September 1 1967, p. 103.

[4]Tony Heilbut, *The Gospel Sound,* p. 22.

[5]Quoted in Arnold Shaw, *The Rock Revolution* (New York: Crowell-Collier, 1969) p. 147.

[6]Quoted in Spitz, *The Making of Superstars,* p. 37.

[7]See Bill Davidson, "Who Killed Your Favorite TV Show?" *Saturday Evening Post* February 27, 1965, pp. 84-7.

[8]See Herman Edel,"Advertising: Spot Music and Advertising Jingles," *The Complete Report of the First International Music Industry Conference,* Paul Ackerman and Lee Zlato, eds. (New York: Billboard, 1969), p. 267.

Chapter 18:
The Erotic Politicians of the
Woodstock Nation
Go Creepy Crawling Toward Altamont

The sixties came together and fell apart in five short months. The end began when Charlie Manson's followers came together to carry out the Tate-La Bianca murders in Los Angeles on the nights of the ninth and tenth of August, 1969; only a week later, on the fifteenth, sixteenth, and seventeenth, the Woodstock Nation came together for the first and only time. Then, finally, the hippies came together to create Woodstock West at Altamont, California, on the ninth of December, to hear the Rolling Stones, and it all came apart. The sixties began with the Beatles and ended with the Rolling Stones. As it often happens in momentous events, this generalization holds in more than one sense. If Charlie Manson thought that the Beatles were sending him secret messages to commit murder, the Rolling Stones found out that they couldn't prevent murder. As it also happens in momentous events, these three have a symbolic quality in that they stand for the social change of the sixties which was inseparable from the music. A full appreciation of the music requires a full appreciation of how and why people "went through changes," as we said at the time. And vice versa.

"Think of us as erotic politicians." Jim Morrison included this instruction in his first press release. "Politicians" refers to social action, and "erotic" refers to personal experience. It now seems to us that the tension between the social and the personal pervaded the sixties, but it did not seem that way at the time, when many people believed that "The personal is the political." (In 1967, R.D. Laing published a book with a characteristic title: *The Politics of Experience.)* Thus, to let your hair grow long was to make a political statement. This made sense for a while, for the same people who wanted the kids to wear their hair short also supported the war, and hated rock 'n' roll.

Nevertheless, to say that "The personal is the political" was to think that wishing would make it so, for these two adjectives stood for the two opposing tendencies of the age. These tendencies were so strong, and so utterly opposed, that people could not balance them indefinitely. The first of these tendencies, the political one, was in fact the centralization of power in the executive branch of the federal government which more or less dates from the Roosevelt Presidency. The people who agitated for the passage of the Civil Rights Act, for instance, believed in a fairly pure form of this centralization. They wanted the federal government to take from the Southern states the right to practice segregation, and to assume the right to impose integration. But this same centralization of power made it harder to stop the war.

For it was the war which de-centralized authority. The fact that very large numbers of people found the war abhorrent, and invested large amounts of time and energy to stop it, with no apparent effect, greatly weakened the social consensus which had existed in the fifties. The kids whose respect for the society was weakened by the enduring presence of the war found it more and more difficult to respect other forms of authority as well. So if straight society didn't want you to wear your hair long, smoke dope, and have orgies, well, that just didn't mean as much as it had in the fifties. Kids had rebelled before this, of course, but by the late sixties the baby boomers achieved a critical mass which created its own internal consensus.

It was all very traditional, of course. Like almost everything connected with rock 'n' roll, the experimentation with drugs and freak clothing in the sixties derived from early nineteenth century European Romanticism. Seymour Martin Lipset apparently noticed this first, when he commented in the early seventies that:

If you read through the literature on youth and student protest historically and comparatively, the extent to which the dominant behavior patterns repeat, ever since 1800 in the United States and Europe is fantastic.
The first such movement in nineteenth century Europe was the Borschenschatten organizations of German students circa 1815, who in protest to life in Germany developed a "counterculture." It took the form of special moustaches, beards, long hair, colorful clothes, unwashed skin, rough clothing. The descriptions of their clothes suggest they looked very much like the hippies of today. They also defended their counterculture in populist terms, i.e., styles of the common people.[1]

The counterculture also had its own American predecessors, most notably Thoreau, from whom Michael Nesmith took a phrase for the title of the song which made Linda Ronstadt a star, "A Different Drum."

More than anything else, it was a form of medical technology which brought about the rise of erotic politics: The Pill. Enovid was synthesized in the lab in 1959, and caused what demographers call a contraceptive revolution between 1965 and 1970, when very large numbers of married women went on the Pill. This ongoing change created much of the sexy atmosphere of the sixties. It was harder for unmarried women such as college coeds to get a prescription for the Pill, but many of them did so. No matter what the numbers, sociologist Ira Reiss says that it was the mere presence of The Pill in society that mattered. "Overall, however, it seems that the pill's importance is likely that of its availability and its use as a female method of contraception. The pill forces females to decide about their own sexuality."[2] Medicine had removed the two great fears about sex, the fear of contracting syphillis and the fear of getting pregnant, and more and more women decided that they wanted sex. In fact, from the best information we have, it seems that male sexual behavior changed very little during the sixties. The change occurred with women.

Actually, the sixties was the second great decade of technological and social change in America; the first was the twenties—which was also a decade of great music. Not coincidentally, sexual mores changed at about the same rate in these two decades. Comparing the sixties with the twenties in this respect, Reiss concludes: "The proportion of females nonvirginal at marriage doubled in the first period from 25 to 50 percent, and in the second period the increase was probably from 50 percent to a current rate of about 75-percent nonvirginity at marriage."[3]

Since women's clothing always expresses the sexual mores of the times, it's worth noting that hemlines rose daringly in both the twenties and the sixties, and that in compensation, fashionable clothing often de-emphasized the breasts in both decades as well. Twiggy, the girl-child, looked a lot like a flapper, so it's appropriate that she starred in a spoof of 1920s musicals, *The Boy Friend* (1971).

Another major change, while not so widespread or long-lasting, also came out of scientific laboratories in the fifties—the use of LSD. Why did people drop acid in order to blow their minds in the sixties (Rimbaud's "derangement of all the senses") and even refer to a musical style as acid rock? Statistics don't help here, but McLuhan does.

McLuhan noticed that both the synapses in the brain and the circuits in a television set work by electricity, and concluded that what we were doing in creating electronic communications was externalizing the circuits of the brain. When such externalization occurs rapidly, as it did in the fifties and sixties, it creates an imbalance. To correct this imbalance, people needed a greater awareness of the internal self as a compensation. So the kids explored the canyons of their minds by dropping acid. Dropping acid may have been a sixties fad, like swallowing goldfish, but it was no random ripple in the history of the world.

Still, relatively few people took acid. More widespread changes occurred when people started smoking dope and wearing crazy clothes. To explain these changes, John Naisbitt's adaptation of McLuhan's work in *Megatrends* offers more help. Having learned from McLuhan's capacity to think up catch phrases to popularize his ideas, Naisbitt uses the phrase "high tech/high touch" to relate social trends to technological change. Although he doesn't believe in McLuhan's hot/cool opposition, Naisbitt does believe that major social trends constitute responses to technological change: "High tech/high touch is a formula I use to describe the way we have responded to technology. What happens is that whenever new technology is introduced into society, there must be a counterbalancing human response—that is, *high touch*—or the technology is rejected. The more high tech, the more high touch."[4] In Naisbitt's terms, dope increases your touch because it makes you more sensually aware. It gives you a giddy, unfocussed sense of well-being and makes it easier to get lost in sex and/or music.

Almost all the changes in their daily lives that people went through in the sixties expressed the desire to create high touch. This is what black society had always had, and its music had great appeal. In addition, though, there was exotic and esthetic high touch. People bought incense and patchouli oil; they blew soap bubbles in the park on sunny afternoons and said "Oh, wow." Men let their facial hair grow, and—what was more revolutionary—some women let their underarm hair grow, and stopped shaving their legs. To be an American in the fifties was to live in a low-touch society, and it was the work of the sixties to re-define America as a high-touch society—or at least as a higher-touch society. As a high-touch—or what McLuhan called a "cool"—phenomenon, hair offered the most visible means of bringing about this change. The Broadway musical *Hair* and the billboards which read "BEAUTIFY AMERICA—GET A HAIRCUT" both make sense in these terms.

The high touch of hip clothing complemented the high touch of body hair. Rex Weiner and Deanna Stillman, the compilers of the invaluable *Woodstock Census*, report that:

For the people we talked to, clothes became as much a personal statement as they ever were for aristocrats at the court of Louis XIV. In Haight-Ashbury, the East Village, and hip ghettos all over the country, people wore clothes that were often as bizarre as they were beautiful—outrageous clothes made of paisley and velvet, silk scarves and embroidered robes, purple bell-bottoms and long, flowing skirts, cast-off military jackets emblazoned with peace symbols and hat blooming with flowers and feathers.[5]

The "hip ghetto" is not a phrase which Weiner and Stillman made up; it was a reality in the sixties, usually in college towns like Madison and Ann Arbor and Berkeley. All the trends of the sixties, especially sex, drugs, and rock 'n' roll, came together in the hip ghettos. A cultural anthropologist named William Partridge lived for a while in a hip ghetto of Jacksonville, Florida, and wrote a book about it.

Partridge begins with a statement about sixties hippies which substantially agrees with what I have said about them, and which bears repeating: "The 'hippie movement' is not in dialectical opposition to American culture. Its adherents are offspring of middle-class white Americans, who were socialized in the American city, suburb, and school, drafted into the American armed forces, and who carry and transmit American behaviors, ideals, and myths."[6] But neither Partridge nor I nor anyone else is saying that people felt good about the society which had produced them. In fact, Partridge says that, "During the time of this study residents of the ghetto generally felt themselves involved in a mission to seek alternatives to the larger American society—a society they viewed as hypocritical, warlike, and inherently evil."[7]

As a social alternative to the neighbors and relatives with whom they had grown up, they formed themselves into what Partridge calls "quasi-bands"—small groups "usually organized around a common means of subsistence."[8] Quasi-bands usually had an "elder" (to use his term again)—an older man who had some street smarts, and sometimes a mysterious past. He "acts as a guide and model during the period of experimentation."[9] Whether the members of the quasi-band went to school or worked, they had to go out and confront straight society every day. No matter what they did, it was a low-touch experience, and when they came back to the ghetto at night, they wanted high-touch experience. They got it in the form of the nightly rap session, during which people sat around on the floor, smoked dope, listened to rock 'n' roll, and rapped. This rap session "Is the most frequent ritual behavior and is characteristic of all the quasi-bands that make up ghetto society."[10] In fact, "Not to participate in the nightly rap session is not to be a member of ghetto society."[11] They told "us and them" stories about past encounters with straight society, but also about good times, too. "It is by keeping these bonds tight and rekindling the memories of the past that the group can exist apart from the larger society."[12]

We can subsume everything that Partridge tells us about the hippie ghetto, and everything we know from our own experience, under the heading of decentralization. Hippies were too much a product of the American middle class to believe that you should do "your own thing" unless it turned out to be a lot like everyone else's thing. Straight, which is to say centralized, society believed in goal-oriented behavior. In the late sixties, though, having goals meant settling for a low-touch life, and hippies didn't want to do that. To deny the meaning of goals was to deny centralized authority, and smoking dope made you unable and unwilling to engage in goal-oriented behavior—as anyone who has ever driven a car while stoned knows.

The figure/ground relationship between television and rock 'n' roll furthered decentralization when people generally stopped watching television. Just as people often didn't use last names, they didn't watch the six o'clock news, either. "Information from the outside world is irrelevant to life in the ghetto, except as it related to the experiences of residents."[13] The networks determined what was on television, but not what was on the record player, so the record player was a lot more important than the television set.

In this context, Woodstock seems like the biggest, if the shortest-lived, hippie ghetto. Because of the publicity at the time, and especially because of the movie, Woodstock has become a key event in the myth of the sixties, and nothing more needs to be said here about the joys and good times of those three days. What does need to be said is how it happened that Altamont followed so soon after Woodstock, and how Woodstock, Altamont, and the Tate-La Bianca murders were all related. When we understand that, we will understand what happened in the sixties, and how the sixties turned into the seventies.

We might begin by noticing how Partridge's comment that hippies transmitted American myths applies to the outbreak of agrarianism at Woodstock. When Max Yasgar came on stage to announce, "I'm a farmer," the assembled multitudes roared their approval. And in the song "Woodstock", sung by Crosby, Stills, and Nash. Joni Mitchell announced the agrarian dream as a duty: "We have got to get ourselves back to the garden." Thomas Jefferson would have loved it.

Yet Crosby, Stills, and Nash were celebrating an industrial garden, for they sang "Woodstock" to hundreds of thousands of people; they could do so because they had at their disposal some very expensive technology in the form of microphones and outdoor speaker systems. Once we think about it, this contradiction between a belief in agrarianism and the enjoyment of technology characterized the festival as a whole. But it was so brief, and the shock of recognition at seeing so many hippies in one place was so great, that it didn't seem obvious.

The use of technology to create a supposedly natural effect appears again and again in the sixties, most strikingly in the way women changed their appearance. They ironed their hair, for example, so that it would look naturally smooth. While Weiner and Stillman say that, "59% of the women we surveyed say that during those years they stopped using makeup altogether,"[14] most women did not stop using it altogether. Rather, they now used makeup to look natural. Mary Quant, the British fashion designer who costumed the sixties, commented in 1966: "Makeup—old style—is out. It is used as expertly as ever but it is not designed to show. The ideal now is to look as though you have a baby skin untouched by cosmetics."[15]

After the movie *Woodstock* came out, Lawrence Dressner wrote a provocative essay on it, *"Woodstock*, A Nation at War," in which he argues that no matter how much people wanted to escape from their society, they couldn't.

One can hardly doubt the sincerity with which participants and movie-goers celebrated the life-style and moral imperatives of peace. They displayed peacefulness, gentleness, in much of their behavior. The combativeness in which youthful peace protesters often indulge was deliberately and consciously avoided by the Woodstock audience, and even more scrupulously avoided by the producers of the film. Yet war is an inseparable strand in the fabric of modern American culture. For many young people it is at least a temporary career; for most it is known through motion pictures, television fiction, and television news.[16]

As a result, for the kids who made up the audience,

Their festival is a paradigm of the military culture of their youth: a ready peacefulness punctuated with orgies of release through the accepted chaos of purposeful war on foreign soil. Their symbol is not the flag, but to their symbols they are sternly and deeply patriotic. Their forms are contemporary: modern technolgies including the technology and programming of television, are carelessly, proudly, assimilated. They have the war they were brought up for. It is a child's war; it is play. Who are more serious, and more proud of that seriousness, than children at play?[17]

The problems which would soon, sooner than anyone at Woodstock could imagine, tear the Woodstock myth apart come across in unexpected ways. On the album, for instance, an anonymous man (Chip Monck, I assume) is making a stage announcement. What he wants to say is, "Don't take the brown acid that's going around. It's causing bad trips." But in August of 1969, no one could say that at a rock festival. He knew that if he had said that, everybody would have put him down for trying to lay his trip on others. So this is what he says, as I transcribe it:

"You may take it with however many grains of salt you wish that the brown acid that's circulating around is not specifically too good. It's suggested that you do stay away from that. Of course, it's your own trip, so be my guest. But please be advised that there's a warning on that one."

The schizophrenic vocabulary betrays the speaker's discomfort. On one hand he uses the hip phraseology of the day: "acid" and "your own trip." On the other hand, he uses the abstractions and passives of corporate and military bureaucracy: "circulating"; "specifically" and—worst of all—"please be advised." However inappropriate his language, it allowed him to disavow personal responsibility for what he was saying.

Monck spoke in this tortured way because he felt himself on the horns of the dilemma for sixties hippies, the contradiction between the belief that "We are brothers and sisters" and the belief that you should "do your own thing." If everybody's "own thing" is exactly equal to everybody else's, then no one can comment on, or judge, anyone else. Everyone is therefore totally isolated from everybody else. Our anonymous speaker felt the urge to keep people from frying their brains on bad acid, but realized that he had no right to do so. Or, as sociologist Sherri Cavan put it more formally in commenting on the assumptions of life in Haight-Ashbury in the sixties: "In effect, the belief in the compatible collectivity of mankind and the value of individual uniqueness may generate a particular set of difficult conditions. Under these conditions, amelioration of incompatible differences between members by any kind of change or compromise on the part of the members makes no sense."[18]

Something else about Woodstock that seems minor actually isn't: the kids who were diabetics didn't bring any insulin along.[19] It was so important to cut yourself off from the straight world by not using last names or status symbols that it seemed only part of a larger endeavor to cut yourself off from biology, too. After all, the Pill was separating women's biology from women's destiny for the first time, and everybody had just seen computers do something that no group of unaided human minds could do—send a man to the moon.

When we think about it, the denial of biology pervades the sixties. The Pill made it possible to enjoy sex without substantial worries about pregnancy, and electric technology made it possible for musicians to play for an audience of half a million. It was the hubris of the times that biology was no longer a limitation or even an imperative. Even when women did get pregnant, they could stay cool about childbirth, as in this story told by the ever-preceptive Joan Didion: "John and Michelle Phillips, on their way to the hospital for the birth of their daughter Chynna, had the limo detour into Hollywood in order to pick up a friend, Anne Marshall. This incident, which I often embroider in my mind to include an imaginary second detour, to the Luau for gardenias, exactly describes the music business to me."[20]

Weatherwoman Bernadine Dohrn played on the widespread feeling in the sixties that people had transcended biology by bringing sex and politics together in a deliberately provocative way, as the following story by Steve Tappis, a fellow participant in the Weather Underground illustrates:

"She would be arguing political points at the table with her blouse open to the navel, sort of leering at J.J.[her lover]," remembers Tappis. "It was a moral thing, just sort of disconcerting. I couldn't concentrate on the arguments. Finally I said, 'Bernadine! Would you please button your blouse!' She just pulled out one of her breasts and, in that cold way of hers, said, 'You like this tit? Take it.' "[21]

The transcendence of biology has to do with more than Dohrn's manipulative combination of sex and radical politics, though; it offers a clue to the incidence of drug abuse. In 1969, Dave Smith of the Free Clinic in Haight-Ashbury commented of the street people, "They will usually take anything given them without asking what it is," and added, "This community has always had serious health problems, but the kids today simply cannot or will not take care of themselves."[22] Of course not; in McLuhan's terms, they felt so over-extended by the media around them that they believed they could do anything they wanted to their bodies.

The final point to be made about Woodstock is that it illustrates one of McLuhan's key principles, that processes are not monolithic, and that they can reverse themselves. Thus, Woodstock reversed a long-standing trend in American popular music, and one to which I have devoted a lot of space in this book, secularization. There are American precedents for thinking of Woodstock in a religious sense. If the Great Awakening in the 1740's represented decentralization of religion in that it represented a violation of the earlier prohibition on worship services held anywhere except in a church, so Woodstock represented decentralization of spiritual values as well. The process of secularization reversed itself into resacralization. A remark by Ralph Gleason, father figure to the Flower Children, about Altamont, applies even more to Woodstock: "The gathering was religious, of course, which is no new comment."[23] We talked about morality a lot in the sixties; did we not condemn the war on moral grounds?

If you listen to the record, you can even find the moment which makes the spiritual quality palpable at Woodstock—it is Sly Stone's set. Sly Stone, who is Sylvester Steward, made his first record "On the Battlefield for the Lord," with a family group, the Steward Four, while still a child. After spending some time with Sly and his group just after Woodstock, Ben Fong-Torres concluded, "So Sly's Family Stone, as well as his family, is firmly rooted in California, in the church, and in church music."[24]

Thus, in Sly's set at Woodstock, we have the secularization of black music which brings the promise of gospel to white kids who had had too much secularization. Sly worked the audience like a congregation, and pulled them together. Everybody loved it because it was so much more uplifting than anything they had ever experienced in church. After the stuffy church services and boring church music they had grown up with, they found it exhilarating to feel the music evoke such communality. When Sly sings "(I Want to Take You)Higher," he sets it up as a call-and-response situation, as black preachers usually do. He says that after he sings "Higher," he wants them to "Say 'Higher' and throw the peace sign up—it'll do you no harm." Conscious that his mostly white audience had had little experience with call-and-response worship services, he reassures them. "A lot of people think it might be old-fashioned. But you must dig that it is not a fashion—it's a feeling." If it's a feeling, who can be against it? The delicious feeling of participating in the music, and of a feeling oneself part of a common cause gave that night, and the survivors of the sixties, a lasting spirituality.

In the sixties, as in life, everything had its opposite. The stronger one tendency became the stronger the opposing tendency became. If peace and love reigned at Woodstock-and they did—they did so despite the fact that manipulation and hatred reigned among Charlie Manson's followers. They fit Partridge's description of a hippie quasi-band well, and Charlie functioned as an elder with a vengeance. Yet this quasi-band went on a two-night murder spree, and it had as much to do with rock 'n' roll as Woodstock or Altamont. Like The Doors, Charlie was testing the limits of reality. The sixties had sympathy for the devil, if you will, and Charlie was so much a part of his times that Didion has this to say about local reaction to the murders.

There were rumors. There were stories. Everything was unmentionable but nothing was unimaginable. This mystical flirtation with the idea of "sin"—this sense that it was possible to go "too far," and that many people were doing it—was very much with us in Los Angeles in 1968 and 1969.... On August 9, 1969, I was sitting in the shallow end of my sister-in-law's swimming pool in Beverly Hills when she received a telephone call from a friend who had just heard about the murders at Sharon Tate Polanski's house on Cielo Drive. The phone rang many times during the next hour. These early reports were garbled and contradictory. One caller would say hoods, the next would say chains. There were twenty dead, no, twelve, ten, eighteen. Black masses were imagined, and bad trips blamed. I remember all of the day's misinformation very clearly, and I also remember this, and wish I did not: *I remember that no one was surprised.*[25]

No one was surprised because Charlie was so much a part of the sixties. Take the bus, for example. Almost everyone who writes about the sixties mentions Jack Kerouac's *On the Road* as a book which inspired Ken Kesey's bus in which his Merry Pranksters travelled. Since these people are usually cribbing from Tom Wolfe's *The Electric Kool-Aid Acid Test*, most of them don't think to mention The Who's "Magic Bus," or the Beatles' bus of *Magical*

Mystery Tour fame—or Charlie's bus. Nevertheless, Charlie's bus was painted in psychedelic colors, and carried a band of merry pranksters who consorted with Hell's Angels, just like Ken Kesey's bus.

Charlie, his followers, and the murders they committed—we'll never know how many—were not some strange aberration from the sixties, nor did their crimes prove that sex, drugs, and rock 'n' roll come from the devil. What their crimes did show, though, was that the dichotomies of the sixties such as the one between high culture and popular culture, or that between the social commitment of The Movement and the extreme individualism of doing your own thing had no possible resolution. Consummate manipulators like Charlie seized upon the rigidity and peer pressure created by these dichotomies and played them for all they were worth. His success shows that while Dylan told us many truths in the sixties, he also told us at least one lie when he told us that people who live outside the law "mus' be honest." It ain't necessarily so, because Charlie lived inside the Gates of Eden, where there are no truths.

Since there were no truths inside the Gates of Eden where Charlie lived, there remained only personal experience. It often happens that when social change occurs, it occurs by intensifying (or speeding up, as McLuhan would have said) a previously existing situation. This is what Charlie did with women. In prison, he had had long discussions with experienced pimps about the techniques for turning women out—turning them into obedient prostitutes. Once Charlie got out, he applied what he had learned there to the women who came under his power. He took advantage of the new Pill-given freedom to intensify the sexist attitudes of middle-class America. If in the fifties women had been visual sex objects—"You can look but you better not touch," in the words of "Poison Ivy"—Charlie made his women into tactile sex objects. They themselves were never allowed to initiate sex, but Charlie made sure that any time he told them to "strip and suck," they would. He was so good at it that he could show them enslavement and make them think it was liberation.

He couldn't have done it without rock 'n' roll, though, and for a while it seemed like he might make it in show business. Although he started gathering slave-girls at Berkeley in the spring of 1967, he moved them to LA that fall, in order to acquire some Hollywood glamor. Since Hollywood has always dealt in illusion, he felt right at home on the movie sets of the Spahn ranch, where they lived. The girls constituted his power base, and he used them to befriend Dennis Wilson of the Beach Boys, and Doris Day's son Terry Melcher. Like a lot of people, he was listening to the Beatles and was writing songs. He made a demo record for the Brothers label which the Beach Boys were thinking about forming.

In 1969 it wasn't just Charlie who was predicting a race war, but only Charlie called it Helter Skelter, after the acid rock cut on the white album. He also grooved to the manic quality of John's voice when he screamed "Rise" on "Revolution 9," and by the ominous tones of George's "Piggies." These phrases later showed up, in blood, on walls and refrigerator doors.

Like a lot of other people, Charlie believed that the Beatles were sending out secret messages which only a few people could decode. This belief, widely shared at the time, was yet another instance of the way popular culture had new and unprecedented affinities with high culture in the sixties. The assumption that only a few people, an elite, can grasp the meaning of a given work is characteristic of high culture, not popular culture, which is supposedly accessible to the average person.

Decentralization took many forms in the sixties as people decided they wanted to do it themselves. Just as people were rolling their own smokes, Charlie and his merry pranksters stole movie cameras and made their own movies. What they made were later to be called snuff films—films of their performances in torturing and murdering helpless women. Nor was this just American narcissism; Ian Brady and Myra Hindly, the so-called Moors Murderers in England, tape-recorded their victims' screams.

Ed Sanders suggests in his book *The Family* that in ordering the murders Charlie wasn't simply working out his power trip, but was taking a paranoid's revenge after getting burned on an acid deal.[26] Whether or not this is true, the murders were horrible enough. Yet horrible as they were, it was creepy-crawling that was symbolic. Creepy-crawling was the name that Charlie gave to a training exercise wherein his minions would break into a house, re-arrange the furniture, and sneak out again undisturbed. The point was to serve notice to the people who lived there that they were not safe from violence and not safe from change. McLuhan once said that war is accelerated technological change, and it's also true that accelerated technological change is war. When the Manson family went creepy-crawling, they were sending messages from the war zone, and those messages said that the war zone was everywhere. Just as the evening news brought the war in Vietnam into middle-class living rooms at night, creepy-crawling brought the war at home into middle-class living rooms as well. It was a way of obsolescing the gap between inside and outside which informs Dylan's songs.

If the sixties began with the Beatles on Ed Sullivan, it ended with the Rolling Stones at Altamont. The Maysles' *Gimme Shelter* mercilessly records two key moments—one offstage, and one onstage—when the sixties came apart. Offstage, the camera catches Bob Weir of the Grateful Dead saying over and over again, "It's really weird, man; it's really weird." There just wasn't anything in the hippie vocabulary which would let him talk about the anxiety that he was feeling. The most gripping moment, though, comes when Lucifer himself, Mick Jagger, loses control over his audience. Great trouper that he is, he works the crowd by using the rhetoric of flower power, and says, "Be cool, brothers and sisters." He had learned much from blacks, and like so many people in the sixties he used "brothers and sisters" without an awareness that it comes from black church services. The trouble was, his audience at Altamont lacked the shared faith, and the shared experience of oppression that makes it real when blacks address each other as "Brother So-and-so" and "Sister So-and-so." (Incidentally, Southern whites did this, too, at least as late as the fifties, when I was growing up in Tupelo.) But the audience didn't have enough shared experience to form a congregation; the consensus that even great performers need wasn't there, so he couldn't stop the violence. Greil Marcus said it well: "A young black man murdered in the midst of a white crowd by white thugs as white men played their version of black music—it was too much to kiss off as unpleasantness."[27] Flower Power hadn't stopped the war, and the Flower Children themselves couldn't come together in peace and love—at least not twice—so in effect the sixties were over. We had brought it all—the violence as well as the joy—back home, and it hurt.

We couldn't understand what happened in the sixties because we couldn't understand the history and the economics of the times. We couldn't understand the power of the inertial force of the hippies' socialization into the middle class. Most of them grew up in the middle class, and most of them returned there in the seventies. We also couldn't understand the history of the baby boom, whose members created great pressure on society by "just being," to use a hippie phrase. And we couldn't understand the economics of prosperity and low inflation which gave people the boundless confidence and trust which was required to stay high and/or mellow.

This boundless confidence and faith made us believe that we could hold together the oppositions of our society: man/woman; black/white; rich/poor; high culture/popular culture; centralization/decentralization; and personal/political. It turned out, though, that these oppositions often manifested themselves as dichotomies, despite all we could do. To make matters worse, the oppositions that people construed as dichotomies, like hip/straight, turned out not to be dichotomies—at least not all the time. As Jonathan Eisen put it in the book on Altamont which he edited:

Altamont was nothing in itself. It was not very special except to make people realize how similar we all are to the society we have no choice but to abhor. For many it destroyed in a few moments the dichotomies our people have been making with increasing relish, and sent them back to thinking about how alike, how close and how reflective everyone is of everyone else, despite the hair, despite the acid and the music.[28]

When people contrast what happened in the sixties with what happened later, they ask what has happened to "the ideals of the sixties." To ask this is to reveal oneself a prisoner of media images, television images of demonstrations and peace marches. The enduring ideals of the sixties were personal, as American ideals usually are. So what the personal ideals of the sixties accomplished was to legitimize hedonism as part of the American way of life. If the consequences of sex, drugs, and rock 'n' roll weren't always what we wanted in the seventies, well, the joy of discovery is always more fun than the work of assimilation. To paraphrase something T.S. Eliot said about literary classics, we know more than we did in the sixties—and the sixties are most of what we know.

Notes

[1]Quoted in *Technology, Power, and Social Change*, p. 85.

[2]Ira L. Reiss, *Family Systems in America*, 2nd ed. (Hinsdale, IL: The Dryden Press, 1976), p. 170.

[3]*Ibid.*, p. 183.

[4]John Naisbitt, *Megatrends* (New York: Warner Books, 1984), p. 35.

[5]Rex Weiner and Deanne Stillman, *Woodstock Census* (New York: The Viking Press, 1979), p. 38.

[6]William L. Partridge, *The Hippie Ghetto. The Natural History of a Subculture* (New York: Holt Rinehart and Winston, 1973), p. xiii.

[7]*Ibid.*, p. 29.

[8]*Ibid.*, p. 39.

[9]*Ibid.*, p. 30.

[10]*Ibid.*, p. 44.

[11]*Ibid.*, p. 51.

[12]*Ibid.*, p. 65.

[13]*Ibid.*

[14]*Woodstock Census*, p. 38.

[15]Mary Quant, *Quant by Quant* (New York: G.P. Putnam's Sons, 1966), p. 156.

[16]Lawrence J. Dressner, "Woodstock, A Nation at War," in *Things in the Driver's Sear*, H.R. Huebel, ed. (Chicago: Rand McNally, 1973), p. 246.

[17]*Ibid.*, p. 251. An incident in Haight-Ashbury noted by Sherri Cavan reveals a similar unstable relationship between peace and aggression among hippies.

The tourist approaches a cluster of Hippies lounging against one of the cars. Only a few minutes earlier, I had been listening to their conversation, which was essentially that love would set the "Straight" world straight. The tourist, with deference and politeness, requests permission from the Hippies to take their photograph. One of the Hippies says to him, "I'd like to take that camera and bash it in your face." Two of three other Hippies nod in apparent agreement; none of them protest the response.

Sherri Cavan, *Hippies of the Haight* (St. Louis: New Critics Press, 1972), p. 75.

[18]Cavan, *Hippies of the Haight*, p. 184.

[19]Robert Stephen Spitz, *Robert in Babylon* (New York: The Viking Press, 1979), p. 454.

[20]Didion, *The White Album*, p. 26.

[21]Quoted in Peter Collier and David Horowitz, "Doing It. The Inside Story of the Rise and Fall of the Weather Underground," *Rolling Stone*, September 30, 1982, p. 23.

[22]Quoted in John Luce, "Haight-Ashbury Today: A Case of Terminal Euphoria," *Esquire*, July, 1969, p. 119.

[23]Ralph Gleason, "Altamont," in *Altamont, Death of Innocence of the Woodstock Nation*, Jonathan Eisen, ed. (New York: Avon Books, 1970), p. 210.

[24]Ben Fong-Torres, "Everybody Is A Star: The Travels of Sylvester Stewart," *Rolling Stone*, March 19, 1970, pp. 33.

[25]Didion, *The White Album,* p. 42.

[26]Ed Sanders, *The Family* (New York: E.P. Dutton, 1971), pp. 334-336.

[27]Quoted in *The Sixties,* p. 303.

[28]Jonathan Eisen, "Introduction," *Altamont: Death of Innocence in the Woodstock Nation.* p. 22. Although Eisen speaks for the audience here, notice how similar Cass Elliot's remarks are even though she speaks as a performer: "Probably the biggest bringdown in my life—it's so hypocritical—was being in a big pop group and finding out just how much it was like everything it was supposed to be against." (Quoted in Ellen Sander, *Trips. Rock Life in the Sixties* (New York: Charles Scribner's Son, 1973) p. 12)

Chapter 19:
A Few Good Words For the Seventies

A song by the Statler Brothers said the seventies were "ten long years of reruns/Even Watergate was nothing new." I think the time has come for somebody to say a few good words for the seventies, which turned out to be the most complicated decade in the history of popular music. Never before had so many different styles appeared in such a brief period of time, and never before had the interrelationships between performers and their audiences undergone so many changes.

A major reason why people don't like the seventies is that the sixties ended before they were over. In 1970, Nixon was still President, and the war still went on. In fact, it got worse, with the invasion of Cambodia and the shooting of the four students at Kent State. Watergate, the energy crisis, and the Iranian hostage crisis left people with unpleasant memories. In discussing the seventies it is fashionable to lament the demise of the ideals of the sixties, but to do so is to misunderstand the sixties. What we were doing in the seventies was assimilating the changes of the sixties—which we will be doing for the rest of the twentieth century.

It's not that we forgot about the sixties; it's rather that the much-ballyhooed changes of the sixties took over only in the seventies; when sixties attitudes became generalized, from a small minority of free spirits, they simply became part of society—which is what happens when a rebellion succeeds. Objecting to the "Whatever happened to the ideals of the sixties" laments, John Rockwell in 1975 wrote in *The New York Times*, "But most everybody in high school looks like a hippie these days; the emblems of a counterculture have become the fashions of the mainstream. What used to be a challenging vanguard, posing musical and political alternatives, has become the establishment entertainment of the day."[1]

The key concept in understanding the seventies is balance. In the sixties we opened ourselves to new experiences of different kinds, but no society can sustain a prolonged opening, so what we did in the seventies was to close ourselves in order for the work of assimilation to continue. As sociologist Orrin Klapp has said, "The natural pattern is alternation, and the more alive a system is, the more alertly it opens and closes. In such a view, closing is not, as some suppose, merely a setback to growth and progress, but evidence that the mechanisms of life are working, that the society has resiliency."[2]

Closure had more than a merely metaphorical meaning in the seventies. In March of 1973, *Fortune* magazine reported that "The ubiquitous monument of urban America in the Seventies is the sports stadium."[3] Although some cities built enclosed football stadiums in the sixties (the Houston Astrodome opened in 1965), it was in the seventies that they turned into the dominant trend. Seattle, Detroit, and New Orleans all built enclosed stadiums; the political powers in those cities knew that a city with a pro football team and a dome projected a positive image.

The tendency toward enclosure appeared also in the construction of shopping malls all over the country. An article in *Forbes* in 1976 stated that, "There is 60 billion invested in shopping centers in the U.S. Centers by far account for the biggest part of retail sales (44%), excluding building and automotive products. There are 16,000 centers in the U.S."[4] In the record year of 1973 alone, some 1,600 shopping centers were built. It is appropriate, then, that in the seventies there appeared a musical style predicated on a particular enclosure with restricted access—disco.

Such enclosures set Dylan's distinctions between inside and outside into concrete, and this split suggests the way the oppositions of the sixties split apart and became assimilated in the seventies. Generally speaking, we can say that rock split into music for football stadiums and music for shopping centers. Not for nothing is heavy metal, probably the dominant style of the seventies, sometimes called "arena rock," for it's about the only kind of music you can play to crowds of over 50,000 people. So Grand Funk Railroad, Led Zeppelin, Black Sabbath, and the others thrived. But there was an audience for soft rock as well, as Carole King proved when she sold 14 million copies of *Tapestry*. James Taylor, Cat Stevens, and the individual singer/writers thrived, too. As a matter of fact, hard rock and soft rock alternated at the top of the charts in the early seventies. On the last album chart for 1969, *Led Zeppelin II* knocked *Abbey Road* out of the #1 position. It stayed there for seven weeks only to give way to Simon and Garfunkel's *Bridge Over Troubled Water*. Then *Led Zeppelin III* almost but not quite knocked *Tapestry* off the top of the chart in 1973. Ellen Wills was right when she wrote in *The New Yorker* in 1972, "The fragmentation of the rock audience is just one symptom of social and political developments that cut pretty deep; I doubt whether one person or one band, no matter how potent, can put it back together—not now, anyway."[5] But Wills was wrong to imply that it needed to be put back together. It was, and still is, hard to understand that what was right for the sixties—especially the rapidly developing myth of the sixties—was not right for the seventies.

It was part of the myth of the sixties which the seventies created that the audience had been unified when in fact there had been the same distinction between hard rock and soft rock in the sixties; there was the difference between the Stones and Donovan; between the Doors and Simon and Garfunkel. Similarly, there was an ambivalence about the relationship between the performers and the audience. It's a measure of the change in this relationship in the sixties that the camera stays on the performers throughout *The T.A.M.I.*

Show, but vacillates between the performers and the audiences in *Monterey Pop* and *Woodstock.* When the freaky costumes of the Flower Children started to rival the freaky costumes of the performers, it created an ambiguity which no one could tolerate for long.

The seventies resolved this ambiguity with yet another split. On one hand, concerts evolved into grandiose spectacles on a scale unimaginable in the sixties. Alice Cooper, David Bowie, and Elton John broke into the big time by sensing the need for spectacle; and groups could put on even bigger spectacles than singles acts, as the success of Queen and Kiss showed. On the other hand, technological changes made it possible to eliminate the rivalry between performers and audiences entirely. The result was disco, in which no one had a sense of the presence of musicians and singers at all—the audience consisted of dancers who were themselves the show.

Both in the case of disco (which broke in gay clubs) and in the case of the concert as spectacle (as the names of Alice, David, and Elton indicate), the aggressive male sexuality of sixties rock split into what we now call gender benders. Alice Cooper's name is Vincent Fournier, but he likes girls anyhow; David Bowie has an androgynous image; and a feminist critic attacked Doors songs like "Twentieth Century Fox" as "cock rock." Before the seventies, only women—and Liberace—put on elaborate costumes, pranced about on stage, and presented themselves to be admired and desired. Now men did that, too, so it was inevitable that audiences whose own sex roles were being transformed by the Pill found a feminine quality in what they did.

The performers who broke in the seventies generally had one thing in common which distinguished them from the performers who broke in the sixties. The giants of the sixties created rock 'n' roll from something else, such as folk music or the blues, but the performers of the seventies did not have to do this. Elton John once said, "My mother introduced me to rock and roll." It seems that one day she brought home records by Elvis and Bill Haley and the Comets.[6] And Jimmy Page spoke for many of his contemporaries when he said, "I've always been a rock musician; I can't play anything else."[7]

Elton's comment about his mother illustrates the way the seventies tended to obsolesce the generation gap. It appears in a September 1971 issue of *Life* in a story on "The Rock Family Affair," which pictured rock stars with their parents. The sight of Grace Slick with her illegitimate daughter in her mother's elegantly furnished living room was not altogether a bad sign. Rock started more and more to appear in a family context, as when couples like John and Yoko, Paul and Linda, Bonnie and Delaney, Carly Simon and James Taylor, and Kris Kristofferson and Rita Coolidge starting performing together. (Carly's ode to marriage, "That's the Way I've Always Heard It Should Be," did well in the summer of 1971.)

Like so many other things, the couples phenomenon told us something about the baby boomers: "In the decade of the seventies, some 32 million Americans had their thirtieth birthdays, an increase of 39 percent over the sixties."[8] Moreover, enclosure as family solidarity in music had even more significance for the teenyboppers who had been born at the very end of the baby boom. In 1973, Sara Davidson observed with her usual astuteness that:

The most successful subteen heroes represent a happy, loyal tight-knit family with which their fans can identify. The Osmonds, the Jacksons, and the Carpenters are members of actual families, and David Cassidy is visualized less as Cassidy the actor—the only child of separated parents—than as Keith Partridge, who lives in a family with lots of other children. All the families appear to be a kind of kids' nation.[9]

In the post-Altamont dissipation of tensions, we began to realize that the generation gap had been overrated all along. In a detailed study of Muncie, Indiana, the city which Robert and Helen Lynd had made famous as "Middletown" in their pioneering studies in the twenties and thirties, a team of sociologists compared the attitudes of families over three generations. When they polled children about their parents in 1976, "More than half of the respondents claimed to be 'quite close' or 'extremely close' to their fathers, and almost two-thirds to their mothers...Indeed, when we take into account the temporary alienation from parents that often occurs in adolescence, the similarity between adolescents and adults raises the possibility that the generation gap has been *narrowing*."[10] So it's not as startling as it might seem that at the 1972 Democratic Convention in Miami young people were carrying signs which read "Long Hairs and White Hairs/Struggle—Unite" and "We Are the Senior Citizens of Tomorrow."[11] After all, Paul Simon's "Mother and Child Reunion" had gone to #4 the previous February.

If young and old could come together in the seventies, then black and white could, too—even in Alabama, as demonstrated by the following vignette from 1972 which Marshall Frady describes. The participants are Johnny Ford, the black mayor of Tuskegee, Alabama, his son John-John—and George Wallace.

Ford then introduced Wallace to John-John. Wallace, leaning forward in his wheelchair, gave John-John a quick little hug, and Ford said, "C'mon, John-John, give the governor some skin," and Wallace and John-John exchanged light soul-spanks with their palms. It was only an idle happening; but in such nuances—trivial, fleeting gestures in the air—are the rise and wane of whole social orders registered, the passing of ages and immense gear-shiftings of history affirmed.[12]

Taken by itself, this incident is startling enough; but when we realize that John-John's mother, and Johnny Ford's wife, was *white*, the incident becomes truly stunning, and bears all the historical weight which Frady gives it. Of course, both Frady and I know too much about the South to believe that the millenium has come; but we both also know that a lot of positive change took place in the South in the seventies.

The image of the South began to improve, too; it was about at this time that Winston cigarettes abandoned its infamous slogan "Winston tastes good like a cigarette should" for "Down Home Taste." One Southerner noted with relief that, "The message about the region was clear: the white South represents home, family, good old values."[13] The rehabilitation of the South became especially clear when the nightmare figure of Bull Connors evolved into the comic figure of the sheriff in Dodge commercials on TV, and then into the Jackie Gleason character in *Smoky and the Bandit* (1977). It was okay to be from the South again, and great rock groups like The Allman Brothers and Lynyrd Skynyrd came out of the South.

Of all the oppositions in American life, the opposition between the sacred and the profane has the most tenuous balance. Dylan's attack on American civil religion in "With God on Our Side" drew the battle lines in the sixties: those who believed in the sacred, also believed in The War, short hair, and asceticism. Those who rebelled against those last three items in various ways, also rebelled against the first. But rebellion against the sacred is a tricky business in America, because it often turns into its opposite. Let us consider the ways of the profane and of the sacred in the seventies.

In an important book, *Getting Saved from the Sixties*, Steven Tipton has shown how the sixties counterculture did not "lose its ideals" at all, but evolved in an understandable way. Werner Erhard's *est* movement, for example, grows out of the sixties because "*est* defines what is intrinsically valuable in a form compatible with counter-cultural ideals, namely the individual's subjective experience of well-being and satisfaction."[14] In urging people to take responsibility for their lives, and in insisting that "Life has no rules," Erhard was turning the individual into what Tipton calls "an omnicausal agent," and secularizing moral concepts with a vengeance. Most of the people who benefit from *est* do not work with ideas or things; they work with people. The sense that work is social interaction which has no rules—hence the individual has to make them up—derives from the sixties, though. To quote Tipton again, "The idea of work as a game goes hand in hand with the notion of one's own life as a work of art. The enterprise of self-perfection, passed down from philosopher and monk to bohemian dandy and hippie, now takes therapeutic form in 'working on yourself.' "[15]

"Working on yourself" meant, among other things, liberating yourself from religious rules as instutionalized in the middle-class family; it meant de-centralizing the psyche, so to speak, and embracing a profane world in which you made your own rules. After all the media exposure which the counterculture had gotten, straight middle-class couples wanted to get liberated, too, especially from their sexual hangups. So in 1970 when John Williamson started Sandstone, a private club in Los Angeles for people who wanted to engage in open sex, "He wanted to assemble a large membership of stable couples, young middle-class sensualists who believed that their personal relationships would be enhanced, rather than shattered, by the elimination of sexual possessiveness."[16] The thing to remember is that by the seventies it was no longer hippies who were having orgies; it was "stable couples"—the same stable couples who were making X-rated movies acceptable by going to see *Deep Throat*, and discussing it at dinner parties. A few years later, many of these same swingers welcomed the opportunities for exhibitionism which disco offered.

At the same time, though, people were embracing the sacred with a new intensity. One of Tom Wolfe's most accurate observations in his famous essay "The Me Decade" was "The hippies had suddenly made religion look hip,"[17] and even someone as straight as he is admitted that there was some substance to all the rhetoric about religious experiences and drugs. By the seventies, though, people wanted to "get there without drugs," and they tried to do so in various ways.

At the San Francisco Zen Center, Tipton found that Zen appealed to sixties youth because it seemed to create a reliable and lasting order out of inner experience. For some people in the sixties, an interest in Eastern religions was a fad inspired by the Beatles; for others, it was a permanent rejection of the Christianity and Judaism they had grown up with. In Tipton's sample, such people usually came from comfortable backgrounds, and often had been over-achievers in high school and college. Their intelligence and self-discipline served them well in Zen meditation.

As usual in America, Jesus was more popular than Buddha, and people found ways to adapt sixties rhetoric to Jesus. As Peter Skolnick says, Jesus became a fad.

"I'll give you a free trip," said one of the saved. "It's really a groovy high. It's called Jesus Christ and it will really blow your mind." The Jesus Movement fueled a spate of fad products, from *Jesus Christ Superstar,* a rock musical of 1971, to Jesus T-shirts, Jesus jockey shorts, Jesus bikinis, and marijuana "roach" holders shaped like crosses.[18]

In Palo Alto, Tipton studied a group of Christian fundamentalists who called themselves the Living Word Fellowship. They did not go around talking about how groovy Jesus was but they too demonstrated clearly the continuities between the sixties and the seventies. "Like the counterculture, the LWF conceives itself set over against the larger society by its direct experiences of the truth."[19] The Jesus freaks differed from the practicioners of Zen in that many of them had been rock musicians and drug dealers in the sixties, and in that "Most of them come from class backgrounds with relatively little money, education, power, or career prospects. Denied social-structural access to conventional status, they turned first to the counterculture and then to the LWF in attempts to attain alternative sorts of status."[20] Like many fundamentalist Christians, the members of LWF practiced speaking in tongues. That seemed like a perfectly reasonable thing to an ex-dealer who told Tipton, "When I began speaking in tongues I remember thinking it was a kind of Nirvana. I was as high as I'd ever been on drugs."[21]

The musicians both reacted to this trend and gave impetus to it. Paul Simon started listening to black gospel music; when he had "Mary Don't You Weep" by the great Swan Silvertones on the turntable, he noticed one of Claude Jeters' interpolations, "I'll be a bridge over deep water if you trust in my name," and got the idea for "Bridge Over Troubled Water."[22] Art sang it as a hymn of hope in his angelic tenor and the single went to #1 in the spring of 1970; the album sold over nine million copies worldwide. As a singles act in 1973, Paul got the Dixie Hummingbirds, also a black gospel group, to back him up on "Loves Me Like a Rock." The success of "Bridge" meant that it wasn't just the nervous Nellies who wanted peace, and a Coke commercial which became "I'd Like to Teach the World to Sing (In Perfect Harmony)," was a hit in two different version in 1971.

In fact, some remarkable religious songs appeared on the charts in the early seventies, as the following table shows.

Religious Hits of the Early Seventies

Song	Artist	Highest Position	Date
"Amazing Grace"	Judy Collins	#15	12/12/70
"Amazing Grace"	Pipes and Drums of the Military Band of the Royal Scots Dragoon Guards	#11	5/20/72
"Put Your Hand in the Hand"	Ocean	#2	3/13/71
"Jesus Is Just Alright"	Doobie Brothers	#35	12/16/72
"The Lord's Prayer"	Sister Janet Mead	#4	4/10/74

These songs combine the old and the new in a way which distinguishes the seventies from the sixties. Along with two new songs by two new groups, we have the archetypal Protestant hymn by Dr. Watts, "Amazing Grace," in a hit version by a clear-voiced folkie *and* in a bagpipe version! First Judy Collins, and then Arlo Guthrie, started ending concerts with "Amazing Grace," and the Nitty Gritty Dirt Band ended theirs with "Will the Circle Be Unbroken." As if this were not enough, an Australian nun named Janet Mead had a #4 hit with "The Lord's Prayer."

The resacralization of the early seventies—as revolutionary a tendency as the secularization of the fifties and sixties—was one of many examples of a Marshall McLuhan prophecy come true. In 1964, he had predicted that television, and electronic media in general, would produce a society of people who wanted involvement in depth. But a major lesson which we learned in the sixties is that we could not have involvement in depth with America as a whole. Our country is too big, too diverse, and too complicated for that. So we decentralized our experience of America into multiple smaller groupings of like-minded people. This decentralization is not to be confused with fragmentation, and it does not necessarily offer cause for alarm. In fact, decentralization often meant an increase in tolerance. The sociologists who studied Middletown in 1977 administered to its high school students the same poll which the Lynds had administered in 1924, so we have an excellent measure of the change in religious attitudes over a crucial fifty-year period in American history. They found that, "With respect to the all sufficiency of Christianity, there was a notable decline. The proportion of respondents agreeing that 'Christianity is the one true religion and all people should be converted to it' was 94 percent in 1924 but 38 percent in 1977."[23] Still, since decentralization and the need for involvement in depth appeared in everything from special interest groups in politics to punk rock, it certainly made the seventies a confusing and often contentious period.

Notes

[1]Quoted in Fred Davis, *Yearning for Yesterday. A Sociology of Nostalgia* (New York: The Free Press, 1979), p. 42.

[2]Orrin Klapp, *Opening and Closing* (Cambridge University Press, 1978), p. 15.

[3]Charles G. Burch, "It's Promoters vs. Taxpayers in the Superstadium Game," *Fortune*, March, 1973, p. 105.

[4]"Why Shopping Centers Ride Out the Storm," *Forbes*, June 1, 1976, p. 35.

[5]Ellen Wills, "My Grank Funk Problem—and Ours," *The New Yorker*, February 26, 1972, p. 81. The odd title of Wills' article is a play on the title of Norman Podhoretz's article from the early sixties, "My Negro Problem—and Ours."

[6]Quoted in *Life*, September 21, 1971, p. 49.   [7]Quoted in Ritchie Yorke, *The Led Zeppelin Biography* (New York: Methuen, 1976), p. 64.

[8]Jones, *Great Expectations*, p. 263.

[9]Sara Davidson, "Feeding on Dreams in a Bubble Gum Culture," *Atlantic*, October, 1973, p. 63.

[10]Theodore Caplow et al., *Middletown Families, Fifty Years of Change and Continuity* (Minneapolis: University of Minnesota Press, 1982), p. 146.

[11]See Nora Sayre, *Sixties Going On Seventies* (New York: Arbor House, 1973), p. 375.

[12]Marshall Frady, *Southerners. A Journalist's Odyssey* (New York: New American Library, 1980), p. 134.

[13]Jack Temple Kirby, *Media-Made Dixie, The South in the American Imagination* (Baton Rouge: Louisiana State University Press, 1978), p. 134.

[14]Steven M. Tipton, *Getting Saved from the Sixties, Moral Meaning in Conversion and Cultural Change* (Berkeley: University of California Press, 1982), p. 187.

[15] *Ibid.*, p. 216.

[16]Gay Talese, *Thy Neighbor's Wife* (Garden City, NY: Doubleday, 1980), p. 333.

[17]Tom Wolfe, "The Me Decade," *New York*, August 23, 1976, p. 35.

[18]Peter L. Skolnik, *Fads* (New York: Thomas Y. Crowell, 1972), p. 162.

[19]Tipton, *Getting Saved from the Sixties*, p. 35.

[20]*Ibid.*, p. 88.

[21]*Ibid.*, p. 57.

[22]See Tony Heilbut, The Gospel Sound, p. 149.

[23]Caplow et al., *Middletown Families*, p. 252.

Chapter 20:
Tradition and the Individual Apple Pie

The cover story for *Newsweek*'s last issue in 1970 begins like this: "Nostalgia for the American dreamland is sweeping the country like a Kansas twister, tossing up people and things we haven't seen or heard from or even thought about since Little Orphan Annie's Sandy first said 'Arf'."[1] The story cites such reminders of the past as advertising layouts for Arrow shirts which look like they came from 1906, and the Broadway revival of the musical *No, No, Nanette*. Even more remarkable, Sears Roebuck sold 200,000 copies of its 1897 catalog at $14.95 each. An interest in the past unquestionably pervaded American popular culture in the early seventies.

The two major films set in the past which have relevance to popular music are Peter Bogdanovich's *The Last Picture Show* (1971), which deals with the moment of transition from the dominance of movies to the dominance of television; and, of course, George Lucas' *American Graffiti* (1973). The soundtrack for these films consisted of hits of the early fifties and the early sixties respectively; for the first time, well-known records were used as counterpoint to, and comment on, the action on the screen. In addition, *The Sting* and *Paper Moon* appeared in 1973 as well; they, too, used popular music to evoke an era.

Also in 1973, Streisand and Redford appeared in *The Way We Were* (her recording of the title song went platinum) and Francis Ford Coppola's *Godfather* movies came out in 1972 and 1974. It's not just that these movies were set in the past; part of what interested us about them was the way they showed the way styles in clothing, cars, and furniture changed over the years.

Television also showed its awareness of national trends; three major shows which began in the early seventies were set in the past. *The Waltons* was the first to appear, in September of 1972; *Happy Days* premiered in January of 1974, and *The Little House on the Prairie* premiered in September of the same year.

When *Newsweek* asked various pundits to explain the surge of interest in nostalgia, they all said that things had gotten so bad in the sixties that people were seeking refuge in escapism—a comment which has the attractive quality of most half-truths. The trouble with it is that such people also say that *any* new trend is popular culture is escapism. What journalists called the "nostalgia craze" was actually something much more important, for it had lasting meaning. This interest in the past, while not unprecedented, signalled a new form of involvement in depth: a desire to understand the relationship between the past and the present. As far as music is concerned, this desire appeared most clearly in the tremendous popularity of Don McLean's "Miss

American Pie," which was *the* single of the fall and winter of 1972. People all over the country were trying to figure out the references, and *Life* did a story on it.

"Miss American Pie" is a mythologized treatment of the ten year period between 1959 and 1969. It features mostly acoustic guitar and piano with strong male harmonizing on the choruses; Dylan's influence is obvious throughout in the internal rhymes and in the use of popular culture to comment on society. To cover so much material in six verses, McLean makes his singer/narrator evolve, and he cleverly collapses similar events into each other. At the beginning our hero is delivering papers and hoping to make it as a performer—"to make those people dance." He is saddened at the news about "his widowed bride," who is both Maria Helena Holly and Jackie Kennedy (minor chords on the piano here). At the end, he is not a performer, but a spectator at a festival, where a generation is in one place; a reference to "Jumpin' Jack Flash" suggests that this is Altamont, but it is also Woodstock, too.

Our magical mystery tour of the ten years when we were "on our own" mentions two singles from the fifties, the Monotones' "The Book of Love" and Marty Robbins' "A White Sport Coat and a Pink Carnation," and two singles from the sixties, the Lovin' Spoonful's "Do You Believe in Magic," and the Byrds' "Eight Miles High." The Beatles appear as the Sargeants and Dylan is the "jester in a cast." Protests take the form of opposing musical styles, between hippies and a "marching band"; but the band "refused to yield." The name "Helter Skelter" evokes Charlie Manson, and fittingly, the final reference, in the sixth verse, is to a dead singer—Janis Joplin.

The chorus bids goodbye to "Miss American Pie," which reminds us of the phrase "as American as apple pie." We are in the South, for the singer drives his "Chevy to the levee," and there are good ole boys there. They sing "This will be the day that I die." Thus, the song is about various kinds of death, despite its generally cheerful tone. Performers die, musical styles die, and eras die.

The tremendous popularity of "Miss American Pie" expressed an awareness that the sixties were over, and that the seventies had begun, for the song treats the sixties as the past. We can surely understand the sadness that Buddy Holly and Janis Joplin died, but where do those good ole boys come in? What are they doing? I think they are at the levee holding a wake for the importance of the Southern tradition in music which had created rock 'n' roll in the first place, and that this is why "the levee was dry." By this I don't mean that the recordings of, say, Muddy Waters and the Staples Singers had stopped being great records, but rather that by their very success they had lost the power to stimulate innovation. After all you can't go on adapting blues songs and secularizing gospel songs forever.

Moreover, the tremendous popularity of "Miss American Pie" was not a fad in the sense that it was a blip on the surface of American consciousness. McLuhan liked to say that media serve as retrieval systems which retrieve the past to us, and in the seventies media brought the past of popular culture to our awareness in ways which affected the style of many films and records of the time. This phenomenon is an important instance of the generalization of sixties trends; what began with the Beatles' white album eventually swept the country "like a Kansas twister."

This fact is all the more important because, historically, popular culture had ignored its past; historical consciousness had heretofore belonged to high culture, as in T.S. Eliot's *The Waste Land,* a poem which requires many footnotes and historical explanations to explain the allusions. If you don't know that Eliot is working a variation of Chaucer in the first line, you are missing something—just as you are missing something in "Miss American Pie" if you don't get the clues to "The Book of Love" and "Eight Miles High." A critic as well as a poet, Eliot make all this clear in his famous essay "Tradition and the Individual Talent."

Eliot begins with a complaint which applies as much to most rock criticism today as it did to poetry criticism when he was writing in 1919: "We dwell with satisfaction upon the poet's difference from his predecessors, especially his immediate predecessors; we endeavour to find something that can be isolated to be enjoyed."[2] Eliot's discomfort grew out of his feeling that there was more to poetry than the myth of Romantic individualism. It is that same myth which imbues most rock criticism today, with the same results, that performers are isolated from the historical process in which they play such crucial roles, and from the audiences which make them important.

What I have called "historical consciousness" Eliot called "the historical sense," and he describes it as follows: "This historical sense, which is a sense of the timeless as well as of the temporal and of the timeless and of the temporal together, is what makes a writer traditional. And it is at the same time what makes a writer most acutely conscious of his place in time, of his own contemporaneity."[3] So an awareness of tradition doesn't mean a disregard of the present; on the contrary, only those artists who have a historical sense can respond to the present at all. In this sense Lawrence Welk is not traditional —he is merely old-fashioned.

For Eliot, tradition is not static; it changes constantly, and what makes it change is true innovation. When somebody does something truly new, "The relations, proportions, values of each work of art toward the whole are readjusted."[4] To have this kind of awareness brings on a sense of competition with the past—just the competition between "ephebes" and "precursors" which brings on the anxiety of influence, according to Harold Bloom.

The movie which makes it clear how significant historical consciousness and the anxiety of influence were in the seventies is Woody Allen's *Play It Again Sam* (1972), which appeared at the height of the nostalgia craze. The movie begins with Woody in a movie theater watching the ending of *Casablanca,* and if you haven't seen that movie, and don't know anything about the Bogey myth, then much of *Play It Again Sam* must remain incomprehensible to you. In personal terms, Woody's character (as well as the historical Woody, I might add) is working out his anxiety of influence as an actor and as a lover from

Bogey. At the end Woody's character is able to accept himself and accept the past as well.

Historical consciousness appeared in a fascinating variety of ways in the seventies. It's implicit, for example, in the Eagles' mournful Topanga Canyon cowboy harmonies which sold so many records. On their daring, surrealistic "Hotel California" the narrator drives to a place where the bizarre characters are all haunted by the memories of the sixties. The memories of the personal disappointments of the past later brought on a revolutionary change which appears in the lyrics of the title song of an album which went platinum. "The Long Run." Working against the tradition of songs like "Then I Kissed Her" and "Sweet Pea," the Eagles deny that if you fall in love, it will necessarily be forever. Only the long run when the present becomes the past will tell if this magic moment will last. A truly startling change in love songs, yet one to which ageing baby boomers responded.

Innovations often occur when a confrontation between the present and the past makes us think about the past in a new way. In the seventies the much-discussed issue of changing roles for women appeared not so much in Helen Reddy's feminist anthem "I Am Woman" as in women's cover versions of songs which men had recorded. Take, for instance, Bette Midler's "Do You Wanna Dance?" from 1973. Instead of repeating the bouncy uptempo style of the original, she slows it down; instead of the driving male vocal, she substitutes a quavering, uncertain female vocal. She makes us think about male and female roles in a new way by psychologizing a frat party song. Bette also did an wistful, emotional cover of Percy Sledge's "When a Man Loves a Woman," in the greatest rock movie yet, *The Rose* (1979). A very different woman, Rita Coolidge, did a gentler version of Jackie Wilson's "Your Love is Taking Me Higher."

Nobody did more of this, or did it more successfully, than Linda Ronstadt. In the albums which Peter Asher produced for her, which defined the state of the art of high-tech LA sound, she often covered songs written or performed by male vocalists. A woman's double-tracked vocal in the seventies sounded startlingly different from a man's single-tracked vocal in the sixties, so that she—like Don McLean—was defining the seventies against the sixties. What had earlier seemed to be the song, satisfying and complete in itself, now turned out to be only one way of understanding the song. Although we didn't realize it at the time, she was claiming for women what had previously belonged only to men—and doing so long before the Go-Gos' "We Got the Beat."

Among others, she covered Dylan's "I'll Be Your Baby Tonight" (*very* sexy when a woman sings it); Neil Young's "Love Is A Rose"; the Miracles' "Tracks of My Tears"; Jackson Browne's "Rock Me on the Water"; Buddy Holly's "That'll Be the Day." Just as imaginative was Dave Mason's cover of the old Shirelles' song "Will You Love Me Tomorrow?" The new sexual assertiveness of women made this a song which, for the first time, sounded right coming from a man.

In the seventies, the past sometimes seemed as real, as immediate, as the present, and women were claiming equal stylistic rights with men. True historical consciousness means a consciousness of the variety in that tradition; in the seventies, this consciousness matched the variety of FM formats to produce the phenomenon known as progressive country.

Between the years of 1969 and 1979, the number of country music stations almost tripled.[5] Country, usually the most traditional of all the styles of American popular music, acquired such general popularity that it could sustain the weight of a metaphor about American society in *Nashville* (1975). After Kris Kristofferson brought the bedroom to the stage of the Grand Ole Opry, country music had a greneral appeal, and Kenny Rogers and Dolly Parton became megastars. In the seventies the historical consciousness which had begun in rock generalized to an awareness of the variety of styles of American popular music. This awareness produced strange bedfellows, so to speak, as when Loretta Lynn and Teddy Pendergrass made a soundtrack album together.

But American history, especially the history of black and white in the South, has time bombs in it, and one of them exploded in January of 1977, in the form of the eight-part television miniseries *Roots*. One of the questions which people who believe that the nostalgia craze was a trivial fad cannot answer is: Why *Roots?* You would think that sensible producers would turn down such material as too controversial, as sure to produce disastrous ratings. But the gamble that the present had so altered our perceptions about slavery that we needed a new presentation of black history paid off; some 130 million people watched and agonized. *Time* magazine it commented " *Roots* and the reaction to it are as much effect as cause."[6] The phenomenon showed the effect of the need for involvement in depth, of the historical consciousness which American have usually attributed to Europe; but now Americans needed the sense of identity which only historical consciousness can give. The pain which *Roots* caused so many people, both black and white, had a cathartic quality. Because of television's capacity to retrieve the past to huge numbers of people simultaneously, that pain helped to heal a national wound.

Notes

[1]*Newsweek*, December 28, 1970, p. 34.
[2]T.S. Eliot, *Selected Essays* (New York: Harcount, Brace, and World, 1960), p. 4.
[3]*Ibid.*
[4]*Ibid.*, p. 5.
[5]Philip K. Eberly, *Music in the Air. America's Changing Taste in Popular Music, 1920-1980* (New York: Hastings House, 1982), p. 264.
[6]*Time*, February 14, 1977, p. 71.

Chapter 21:
The Individual Strands of *Tapestry*

Carole King's *Tapestry* album was far and away the biggest-selling album of the early seventies, and is now the third biggest seller of all time, right behind Michael Jackson's *Thriller* and the soundtrack from *Saturday Night Fever*. Its success can help us begin to sort out the proliferation of styles and artists which characterized the seventies.

As a seminal figure in Brill Building Pop during the early sixties, Carole was associated with New York, and New York professionalism, from the very beginning of her long career. Her great successes as part of the Goffin/King songwriting team with "Will You Love Me Tomorrow?" and "Loco-motion" came during the period of assimilation after the surge of Southern rockers in the fifties, so it makes sense that she would enjoy another successful phase during the period of assimilation after the intensity of the sixties.

As we know, the early sixties witnessed a resurgence of New York music with groups like Dion and the Belmonts, and styles like the Twist coming from the Big Apple. Similarly, in the early seventies many of the varieties of popular music that could conceivably be called rock in the seventies were in a New York state of mind. Carole played piano on James Taylor's *Sweet Baby James*, and although he was originally from the South, he lived in New York, and married a New York girl, Carly Simon. Jim Croce, an Italian kid from Philadelphia (like Fabian and Frankie Avalon), was discovered while he was gigging in New York. In the seventies, for the first time in rock history, New York actually produced a major rock 'n' roll band—Blondie—and a group which did very well for a while, the Village People. If the Village People were the Monkees of the seventies, Barry Manilow was the Johnny Mathis of the seventies; he was from Brooklyn, and he stayed on the charts from 1974 on. Moreover, two trends of the seventies, disco and punk, began in New York, and the greater metropolitan area contributed Bruce Springsteen and Billy Joel, with their distinctly East Cost sensibilities.

The prominence of keyboard players marks a major distinction between the seventies and the sixties. If the hallmark of the sixties was the hot guitar player like Jimi Hendrix or Eric Clapton, then the hallmark of the seventies was the hot keyboards player, like Elton John. In addition to Carole, Barry, Billy, and Elton, keyboards virtuosos Rick Wakeman and Keith Emerson became individual stars within Yes and Emerson Lake and Palmer respectively. Then, too, Bruce Springsteen uses two keyboards, piano and organ, in the E Street Band. The synthesizer had a lot to do with the keyboards resurgence, and Pete Townshend used it on *Who's Next;* Stevie Wonder got rave reviews, and great sales, for *Songs in the Key of Life.* But Carole doesn't play a synthesizer on *Tapestry;* she plays an acoustic piano. Producer Lou Adler didn't double-track her voice—he said he was trying for a "bare sound." He certainly got it, and the success of that bare sound was the first clear voice of the seventies.

Two other albums in addition to *Tapestry* represent the rise of the individual singer/songwriter in the early seventies: James Taylor's *Sweet Baby James,* and Cat Stevens' *Teaser and the Firecat.* These three very successful albums have a lot in common; they mostly use acoustic instruments with hardly any noticeable studio effects. The strength of the albums lies in the writing and in the vocals. What we have here is the quiet after the storm of the sixties, and Carole, James, and Cat all take notice of the passage of time. Carole says that her life "has been a tapestry" in the song of the same name, James says that he has seen "Fire and Rain"; Cat welcomes the passage of time on "Changes IV" and expresses hope for the future on "Peace Train." The contrast of the present with the past, which is related to the so-called nostalgia fad on the early seventies, appears on each album as well. Carole covers two of the great songs which she wrote as part of the Goffin/King team. "Will You Love Me Tomorrow?" and "(You Make Me Feel Like a) Natural Woman". James does the old Stephen Foster favorite, "Oh Susannah" in order to play up the reference to the suicide of a girl named Susanne in "Fire and Rain." As for Cat, he does the hymn, well known in England, "Morning Has Broken." Still, each album has its own individual features.

Although people do not usually think of Carole as a feminist, much of *Tapestry* expresses a woman's perception of male attitudes and male music. For one thing, there's the opposition of the piano to the guitar. A piano, which you can't easily carry around, suggests home, stability, and a settled way of life, as opposed to the portable guitar. Hence the appropriateness of her comment in "So Far Away" that "One more song about movin' on the highway" can't say anything new. Historically, it has been men who have sung songs about moving on, and this comment is directed toward Dylan as well as toward Steppenwolf's "Born to be Wild," If the lyrics and instrumentation of "So Far Away" react against macho rock, "It's Too Late" reacts with equal force against cheerful songs like the Beatles' "We Can Work It Out." This song, sung movingly and quietly, anticipates Paul Simon's witty/melancholy "50 Ways to Leave Your Lover," in accepting the fact that you *can't* always work it out, and that life will go on anyhow. As for "Smackwater Jack," it sounds a lot like Jim Croce's hit, "Big Bad Leroy Brown," but unlike that song it's a morality tale about macho violence. Carole can even react to her own work of the sixties; "Way Over Yonder" is a gospel expression of the need for escape in "Up On the Roof."

James Taylor comes from North Carolina, and he has such a confident feel for the blues that he can even sing at the easy rocking tempo of downhome blues. "Lo and Behold" flows easily, as does "Steamroller," yet both of them have contemporary lyrics. Most impressive of all, though, is "Oh Baby, Don't You Loose Your Lip on Me," which sounds like a blues improvisation that a much older man could have been proud of. Remarkably, though, hardly anything else on the album sounds bluesy at all. The singles, "Sweet Baby James"; "Country Road"; and "Fire and Rain" have literate, imaginative lyrics (I especially appreciate the way he rhymes "Boston/frostin'"), and strong backup work.

If James is Southern, Cat is Greek, and *Teaser and the Firecat* is surely the only album of the seventies which has part of a song printed in Greek on the lyrics sheet. Cat also uses the bouzoukia, a Greek folk instrument something like a mandolin, on "Rubylove." What we have mostly on this album, though, is his clear, rich voice and acoustic guitar. In this respect, he resembles James a lot, but the two men differ greatly as lyricists. Unlike James, Cat writes vague, spacey lyrics in free verse so that he creates a romantic atmosphere—the epitome of early seventies mellow—without making a personal statement.

Given that these are talented performers beautifully recorded, what made the singer/songwriter so important in the early seventies? One way of a answering that question is to say that these are the kinds of records you like to put on when you come home from work to an empty apartment. It's not coincidental, I think, that Gilbert O'Sullivan's "Alone Again (Naturally)" went over so big in 1972. When you live alone, you often don't want to listen to hard rock by yourself, because its party atmosphere and invitation to the dance make for frustration. Often, what you want in that situation is to listen to Carole King's reassuring "You've Got a Friend."

In the seventies a greater percentage of the American population lived alone than ever before. They did so in a variety of situations, of course. As they got out of college, lots of baby boomers moved into apartment complexes for swinging singles, like Marina del Rey in Los Angeles. "In a sense the singles ghettos in the cities were not that much different from the youth ghettos in the colleges: removed from the proximity and therefore scrutiny of the older generation, they were free to develop values that place them outside the adult population."[1] They were also free, in Dylan's words, to do anything they wanted to do but die, and there was a lot of loneliness and anxiety in their lives, especially for women; four out of five amphetamine prescriptions are written for women.[2] So the warm, sincere singers helped to assuage those negative feelings.

Several statistics pertaining to living arrangements doubled in the seventies. The proportion of unmarried women aged 25-29 doubled; not unrelated to this is the fact the national divorce rate doubled as well.[3] Those glum facts made for a lot of Eleanor Rigbys. Not everybody was living alone, though; between 1970 and 1976, the number of couples living together also doubled, from 327,000 to 660,000.[4] This change, another form of decentralization in its disregard for established authority, didn't mean that those couples stopped listening to rock 'n' roll, but it did tend to produce a change in their expectations about that music. Living together means, among other things, that you can have fantastic sex with someone but still have arguments about emptying the kitty litter box. Such a realization can manifest itself as a preference for understatement rather than promises about eternal love.

So much was going on at any given time in the seventies that no one trend ever took over for long, so we need a way of distinguishing the different audiences for the different styles. To do this we don't need absolute distinctions, only relative emphases, since different styles work best in different modes. One way of doing this is to measure the success of the act in the three ways of getting exposure: radio airplay, concerts, and albums. It is possible to distinguish in very general terms the singer/songwriters, the heavy metal groups, and the British art rockers according to these outlets. The short, quiet songs of Carole, James, and Cat lent themselves well to radio airplay, and all three artists enjoyed very respectable chart activity in the seventies. By contrast, the heavy metal groups had very little chart activity, since their songs were too long to fit on playlists, and the kids couldn't play their radios loud enough to satisfy them anyhow. So the heavy metal groups gave dynamite concerts. British art rockers also had little chart activity, and gave some profitable concerts tours, but their strong suit was the album—Pink Floyd's _Dark Side of the Moon_ stayed on the album chart for a staggering ten years!

Notes

[1]Jones, _Great Expectations_, p. 175.

[2]_Ibid._, p. 172.

[3]_Ibid._, pp. 179 and 183.

[4]Eleanor D. Macklin, "Review of Research on Nonmarital Cohabitation in United States," in _Exploring Intimate Lifestyles_, Bernard I. Murstein, ed. (New York: Spring, 1979), p. 205.

Chapter 22:
Rock Starts to Compete With Television

In the seventies, first Mick Jagger and then Bruce Springsteen appeared on the cover of *Time,* and rock became assimilated into the straight media, and thus into the modern world. Now it was no longer just *Rolling Stone* which reported on the comings and goings of rock stars; it was also *People* and even *The National Inquirer.* Thus it happened that rock started to compete with the omnipresent fact of the modern world, television. By this, I don't mean that major acts like Bob Dylan and the Rolling Stones appeared on *Saturday Night Live,* although that was surely a sign of the times. Rather, I mean the re-definition of rock implicit in the way a young fan from Milwaukee talked about a Kiss concert: "I think their music's pretty good, but mostly I come for the show. They have flames, smoke, and explosions, and I go for that stuff."[1] You bet he does—you just can't make smoke, flames and explosion spectacular even on a 25-inch color screen. This kid has watched television all his life (as Steven Spielberg once put it, television is like a third parent for modern kids), and he can listen to rock on FM stereo 24 hours a day. What he wants at a concert, then, is something he can't get at home—something "outrageous."

So the time had passed when acts could just show up and play, as the the Beatles had done at their famous Shea Stadium gig in August of 1965. The audiences wanted more than just the opportunities to see their favorite performers in person—they wanted spectacles. Three major acts of the seventies, Elton John, Alice Cooper, and David Bowie, gave them spectacles.

All three made major innovations in performance style, yet all three also showed the effects of historical consciousness in ironic yet nevertheless revealing ways. To take only one example for each, Elton contributed "Crocodile Rock" to the nostalgia style; Alice began concerts with a tape of Kate Smith singing "God Bless America"; and David has his backup singers quote a line from "A Day in the Life" on "Young Americans." All three began the use of ever more elaborate costumes and sets, and they made sexual ambiguity trendy. Let's take them in the order in which they appeared on the charts.

Elton is the top artist of the seventies. His astonishing record includes five #1 singles between 1970 and 1975, and seven straight albums which went to #1 on the album charts. These numbers are all the more astonishing since his lyricist Bernie Taupin does not himself perform. This very successful collaboration sometimes produces some odd effects. For the moment, though, we want to notice how Elton made it as a performer. When he legally changed his name from Reg Dwight to Elton John, he chose Hercules as his middle name, and Reg Dwight is to Elton John rather as Clark Kent is to Superman. Reg Dwight was a shy, dumpy, near-sighted kid who studied piano at the Royal Academy of Music; Elton John is a manic rocker with over-sized spectacles and platform shoes who plays a sequined Steinway. Here, for example, is a description of how he looked at the final concert in his 1974 tour: "There he was!—banging away at the piano in some kind of cockamamie papal purple robe with magician smoke (from a dry ice pump) hissing up around him and a four-foot ostrich plume slanting and swaying up from the glittering top hat at a wild angle."[2] When Elton John does a cameo appearance in the movie version of *Tommy* (1975), his costumes and performance are as overdone as everything else in that memorable film.

Any armchair psychologist can guess that shy Reg needed these props, and the manic energy, as a mask for his anxieties. What's much more significant, though, is that the paraphernalia which would have alienated audiences in the sixties delighted audiences of the seventies. Not since the heyday of Jerry Lee Lewis and Little Richard—the obvious comparisons—had a pianist overcome the physical limitations of playing his instrument to seize and hold the attention of the audience. But like any major performer he needed strong material, and he got it by working with Bernie Taupin. As it turns out, they are both mid-Atlantic men, as surely as Mick Jagger and David Bowie are.

Elton and Bernie produce remarkably consistent songs. With a few exceptions, like "No Shoestrings on Louise," on which Elton sings like Mick Jagger on "Dead Flowers," and "Jamaica Jerk-Off," their tribute to reggae, their songs feature strong lyrics, with Elton's warm voice and confident piano mixed up front. No matter what the subject of the lyrics or the key of the music, what comes across most frequently is their fascination with American popular culture.

Although Elton started out playing in a band called Bluesology, I don't hear any significant traces of the blues in his music. There's a strong gospel feel, though to such songs as "Border Song"; "Son of Your Father"; and "Rotten Peaches." After he started recording in America, he had access to real gospel singers, and used a choir directed by gospel great Rev. James Cleveland for "Boogie Pilgrim" and "Where's the Shoorah?"

The interest in gospel suggests an interest in, and sympathy for, the outsiders of society which is common enough among rock musicians. Thus, Elton and Bernie do a number of songs about outsiders in nineteenth-century America, especially in their most fully realized concept album, *Tumbleweed Connection*. The album sleeve itself is an elaborate production, and bears witness to the importance of the album as opposed to the single in the early seventies. It has pictures of Elton and Bernie at a nineteenth-century railroad station on the cover, and features the complete lyrics to the songs printed in nineteenth-century typography and appropriate illustrations in the style of nineteenth-century engravings.

If the lyrics and the illustrations refer to nineteenth-century America, the album as a whole offers a tribute to twentieth-century America, specifically to Bob Dylan and The Band. Thus, "Ballad of a Well-Known Gun" de-mythologizes "John Wesley Harding." The lyrics of "My Father's Gun" form a dramatic monologue on the part of a Confederate soldier, and thus resemble "The Night They Drove Ole Dixie Down," on *The Band*. The singer mourns the loss of a brother on "The Night..." whereas Elton mourns the loss of his father on "My Father's Gun." He's going to take a "riverboat," whereas The Band's song refers to the Robert E. Lee. But there's a curious thing about "My Father's Song," and it happens more than once with Elton and Bernie. The singer vows to avenge his father, and "wear the colour of the greys" in order to "plant the seeds of justice." They don't seem to understand that while those words have a fine ring to them, they still constitute a defense of slavery. Such a misunderstanding can happen occasionally when people try to deal with the history of another country in another century. A similar problem occurs on "Burn Down the Mission," which deals with a populist insurrection in the Southwest. Bernie uses a distinctively British word, "keep," for "courtyard," and it sounds out of place. However, nothing like this mars "Country Comfort" which is a masterpiece; it begins slowly, with just Elton and his piano, and then a steel guitar and country fiddle join in. Thus the instrumentation complements Bernie's Wordsworthian lyrics.

You can understand why a mid-Atlantic man would call an album *Madman Across the Water;* as it happens, though, it contains only one American song. This is "Indian Sunset," which uses a Indian chant style, and probably was written under the influence of "Indian Reservation" by Paul Revere and the Raiders. On *Honky Chateau* the problem of coordinating Bernie's lyrics with Elton's musical ideas appears again on "Honky Cat," where the sharp bite of a brass section (French studio musicians) contrasts with the American pastoralism of Bernie Taupin's lyrics. The steel guitar makes "Slave" a more successful American song. Their sympathy for the emancipation of blacks comes across in "One Horse Town," whose lyrics are related to "Burn Down the Mission." Although the lyrics deal with nineteenth-century Alabama, the instrumentation includes an electric piano, a synthesizer, tubular bells—and features a cello solo! The music never makes us think of the South, or of the nineteenth-century at all. Speaking of the past, "Crocodile Rock" evokes the fifties, which is to say America in the fifties, with its staccato thirds and its reference to the time when "rock was young."

Neither Elton nor Bernie has any interest that you can hear in American music; what they really care about is American movies. Once you think about it, you realize that rock and movies have a natural affinity, for the amplification of volume in rock corresponds to the enlargement of the image in movies.

Elton and Bernie were so taken with American movies that they appear in the names of some of their albums. Although the name *Don't Shoot Me, I'm Only the Piano Player* comes from Francois Truffaut's *Shoot the Pianist* (1960), the cover shows a theater which has a poster advertising the Marx

Brothers' *Go West* (1940). And the title of *Goodbye Yellow Brick Road*, also from 1973, makes an obvious movie reference. Then too, some individual songs rely on movie references in various ways, such as "Teacher I Need You," with its references to John Wayne and Erroll Flynn; "Candle in the Wind," a tribute to Marilyn Monroe. "Roy Rogers" suggests that Bernie and Keith Richards shared a childhood idol. A final movie reference brings us back to the fifties, when Bernie celebrates Elvis on "Idol," and Elton's cocktail lounge piano reminds us that he was performing in Las Vegas at the time.

"Starring Elton John" reads the marquee on the cover of *Don't Shoot Me...*, and Elton and Bernie show the effects of stardom by writing a series of songs whose lyrics have as their topic the act of songwriting. Their first charted song, "Your Song," may serve as a case in point. Continuing what Paul Simon had begun with "Homeward Bound," they made the self-conscious song into a subgenre. In this they were not so unique; in fact, they were part of a trend, for self-conscious songs appeared on the charts again and again in the seventies.

Self-Conscious Songs of the Seventies

Artist	Song	Year
Grand Funk Railroad	"We're An American Band"	1973
Dr. Hook	"Cover of Rolling Stone"	1973
Paul McCartney and Wings	"Band on the Run"	1974
Barry Manilow	"I Write the Songs"	1975
Jackson Browne	"The Load Out"	1978
Lynyrd Skynyrd	"What's Your Name"	1978
Dire Straits	"Sultans of Swing"	1979
Willie Nelson	"On the Road Again"	1980

"Your Song" is a love song, and "Bennie and the Jets" is about a rock group, but "I'm Going to be a Teenage Idol" expresses pure individual ambition of the kind that the major stars have, and the fans fantasize about. Elton and Bernie feature themselves in *Captain Fantastic and the Brown Dirt Cowboy*. The lyrics sheets to the album amount to a scrapbook complete with family snapshots and chatty commentary. The title song begins with their childhood, when Elton was "hardly a hero" and Bernie wondered, "Are there any chances in life?" and ends with their present fame. "Bitter Fingers" expresses their lingering resentment at the treatment they received in Denmark Street, London's equivalent of Tin Pan Alley. Collaborating on songwriting is like a marriage, people say, and Bernie and Elton celebrate their work together, so that the album ends on a positive note.

It is no criticism of Elton to say that his music changed relatively little in the seventies. He used different sound textures by playing on the organ, the mellotron, and the synthesizer as well as the piano; you hear choruses and strings on some of his songs. Still, his songs are clearly recognizable as Elton John songs—which is one reason why people like them so much.

Alice Cooper did not have the staying power of Elton John, but he certainly caused more furor. In 1973, he was the top-drawing act in the world, and now that the seventies have passed, it's easy to wonder why. The group sounds like just another garage band, and "I'm Eighteen" could be another remake of "Satisfaction" without Keith's riffing guitar. But for more and more performers during the seventies, the records were becoming secondary to the concerts, and it fell to Alice Cooper to begin this major trend. And when you listen closely to "I'm Eighteen," you realize that the singer is no Fabian— the voice is too deep, and the snarl too guttural. Similarly, if "School's Out" seems like the title for another Beach Boys song, the lyrics announce, not just that school's out for the summer, but that school's out "forever," and so the song turns into a proclamation of anarchy.

There's no simple, easy response to Alice Cooper. He wore mascara and a dress, but he often had a stubbly beard and he certainly had no effeminate mannerisms. He sang hard rock, but at home he liked to listen to Burt Bacharach albums. It also turns out that Alice Cooper, aka Vincent Furnier from Phoenix, is an intelligent perceptive person who knew what he was about. Given these complexities, and given the importance of movies for rock in the seventies, a good way of understanding the response which Alice Cooper evoked is to think of the similarly intense response which *The Exorcist* (1973) evoked. There was much in our recent social and political history that needed to be exorcised, and the movie provided a surrogate exorcism which people found deeply satisfying, if also deeply disturbing.

Alice Cooper as an exorcist? Why not? He once confided to journalist Bob Greene that, "Mothers come to me with their kids and say, 'Sing it,' and it's always 'Dead Babies.' "[3] Clearly, something is happening here, when mothers bring their children to sing "Dead Babies" for Alice Cooper.

It is not just coincidence that about this time kids started telling dead baby jokes. As jokes often do, these jokes were serving an important function. At this time the birth rate was falling (it hit an all-time low in 1976), while the number of abortions performed each year was dramatically rising. It is not just that these things were happening, they were receiving widespread publicity, and causing great controversy. If adults sometimes felt confused, it is little wonder that the kids started feeling like an endangered species. They surely wondered whether they were wanted or were just accidents. So by singing "Dead Babies" they could face these anxieties without seeming to do so. It was just a song—wasn't it?

Alice's principal significance is that he made the stage shows as provocative as possible. Alice and his manager Shep Gordon realized that "The mass circulation general press would print *anything* about a rock and roll group if it was sufficiently disgusting and opposed to standard morality."[4] Thus, Alice Cooper represents a key moment in the long, important, and little-understood history of the manipulation of the press by rock stars. Alice and Shep did what the Stones had done, only they did it a lot more audaciously than the Stones had ever wanted or dared to do.

On the Billion Dollar Babies tour in 1973, for example, Alice came out in a dress with what looked like blood stains at the crotch, hacked up baby dolls, massaged the breasts of a mannekin, went down on her(it?), and then attacked her(it?) with an oversized toothbrush. These antics drove the kids crazy, of course, because they certainly hadn't seen anything like it during the thousands and thousands of hours which they had spent watching TV. As if this were not enough, they had a guy dressed as Santa Claus come out, and while the tape played the most popular recording ever made—Bing Crosby's "White Christmas"—they pretended to kill him. Only after doing in Santa Claus did Alice go through the most famous/infamous part of the show and go under the guillotine. Of course, it was only a dummy that got its head chopped off, but the head looked real enough when the members of the band brought it to center stage, and it dripped what looked like real blood. The group did understand, though, that popular performers must respect limits, even if they seem to flaunt them, so Alice came back for an encore to reassure the kids that it had all been in fun.

In understanding the dynamics of the Billion Dollar Babies tour, the appropriate movie analogy is not so much with *The Exorcist* as with the horror movies which followed it, such as *Halloween* (1978). People have noticed that such "splatter movies," as they came to be called, follow a definite pattern: Teenage sex is followed by violence against teenagers. This sequence occurs so often that people have speculated that it assuages guilt feelings among the audience. The sociological studies which show that kids have guilt feelings about sex even when they don't do anything which they themselves consider improper seem to justify this speculation. What it comes to is that splatter movies let teenagers have their cake and eat it too.

This is what Alice Cooper did as well, and he had an unusual understanding of what his show did, and how it affected his audience. Once, when the city fathers were trying to ban his concert, Shep called him in to persuade them to let the show go on, and here's what he said: "We make our shows a morality play, in which I misbehave, and then I am punished, and then I am executed. The kids realize that—even if they can't put it into so many words, they realize it." So, like other phenomena of the time, like *The Exorcist* and splatter movies and dead baby jokes, Alice was creating a cathartic experience which helped to relieve the stresses of social change. Whatever television could do, it couldn't provide catharsis—the very size of its audience precluded extreme, intense experiences. (As Gil Scott Heron put it so memorably, "The revolution will not be televised.") Only after Alice showed what rock could do did television provide something like catharsis for the tensions of the time, with *Saturday Night Live* (which premiered in 1975), and *Roots*, which had a subject of exceptional importance.

Alice's success also made freakish clothing and freakish behavior more acceptable in the hinterlands than it had ever been in the sixties. The following comments by astute journalist Bob Greene about the freaks at a party after Alice's concert in Buffalo, New York, show how Alice fostered the assimilation of the sixties by the seventies: "It was the kind of scene that used to appear in wirephotos from the most consciously decadent San Francisco drag clubs; but Alice Cooper had made it acceptable for the children of heartland America, and here they were, at his New Year's Eve party."[6]

What Alice began, David Bowie developed. Indeed, Myles Palmer thinks that he's more important than that: "The first line of ¢Space Oddity' was a signal for the seventies to begin, and David Bowie became the premier influence on young songwriters."[7] Even though Palmer is exaggerating, David is certainly the consummate British performer of the seventies, as crucial for England as Bruce Springsteen is for America. If other performers reacted against the sixties, he fulfilled the sixties, for his work would make no sense without those years—and our knowledge of them. David, and only David, combined the songwriting genius of the Beatles, the irony and ambiguity of the Stones, and the chameleon-like evolution of Dylan. If the Beatles made the first concept album, David not only made concept albums, he performed them as concept concerts—something the Beatles never did. If you never knew what the next Dylan album was going to sound like, you never knew what the next David Bowie concert was going to sound like or look like. No one sound, or style, or look can define him, because they are all valid but partial personas for him. He is the only rock performer who has appeared successfully in movies and on Broadway. Sometimes he was a rocker, and sometimes he was a crooner; sometimes he was straight and sometimes he was gay.

Given all these ambiguities, it is important to specify why David was so right for his times. In his case, a clue comes from Tom Wolfe's "The Me Decade." Wolfe explains the self-involvement of the seventies by quoting the advertising line "If I've only one life to live, let me live it as a blonde," and saying that people were filling in the blank in the line, "If I've only one life to live, let me live it as a —————." The point is that David had the capacity to fill in more blanks than anyone else. Nicholas Schaffner very neatly describes his multiple identities when he says, "Bowie strove continually to reinvest himself alternately homo-, hetero- and bisexual, in much the same way that he could (and would) reinvest himself as a Mind revivalist, a soul singer, a Continental crooner, a movie star, or a film director; the bisexual space oddity just happened to be the persona through which we made Mr. Bowie's acquaintance."[8] Or, as David himself once put it in his usual provocative manner, "Sometimes I don't feel like I'm a person at all; I'm just a collection of other people's ideas."[9]

In addition to his talent, David could have been a hero simply because of his presence. For this he has two factors to thank—his face and his lack of family. He has the kind of classically Aryan face which we saw again and again in *Chariots of Fire* (1980), for instance. His face is, in fact, so pure that it has no defining features, and thus he can come on as androgynous. Moreover, he can adopt a persona as a space oddity or as a Thin White Count because we have so little information about him. His father died in 1969, and his mother refuses to speak to the press about him; his sister got married and moved to Egypt (he says), and his brother (if he is still alive) is in a mental institution. Thus, we don't have any demythologizing photos of little David like the ones we have of Elton and Bernie, and there's nobody to tell us what he was like when he was little. So we have yet another paradox about him: although he is very much a product of Britain in the sixties, he seems to have come out of nowhere—or from Mars.

Actually, we can tell where David came from by listening to his *Space Oddity* from 1969, where his musical debts are readily apparent. The title song takes the bolero rhythm from the Jefferson Airplane's "White Rabbit," and uses tape effects like the ones on "Revolution 9." The next song, "Unwashed and Somewhat Slightly Dazed," sounds a lot like early Dylan, and comes complete with harmonica. (Not for nothing did David write "Song for Dylan.") "Letter to Hermione" and "An Occasional Dream" amount to homage to Donovan. As to the Beatles, "God Knows I'm Good" is a folkie's version of "Eleanor Rigby," and "Memory of a Free Festival" ends with everyone joining in, like "Hey Jude." In addition, "Cygnet Committee" has an unrecognized importance, for it hints at David's admiration for Anthony Newley, and forms something of a reprise for "Space Oddity"; it has apocalyptic intimations which may well come from "The Eve of Destruction," and in fact Ziggy himself could have sung the line "I gave them all."

In short, *Space Oddity* is a typical first album for a talented performer; what you expect is that David will proceed to develop his own, distinctive style. But this just did not happen; there *is no* distinctive Bowie style; "Unlike, say, Lennon, Dylan, or Townshend, Bowie did not purport to be 'authentic.' "[10] David did not need to be "authentic" or "natural," or any of those other terms of Romantic praise because he was a creature of the seventies, when people more or less consciously understood that the sound they were hearing was in no meaningful sense "natural" or "authentic." And since the sound defines the musicians, people had less interest in whether the musicians were "natural" or "authentic." After all, David was just demonstrating different ways of being far out. Specifically, he demonstrated those ways of being far out on two of the most complex, and most fully realized albums of the seventies, *Ziggy Stardust*, June, 1972, and *Diamond Dogs*, April, 1974. Almost everything about these albums involves a series of puns, associations, and references.

Take the full title of the Ziggy Stardust album, for instance: *The Rise and Fall of Ziggy Stardust and the Spiders of Mars*. To begin with, it refers to the Bertold Brecht-Kurt Weill 1927 opera, *The Rise and Fall of the City of Mahogany*. The Doors may have aroused his interest in *Mahogany* when they recorded "Alabama Song" from it on their first album. David himself made this connection when describing his White Light Tour from 1976: "I've reverted to pure Brechtian theater and I've never seen Brechtian theatre used like this since Morrison and the Doors, and even then Morrison never used white light like I do."[11]

Like *Ziggy Stardust, Mahogany* is a dystopia—a corrupted utopia. The name seems to have provided the name for Ziggy's backup group; Leocadia Begbick, a madam, sings that it means "Spiderweb": "It will be like a web/ Spun out to catch all the plump juicy insects."[12] One other noteworthy feature of *Mahogany* is that during a brief play within the play, God comes down to Mahogany, just as Ziggy comes down to Earth.

A sense of decadence and a foreboding of fascism pervades Brecht's play, and must have provided David with seductive analogies to what he sensed in London in the early seventies. In general, the German connection is an important one for David; he had read enough Nietzsche to feel justified in thinking of himself as the "blond beast," the future superman whose coming Nietzsche prophesied. David collected Nazi war relics, and actually lived in Berlin in the summer of 1976, but more than biography is at stake here. No one else among his contemporaries sensed the similarities between the spectacle of Nazi party rally in *Triumph of the Well* (1935), and the spectacle into which the rock concert had evolved in the seventies. Certainly, no one had the audacity to mention that similarity, as David did: "Rock stars are fascists, too. Adolph Hitler was one of the first rock stars."[13] David is a past master at making provocative statements, of course, but he has a serious purpose here—to connect the past and the present. The Nazis were such monsters that we like to think of then as safely relegated to the past, but David isn't letting us get away with that. True to his subtle historical consciousness, he is insisting that the present has grown out of the past, and that to understand the present, we must assimilate the past.

Ziggy Stardust also grows out of the more immediate past as well. The name "Ziggy" comes from the name of Iggy Pop, whom David greatly admires, and "Stardust" has a set of associations. For David's audience, "star" means "famous performer," and only secondarily "celestial body." When the astronauts became celebrities—a process which Wolfe describes with devastating wit in *The Right Stuff*—for journeying among the stars, the ambiguities accumulated rapidly. Then too, these more recent meanings are also played off against the associations of celestial bodies and romance in popular songs, such as "Blue Moon"; "Wish Upon a Star"; "Catch a Falling Star"; and—obviously— "Stardust." The New York-Hollywood tradition which these songs represent is very important to David, who admires the greatest interpreter of that tradition. In 1976, he announced, "I want to be a Frank Sinatra figure, and I will succeed." As for the more recent past, astrological imagery grew into a virtual obsession for Jimi Hendrix, as his song titles "Third Stone from the Sun", "Moon, Turn the Tides", and "Astro Man" suggest.

Concept albums also came from the late sixties, and not just from the Beatles. David has been greatly affected by Kinks, whose 1966 hit "Dedicated Follower of Fashion" makes the kind of social commentary which he developed. Two of their concept albums clearly anticipate Ziggy Stardust: *Arthur (Or the*

Decline and Fall of the British Empire), from 1969—a suggestive title—and *Lola Vs. Powerman and the Moneygoround* from 1970. Both of these albums have to do with society and pop music and their interrelations. In particular, the cut released as a single from the second album. "Lola," plays on just the kinds of technological ambiguity ("electric candlelight") and sexual ambiguity (Lola is a drag queen) which set up major oppositions on the albums.

What of Ziggy himself? The precedents begin with "Johnny B. Goode," and Ziggy is certainly Johnny taken at a higher level—both literally and metaphorically. The song "Rock 'N' Roll Suicide" reminds us of the deaths of Janis Joplin, Jim Morrison, and Jimi Hendrix. In particular, Janis seems to have died for the people as Ziggy presumably did; her fans in effect forced her to live up to the role of hard drinkin', hard livin' mama which she had created. Like Ziggy, she took it all too far. Although Janis did not play guitar, Eric Clapton did—"boy could he play guitar," as the song has it. It's hard to believe that David failed to see one of the many graffiti in London which proclaimed, "Clapton is God." Clapton was certainly a guitar-playing deity, and in the early seventies it seemed as though his addiction to heroin and Patti Boyd Harrison were going to make a rock 'n' roll suicide of him.

The question which interests us here, though, is not what David started with, but what he did with it, for it is the final result, the album itself, that matters. The album has two sides, and just about everything on it has its opposite, which negates or undercuts it. Ziggy is a Messiah, but a reluctant one, for he's afraid he'll blow their minds—or so the kids think. Ziggy is a Messiah who engages in a secular calling—he plays guitar. But he can't play guitar, because the electricity is failing.

The overriding opposition, though, is the opposition between Heaven and Earth. In terms of Heaven, the album deals with the Second Coming and the End of the World; in terms of Earth, the album deals with rock stars and the energy crisis. Neither of these meanings ever quite cancels the other out: "Clapton is God" fuses them into one. Thus, the songs are sung either by Ziggy, representing Heaven, or the kids, representing earth. (The exception, "Ziggy Stardust," is sung by his band, who mediate between Ziggy and the fans.)

We might call Side I "Promise." It begins with a kid's survey of the situation on earth ("Five Years") and Ziggy's decision to descend ("Soul Love"). The rest of Side I belongs to the kids who freak out together ("Moonage Daydream"), talk of Ziggy ("Starman"), and of the hope which he brings ("It Ain't Easy'). Side II, "Fulfillment," begins with an account of Ziggy in concert ("Lady Stardust"). The spiritual ambiguity (Is Ziggy God or Man?) generates a second ambiguity: Is Ziggy a man or a woman? On "Star," Ziggy dreams of becoming human "like a regular superstar," is warned of the fate which may befall him ("Hang On To Yourself"). Ultimately, he meets indifference from fans who are into a heavy sex trip ("Suffragette City"). The refrain "Leave me alone" suggests that this song may derive from the scene in *Blow-up* in which David Hemmings meets nothing but indifference when he takes his proof of a murder around swinging London. Ziggy's death ("Rock 'N' Roll Suicide") is more than death, of course; it is suicide as crucifixion as reassurance. The change from electric guitar on the previous songs to acoustic guitar here may suggest that we have here Ziggy's thoughts and reminiscences after "death." Ziggy reached out to his fans, and reassured them that they were not alone—unlike the lonely people in, say, "Eleanor Rigby."

Although this explanation clarifies the general use of the oppositions which I've mentioned, it fails to do justice to the complexity of the individual songs. On "Five Years," for instance, David creates a riffing effect, first with piano, and then with strings, instead of guitar. The tension builds until it is released on the phrase "five years"—thereby suggesting death will come as a relief. The album thus both begins and ends with death, and the music draws us in until we celebrate that death, and turn it into transcendence. Similarly, "Soul Love," Ziggy's first song, begins with a vision of his mother at his grave— the clearest Christ reference on the album.

The stylistic variations begin with "Moonage Daydream"; since "moonage" here means "teenage"—it's the kids' song—and is done in heavy metal. David acknowledges his debts to the Kinks on "Starman," which he sings like Ray Davies, and which has a satirical edge, just as "Dedicated Follower of Fashion" does. References abound on "It Ain't Easy"; the Stones have a song by the same name, and the lyrics refer to "Satisfaction," as well as "Hootchie Kootchie Man," and a song from Elvis' first album, "Tryin' to Get to You." "Suffragette City" is an homage to Lou Reed, yet David undercuts that homage—typically— by the famous/infamous line "Wham bam thank you ma'am," which makes it a heterosexual song. Since the Beatles were the ultimate superstars, Ziggy's career as a star has some references to the Beatles. David sings "quite out of sight" in multi-tracked Beatlesesque harmony, and the music of "Star" hints at "Get Back" and "Lovely Rita."

Thus, the album re-tells the story of the life of Christ, rather as *Jesus Christ Superstar* does, but at the same time subverts that story by insisting on its ambiguities, and by making the very means of telling the story ambiguous through references to its origins. No wonder *New Musical Express* called David "T.S. Eliot with a rock 'n' roll beat."[14]

Clearly, *Ziggy Stardust* is a major accomplishment, possibly the most innovative album of the seventies, but its subtleties limited its appeal. Thus, the Ziggy Stardust tour gave the album some badly needed support. The importance of concerts is indicated by David's chart activity—or relative lack of it. In the seventies, he had only one #1 song ("Fame"), and no #1 album (although *Diamond Dogs* and *Station to Station* got to #5 and #3 respectively.) His extraordinary media coverage did not translate directly into radio airplay and record sales.

The tour made it apparent that David owed a lot to Alice Cooper, if only in terms of the support of his label. David Douglas points out, "Without a doubt, the success of the outrageous Cooper was one of the considerations that prompted RCA to risk so much on Bowie's first US tour."[15] There was an important difference in their audiences, though. Alice was a very American act in his assault on propriety and Kate Smith and Bing Crosby; kids in the hinterlands could get off on it, so he could play places like Utica, New York, and Nashville, Tennessee. David's was a more European show, so he tended to stay in the big towns, like New York, Philadelphia, and Los Angeles. In these places, the freaks could accumulate into a critical mass, and as a result. "The audience didn't come just to see Bowie or to hear the music. He provided them with a forum where they could show each other and Bowie the outfits they had come up with."[16] As Ziggy, Bowie had orange hair, came on stage to the strains of Beethoven, and during "Suffragette City," he made sure that people would remember him. He had announced in 1972 that he was gay, and

Bowie took his play with sex roles to where it counted most; he dredged the mass subconscious to create his effects. Of all the elements (theatrical and otherwise) that eventually became part of the Ziggy stageshow, the mock-fellatio performed on Ronson's guitar was the most popular and sensational, effectively subverting the image of guitar as phallus, and the whole macho world of rock 'n' roll...The image of the blow job...was infinitely more powerful and disturbing because there was no gender limitation implied.[17]

The Ziggy Stardust tour made David the star he believed he was, since he had made it in America. In fact, David is even more of a mid-Atlantic man than Mick Jagger, as his choice of an American producer, Tony Visconti, suggests. Visconti recalls that in about 1970 that what he, David, and Marc Bolan used to do "Was get high and listen to Beach Boys albums and Phil Spector albums—we all had that in common, that we loved the Beach Boys."[18] It's not surprising, then, that in the seventies David alternated between making American albums and British albums. If "Song for Bob Dylan" and "Andy Warhol" tend to make *Hunky Dorey* an American album, then it follows that *Ziggy* is a British album, and its conception and references are indeed primarily British.*Aladdin Sane*, written and recorded in America and featuring such songs as "Drive-In Saturday" and "Panic in Detroit" is an American album. Then, *Pin-ups*, which consists of David's covers of songs by British groups, is clearly British, as is *Diamond Dogs. Young Americans*, with its title and soul sound, is obviously American.

Then, in 1976, he made an important announcement: "I want to be a Frank Sinatra figure, and I will succeed."[19] (Earlier, he said he had written "Life on Mars?" around the chords for "My Way.") In naming Frank as his precursor, David was transcending such petty matters as citizenship (Sinatra belongs to the world) and musical style. By this time, he had gone through so many changes that we began to realize that he was not any one person.

With this in mind, let's return to his other crucial album, *Diamond Dogs* (April, 1974). He wanted to make a musical version of George Orwell's *1984*, but Orwell's widow refused to grant him the rights to the property, so this is the result. To Americans this book seems like an odd choice, even for David.

But David's album, like Orwell's novel, grows out of a peculiarly British paranoia about government bureaucracy. "This fear has long been a major one in Britain—a physically small country with a strong centralized government—and regularly emerges as a topic in fiction, films, and television, producing such works as Orwell's *1984* and the recent BBC-TV series *1990*, whereas in America, with its various States still retaining some autonomy within the federal system, the same fear is less intense."[20]

Guy Peelaert's cover for *Diamond Dogs* shows us David's head and torso on the feet and hindquarters of a dog. If *Ziggy Stardust* played on the human/divine ambiguity, then *Diamond Dogs* plays on the human/animal ambiguity. It is this ambiguity that causes people to speak of it as an unpleasant album. This ambiguity also forces unpleasant juxtapositions, as when David proclaims, at the end of "Future Legend," "This ain't rock 'n' roll—this is genocide"— and the crowd roars in approval. Is the crowd roaring in approval of its own death, or the death of some other group? Either way, the response disturbs us.

"Future Legend" creates the usual distopian setting for one of David's albums, and for the first full-length cut he found inspiration in the Stones' distopian song of decadence, "Live With Me," and included an appropriate reference to Donovan's "Season of the Witch." He has none of the Stones' irony. As though in compensation, on "Sweet Thing," he undercuts his own song by emphasizing the artificiality of what he is doing—"My set is amazing"— even as he is doing it. The hit from the album, "Rebel Rebel" is the "Louie Louie" of the seventies, and is supposed to remind us of the Troggs'"Wild Thing." Yet he juxtaposes garage band music against a dramatization of his old trick of sexual ambiguity. He sings both the part of the father upset about the sexual ambiguity of the child, and of the child.

To go from side I to side II is to go from garage band music to an anthem, "Rock 'n' Roll With Me." This song, and the next two, seem to be sung by the rebel child himself/herself. The swelling, melodious music promises youthful hope, as does the phrase "the door which lets me out," but the purpose of the song is to set up expectations which the rest of the album undercuts. "We Are the Dead," the longest and most complex song on *Diamond Dogs*, destroys hope and speaks of alienation. The key line, "Because of all we've seen and said we are the dead." seems to combine the paranoia of "Desolation Row" with the urban despair of T.S. Eliot's "The Hollow Men," which begins, "We are the hollow men." In general, these are David's most difficult lyrics. Although they do not lend themselves to ready summary, they have the eye imagery of "The Hollow Men," and are written in the same kind of loose free verse as Eliot's poem. The rebel child, nostalgic for the rebellion of the sixties, warns of the "savage shore" on "1984," to the incongruous sounds of a funky guitar borrowed from Curtis Mayfield's "Shaft." Presumably the rebel child is shafted, because we hear no dissenting voices on "Big Brother." There's incongruity galore, though, because on this album which so sternly denies transcendence, "Big Brother" begins with a choir. David's multi-tracked voice sings it as a hymn of submission to totalitarianism, complete with tambourines, and the album ends with a tape loop of the middle syllable of "Big Brother" which repeats and then fades.

Although *Diamond Dogs* hardly sounds like the kind of thing from which great concert tours are made, David carried it off by presenting it as a theatrical experience.

Mark Ravitz's elaborate set loosely based on Fritz Lang's *Metropolis* [1927] transformed the arena stage into the ravaged townscape of *Diamond Dogs,* and each number was a set piece, choreographed by Tony Basil (with the band, now led by guitarist Earl Slick, kept hidden behind a screen). There was movable catwalk, from which Bowie, wrapped in a trench coat, crooned "Sweet Thing" and "Candidate" under the glare of a streetlight. For "Cracked Actor" he donned a cape and shades, to address the skull that he clutched at his crotch. During the sophisticaited, S&M-flavored dance routines of "Diamond Dogs," David's backup singers tied him up with their "leashes." "Big Brother" was highlighted by a giant mirrored pleasure dome; but the piece de resistance was "Space Oddity," for which Bowie entered an actual space capsule, hoisted over the cheering throngs by a glorified cherrypicker as he sang his first hit into a red telephone.[21]

By singing in a space capsule, David had gone about as far as he could go, and it was time for another change. Indeed, he kept changing throughout the seventies. These changes in his persona were more than mere whims, as the changes of any major performer are. David had the talent and inclination to evolve, both musically and theatrically, at a time rock 'n' roll had established itself as a style. As a result, he could take rock as a given, and ring changes on it. In doing so, David—along with Elton and Alice—made theatricality a major characteristic of seventies rock.

Notes

[1]Quoted in Colette Dowling, "An Outrage Called Kiss," *New York Times Magazine,* June 19, 1977, p. 18.

[2]Ed McCormack, "Elton's Tour Ends: Tears, Lennon, and Whatever Gets You Through the Night," *Rolling Stone,* January 2, 1975, p. 9.

[3]Quoted in Bob Greene, *Billion Dollar Baby* (New York: Atheneum, 1974), p. 257.

[4]*Ibid.,* p. 174.

[5]*Ibid.,* p. 236.

[6]*Ibid.,* p. 361.

[7] Myles Palmer, *New Wave Explosion* (New York: Proteus Books, 1981), p. 51.

[8]Nicholas Schaffner, *The British Invasion* (New York: McGraw-Hill, 1983), p. 170.

[9]Quoted in Kate Lynch, *David Bowie, A Rock ¢N' Roll Odyssey* (New York: Proteus Books, 1984), p. 54.

[10]Schaffner, *The British Invasion,* p. 170.

[11]Quoted in Lynch, *David Bowie,* p. 116.

[12]Bertold Brecht, *Collected Plays* Vol. 2 (New York: Vintage, 1977), p. 88.

[13]Quoted in Lynch, *David Bowie,* p. 117.

[14]See *ibid.,* p. 72.

[15]David Douglas, *Presenting David Bowie* (New York: Pinnacle Books, 1975), p. 54.

[16] *Ibid.*, p. 82.

[17]Lynch, *David Bowie*, pp. 62-3.

[18]Quoted in John Tobler and Stuard Grundy, *The Record Producers* (New York: St. Martin's Press, 1982), p. 171.

[19]Quoted in Schaffner, *The British Invasion*, p. 180.

[20]John Brosnan, *Future Tense, The Cinema of Science Fiction* (New York: St. Martin's Press, 1978), p. 113.

[21]Schaffner, *The British Invasion*, p. 179.

Chapter 23:
A New Jersey Outlaw

If you were a crow, and you flew directly south from Battery Park at the southern tip of Manhattan, you would fly directly over Asbury Park, New Jersey. On a map, Asbury Park is right beneath Manhattan. This relationship may serve as a helpful image for Bruce Springsteen's relationship to New York City, for local folklore has it that New Jerseyites are crude and uncultured in comparison to sophisticated New Yorkers. As a would-be rock 'n' roller trapped in parochial school; as a New Jersey kid growing up south of Manhattan; as a working-class kid wanting to prove himself to adults who have made it, Bruce Springsteen experienced in his gut the feelings which make him fit into a classic American role—the outsider, the outlaw on the run.

Like Huck Finn, Bruce's many characters light out for the territory; like Huck, they seek release in the river. But Bruce matured in the seventies, and in movies as in what we call real life, the frontier had closed—there was no longer any territory to light out for. In his biography of Bruce, Dave Marsh poses this problem as a paradox: "America has eclipsed its frontiers...but in Springsteen's songs that frontier made a reappearance, both everywhere and nowhere."[1] Marsh also quotes a comment by Norman Mailer which is very much to the point here: "There was a message returned to us by our frontier that the outlaw is worth more than the sheriff."[2] The trouble is, outlaws have fallen on hard times lately, even in the movies. Even if you go to some other country, they catch up with you there, too, as in two movies very relevant to Bruce's music: *The Wild Bunch* (1969); and *Butch Cassidy and the Sundance Kid* (1970).

So all that's left is the great Romantic refuge, the night. And by definition the night offers only temporary relief, and thus a certain tragic desperation lurks in Bruce's music. Marsh himself hints at this tragic quality when he says, "Despite the legitimate claims of others to be taken seriously, Bruce Springsteen often seems like the last rock star, or at least the last one innocent of cynicism."[3] As the last one innocent of cynicism, Bruce resembles the last gunslinger and thus takes on a heroic stature because of his dedication, his energy, and above all, because of his love for his audience. All the great performers need their audiences: Bruce, and only Bruce, loves his.

A true child of the seventies, Bruce has an exceptionally intense historical consciousness; "Miss American Pie" came out just before he started work on his first album. The tradition of rock 'n' roll which he inherited has such immediacy for him that he does not distinguish between the past and the present: "We don't play no oldies. They may be old songs, but they're not nostalgic, really."[4] The price you pay for such historical consciousness is the anxiety of influence. In Bruce's case it was the anxiety of influence suffered by a New Jersey kid wanting to make it in the big time in Manhattan—so he suffered from a feeling of inferiority to the songwriter associated with Manhattan when he was in high school: Bob Dylan.

Bruce has said of Dylan's work, "It's *the* greatest music ever written, to me. The man says it all, exactly the right way. Incredibly powerful. You don't get no more intense."[5] In the early seventies, Bruce—like Don McLean and just about everybody else—was in awe of Dylan. He looks a little like Dylan, and has a surname which some people take as Jewish; like Dylan, he's not a singer—he's a vocal stylist. As if all this were not enough, Bruce auditioned in the office of John Hammond, Columbia's legendary talent scout—and he had just been reading about Dylan's audition in that same office ten years earlier.

Thus, we have to understand that much of the internal dynamics of Bruce's evolution through the seventies comes from his need to define himself against Dylan. But of course this need has larger resonances as well; the opposition of Bruce and Dylan corresponds to the spatial opposition of New Jersey and Manhattan as well to the temporal opposition of the seventies and the sixties. Other artists in the seventies were defining themselves against the sixties, but nobody else took on, and matched Dylan. With only slight rhetorical exaggeration one could say that Bruce was to the seventies what Dylan was to the sixties. Just as lots of acts had more Top 40 hits and sold more records than Dylan in the sixties, so lots of acts had more Top 40 hits and sold more records than Bruce in the seventies. But the fact remains that, like Dylan, Bruce set the standards for his times.

Growin' Up

You often sense Dylan's presence when you listen to Bruce's first album, *Greetings from Asbury Park, N.J.* Although the title of cut one on side one, "Blinded by the Light," comes from Simon and Garfunkel's "Patterns," the style is recognizably Dylan's. "Blinded by the light" has long, 20-syllable lines with three rhyming words in each line (an exceptionally demanding form for a young songwriter); several lines have Dylanesque phrases consisting only of nouns, such as "Madam drummers bummers" and "fleshpot mascot." There are bizarre pieces of advice like "Dethrone the dictaphone" which seem to derive from "Subterranean Homesick Blues," and some phrases which surely do, like "go-cart Mozart was checkin' out the weather chart."

Clearly, Bruce is in love with the sound of words for their own sake. Where did his get this love? How did it happen? Although his lyrics refer to Asbury Park, the overall style of his early music doesn't grow out of his society in any clearly recognizable way. Still, one line toward the end of "Growin' Up" hints at the precarious balance which Bruce had already achieved. He says that his feet "took root in the earth," and that he got himself "nice little place in the stars." Only Elvis had something like Bruce's capacity to live within his society yet transcend it at the same time. No wonder that, following Dylan again, he says in "Mary Queen of Arkansas," "Well I'm just a lonely acrobat." There's other evidence of Dylan on *Greetings*, such as the debt of "Growin' Up" to "The Chimes of Freedom," and the possibility that "Mary Queen of Arkansas" is a confused rewrite of "Sad-Eyed Lady of the Lowlands." And on "The Angel" he even tries to sing like Dylan. Although the young Bruce does better as a vocal stylist than as a songwriter, he already differs from Dylan in one important respect. Unlike the early Dylan, whose work divides into anger songs and compassion songs, Bruce seems never to have written any anger songs at all. He never lashes out at the oppressive society around him, and he never puts down women. As a result, he has a lasting and deeply appealing quality of wholeness and goodness.

Despite the problems in the lyrics on *Greetings*, though, there's also evidence of the genius that Bruce would become. Without Dylan's knowledge of poetry and folk music, Bruce doesn't use a verse and chorus structure; except for "Growin' Up" which is in couplets, he writes free verse. Unlike Dylan, Bruce vacillates between creating an "I," a narrator, a hero, who is not exactly self-absorbed, but rides off in all directions emotionally; and creating situations with bizarre characters, like "Spirit in the Night."

If the young Bruce was blinded by the light, it was the neon glow of Manhattan that did it, as the very names of the songs indicate. On *Greetings*, we have "Does This Bus Stop at 82nd Street," and "It's Hard To Be A Saint in the City," and "Incident on 57th Street" and "New York City Serenade" on his second album, *The Wild, Innocent, and the E Street Shuffle*.

There's a big city quality about the musical style of the first two albums which may represent Bruce's reaction against the hard rock of the sixties. "Spirit in the Night," on *Greetings*, has a jazzy feeling, and Bruce tries out different sound textures on *The Wild...* It may well be true that, as people say, Bruce was influenced by girl group rock and Phil Spector's wall of sound, but you'd never know it to listen to these albums. The imaginative "Wild Billy's Circus Song," for instance, plays off a tuba against an accordion, and "New York City Serenade" has romantic violins. There are still echoes of Dylan here, as when he tells Rosalita that he's not here to "liberate you, confiscate you," a turn of phrase which comes straight from "It Ain't Me Babe," Still, this is more of an instrumental album than a verbal album.

By listening closely, we can find some of the characteristics of Bruce's writing on the future masterpieces. One key to his style is displacement, the displacement of qualities which belong to one thing onto another thing. On "The Angel" a motorcycle is a "hunk metal whore," and on "It's Hard to be a Saint in the City," there are silver studs on his duds "like a Harley in heat." To displace male sexuality onto a motorcycle is not exactly new, but for Bruce it's an instance of something more general.

As a south Jersey version of Huck Finn and Daniel Boone, Bruce has to get away; lighting out for the territory is his great theme. So it's appropriate that such a traditional American impulse first appears in his work as a quotation. Movies are very important for Bruce, and the line from "Mary Queen of Arkansas," "I know a place where we can go," is what Sal Mineo says to James Dean and Natalie Wood in *Rebel Without a Cause*. Here we have the promise of what Henry James, whom Bruce has surely never read, called "the great good place." This is the American dream that haunts Bruce's heroes. The guy tells Sandy that he's leaving on "4th of July, Asbury Park (Sandy)," and a circus barker entices Billy to leave on "Wild Billy's Circus Song."

Grown Up

Bruce got out of Asbury Park, and went across the river to record *Born to Run*, his breakout album, at the Record Plant in Manhattan. He made the change from the small 914 Studio where he recorded the first two albums at the urging of Jon Landau, who wrote the famous line "I have seen the future of rock and roll, and its name is Bruce Springsteen." Jon seems to have helped Bruce find himself, for it is as though Bruce had been playing a beat-up acoustic guitar, and then switched to the Fender Esquire which he's holding on the cover of *Born to Run*. Certainly, there were advantages to starting out in Asbury Park, and Landau himself said, "For twelve years, Bruce had the time to play every kind of rock and roll. He has far more depth than most rock artists because he really has roots in a place—coastal Jersey, where no record scouts ever went."[6] But such isolation also had its disadvantages, for Bruce needed the kind of stimulating environment which Dylan has found in Greenwich Village. I have the feeling that before he met Landau, Bruce had never known anybody he could talk to about the visions inside his head. Of course, he was, and is, very close to his fellow musicians from Jersey, but musicians are notoriously non-verbal, and Bruce was supposed to be the leader of the band— they looked to him for advice. So Landau put him in a good studio with a crack engineer, Jimmy Iovine, and helped him figure out what he was about. Bruce did the rest.

The album opens with "Thunder Road," which brings together and unifies into a single powerful experience the promises of the first two albums. Like the songs on those albums, it has a variety of sound textures, since it begins with delicate piano arpeggios and then blossoms into full-throated rock. It also reprises the situation of "4th of July, Asbury Park (Sandy)," in which the Boy asks the Girl to get out of town with him. But now there's more to it than just lighting out, for we have the Boy who confronts the Girl, the Car, and the Night. These three elements come together one way or another in virtually all of his masterpieces. For Bruce, the freedom from Asbury Park, from the working life, which the Car promises him becomes an image for the promises of the covenant in which the Boy devoutly believes. In biographical terms one could say that Bruce displaced onto the American Dream the faith which the nuns pounded out of him. This happened because American civil religion has historically displaced religion onto democracy in a manner very consistent with Bruce's songwriting style. As the Boy tells the Girl: "Show a little faith, there's magic in the night." The religious metaphor gets further displaced onto the Car when all the redemption he can offer her "is beneath this dirty hood"; a fallen angel in a used car lot, he promises that they can "trade in these wings on some wheels." Of all the artists who broke in the seventies, only Bruce had developed Dylan's meditations on American civil religion, and on America's covenant with God. One result was a lasting rock classic, the "Satisfaction" of the seventies, "Born to Run."

Dylan is still with us in "Born to Run." The phrase "suicide machines" in which we ride "through mansions of glory" comes from "Desolation Row." The Boy, the Girl (named Wendy this time), and the Car, and the Night combine to create frenzied flight; this time there's no displaced religiosity because it's a "runaway American dream," although there's displaced sexuality in the phrase "my engines." There's desperation ("We gotta get out while we're young"), and one sharp, rich image after another. This is "Highway 61 Revisited" not just as a distant image of violence, but as immediate experience. But it is an experience shared with others, and this is the essential difference between Bruce and Dylan as the two great lyricists of our time. Almost all of Dylan's songs in which there's an "I" present the hero (if that's the right word) either in isolation or as an observer. This holds true even for "Desolation Row." In Bruce's lyrics the hero either shares the experience with others, or pleads with a girl to share it with him.

Bruce shares the song in another sense—he shares it with the E Street Band, for "Born to Run" is heavy-duty rock 'n' roll, with a full rich seventies sound that's unlike anything on *Blonde on Blonde*. You can say that this is how Bruce overcame his anxiety of influence from Dylan. Bruce was saying in effect to Dylan, "No, I'll never write a 'Sad-Eyed Lady of the Lowlands' but you'll never write a 'Born to Run'." In effect, he's balanced Dylan with Phil Spector's wall of sound-say, the intense passages of "You've Lost That Lovin' Feeling." Only a genius could have married a Phil Spectorish sound to Dylanesque lyrics to create a magic which doesn't sound like either of them.

I have mentioned that Bruce has encountered the covenant, and thus has become part of its tradition. We can compare "Born to Run" with other American classics, such as "Over the Rainbow," as sung by Judy Garland. Both songs express the longing to get out, to find the great good place, but with what a difference in style! When Judy sings about bluebirds, it points up the difference between their freedom to move and her lack of that freedom. This pathos also appears in "Somewhere," the wistful duet which Tony and Maria sing toward the end of a movie about kids in Manhattan which was probably often on Bruce's mind, *West Side Story* (1961). Like Tony, Bruce's hero is not alone, but unlike him, he can move. In fact, since he is born to run, he is condemned to move. But movement means energy, and there is an undeniable energy, if not exactly joy, in "Born to Run."

As a piece of recorded music, "Jungleland" is more ambitious and more complex than "Born to Run." It begins with violins and piano, builds to great intensity, and then ends with Bruce's whispered delivery of the final lines. In "Jungleland" Bruce makes a connection between Manhattan and New Jersey for the first time, moving from the Rangers in Harlem to the story of the Magic Rat who crosses the Jersey state line to get the barefoot girl, and then goes back to Harlem where, ominously, "The Rat's own dream guns him down." There's another, unnamed, couple, "beneath the city" (does that mean Asbury Park?), but this is mostly a New York song. The reference to the "poets down here" (the only time Bruce has ever used the work "poets" in a lyric) suggests a degree of self-consciousness about its construction, and its relationship to other music about New York. For one thing, Clarence Clemons' sax solo has a wistful, yearning quality, yet with a raw edge, which often gives Bruce's music a big city feel usually absent in rock 'n' roll bands. For another, the title of the other New York song on the album, "Tenth Avenue Freeze-Out" may come from the title of the ballet "Slaughter on Tenth Avenue" which Richard Rodgers wrote for *On Your Toes* (1936); the lyrics to "Jungleland" refer to a ballet "being fought out in the alley."

"Jungleland" is also noteworthy because it is Bruce's only song which owes something to a British song—the Stones' "Street Fightin' Man," which also happens to be virtually the only British song which he has done in concert. When the kids' frustration breaks out, they "flash guitars just like switchblades"; there's nothing for a poor boy to do but play in a rock 'n' roll band.

The fate of the Magic Rat becomes symbolic on Bruce's next album; it's not by chance that he called it *Darkness at the Edge of Town*, for the words "dark" and "darkness" recur throughout the songs: "dark cloud" ("The Promised Land"); "in the darkness" ("Streets of Fire"); "the darkness of your room" ("Adam Raised a Cain"); "darkness of Cathy's hall" ("Candy's Room"); "the house is dark" ("Racing in the Streets"). This is not exactly a concept album, but it has certain unity of mood, and "Racing in the Streets," a pivotal work in Bruce's career, sets that mood.

The ambivalence of speed pervades *Darkness*. The anguish of belief in lighting out for the territory where there's no longer any territory to light out for, the frustration of coming after great artists who may not have left you anything to say, has no outlet. The problem is not that there's nothing to believe in, as it was for Jack Kerouac and the Beat Generation, so that you seek one sensation after another to prove to yourself that you're still alive; the problem is that you do believe, and believe passionately ("The Promised Land"), and that you live the right way. The problem is that when you break out of your stuffy home town and the stuffy life of your parents, lured as you are by the promises of the covenant, you have to pay the price. The Bible verse, "A pearl of great price is not to be had for the asking," resonates though *Darkness*, especially Side Two. Bruce takes the standard high school Romeo's line when he tries to get his girlfriend into bed, "Prove you love me," and makes it obsessive; no relief or satisfaction is possible when you have to prove it all night.

If "Darkness at the Edge of Town" gives the album its title, "Racing in the Streets" gives it its theme. It is Bruce's only song which plays itself off against another song—"Dancing in the Street." The chorus of this song, which was a hit in the sixties both for Martha and the Vandellas and for the Mamas and the Papas, is: "Summer's here and the time is right/ For dancing in the street." Here we have the Boy, the Girl, and the Night, so Bruce fits the song into his imagistic scheme of things by changing "dancing" to—what else?— racing. More important, he changes the tone of the song. Whereas in the sixties, the uptempo original sent out a call to kids "around the world" to celebrate summer, Bruce sings his song like a dirge, slowly and mournfully. I think Bruce needed a well-known song to push off from, as it were, for he is working against the traditional presentation of the car in rock 'n' roll, In "Racing in the Streets," racing is not fun, fun, fun, as it is with the Beach Boys; the car does not give you a way to catch your baby, as in "Maybelline"; rather, it separates you from your baby, who is alone and who "hates you for just being born." Before Dylan, only poets alienated from American popular culture like Karl Shapiro had dealt with the car's potential for alienation and destruction.[7] Yet in some major songs by so ardent a populist as Bruce Springsteen, the trinity of the Car, the Girl, and the Night starts to come apart.

Clearly, something is happening here, and Bruce is doing more than engaging in a technical exercise, just as Eliot was in *The Waste Land*. Just as Eliot was creating haunting images and situations to respond to the despair of Europe in the wake of World War I, so Bruce—very much in the spirit of Jackson Browne's "Running on Empty"—is creating haunting images and situations to respond to the energy crisis of the seventies.

For the energy crisis forced us to rethink our relationship to the car. The Arab oil embargo made us realize that the car had not liberated us as much as we had thought; rather, it had gotten us into a entangling foreign alliance more binding than anything George Washington could have imagined in his farewell address.

Americans had long led the world in the production and use of cars. In personal terms, cars enabled us to get away from our families and home towns; in economic terms, they enabled us to dominate the world market. But "By the early 1970s, saturation points had been reached in both the domestic and world market for motorcars."[8] As if this weren't bad enough, foreigners were starting to beat us at our own game; by 1971, Japanese cars were outselling Fords and Chevrolets in the epitome of the car culture, Southern California.[9] At about this time, the Vega plant in Lordstown, Ohio, opened with a lot of hype about how advanced and sophisticated it was. But it was plagued by breakdowns and a much-publicized strike. Management in Detroit responded, not by learning from the competition, but by putting the squeeze on their dealers. This crude power play predictably produced a revolt on their part.

One Ed Mullane headed the insurgent Ford Dealers' Alliance, and asked a question which has a startlingly specific relevance for Bruce: "When I grew up in New Jersey, the automobile was the one product that universally signified success in America. What has happened to Paradise?"[10] Bruce's work in the late seventies represents his way of showing us how to deal with that dilemma.

Returning now to "Racing in the Streets" with its more general significance in mind, we notice that if the chorus comes from "Dancing in the Street," the verses derive from a brilliant, prophetic film which got poor distribution, *Two-Lane Blacktop* (1971). (Remember that Bruce's heroes always ride the two lanes and backstreets—never the interstate.) This movie starred James Taylor and the late Dennis Wilson as buddies who make their living by racing the hot rod which they built themselves. It was the first movie to use rock music to comment on the action, and some of the people who worked on it went on to work on *American Graffiti.*

Bruce evokes the situation of *Two-Lane Blacktop* with wonderfully economical details, such as the Seven-Eleven store where his hero works, but adapts the ending to his own recurring images. In the movie a remarkable visual effect at the end makes it clear that James Taylor goes crazy—that the need for motion in and of itself comes from a nihilism inherent in the American experience. Bruce's hero, by contrast, rides to the sea with the Girl, to "wash these sins off our hands." What sins? Sins of inadequacy and despair which they feel they have committed by identifying themselves so completely with the car.

Unlike the use of "Dancing in the Streets," the use of *Two-Lane Blacktop* in "Racing in the Streets" is not a unique phenomenon, for "Bruce came to understand himself and his songs better by viewing the works of filmmakers who could depict almost identical situations a dozen times and yet make each one of them different."[11] Bruce once explained the lack of complete narratives in his songs by comparing their effects to the effects which a movie camera can create: "You pick up the action, and then at some point—psst!—the camera pans away, and whatever happened, that's what happened. The songs I write, they don't have particular beginnings and they don't have endings. The camera focuses in and then out."[12] "Born to Run" and "Jungleland" offer prime examples of what Bruce is talking about here. Of course, since Bruce is who he is, he saw and drew on the films of the common people. He once said of his songs, "They always had a sort of drive-in quality to them."[13] Among the movies which Bruce and his buddies saw in drive-ins around Freehold and Asbury Park in the late sixties were spaghetti westerns like *A Fistful of Dollars* (1966), which made Clint Eastwood an international star and which was directed by Sergio Leone.

There are several reasons why Leone's movies affected Bruce as they did, and one of them has to do with the fact that Bruce's mother was a Zirilli before she got married. Although the Italian connection doesn't matter as much to Bruce as it does to Sinatra, it is still there. Italians have to deal with the Catholic church in one way or another, and Bruce hated parochial school (which is why he put the bald, pregnant nuns in "It's So Hard to be A Saint in the City"), so he could appreciate the anti-Catholic sentiment which runs throughout Leone's films.[14] Leone's movies present the church as a negative force in society, and the community as a positive one. It was easy for Bruce to transpose what he saw on the screen onto the community feeling among the south Jersey musicians whom he knew. Finally, and most important of all, Leone breaks with the Hollywood tradition which makes gunslingers settle down at the end of the movie, or die. In Leone's movies, the Man With No Name, the Clint Eastwood character, keeps riding off into the sunset; he is on the move, as Bruce's heroes are. One could say, then, that in his songs Bruce has set some of the principal features of Leone's movies in the context of south Jersey and the American civil religion.

Bruce didn't just see Leone movies, though, and the names of several of his songs come from the names of movies. He has said that he didn't even see the Robert Mitchum movie *Thunder Road* (1958), which inspired the song of that name. "I never saw the movie, I only saw the poster in the lobby of the theater. I took the title and I wrote this song."[15] Similarly, he took only the title of the Lee Marvin thriller *Point Blank* (1967) for the song of the same name. He does seem to have seen *Badlands* (1973) though, because his song of that name recapitulates some of the plot points in that movie about a couple who go on a killing spree. "Jackson Cage," on *The River*, does the same thing with a similar movie *Jackson County Jail* (1976), in which Yvette Mimieux and Tommy Lee Jones go on the lam from prison.

"Cadillac Ranch" makes two predictable references to car movies, and does something unpredictable with them. It refers to James Dean in *Rebel Without a Cause*, and to Bert Reynolds in *Smokey and the Bandit* (1977), but the title does not come from a movie. It comes from an installation of the kind called "earth art" by conceptual artists in the seventies. "Cadillac Ranch" consists of 10 Cadillacs buried in a row at a 45 degree angle in a field just off Route 66 outside Amarillo, Texas, and is reproduced on the lyric sheet for *The River*. When the lyrics say that James Dean and Bert Reynolds are going to the Cadillac Ranch, it means that they are going to a graveyard for cars because the car culture is dying.

"Cadillac Ranch" is the creation—if that is the right word—of a group of artists who call themselves the Ant Farm, and who have been described as "hell-bent on the destruction of American values."[16] Since cars have symbolized so much about American values, the Ant Farm liked to destroy them. On Independence Day, 1975, they staged *Media Burn*, an event in which a car was driven through a wall of burning television sets in the parking lot of the Cow Palace in San Francisco.[17] It's hard to imagine anything more different from the spirit and execution of the Ant Farm than Bruce's music, but what's fascinating is that during the seventies they could come together.

But "Cadillac Ranch" has a disconcerting contrast between its gloomy lyrics and its sound, which resembles Rolling Stones raunch, and which features Roy Bittan's extravagant glissandi on the piano. This good time sound, and the couplets with the easy rhymes like sun/done make "Cadillac Ranch" an unusually accessible song, and the night I heard Bruce do it he had the audience on its feet, grinning and clapping in time. They either didn't know, or had forgotten, what the Cadillac Ranch meant.

The car dies and is buried; you can't use it to get away, so you have to accept your situation. *The River* begins with affirmations of family, "The Ties That Bind," and "Independence Day." These songs continue the somber mood of "Racing in the Streets." Just as "Racing in the Streets" plays itself off against "Dancing in the Street," so "Independence Day" plays itself off against Bruce's own early song "4th of July, Asbury Park (Sandy)." The event calls for celebration, but Bruce personalizes the national holiday. Getting away no longer has to do with distance and movement. As so many baby boomers were doing at the time, Bruce's heroes were growing up. These songs express, and evoke, complex feelings about personal identity and family relationships. They offer no easy answers, just as Dylan's "May You Stay Forever Young" doesn't. Is that song Dylan's blessing to his fans—or is it the curse of Dorian Gray?

Thus, you can say that on *The River* Bruce is recapitulating at a higher level "Growin' Up," from his first album. Growing up is a way of getting out of Asbury Park, but it is often a painful way, and this contradiction splits *The River* into two styles. First, there are catchy boy-girl songs like "Crush on You," and "Ramrod," which would sound campy if anybody else but Bruce did them. "Crush on You" is Bruce's homage to the girl group sound in its combination of infectious melody and simplistic lyrics. As for "Ramrod," it's the first time Bruce has used the displacement of sex onto mechanical parts in a self-conscious way. Something very similar is going on "I'm A Rocker," which comically creates an identity out of the artifacts of popular culture. In these songs Bruce is creating a distance between himself and his material; he asks us to enjoy the songs, but also to appreciate, in an affectionate way of course, how silly they are.

Bruce's earlier heroes had celebrated the moment which had consisted of the trinity of the Girl, the Car, and the Night. Now that that trinity has been torn asunder by the interrelated disasters of the energy crisis and growing up, something new appears to replace it: narratives. Three key songs on the album, "Independence Day," the opening song; "The River," the title song; and the final song, "Wreck on the Highway," are all narratives. Like the Eagles' "The Long Run," they accept the fact that time passes, and that time changes people. Thus, they have none of the good time sound and easy rhymes of "Ramrod." Taken together, they form a trinity of the key moments in a young man's life. As we know, "Independence Day" reinterprets getting away from one's parents as painful and troubling. On "The River," our hero gets Mary pregnant, and as working-class heroes do, he does the right thing by her. So the wedding day dream doesn't come true: "No wedding day smiles, no walk down the aisle." Although the river is dry—an echo of "Miss American Pie"?—he and Mary go to it anyhow to seek the redemption which the car used to give them.

"Wreck on the Highway" concludes the album, and Bruce's first mature period, with a rich and suggestive image. There had been lots of car wrecks in movies in the seventies from which Bruce might have taken the idea. Robert Altman usually includes one in his movies, such as the ones in *Nashville* and *Wedding* (1978).Our hero, presumably the same Boy as in "The River," sees a wreck on the highway, and the body of a young man lying beside it while driving home from work. Clearly, he is seeing his double, and the visions of his dead youth keep him up past the dawn. For, as Eliot wrote in a memorable line, "In my end is my beginning," and if Dylan was with Bruce on the first song on his first album, he is with him here on the last song on his greatest album. Dylan's "Visions of Johanna" have become Bruce's visions of youth and freedom. In this allegory, comparable to the allegories on *John Wesley Harding*, Bruce has done with Dylan what he had done with other people's material—he had worked it into his own imagistic structures and thereby made it his own. Bruce had passed thirty, and he had grown up.

Notes

[1]Dave Marsh, *Born to Run. The Bruce Springsteen Story* (New York: Dell Books 1981), p. 40.

[2]Quoted in *ibid.*

[3]*Ibid.*, p. 226.

[4]*Ibid.*, p. 118.

[5]Quoted in Paul Gambaccini, *Bruce Springsteen* (New York: Quick Fox, 1979), p. 51.

[6]Quoted in Marsh, *Born to Run*, p. 51.

[7]See Laurence Goldstein, "The Automobile and American Poetry," in *Michigan Quarterly Review*, Special Issue, "The Automobile and American Culture," 1980, pp. 619-638.

[8]James J. Flink, *The Car Culture* (Cambridge: MIT Press, 1975), p. 211.

[9]*Ibid.*, p. 211.

[10]Quoted in Emma Rothschild, *Paradise Lost. The Decline of the Auto-Industrial Age* (New York: Random House, 1973), p. 5.

[11]Marsh, *Born to Run*, p. 209.

[12]Quoted in Gambaccini, *Bruce Springsteen*, p. 110.

[13]Quoted in *ibid.*, p. 112.

[14]Here and below, in my remarks on Leone's movies I am drawing on Christopher Frayling, *Spaghetti Westerns. Cowboys and Europeans from Karl May to Sergio Leone* (London: Routledge and Kegan Paul, 1981)

[15]Quoted in Gambaccini, *Bruce Spingsteen*, p. 86.

[16]*Domus*, May 5, 1973, p. 27.

[17]On *Media Burn*, see *Studio International*, vol. 190 (September-October, 1975), p. 157.

Chapter 24:
High Culture as Popular Culture, II

When The Who performed *Tommy* at the Metropolitan Opera House in New York in 1970, the group was participating in the transition from the sixties to the seventies. If Pete Townshend and Jim Morrison had been interested in the literature of high culture in the sixties, in the seventies some very popular groups were interested in the music of high culture, and their music made some of the demands on their audiences which high culture had made in the past.

Considering the importance of New York in the seventies, we can begin with choreographer Twyla Tharp; in 1973, she renounced the ascetic minimalism of her work in the sixties, and did "Deuce Coupe," a ballet for a medley of Beach Boys songs. In 1977, she followed up this tour de force with a ballet for a medley of Paul Simon songs, and included a solo for herself for "Fifty Ways to Leave Your Lover." (Paul Simon now sits on the board of the Twyla Tharp Dance Foundation, Inc.) She has also created "Eight Jelly Rolls," to the music of Jelly Roll Morton, and "The Bix Pieces," to the music of Bix Beiderbecke.

But most of the interaction between popular culture and high culture in the seventies began in England, with three major groups: Emerson Lake and Palmer, Yes, and Pink Floyd. Art rock, as the work of these groups, along with that of The Moody Blues and King Crimson, came to be called, arose because of the strong force of British musical tradition. In the sixties the major British groups had adapted American popular music with startling results, but such adaptations could continue only so long. No group could repeat the Stones' awesome assimilation of black blues, and no group needed to. As Greg Lake once said, "I think it's a question of heritage. European musicians tend to come from a classical heritage. American bands tend to come from a blues-based heritage."[1] Steve Howe, lead guitarist for Yes, once said that at home he mainly liked to listen to—not Keith Richards or Eric Clapton or even Muddy Waters—but Julian Beam.[2]

Indeed, the members of these three groups had strong backgrounds in high culture. It goes without saying that The Nice, Keith Emerson's first group, was formed in art school; they put out an album called *Ars Longa, Vita Brevis*. The three founding members of Pink Floyd—Roger Waters, Syd Barrett, and David Gilmour—came from the venerable university town of Cambridge, and in 1971 Pink Floyd became the first rock group to be invited to play at the Montreux Classical Music Festival. Rick Wakeman and Tony Kaye, of Yes, attended the Royal College of Music, and Roger Dean had studied at the Royal and Canterbury Schools of Art. Patrick Moraz, the keyboardist who replaced Wakeman for a time, also had classical training.

It's not surprising, then, that Emerson Lake and Palmer and Yes recorded classical music. *Yessongs* begins with an adaptation of Stravinsky's "Firebird Suite," and *Fragile* includes "Cans and Brahms," adapted from Brahms' Fourth Symphony. Emerson Lake and Palmer recorded all of Mussorgsky's "Pictures at an Exhibition" in 1972. The "Toccato" on their *Brain Salad Surgery* album of 1973 comes from the Fourth Movement of the First Piano Concerto by Brazilian composer Alberto Ginastera—and is so credited on the liner notes. For their *Works* album from 1977, Carl Palmer orchestrated an except from Prokofiev's "Scythian Suite," and adapted Bach's "Two Part Invention in D Minor." They also released a version of Aaron Copland's "Fanfare for the Common Man" as a single in 1977.

British art rock in the seventies occasionally represented something unique in a musical style which did not derive from Southern evangelical Protestantism: secularization. Specifically, British art rock often secularizes the organ and choral music with which these well-educated boys grew up. Yes Bassist Chris Squire, for instance, had a bass tuned to the deepest organ tones for extra depth.[3] It no doubt reminded him of the organ in St. Andrews Church where he had sung in the choir. He once said of that experience: "I suppose the actual understanding of, and spiritual feeling towards, music is something that's stayed with me, although it was not church music we were dealing with."[4] Yes biographer Dan Hedges accurately characterizes Side I of *Close to the Edge* as "A thundering, sonic impression of Chartres Cathedral on Easter Sunday morning."[5] Although Yes' music is more clearly religious than that of any other group in the seventies, Emerson Lake Palmer recorded their share as well. "The Only Way (Hymn)" on *Tarkus* uses themes from Bach, and Keith plays it on the organ of St. Mark's Church; similarly, they begin their most fully realized album, *Brain Salad Surgery*, with "Jerusalem." The lyrics come from the opening of William Blake's *Milton*, and after Charles Parry set them to music in 1916, the work became the unofficial British national hymn— roughly the British equivalent of "The Battle Hymn of the Republic."

The huge American audiences which went to Yes and ELP concerts and bought the albums knew very little of this. What makes the commercial success of this music so interesting is that we have in it a merger of secularization with its opposite tendency, resacralization. The kids who wanted to hear Judy Collins sing "Amazing Grace" also wanted to hear something more than an electric guitar doing a 12-bar blues when they went to a concert.

This resacralization is also related to the status of the individual performers. If we think about it, we realize that the great musical personalities from Beethoven and Liszt to Sinatra and Jagger have usually performed secular music. (Elvis is an exception to everything.) Religious music glorifies something greater than an individual, so that the individual performers mostly serve as a medium for the transmission of the music. Rick Wakeman once admitted that he was a star, and added, "But when somebody says, 'Yes,' you think of the music and not so much of the people in the band."[6] This generalization certainly applies to Pink Floyd, whose music often laments the alienation of people who have to live in a godless world: "Pink Floyd's faceless components could—and sometimes did—walk unrecognized among the audiences at their own marathon concerts."[7]

Just as British secularization met American resacralization in a mutually reinforcing system, so British anonymity met American technology in a mutually reinforcing system. Keith Emerson's The Nice was the first group to use a Moog synthesizer; in 1970, he described it in a telling phrase as "like a recording studio condensed into one machine."[8] However, for some time he felt frustrated because the early Moogs were monophonic—that is, they could play only one note at a time, and thus no chords. Only the polyphonic Moogs of the early seventies (which Stevie Wonder and Pete Townshend also used with great success) made ELP's concerts and albums what they were. Similarly, Steve Howe of Yes was one of the first guitarists to use Walter Sears' guitar synthesizer; it had a tracing device which enabled the guitarist to play one note, and then a second, while a tone connected the two. The effect was often to make the guitar sound more like an organ.[9]

When people listened to performers play music on such complex equipment, they found it increasingly difficult to hear a connection between the performers and what they were playing. That is to say that the music took on a life on its own as it had never done in the sixties, but that is not to say that synthesizer music did not have a history of its own, and that that history did not affect the way the audience listened to ELP, Yes, and Pink Floyd.

An early version of the synthesizer was called the theremin, and "the way in which most people hear almost any piece of electronic music has been indelibly coloured by the spine-chilling wail of a theremin in *They Came from Outer Space* (1967), or the roar of monsters from the id in *Forbidden Planet* (1956)."[10] Theremins were even featured as part of the space ship as well as on the sound track in *The Day the Earth Stood Still* (1951). Since people associated electronic sounds with outer space, they found it easy to call this music not just "far out," but also "spacey." No wonder the space oddity himself, David Bowie, took up the synthesizer, and that Yes included a song called "Starship Trooper" on *The Yes Album*. Roger Dean's multi-panel painting on the cover of *Yessongs* looks like a matte for a Hollywood space epic.

The album which takes the space-computer-synthesizer age the most seriously is ELP's *Brain Salad Surgery*. As an artifact, the album sleeve attests to the importance of albums in the seventies, for it is even more elaborate than *Tumbleweed Connection*. The austere front cover displays the name of the album in white letters on a black background, but the back cover features a painting by the Swiss surealist H.R. Giger of a skull imbedded in a bizarre mechanical device. It thereby states non-verbally the album's recurring opposition of the human and the mechanical. However, when you open the two halves you find another painting, this one of a sleeping woman with the infinity symbol on her forehead. Nothing is ever completely what it seems here, for *Brain Salad Surgery* plays off one opposition after another.

Blake's familiar (to English audiences at least) lyrics for "Jerusalem" repeat the opposition of the human and the mechanical, and combine it with the opposition of the sacred and the profane. The "Toccata" follows, and separates "Jerusalem" from "Benny the Bouncer"; it opposes instrumental music to vocal music, as the "Second Impression" separates the "First Impression" from the "Third." It gets more complicated still, because the "Toccata" also opposes the high culture of the present to the popular culture of the past (the tinkly piano on "Benny the Bouncer").

Taken together, the three "Impressions" have a collective title of "Karn Evil 9," and the pun suggests the debt which the album owes to *Sargeant Pepper* and to *Magical Mystery Tour* for its showbiz conceit. But ELP are no band on the run; the show on their album is a "show that never ends." The show creates myth in a shimmeringly ambiguous way by pulling "Jesus from a hat." They present a manipulative totalitarian world as a fulfillment of Blake's dire prophecy about Satanic mills, and thus their album has much in common with *Diamond Dogs*.

After the instrumental "Second Impression," the music turns more ominous in the concluding "Third Impression," and also shows the conceptual link between synthesizer music and movies. The "Third Impression" involves a dialog between man and computer which surely derives from the conversations between Keir Dullea and HAL in *2001: A Space Odyssey* (1968). But to say this is not to say that the piece is derivative, for in it ELP recapitulate the martial and apocalyptic imagery of "Jerusalem." The computer claims, "I am yourself," rendering the human/mechanical and sacred/profane oppositions dramatically ambiguous. At the end, the synthesizer starts hopping back and forth between the speakers; it goes faster and faster and faster..and then stops. We are left to challenge it if we can, reeling from the conceptual audacity and instrumental virtuousity of this extraordinary album.

Pink Floyd dazzles us, too, but in a different way. They have no interest in classical music; rather, they tend to think in terms of sound textures, rather than overall concepts or narratives. You can hear this on *Atom Heart Mother* from 1970, where the title piece takes up all of side I. It begins with an ostinato bass rising to a crescendo against wind sounds. This piece of program music is divided into sections which apparently represent the stages of the development of the fetus from conception ("Father's Shout") to birth ("Remergence")—which sounds something like an airliner taking off. Although there is a distant, spacey soprano who turns into a chorus thanks to the magic of technology, "Atom Heart Mother" has no lyrics at all, so we know that it's supposed to represent something only by reading the liner notes. "Echoes" on *Meddle* is a similar long piece; it has only a brief, vague lyric.

As Pink Floyd evolved in the seventies, Roger Waters' lyrics grew conceptually more important. I think this change helps to explain the phenomenal success of *Dark Side of the Moon*, which stayed on the album charts for ten years. There the lyrics have become more important, but are still hardly more than suggestive. Pink Floyd fans are tenacious and devoted, but I doubt they paid much attention to the lyrics before *The Wall*. A British fan once said, "I think the Floyd must be...you hear things on Floyd on acid, well I do, that I don't hear when I'm straight."[11] David Gilmour's slow, lyrical guitar style and the synthesizer effects make for great listening while stoned, either at home or in the concert hall. Hardly anybody listened to Pink Floyd on the radio, that's for sure.

The famous cover of *The Dark Side of the Moon* shows a prism which splits a beam of white light into a rainbow. When you open the album, you find that that rainbow is also a readout for an oscilloscope which shows heartbeats, and "Breathe" begins the album with what sounds like a heartbeat. Conceptually, then, the album connects the individual with the cosmos—the dark side of the moon represents dark moods. The lyrics deal with alienation and the loss of faith, the abstractions of time and money. The extreme is "Brain Damage," where lobotomy is a solution to madness.

The Floyd could not have done all this without considerable help from the past, and they got it from *Sargeant Pepper*, just as ELP did. Just as "Good Morning Good Morning" begins with the sound of chickens and the middle section of "A Day in the Life" begins with an alarm clock, so "Time" on *The Dark Side*...begins with lots of clocks chiming, and "Money" begins with the sound of cash registers. In both cases, taped ambience sounds state the theme of the song which follows.

"The Great Gig in the Sky," another of the Floyd's wordless compositions with a soprano solo, connects *The Dark Side*...to their next album, *Wish You Were Here*. If the Beatles used the music hall as a conceit, the Floyd use rock stardom as a conceit. The Floyd feel so distant from their audiences that they never offer to take them home, though. The Floyd use the separation between rock stars, i.e., themselves, and their audience as a metaphor for alienation. Whereas "Money," on *The Dark Side*...mentions only the alienating effect of money and greed in general, "Have A Cigar" on *Wish*...is a dramatic monologue by a promoter at a party who is gloating over the proceeds.

It is clear by now that Pink Floyd depended greatly on the technology of studios and synthesizers and mammoth PA systems to make their music. Their concern with alienation from their audience is all the more poignant and forceful, because the very devices which caused their extraordinary success also caused their alienation from the audience. It compounds the irony to realize that *The Wall*, which took that alienation as its theme, also gave them their greatest success in conventional terms. Not only did the album go platinum, it even gave them their first #1 single, "Another Brick in the Wall." (The movie did well, too.)

In a 1982 interview, Roger Waters showed exceptional honesty in talking about this dilemma. The way he generalizes the band's situation makes what he has to say a profound comment on the modern world, and the role which rock 'n' roll plays in it.

Being a rock 'n' roller is a dominant image of success in our society, but it is a cage because the constraints are often just as great as they ever were.

In *The Wall* I've tried to communicate the idea that the relationship we've had between us, between 'us' in our lead role on stage, and 'them' the audience, has been a false one which neither of us has entirely understood.

I'm talking about the difficulty in those circumstances of making any sort of contact with the audience which had to do with music. Audiences at those vast concerts are there for an excitement which, I think, has to do with the love of success. When a band or a person becomes an idol, it can have to do with the success that person manifests, not with the quality of work he produces. You don't become a fanatic because somebody's work is good, you become a fanatic to be touched vicariously by their glamour and fame. It somehow brightens up your life. Stars—film stars, rock 'n' roll stars—represent, in myth anyway, life as we'd all like to live it. They seem at the very centre of life. And that's why audiences still spend large sums of money at concerts where they are a long, long way from the stage, where they are often very uncomfortable, and where the sound is often very bad. I mean, sometimes the sound is so bad the only *honest* response would be for the audience to walk out and demand their money back. They don't however because they're in The Presence, therefore everything has to be wonderful so they pretend it is, even if it's not.... My theatrical wall exists to make the statement: "look, what's going on here is not what it seems."[9]

As with Elvis, so with Pink Floyd: Success brought its own defeat. The difference was that the Floyd were working in the self-conscious era of rock, so they made an album about rock as success as alienation and called it *The Wall*.

Although *Animals* now sounds pretty weak, one song on it, "Dogs," has a line that's especially important for the origins of *The Wall*: "Deaf, dumb and blind, you just keep pretending." Well, there's only one deaf, dumb, and blind kid, and that's Tommy. If the Floyd started out sounding something like Procol Harum, they wound up sounding something like The Who. But unlike Tommy, Pink doesn't want to be a savior; his success as a rock star has made him one—and that's his problem. Of course, by 1979 no one could make a double album about a rock star and his relationship with his audience without a reference to David Bowie. "In the Flesh" refers to "That space cadet glow" which the audience seeks, and on "One of My Turns" Roger Waters even sings like David on "Rock 'N' Roll Suicide," which the song resembles. But Ziggy's rock 'n' roll suicide has the quality of crucifixion, whereas Pink is everyman put on trial for having feelings. Thus, Ziggy and Pink both express the distinctly British paranoia about totalitarianism, but the relationship between democracy and elitism involved also affects Americans deeply. The Floyd are also very European in their attack on education in the hit single, "Another Brick in the Wall (Part 2)" when the working-class kids want "no thought control"; no American writing about high school would worry about thought control.

David always had too much presence, too much classic star quality to make good on his claim to have reverted to the ensemble experience of "pure Brechtian theatre," but an anonymous band like the Floyd could do so, and did, in *The Wall* concerts. They actually built a wall (the front of the album also looks like a wall), used huge, grotesque puppets, and projected images. Brecht would indeed have loved it, because the point, as in his concept of anti-Aristotelian theater, was not simply to entertain the audience, but to challenge it, to raise its consciousness. The album also grows out of the group's own history. Their interest in portraying the life cycle, which began with "Atom Heart Mother," expands into the biography of Pink as he is born into an uncertain world ("Thin Ice"), goes to school ("Another Brick in the Wall"), enters puberty ("Young Lust"), deals with the effects of success ("Comfortable Numb"), and is tried ("The Trial").

The album also has some familiar Pink Floyd touches. "Another Brick in the Wall (Part I)" has taped sounds of children playing, and there is a recorded, half-audible conversation ("This is the United States calling") at the beginning of "Young Lust." Yet "Young Lust" also sounds more like rock 'n' roll than most of Pink Floyd's music, and in general the music is darker and more ominous than it had been in the past. This is in itself a remarkable tribute to their capacity to grow and develop when it would have been very easy for them to let self-consciousness lapse into self-indulgence. Judging from the rawness in their music, and the dark visions of no future in their lyrics, you might even think that they decided to do what the Sex Pistols tried, and failed, to do.

Aside from the memorable hit single, the two strongest and most ambitious songs on the album are "Waiting for the Worms" and "The Trial." The relentless lyrics of "Waiting" depict future totalitarianism not as an esthetic triumph, as David would have, but as lowly creatures who will rid England of its minorities. "The Trial," with its references to "the final solution," owes something to Kafka, but it is staged as a Gilbert and Sullivan operetta turned inside out. The worms have now taken over, and Worm sits in judgement on Pink; he and the prosecuting attorney sing in dark, melodramatic British voices.

Pink Floyd's concert tour for *The Wall* marked, if not the end of the great era of amibitious concerts and ambitious assimilation of high culture and popular culture, at least its climax. ELP and Yes had already broken up, and Pink Floyd broke up soon afterwards. Economic and other considerations tended to confine such groups to the seventies. This generalization does not hold for the mirror image of art rock, which made fewer demands on its audience.

Notes

[1]Quoted in Eric Gaer, "Emerson Lake and Palmer, A Musical Force," *Downbeat*, May 9, 1974, p. 14.

[2]See Michael Brooker, "Yes' Steve Howe," *Guitar Player*, April, 1973, p. 25.

[3]Leonard Ferris, "Yes' bassist Chris Squire," *Guitar Player*, October, 1973, p. 17.

[4]Quoted in Dan Hedges, *Yes, The Authorized Biography* (London: Sidgwick and Jackson, 1982), p. 15.

[5]*Ibid.*, p. 68.

[6]Quoted in *ibid.*, p. 116.

[7]Schaffner, *The British Invasion*, p. 139.

[8]Quoted in *Rolling Stone*, April 16, 1970, p. 21.

[9]On Steve Howe's interest in the guitar synthesizer, see Joe Bivora, "Steve Howe, Walter Sears, and the 'Synthesar'," *Guitar Player*, May, 1976, p. 14.

[10]Andy Mackay, *Electronic Music* (Minneapolis, MN: Control Data Publishing, 1981), p. 86.

[11]Quoted in *Pink Floyd Lyric Book* (London: Pink Floyd Publishers, 1982), pp. 14-15.

Chapter 25:
How the Other Half Rocks

"Heavy metal, mon amour, where do I start?"[1] Thus Robert Duncan in *The Noise*. It's a good question. There's been less criticism written about heavy metal than about any other style of rock, and we can readily understand why. For no other style of rock does McLuhan's dictum "The medium is the message" make more sense. With heavy metal, the experience is everything—the pounding bass and drums, the screaming guitar, the prancing lead singer, and most of all, most important of all, the volume turned up so high that you don't so much hear it as feel it. I remember that when I saw Grand Funk Railroad for the first time, in 1969, I noticed that they had a separate mike for the bass drum, and I realized that something new was happening here.

Heavy metal gives you an experience which purifies the mind; you can't think or say anything at a heavy metal concert. The sound drives away all the petty memories and anxieties which plague us so much of the time. A heavy metal concert creates a special place, set apart from the ordinary world. In this sense heavy metal is the most complete example of rock 'n' roll as Mardi Gras. It was, after all, Grand Funk which promised to "help you party it down."

If heavy metal is not loud, then it is nothing at all. If heavy metal is the experience of heavy metal, then it exists in the moment, and it has been hard for people to have any clear idea of its history. For instance, you often read statements to the effect that heavy metal begins with two power trios from the late sixties, Cream and The Jimi Hendrix Experience. Certainly, Eric Clapton and Jimi Hendrix were overpowering guitarists, but their significance certainly transcended that of the groups in which they played, for the only major heavy metal trio of the seventies was Grand Funk Railroad.

Actually, the Stones which were often the model for heavy metal groups. Their combination of solid but anonymous rhythm section, hot guitarist, and flashy lead singer re-appears in Led Zeppelin and Van Halen, as well as in many other groups. Keith was at least as strong an influence on heavy metal as Clapton or Hendrix. Take "Satisfaction," and the way you can never forget the opening riff. If you play "Satisfaction," and then play Deep Purple's "Smoke on the Water," and Ted Nugent's "Cat Scratch Fever," you'll hear the similarities in the riffs, and the way they're used. Black Sabbath's "Paranoid" derives from "Paint It Black," and their "War Pigs" resembles "Sympathy for the Devil," but without Mick's teasing irony.

286

Heavy metal also has significant affinities with art rock. Both styles came from England, and peacefully coexisted at first. In 1970, Black Sabbath and Yes were sharing the same bill at venues like the Cardiff Arts Centre Project. In the British context, it seemed perfectly reasonable for Deep Purple to put out a record called *Concerto for Group and Orchestra*. After all, their lead guitarist Ritchie Blackmore had had classical training; he once said that he used a Bach chord progression on the "Highway Star" solo on *Machine Head*.[2]

Like art rock, heavy metal depended on technology, and was clearly a function of developing sound systems. Lloyd Grossman puts it very forcefully: "The equation was simple: better equipment made it possible to play to larger crowds, larger crowds meant more money. There was an impetus to develop bigger and better speakers and amplifiers for on-stage use, and these more powerful amplifiers made new sounds possible: Led Zeppelin couldn't have existed in 1965."[3] You can't get that kind of reproduction on car speakers, so heavy metal depended on albums and concerts, just like art rock did. Even Led Zeppelin didn't do a whole lot better on the charts than Pink Floyd; but this is not exactly surprising when you realize that they never released so much as one single in Great Britain. In America, "Whole Lotta Love" got to #4 in late 1969, but in the seventies the group placed only four songs on the charts, and only one of those got as high as #15. (Led Zep was so extraordinary that they got a lot of FM airplay anyhow.)

Like art rock, heavy metal tended to be relatively anonymous; it has produced a few distinctive personalities, mostly lead singers and guitarists, but the technology which has made so many rock stars turns upon them when driven to the max; Duncan calls heavy metal "faceless." The experience of heavy metal in the seventies was more important than the performers who produced that experience.

Then, too, early art rock had a certain effect on heavy metal. Brian Harrigan and Malcolm Dume, authors of the authoritative *Encyclopedia Metallica*, say that "The Nice played a major part in the development of the pomp-school of heavy metal and certainly Emerson's influence was enormous."[4] It wasn't, of course, Emerson's repertoire that influenced heavy metalists, but his extravagant costumes and the way he attacked his organ.

Like art rock, heavy metal often displeased the critics. They often thought that art rock was too pretentious, but that heavy metal was too unpretentious. *Rolling Stone* first split with its readers soon after Altamont when it denounced Grand Funk. It didn't matter much, because the fans went out and bought millions of Grand Funk records anyway.

The crucial difference between art rock and heavy metal, though, is that art rock is complex and heavy metal is simple. The thing is, you can't just crank up the amplifiers and play anything you want. Keith Richard once commented that Mick Taylor left the Stones because their music didn't offer him enough of a challenge, and Eddie Van Halen had this to say about the need for simplicity in heavy metal. "Well, the thing is, in rock and roll you only have so many chords. If you start playing chords like this [plays 7ths and 9ths] in rock and roll, forget it! They have emotion, but they don't fit rock and roll. They're so dissonant that the vibrations of the overtones with that much distortion sound like shit. That's why most rock and roll songs are simple—straight major or minor chords. You start dickin' with chords like 7ths and 9ths through a blazing Marshall, and it will sound like crap."[5] This need for musical simplicity may account for AC/DC's love of the fifties, from which they often plagiarize. Their song "There's Gonna Be Some Rockin'" comes from "Ready Teddy" and "Rockin'" from "Tutti Frutti." Even Led Zeppelin made a fifties number, "Hot Dog"; it features a boogie-woogie piano and Robert's Elvis imitation.

Like art rock, heavy metal came from England, a country where radio airplay doesn't matter so much anyhow. Led Zeppelin, Black Sabbath, Deep Purple, Judas Priest, Urian Heep, Bad Company, and Humble Pie all came from England. Thin Lizzie came from Ireland, and AC/DC came from Australia. The predominance of the British Empire in heavy metal has led British heavy metal freaks like Harrigan and Dume to claim that "true HM has and probably never will really exist in the states."[6] These people would point out that even Foreigner, a New York band, was formed by an Englishman, Mick Jones. Of course, to say that heavy metal doesn't exist in America is to ignore Aerosmith, Blue Oyster Cult, and the J. Geils Band, for openers. Yet there's something to be said for the British origins of heavy metal, and it needs to be explained.

As is usually the case, the differences between British and American music has to do with the radio monopoly of the BBC in England and the Top 40/progressive FM formats in America. In England, a band can make it without radio airplay, but an American band cannot. In England, gigs in clubs and concert tours can keep a band afloat, and as a matter of fact Black Sabbath played for a while at the Star Club in Hamburg, Germany, which was immortalized by the Beatles. Black Sabbath bassist Bill Ward once said of those gigs, "It used to drive us mad to think, we were working so hard, playing our guts out, while these guys were sitting around chattering. So we turned the volume louder and louder until it was impossible for anyone to have a conversation. That seemed to work."[7]

It matters more than it might seem to start out in a place where you have to play loud. Playing very loud just isn't the same as playing loud. There's more to it than turning the knobs on the amplifiers, for you have to learn to control feedback, and to condense and clarify your songs. To play to 20,000 people and more in an arena at 120 decibels, you have to dominate the audience—"On Your Feet or On Your Knees". (At this volume, the music seems more like a force of nature than something manmade, which may be why Deep Purple called one of their albums *Stormbringer.*) Thus, the abortive movement of the early seventies which the British critics called "pub rock" helped heavy metal bands develop their shows.

American bands rarely have this experience because their audiences in bars and clubs where bands start out are used to listening to rock 'n' roll on the radio, which they can turn down when they want to. They do not want deafening volume in such a casual setting. American bands in the seventies knew that they *had* to get on the radio to make it, their managers and their labels put pressure on them to write a hit single. This media situation strikes the British as odd, and Mickie Most, the Dick Clark of England, once went so far as to say that the single was "purely a promotional tool."[8] The magic combination of album, hit single, and concert tour took on ever greater importance in the competitive atmosphere of the seventies, and no American band could safely ignore any of the three points on that triangle. The defenders of the purity of British heavy metal ask us to "Take REO Speedwagon: ever since this Illinois five-piece launched their vinyl career in 1971 with *REO Speedwagon*, they have enjoyed steadily increasing success in the States with a sound that combines sweet melodies with a rock 'n' raunch approach to riffing."[9] An even better, and earlier, example is Kansas, which scored big in the late seventies with "Carry On Wayward Son" and "Dust in the Wind"; those guys sound for all the world as though they had learned to sing by listening to Yes albums. Harrigan and Dume even think that Cheap Trick stole riffs from AC/DC and Aerosmith "By using them to beef up what were, when all is said and done, pop songs of the variety one would expect to hear from the likes of the Move, ELO or the Beatles."[10]

One obvious response to this British chauvinism about heavy metal is to say, "Yes, but what about Van Halen?" The British would probably point out that Van Halen is not, strictly speaking, an American group. The founders, Eddie and Alex Van Halen were born in Holland, and as most musically gifted kids in Europe do, they took lessons in classical music. David Lee Roth, though, is an American free spirit if there ever was one, so the group is the most important recent example of what happens when European talent meets American individualism and American technology.

But there are differences within heavy metal, too. Black Sabbath has a heavy sound, to go with its Satanic trip, while some other bands have a brighter sound, and their songs have lyrics which are cheerful while remaining macho. I'm thinking here of songs like Brownsville Station's "Smoking in the Boys' Room," and Thin Lizzie's "The Boys Are Back in Town."

Although heavy metal created its own rock 'n' roll carnival, it was not completely separated from the world outside, and was even insidiously dependent on it. It took a lot of semis to haul all those amps from town to town, and those semis in turn depended on the interstate system which was completed in the seventies. Just as heavy metal flounders at low volumes, so the semis have to stay on the interstates. Ultimately, it was the interstates that made the major tours of the seventies possible.

Robert Duncan says something else important about the implications of the volume which heavy metal requires.

If *loud* meant passion and acting out, there was a line it crossed and a balance it tipped as it coursed the circuits and tubes of the Marshall amp stacks, and when the loud *est* ness of heavy metal came out the other end, into the arena, it was a series of sonic body blows, true violence and trauma, and finally something quite the opposite of passion. In fact, the loud *est* ness of heavy metal was a deadening of passion, a deadening of the senses, of the laughing irrational, no less than the rational, a deadening, period.[11]

What Duncan is saying is that passion amplified to such a volume reverses itself and deadens passion, just as individualism amplified to such a volume reverses itself into anonymity. The same thing applies to another form of popular culture which did great business in the seventies, X-rated movies. Like heavy metal, X-rated movies were about passion; if heavy metal simplified music, X-rated movies simplified passion, and they blew up the organs involved to such size that they tended to deaden passion.

Ted Nugent has said that heavy metal is not so much about passion as aggression. "Everyone has a form of positive aggression in them left over from when we had to hunt to survive. In the synthetic world of today, no one has an avenue to expose their aggression—unless they shoot people or beat their wife. That's bad. I get it out of my system by hammering on my guitar on stage. Those who come to a Nugent concert get it out with me."[12] It's indicative that Ted Nugent is an enthusiastic member of the National Rifle Association, for heavy metal, hunting, and other working class interests go together. (Ozzy Osbourne is also an enthusiastic hunter.)

The lasting popularity of heavy metal throughout the seventies is symptomatic of the spread of sixties attitudes to high school kids and working class kids, so we need to know something specific about this process. Reporting on an extensive survey of American young people in 1973, the consulting firm of Daniel Yankelovich stated that "Gradually, the New Values and a sense of personal entitlement are seeping into the consciousness of all young people, not just college youth."[13] As a result, belief in "Traditional American values"— like work—declined among working-class kids even while they were riding around in their pickups with American flag decals. "In 1969, 79 percent of the non-college young believed that 'hard work would always pay off,' a view held by only 57 percent of college youth. Now [in 1973] the same traditional feeling about hard work as the royal road to success is supported by only 56 percent of non-college youth."[14] A 20 percent decline in the belief in the value of hard work in only four years is a substantial change. Since the labor force was increasing rapidly, these kids wanted to go for the gusto—and heavy metal sure had lots of gusto.

There's a more specific source for the aggression which Ted mentioned. The working-class kids who went to his concerts had felt left out in the sixties; they had seen their older brothers and friends go off to Vietnam while college kids burned American flags. They had felt put down and left out, but now they had a musical style they could claim as their own. In fact, working-class reaction against flower power helped to form heavy metal. Ozzy Ozbourne declared, "The hippies said, 'The world is so beautiful, man.' You only had to look around to see how crappy it was.... We didn't want to go through any of that phoney bollocks."[15] The American counterpart to Black Sabbath

in this regard is Lynyrd Skynyrd, of course. Their "Sweet Home Alabama" defends George Wallace, and attacks Neil Young for his "Southern Man." Probably the most explicit example of the way heavy metal reacted against the sixties, though, is a song on Blue Oyster Cult's *Agent of Fortune*. It's called "This Ain't the Summer of Love."

Heavy metal didn't just react against the sixties; it surpassed the sixties, at least in terms of numbers. In 1973, Led Zeppelin broke several attendance records which the Beatles had set. What the Beatles were to rock 'n' roll, Led Zeppelin was to heavy metal. Like the Beatles, Led Zep were phenomenally lucky in their management and in their stable personalities, but there was more to their success than that.

One of the reasons for the extraordinary creativity of Led Zep—aside from sheer talent—was age. Born in 1944, Jimmy Page was a little older than the other leaders of heavy metal groups in the seventies (Ozzy Osbourne, for example, was born in 1948), and by the late sixties he had played in hundreds of studio sessions. He knew how to use the studio, so that the group never relied on anyone the way the Beatles relied on George Martin. By the time the Yardbirds broke up, British musicians were calling Jimmy a "stone professional" because he could play in any style they'd ever heard. So we can say that Led Zep unlike Black Sabbath, was not reacting against the sixties so much as growin out of and drawing on that great legacy. Since they had already proved themselv as professionals before they formed the group, they show little of the stylis uncertainty that you hear on the early Stones albums.

People have noticed that the very name of Led Zeppelin includes opposition of "light" and "heavy." Practically speaking, this amounts to opposition between the electric guitar and the acoustic guitar, and app on the first two cuts of their first album. *Led Zeppelin* begins with "G Times, Bad Times," and Jimmy makes his presence known with a scorc guitar solo. However, the next cut is "Babe I'm Gonna Leave," and fea Jimmy's fluid arpeggios on acoustic guitar. Robert Plant doesn't have the of a folk singer, so the overall effect is not unlike that of "Lady Jane their covers of two Willie Dixon songs, "You Shook Me" and "I Can't You," show, they can play the blues, but they never had a commitm this or any other style. What made Lep Zep so great is that while the defining the heavy metal sound, they never let it limit them. John Paul organ solo on "Your Time Is Gonna Come" wouldn't disgrace Keith Er and Led Zep is surely the only heavy metal group which uses a ta "Black Mountain Side."

A seventies classic, "Whole Lotta Love," begins *Led Zeppelin I* Jimmy's usual fabulous guitar work, and Robert Plant's infamous to give you "every inch of my love." But this is Led Zep, not you band, so Jimmy exploits the studio. He puts echo and reverb on t and during the percussion break, the sound jumps back and forth the speakers. "Whole Lotta Love" and "The Lemon Song" are as r raunchy as anything ever recorded. But the other two cuts of *Lea*

II are quieter; "What Is and Never Should Be" and "Thank You" are love songs. Similarly, "Bring It On Home" on side two begins and ends in a bluesy style, complete with harmonica, but turns into hard rock after the first verse.

The group also departed from the usual heavy metal formula enough to include a traditional folk song "Gallows Pole," on *Led Zeppelin III*, and British folkie Sandy Dennis, of Fairport Convention fame, sings on "The Battle of Evermore" on Runes album. This imaginative use of folk music both indicates the way their style grew out of the sixties, and gives us a clue to the origin of the mythological element in their lyrics. So the line "Valhalla I am coming" on "Immigrant Song" anticipates "Stairway to Heaven."

Robert has said that when he was writing "Stairway to Heaven," the words just "came to" him. Maybe so, but Neil Sedaka had a hit with a song by the same name in 1960, and in 1946 there was a British movie called *Stairway to Heaven*. "Stairway to Heaven" is the consummate Led Zep cut, of course, and it shows off all the band's strengths. Its protests against the commercialization of religion and its intimations of utopia are a last statement of sixties attitudes. (It's probably not coincidental that the next cut, "Going to California" evokes memories of the Summer of Love.) "Stairway to Heaven" has an acoustic beginning, which Jimmy then turns into a guitar army, and Robert's vocal control gives him the ability to draw out syllables while singing at full voice. "Stairway to Heaven" just may be the most completely satisfying rock song ever recorded.

Jimmy had always been a much more melodic musician than, say, Keith Richard; he tended to use imaginative runs in his solos rather than riffs. Therefore, it's not a complete surprise to hear his acoustic guitar backed with a string section on "The Rain Song." By the late seventies, Led Zep acknowledged that they had said what they had to say on *Swan Song*. The key song on that album is "All My Love," a religious, lyrical, and melodic reply to "Whole Lotta Love." It is, in short, all the things a heavy metal song is *not* supposed to be.

Heavy metal relies so much on playing very loud and freaking out that many groups stopped innovating after they achieved a certain level of success. Not so with Led Zep. Blessed with talent, professionalism, and Peter Grant's astute management, Led Zep kept growing and developing to the end. They set the standards for heavy metal, and hardly anybody else ever measured up to them.

Notes

[1] Robert Duncan, *The Noise* (New York: Ticknor and Fields, 1984), p. 37.

[2] See Jas Olbrecht, *Masters of Heavy Metal* (New York: Quill/A Guitar Player Book, 1984), p. 54.

[3] Lloyd Grossman, *A Social History of Rock Music* (New York: David McKay, 1976), p. 124.

[4]Brian Harrigan and Malcolm Dume, *Encyclopedia Metallica* (London: Bobcat Books, n.d.), p. 13.

[5]Quoted in Jas Olbrecht, *Masters of Heavy Metal*, p. 155.

[6]*Encyclopedia Metallica*, p. 33.

[7]Quoted in Chris Welch, *Black Sabbath* (London: Proteus Books, 1982), p. 19.

[8]Quoted in *The Record Producers*, p. 135.

[9]*Encyclopedia Metallica*, p. 38.

[10]*Ibid., p. 44.*

[11]Duncan, *The Noise*, p. 47.

[12]Quoted in *Masters of Heavy Metal*, p. 91.

[13]Daniel Yankelovich, *The New Morality.A Profile of American Youth in the 70's* (New York: McGraw-Hill, 1974), p. 28.

[14]*Ibid.*, pp. 30.31.

[15]Quoted in Welch, *Black Sabbath*, p. 20.

SECTION IV
1974-1984

Chapter 26:
Disco, A New Beginning

What 1954 meant, and what 1964 meant, 1974 meant as well: The beginning of a new era in popular music, one which drew on the past to create a new synthesis. Although disco made lots of money for lots of people, it produced no major new stars, as previous eras had produced Elvis and the Beatles, and it did not take the charts by storm, as earlier styles had. Major acts like Fleetwood Mac and the Eagles were hardly affected by it. And the most famous disco group, the Bee Gees, had been putting hits on the charts since the late sixties. What disco meant was a major reorganization of the relationship between the performers and the audience; this reorganization also demanded substantial reorganizations in the way popular music was merchandized to the people who listened to it.

Let's begin with the tetrad chart for disco:

Disco: 1974-79

Medium:	Sociology:	Enhances:	Obsolesces:
12-in singles	gays/blacks	Narcissism	Isolation

Retrieves:	Reverses Into:
Formal Dancing	MTV

It is a commonplace that disco began in gay and black clubs, primarily in New York City—there is no particular mystery about that. The question to ask about disco is: Why did it happen that a style which arose in a setting so foreign to the experience of most Americans became a major national style? The usual answer is that, "People wanted escape," but as usual escapism as the explanation for the rise of a style begs the question: Why this particular style, and not some other one? To explain the rise of disco, we need an explanation of the needs of the audience which the music satisfied, and that explanation depends on an understanding of the Watergate crisis. What the Army-McCarthy hearings were to the music of the fifties, and what the assassination of President Kennedy was to the music of the sixties, Watergate was to the music of the seventies.

Robert Duncan has said, wisely, that, "Indeed, if rock 'n' roll is the sound of perpetual adolescence, making of adolescence a model for the whole of life, then Nixon was surely the father figure who filled out the metaphor and finished the equation for an entire generation of rock 'n' roll adolescents, mama's boys and girls."[1] Duncan comments that he was born the day Nixon was first elected Vice-President. And consider the baby boomers who were born in 1950 and thus were 24 when Nixon resigned on August 9, 1974; Nixon had held high national office for more than half their lives. It was only when he resigned that they could say with Neil Young in "Ohio," that "We're finally on our own." Only when Nixon resigned were the sixties finally over.

When Nixon resigned, he did it on television. In fact, he was our first television politician; his career began on television and ended on television. If Nixon and television had prospered together, and if Nixon was the father figure to the rock 'n' roll generation of baby boomers, this reminds us yet again that television was the ground against which the figure of rock 'n' roll defined itself.

To understand Watergate we need to think of it not as a suspense thriller, as in *All the President's Men* (1976), but as a sitcom which finally lost out in the ratings game. (As a matter of fact, this is more or less what Nixon said in his resignation speech; he never admitted that he had done anything wrong—just that he had lost his political support.) If Nixon was a father figure to the rock 'n' roll generation, we can assimilate him to the father figure which that generation knew best—Robert Young, on *Father Knows Best*.

After beginning on radio in 1949, *Father Knows Best* went to television in 1954, and it was such a consummate media image of the way the Establishment wanted to think of The American Way Of Life that in 1959 the Treasury Department commissioned the producers to film a special episode to promote a Savings Bond drive. They agreed, and the episode was shown in schools, churches, and the like all over the country. Given these facts, I would be astonished to learn that Nixon never watched it. But even if he didn't, thinking of Nixon as a father figure in a fifties sitcom offers a way of bringing together Nixon and the kids, television and rock 'n' roll, into a single process of historical evolution.

Any television genre as durable as the sitcom must satisfy important needs, and here is what television historian David Marc says about the function of the sitcom in this regard:

In the fifties and sixties, the sitcom had offered the Depression-born post World War II adult group a vision of peaceful, prosperous suburban life centered on the stable nuclear family. A generation that had grown up during hard times, and that had fought what Herbert T. Gillis always referred to as "The Big One," had seen its desires fulfilled on the sitcom.[2]

Surely no television show ever showed the world as Nixon wanted it to be so convincingly as *Father Knows Best*. In this dream world without sex, drugs, and rock 'n' roll, Nixon cast himself as father, and then cast his constituents as children.

The sitcoms were not all fun and games; although Marc does not connect Nixon to them, he uses one of Nixon's favorite words in commenting that, "In these shows...actual humor (jokes or shticks) is always a subordinate concern to the proper solution of ethical crises."[3] Marc adds that, in general,

"These shows are bound together by their unwavering commitment to didactic allegory."[4] In an allegory, the part stands for the whole, and the white, stable, nuclear family of fifties sitcoms stood for the whole of America. The problem-oriented sitcoms created a microcosm of moral—i.e., male—order as a limited version of American civil religion. That order was continually confronted with crises, which were usually caused by women and children. These crises never succeeded in disrupting the order of the world, of course, for Father Knew Best.

Nixon's concept of American life was indistinguishable from the image of American life as presented on the sitcoms. Like the sitcoms, his political career began during the McCarthy Era; Nixon shared with the sitcoms the premise that what was good was American, and that what was bad was Un-American. Thus, when Nixon trivialized and sentimentalized the issue of slush fund payments in the Checkers speech, he was doing just what the sitcoms did with substantive issues. Even the issue of credibility, which he offered as his reason for continuing The War when a majority of Americans wanted it stopped, makes sense as a global version of a continual concern of sitcom families: What will the neighbors think?

But since he believed that he would make his mark on history in foreign affairs, he never bothered to revise his understanding of American life as *Father Knows Best*, with himself in the title role. Thus, when the baby boomers insisted on growing up—that is to say, when they stopped acting like the Beaver—Nixon had only two possible courses of action, and he chose them both. He called them names, and in doing so garnered a lot of support from his contemporaries who also felt angered and confused at the passing of sitcoms. Then, when the kids continued to deny that he knew best, he proceeded to shut out the annoying, unsitcomlike world. He withdrew to the White House and Palm Beach and San Clemente.

Although Robert Young remained a powerful prototype for the old Nixon, there was a new Nixon as well. Surprisingly, the new Nixon had many of the qualities which characterized hippies, and his administration self-destructed for reasons which have instructive analogies with the way hippiedom self-destructed. There are family resemblances between the hippies and their father figure. Just consider this statement by Jonathan Schell about Nixon: "What had gotten the President into trouble from the start had been his remarkable capacity for fantasy."[5] Surely the capacity for fantasy was a valued trait among hippies.

Like the hippies, Nixon tended to turn social issues into matters of perception and psychology, not economics and organizations. If the hippies talked about where their heads were at, Nixon talked about The War as a test of American character—not as a matter of military stategy. If the hippies adopted special costumes to show where their heads were at, Nixon's obsession with football expressed his need to believe in a world in which you could always tell the good guys from the bad guys by the color of their shirts. Like the hippies, Nixon thought that ecology was a major national concern, and said so in his first official statement of 1970. Like the hippies, Nixon thought of himself as an outsider struggling against a powerful and implacably hostile Establishment. Like the hippies, Nixon was a now person; he lived for the moment, and whatever he said or did at any given moment had no necessary relationship to what he said or did at any other time. As President-Elect he promised to bring the People together, and then worked to divide them. He promised to end The War, and then extended and widened it. As Schell says, "The manner in which the Administration reversed itself had been as remarkable as the substance of the reversal. It had come like a change in the political weather. No known events had precipitated it. No explanations were offered for it afterward. The President never alluded to any change. Rather, he and his spokesmen talked as though the new mood of the Administration had always been its mood."[6]

Where the new Nixon met the old Nixon was in the matter of media images. If the kids modelled demonstrations on media images of demonstrations, Nixon modelled domestic policy on the only media images of domestic life which he knew—sitcoms. When external events failed to offer the neat resolutions of sitcoms, he created them himself. As his Presidency progressed, he more and more rarely had any experiences which he had not arranged for himself. His aide Alexander Butterfield later testified, "The President often, of course, was concerned whether or not the curtains were closed or open; the arrangements of state gifts; whether they should be on that side of the room or this side of the room; displayed on a weekly basis or on a monthly basis."[7]

In effect, Nixon thought of his life as a didactic allegory. He believed that he embodied Order, and this is how he justified his extraordinary narcissism. Ken Kesey's Merry Pranksters loved to tape-record their conversations, and take home movies of themselves—as did Charlie Manson's rather less Merry Pranksters. But none of them had anything on Nixon.

"At least as great as the President's passion for meticulously prearranging events was his passion for recording the meticulously arranged events as they occurred. The President placed himself under the scrutiny of several overlapping systems of surveillance. Secret Service agents, White House 'ushers,' military aides to the President, and White House switchboard operators were required to note down every meeting he held, every phone call he initiated or received, and, generally speaking, every move he made. At the end of each day, the notes were turned in to a central office, where a Presidential 'diary' was put together."[8]

And so it went. Nixon and his men talked a lot about "images" and "scenarios," and they drew on their public relations backgrounds when they wrote the script for the 1972 Republican Convention in Miami. The platform for that convention asserted that, "It is so easy to forget how frightful it was."[9] This statement, like so many others from the same source, runs counter to human psychology. Surely the point about frightful times is that they are hard, not easy, to forget. But this attitude makes perfect sense in terms of the sitcom mentality. Robert Young didn't let his kids take the easy way out, the Beaver never got to take the easy way out, and Nixon as sitcom father supreme wasn't about to let America take the easy way out of The War.

No one has ever understood that Nixon's oft-repeated boast that he understood Middle America was nothing more than an intuitive understanding of *Father Knows Best*. But *Father Knows Best* was never "realistic" in any meaningful sense. At most, it presented an ideal which a significant number of powerful people believed in. Rock 'n' roll, and all that it represented, challenged the hegemony of that ideal. Nixon, however, was too committed to it, and too unstable, to do anything more than to combine the worst features of the fifties and the sixties. The rest, fortunately, is history.

Scriptwriter William Goldman decided to stop the action in *All the President's Men* before the Ervin Committee began its investigations, and let the teletype narrate the happy ending. The story built and built and built for several years; like a sitcom, it seemed to go on forever. Theodore White has aptly described the way Watergate dominated the news in the summer of 1973.

The scandal was front-page on all newspapers across the nation—not since World War II had any single matter for so long and with such a grip on the emotions led editors to such display. In the *New York Times* alone, the story was front-page all through May, June and July, its editors dropping it from their front page only one day each month, as if to give their readership a breathing spell. And for those whom the daily press and television missed, there were the vivid poster covers of the news-weeklies, spread on 126,000 magazine stands across the nation, from corner drugstore to supermarket.... Whether one listened or one turned away, ...whether one preferred the morning paper headlines or the evening electronic news—the entire news system was announcing the Greatest Show on Earth.[10]

And it got worse. That fall, the Yom Kippur war broke out, and the Arab oil embargo caused lines at gas stations. On the political front, Spiro Agnew resigned as Vice-President, and Nixon fired his Attorney General, and the Special Prosecutor, in what has come to be known as the Saturday Night Massacre. This action evoked what Nixon's men called a "firestorm," and White was not overstating the case when he wrote, "The nation was full of questions; nothing made sense; it was a time of chaos."[11]

It was a time of chaos in two respects. First, the President, who is supposed to respond to the People, isolated himself from them, and from the legal system. Second, Watergate caused extreme tensions in that it went counter to the tendency toward decentralization of the seventies. Just at the time when people wanted to end the war, get rid of Nixon, and get on with their lives, they couldn't. One baby boomer quoted by Landon Jones no doubt spoke for many when he said, "Watergate was when I started getting cynical."

The antidote to such feelings was disco. Not for the first time when people turned away from bad news on television they turned to music. Disco transformed the passive, frustrated television audience of the Watergate Hearings into performers. If television, on sitcoms and elsewhere, could only hint at sexuality, disco flaunted it. If the networks controlled television, no one controlled what went on inside the discos.

Disco celebrated the fact that we had survived Nixon; it is not coincidental that the first song in *Saturday Night Fever* is a survival song: "Stayin' Alive." In 1979, Gloria Gaynor had a big hit with "I Will Survive." Nixon had gone and we could ignore politics for a while. It was a glorious, liberating feeling.

With the rise of disco we broke through to the other side of the cherished American belief in the power of images to refer to something in the external world. Disco was the first musical style to accept images as valid in themselves, and as not necessarily referring to anything else. Artificiality—conscious, deliberate artificiality—was the order of the day not just in the music, but also in the setting in which one heard the music, and in the costumes which one wore. At Xenon, a popular New York disco, patrons could bump against huge "pinball bumpers" as they danced, making lights flash, or hold onto plastic ribbons of light called "electronic maypoles."

It is this acceptance of artificiality that explains the popularity of The Village People. Like the disco in general, they rapidly transcended their gay milieu. The fact that they had four albums go platinum means that they appealed to straights as well as gays. By the late seventies people could accept their costumes as just costumes and not as statements of sexual preferences. The Village People even found an audience among children, who saw them as cartoon figures. It was perfectly reasonable for the Muppets to do "Macho Man."

Something has happened to the star system when a major group has a cartoon-like quality, as Sha Na Na had in the sixties. Disco merged the performers and the audience; it decentralized music by obsolescing the star system. The word "discotheque" was formed by analogy with the French word for library, "bibliotheque," and one no more has a sense of the presence of the performers in a disco than one has of the presence of the authors in a library.

Although disco created some stars, like Donna Summer, they were stars in a mostly abstract way. Nobody ever thought about what a great singer she was while listening to "Love to Love You Baby." The dancers *were* the performers, which is why Steve Rubell screened people so carefully before he let them into Studio 54. One commentator at the time said, "There is here a standard of conformity to the outrageous; one must put on a passing pleasing show."[12] The lucky few whom Rubell let in may have noticed a statue of the Greek god Narcissus in the foyer of Studio 54, for the point of disco was that all the dancers could think of themselves as stars.

The narcissism of disco was no more coincidental than the theme of survival in its music. Why did straights adopt the costumes and the precious posing which in the past had characterized gays? The answer, I think, is that disco became a national craze only after two years of incessant reporting by the news media about the most narcissistic President in American history. True to the American Way, then, disco represented a democratization of narcissism.

In obsolescing the star system, disco also obsolesced isolation. In the late seventies, lots of people were listening to Pink Floyd, say, in the isolation created by headphones. But nobody ever listened to "Stayin' Alive" on headphones. Disco is body music, not head music, and can really be enjoyed only in the company of other people. As one disco entrepreneur put it in 1975, "People are into people again, and that's what discos are all about."[13]

In discos, you were putting yourself on display, and to get people's attention it was not enough to move around aimlessly and do your own thing, as it had been at the Fillmore in the sixties. When we notice how seriously John Travolta and Karen Gorney rehearse for the dance contest in *Saturday Night Fever*, and when we recall how quickly the Arthur Murray Studios started offering disco lessons, we realize how much disco dancing had in common with formal dances like the minuet. One dance teacher pointed out that, "The steps [for the LA Hustle] are highly choreographed, and the rest of the body's motion is high stylized." Like the minuet, the LA Hustle was not done with a partner, "But with one or more (preferably a lot more) people all moving in the same direction, all doing the same step at the same time. Hopefully."[14]

Disco obsolesced the isolation of individuals from each other on the dance floor, as well as another holdover from the sixties, the generation gap. Disco was the first innovative popular music since the twist which parents and their kids could enjoy together. After one disco franchiser held his daughter's wedding reception at his disco in Meadville, Pennsylvania, he commented, "The older people were particularly fascinated. I think they came more to see the disco than to the wedding."[15]

Yet not all age groups liked disco. Although there were a few teen discos, the kids in high school and junior high school were listening to Kiss and Barry Manilow. Disco was too physical and too sexual for them; it demanded listeners who were more comfortable with their bodies than teenagers usually are. In short, it demanded baby boomers, and was the last distinctive style which they made popular.

"Now the music market that mattered was the 18-34 group, which, at the end of the seventies, corresponded almost exactly to the baby-boom cohorts. These were the same people who had discovered the Beatles, only they were out of school and were bringing their musical values to adult life. Disco, moreover, was the consummate modern style."[16]

The implied audience for disco consisted of stoned, flashily dressed dancers of assorted sexual preferences in the urban, high-tech environment of a club. This new implied audience necessitated a re-definition in just about everything associated with the music. Take drugs, for instance. If heavy metal freaks took sopors to get them through the weekend at a Black Sabbath concert, disco dancers took amyl nitrate poppers to pump themselves up for ever greater exertions on the floor.

These re-definitions did not come out of nowhere, of course. Discos had been in existence for some time before they started to satisfy the needs of a mass audience in America. As Albert Goldman points out in his excellent book on disco, the discotheque came from France, as the very name suggests. It arose in occupied Paris during World War II, when the Nazi forbade jazz as a decadent art form. So in certain bistros the owners would play jazz records, both as an act of defiance and as a shrewd way to draw patrons. There was thus a certain secretive quality about discos from the very beginning, which carried over to the gay discos in New York and elsewhere.

The European connection retained its importance when disco came out of the closet/underground. A Swiss-Italian, Giorgio Moroder, wrote and produced Donna Summer's "Love to Love You Baby" in Munich, West Germany, and Alex Cerrone's "Love in C Minor" came from Paris. Jacques Morali formed the Village People. "Dancing Queen" by Sweden's ABBA went to #1 on both the disco and pop charts.

We can account for the European origins of some disco records by noticing the way an advantage can also be a disadvantage. So many British kids have envied the variety of radio programming in America that it's easy to forget that mass broadcasting has its drawbacks—one of which is censorship. Knowing that airplay had negligible significance, European producers could make their records for clubs as lascivious as they wanted. As Goldman comments, "The Europeans had an advantage in that they were geared to produce smaller quantities of records and didn't have to worry as much about violating moral standards. European packaging, for example, was so daring that when an American company licensed a new record, often the jacket would have to be redesigned and toned down."[17] Americans may have remembered some wicked passages on Muddy Waters and Hank Ballard records, hardly any of them had ever heard a woman produce anything like Donna Summer's orgasmic moans on "Love to Love You Baby," or the female chorus sighing "Love me" on Cerrone's "Love in C Minor." Women's sexuality on records was something new and titillating and would never have made it on the radio had the records not been first broken in clubs.

European producers were able to make records which topped the charts in America because they relied on the international sound of the synthesizer. The synthesizer was the vital element in the way disco records were produced and in the way they sounded. Juergen Koppers, Donna Summer's engineer for "I Feel Love," once explained the procedure for producing her highly successful disco sound.

"The first thing we laid down a click track with a metronome, to trigger all the synthesizers and sequencers later. And second thing we do is to get a kind of bass drum sound with a synthesizer. And record it straight...four-on-the-floor...all the way through for five, eight, even 10 minutes. And the same thing with the snare; a separate overdub with synthesizer—no natural snare, just a big Moog. The same thing with high-hat. In the end we decided that the synthesizer bass drum was not strong enough, so we added a real bass drum; I mean that actually was the only natural overdub on 'I Feel Love.' "[18]

Not only do you get metronomic regularity with a synthesizer rhythm track at the necessary 125-160 beats per minute, you also get tapes which you can manipulate and repeat at will. (This assumes, of course, that you're working on a 24-track board, for a studio equipped with anything less will not produce good disco sound.) This latter point is especially important, for Koppers added that on "I Feel Love," "The first overdubs were like maybe seven minutes—because it was always a *repeat*; a certain sequence that repeated all the time. When Donna was singing, she just sang for the first three minutes or whatever. And then everything I told you, the whole arrangement, is the *mix* afterwards!"[19]

When producers recorded actual drums to get a rhythm track, they compressed the sound—i.e., they cut out part of it, making it sharper—or they used equalizers, which is what Koppers did. "Well the way *I* did it—in the recording I boosted like 12 dB at 60 Hz, 10 dB around 3 kHz, and even 10 dB at 8 kHz. And the whole thing over again in the mix! So you can imagine...it has nothing to do with natural sound—no kick drum would sound like that!"[20] As a matter of fact, the drum beat in many disco records sounds more like a pistol shot than anything else.

But it is just here that Naisbitt's principle "high tech/high touch" comes into play. If the instruments sounded impersonal, the singing was as personal as you can get. Donna Summer's five-minute orgasm on "Love to Love You Baby" is the most obvious case in point, but there's more to it than this. Once you got your rhythm tracks down, you could add just about anything you wanted by way of sweetening. This lack of coordination between the rhythm and the melody enabled the Bee Gees to sell lots of disco records while keeping essentially the same vocal style they had been using for years. Or, you could use classical sources, as Walter Murphy did on "A Fifth of Beethoven," and as Tuxedo Junction did when they went to Emerson Lake and Palmer's favorite composer, Mussorgsky, for "Volga Boatmen" and "Night on Disco Mountain." Tuxedo Junction was also eclectic, going back to the Glenn Miller tradition which their own name evokes for "Chattanooga Choo Choo" and "Moonlight Serenade." A lot of Motown music fit well into the repetitive disco format, and Gloria Gaynor recycled the old Four Tops standard "Reach Out I'll Be There."

It was also possible to give the disco treatment to current hits. The Stones' "Miss You" and Rod Stewart's "Do Ya Think I'm Sexy?" were hits both in their rock versions and in their disco versions. Engineer Jim Burgess did the disco remix of "Do Ya Think I'm Sexy?" and here's how he explained the process: "Basically, I changed the balance in the rhythm tracks of the song, which had more of a rock sound on the bottom. For example, the bass had to come up, and I believe we used a Kepex [noise gate] on the snare, to make it cleaner sounding. At the end of the song I extended the vamp by recycling a few bars and pushed up the cowbell to make the instrumental section more effective."[21]

If the implied audience for disco was a bunch of stoned dancers, then there arose a problem with what the record companies call "product." These were not teenagers at a prom, and they wanted to dance for more than three minutes. Although a lot of bands were making tracks longer than three minutes, you couldn't dance to "Stairway to Heaven," say, or "Layla," because the music was too complicated and the time changes too tricky. As usual, a new implied audience requires a new format for the reproduction of the music; the new format for disco soon appeared, in the guise of the 12" 45. This was, of course, a new use of an old medium. The 12" 45 was first issued in July 1975 by Atlantic Records; since the label still thought of radio airplay as the key to record sales, it thought of the single in this new size as a purely promotional item. Independent labels had a flexibility which enabled them to respond to new trends, and by May of 1976 small Salsoul Records of New York released a 12" single for the commercial market.[22]

Since disco records were too long, and the lyrics too lascivious, for many radio stations, somebody had to choose and program them in the clubs. That somebody turned out to be the new star which disco created, the live DJ. Just as there had been disco throughout the sixties, so there had been DJs for a long time. At the big time discos what went on was the interaction between the DJ and the dancers on the floor, and the music was the medium through which this interaction took place. The great DJs could sense the mood of the floor, comment on it, and reflect it back through the choice and sequence of the records. If the dancers merged the previous roles of audience and performer, then the DJs merged the previous roles of record producer and radio program director. There was a certain compensation in this; as more and more FM stations became completely automated, they needed fewer DJs at the same time disco needed more of them.

One of the great innovators in the DJ trade was an Italian guy from Brooklyn named Francis Grasso, who is credited with inventing the trick of "slipcuing." Using headphones, he would locate the best spot to make a splice between two records, and hold the record motionless as the turntable revolved beneath it until just the right second to let it go. Like a record producer, he had equalizers and speed controls which allowed him to match the tempos of two records and play them simultaneously while compensating for any loss of highs. Another popular technique was flanging—the practice of playing two copies of the same record at the same time while slowing down one turntable to get a slight delay effect. Clearly, Grasso represents an early stage in the development of disco, and some of his manipulations of the sound became unnecessary later as producers figured out how to create a consistently successful disco sound. The DJ nevertheless retained his unprecedented importance.

Disco Djs didn't function as "personalities," as the Top 40 DJs had, so a lot depended on their record libraries. Since everything broke so fast in disco, they formed record pools to keep their collections current. By 1977 there were something like 28 record pools in America with over 3,000 member DJs. The first one was formed in New York in December of 1975. Since disco mattered a lot to Motown, that label sent 50% of all its new releases to record pools; in return for the records, the DJs had to fill out a rating sheet. These record pools provided the labels with a new way to get feedback from the audience about particular records. Thelma Houston's "Don't Leave Me This Way" got rave reviews from the DJs, and went to #2 on the disco charts even before the 12" single was released on December 14, 1977. A month later, it had gone to #1 on the pop charts. Never before had record executives had such a quick, reliable way of finding out, and promoting, what was hot. (This was also a *cheap* way of marketing—a fact which accounts for the appearance of a lot of new disco acts.) Still, this was only a partial reorganization of marketing procedure, for the disco market remained primarily a singles market.[23]

Since disco created a complete entertainment environment, it occurred to a number of people that they could do with disco what McDonald's had done with hamburgers: they could franchise. As Mike O'Harro, the disco king of Washington, once said: "You'll be able to know that you can get a good time anywhere by just walking into a disco, because it will be just like every other disco."[24] To use a fashionable word of the seventies, O'Harro was selling a lifestyle. Capitalizing on the success of his Tramps disco in Washington, he also marketed Tramps cigarettes, necklaces, T-shirts, and shoes. Successful discos turned a phenomenal profit; Infinity, a disco in SoHo, earned back its start-up costs in less than seven weeks.[25]

When discos spread to Middle America, they started to change. The dancers were predominantly straight, not gay; they did fewer drugs and wore more restrained clothing; and they liked styles of music other than disco. Thomas Jayson, of Bridgeville, Pennsylvania, understood all this, which is why his disco franchise, 2001, enjoyed such success. They supplied plans, and advertising, and even the macrame wall hangings, and they insisted on the equivalent of what the radio stations call "day-parting," the practice of playing different kinds of music depending on the time of day. Jayson's franchises played Boston Pops selections (!) between 8:00 and 9:00, then starting mixing in some Top 40 numbers, and only toward 11:00 did they play real disco singles.[26]

And so it goes in America. When a style hits, it creates new stars, makes fortunes for entrepreneurs, and forces the industry to make adaptations. But by the same token, as it becomes successful, it adapts to the existing musical and social environment. (Whether or not you think this is deplorable depends on whether or not you are a purist.) Disco broke quite rapidly, and then faded quite rapidly as a trend-setter. Although it did not disappear by any means, it did lack staying power, primarily because it required a special environment, and was to such a great extent a reaction to Nixon. As his memory began to fade, and as recession began to make itself felt at the end of the seventies, the need to dance felt less intense.

Notes

[1]Robert Duncan, *The Noise,* p. 199.

[2]David Marc, *Demographic Vistas* (Philadelphia: U. of Pennsylvania Press, 1984), p. 14.

[3]Ibid., p. 15.

[4]*Ibid.,* p. 16.

[5]Jonathan Schell, *The Time of Illusion* (New York: Vintage Books, 1976), p. 329.

[6]*Ibid.,* p. 73.

[7]Quoted in *ibid.,* p. 285.

[8]*Ibid.*

[9]Quoted in *ibid.,* p. 277.

[10]Theodore White, *Breach of Faith* (New York: Atheneum, 1975), p. 234.

[11]*Ibid.,* p. 244.

[12]Sally Helgesen, "Disco," *Harper's* October, 1977, p. 20.

[13]Unnamed speaker quoted in *The New Yorker,* February 16, 1976, p. 28.

[14]Quoted in *Rolling Stone,* August 28, 1975, p. 46.

[15]Jesse Kornbluth, "Merchandizing Disco for the Masses," *New York Times Magazine,* February 18, 1976, p. 45.

[16]Landon Jones, *Great Expectations,* p. 267.

[17]Albert Goldman, *Disco* (New York: Hawthorn Books, 1978), p. 138.

[18]Quoted in Paul Lawrence, "Disco and Beyond—Juergen Koppers," *Recording Engineer/Producer,* February, 1981, pp. 33-34.

[19]Quoted in *ibid.,* p. 34.

[20]*Ibid.*

[21]Quoted in Crispin Cioe, "Discotech I: How the Big Boys Fix the Mix," *High Fidelity,* July, 1979, p. 73.

[22]I take this information about the 12" 45 from Mary E. Stibal, "Disco—Birth of a New Marketing System," *Journal of Marketing,* October, 1977, p. 86.

[23]I take this information on the marketing of disco from *ibid.,* pp. 82-88.

[24]Quoted in Helgesen, "Disco," p. 21.

[25]See *Forbes,* June 1, 1976, p. 48.

[26]On Jayson and disco franchising, see Kornbluth, "Merchandising Disco for the Masses," p. 22.

Chapter 27:
The Other Side of Disco: Punk

Punk started happening at about the same time as disco, and expressed the same innovative spirit. Punk and disco both came from New York, and they produced the first commercially viable New York groups, the Village People and Blondie. They both promised to satisfy the need for universal stardom, which in fact meant celebrityhood as amateurism. Both styles were commentaries on one of the few truly provocative statements by Andy Warhol: "In the future everyone will be famous for fifteen minutes." Patti Smith paraphrased this as, "This is the era when *everybody* creates."[1] When everybody creates, there are no celebrities, and art is anonymous. Warhol himself said as much, and anticipated the punk celebration of egalitarian creativity when he commented, "I think it would be so great if more people took up silk-screens so that no one would know whether my picture was mine or somebody else's."[2] Substitute "guitars" for "silk-screens" and "music" for "picture," and you have the Sex Pistols' attitude toward rock 'n' roll. If you believed that everybody could be a star, and did your creating behind a microphone, you were into punk. If you believed that everybody could be a star, and did your creating on a dance floor, you were into disco.

Thus, disco and punk complemented each other, which is to say that they used opposite means to achieve the same end. If disco had glitter, punk had shock. If disco often flaunted sexuality, much of punk rock denied sexuality or feeling of any kind. If disco had Studio 54, punk had CBGB's. If disco had roots in black music, especially Motown, punk renounced black music— it was the whitest music ever. (This was the principal reason why you couldn't dance to it.) If disco enjoyed great commercial success, punk did not, by and large. If disco had Mike O'Harro as its principal entrepreneur, punk had his counterpart in a Mid-Atlantic man named Malcolm McLaren who briefly managed the New York Dolls before he returned to London and formed the Sex Pistols.

Like Beatlemania, punk existed in two versions, the American version and the British version. A major difference between them is that punk was genuinely popular in England, whereas it was not in America. Moreover, the punk movement in England was more complicated because it represented genuine social protest on the part of kids with genuine grievances. Yet another major difference had to do with the role of clothing, and that takes us to the origin of punk in the New York Dolls.

Nobody ever said that the New York Dolls were very good musicians, but they had the aggressive self-consciousness which often passes for personality in New York. They dressed in drag, which wasn't so terribly wierd in New York in the early seventies; after all, it was the age of glitter rock, and the Stones had done it in 1968. As Myles Palmer has said, "Just as Jayne Mansfield was a caricature of Marilyn Monroe, and Bette Midler was a caricature of a drag queen, so The New York Dolls were a caricature of the Rolling Stones, and not thought to be important in themselves."[3] We do have trouble taking seriously any group which includes hair and makeup credits on the liner notes of their albums, as the Dolls did. Their derivative relationship with the Stones comes across very clearly on "Looking for a Kiss," for instance; David Johansen must have realized that Mick's posturing and his ironic poses would work very well in the New York gay milieu. The Dolls also covered the fifties novelty song "Stranded in the Jungle," which reminds us that they also learned something about camping it up from another New York group, Sha Na Na. Finally, it's worth noting that in imitating the Stones, the Dolls were doing what the Stooges had done before them.

The New York Dolls played some gigs at the Mercer Arts Center in lower Manhattan, which gives us an important clue to the meaning of American punk. In a way that would make sense only in New York, American punk resembled British art rock in its awareness of high culture. It was because of this awareness that when a guy from Delaware named Tom Miller moved to New York, he changed his name to Tom Verlaine, and became the guitarist/ vocalist for Television. The last time somebody from the provinces took the name of a European poet, it was Bob Dylan, and the anxiety of influence about Dylan—the feeling that if Dylan made it this way I can, too— pervaded New York punk.

Patti Smith especially suffered from the anxiety of influence about Dylan. She adopts a Dylanesque drawl on Van Morrison's "Gloria," and her surrealistic—not to say incoherent—liner notes for *Horses,* the album on which that song appears, obviously imitate the ones which Dylan wrote for *Highway 61 Revisited.* (In covering a song by a major male singer, Smith was doing what other women in rock such as Linda Ronstadt, Rita Coolidge, and Bette Midler were doing in the seventies.) So it's only fitting that on *Wave* she covered the Byrds' "So You Want to be a Rock 'n' Roll Star." She certainly wanted to be a rock 'n' roll star.

Dylan created the persona of the rock 'n' roll star as an artist which Smith presents. She includes a lot of Art on her albums; for instance, *Wave* features a quotation from Jean Genet as an epigraph, and she herself proclaims, on "Rock 'n' Roll Nigger," that "I'm an American artist." If she is an artist, she is a primitive, for her work has a certain undeniable force for all its derivative qualities. Is Patti Smith the Grandma Moses of rock 'n' roll?

Mick Jagger and Dylan loomed large in the consciousness of the New York punks not so much because they lived in New York from time to time but because they are primarily stylists, not vocalists or instrumentalists. Whatever presence is, Mick Jagger and Dylan have it. As a result, it is easy to get attention by exaggerating one feature or another of their performance styles in a quasi-parodistic way, and that the New York punks did.

Smith and Verlaine and the New York Dolls found out what many other American artists have found out, namely that if your Art makes people uncomfortable, people will stay away in droves. It's significant that Smith's only hit, "Because the Night" was written by Bruce Springsteen, and that Blondie broke as a crossover group. But the defenders of punk raise an interesting objection here. Ellen Wills says of her friend, *Village Voice* columnist Bob Christgau, "He argued that people who put down the punk bands as 'fascist' were really objecting to their lack of gentility."[4] So people who found punk offensive or annoying were simply betraying their middle-class origins, and what true rock 'n' roll fan would want to do that? The interesting thing about Christgau's argument is that, like so much else in New York punk, it comes from high culture—specifically the New York art world with which American punk had connections at the Mercer Arts Center, at Andy Warhol's Factory and elsewhere. Fortunately for us, Tom Wolfe has discussed the history of this argument in *The Painted Word.*

In his witty, iconoclastic way Wolfe points out that the success of the style of painting known as abstract expressionism was possible because no more than 10,000 people—*le monde,* as Wolfe calls them—all over the world cared about abstract art in the fifties, and thus "Success was *real* only when it was success within *le monde.*"[5] These people constituted an ingroup which thought of itself as an avant-garde in revolt against middle-class taste. To those people who thought that the paintings of Jackson Pollock, for instance, were ugly, critic Clement Greenberg replied, "All profoundly original art looks ugly at first."[6] Such a principle summed up and fostered the attitude which Wolfe paraphrases in this way, "If a work of art or a new style disturbed you, it was probably good work. If you *hated* it, it was probably great."[7] Such anti-middle class attitudes, which were ultimately anti-art attitudes, culminated in conceptual art. In conceptual art, the idea was the only thing that mattered—the art work did not have to exist at all. In conceptual art, there were no art objects or performances—only mind games.

We can understand New York punk and Christgau's defense of it in this context. Conceptual art and punk were interrelated the way Pop Art and Dylan had been interrelated ten years earlier. The key attitude which conceptual art and punk have in common is their disdain for technique; only if technique is irrelevant does everybody have the chance to be creative. Thus punk sounded like a populist movement, but it used a high-culture rationale for what it was doing, and thus it could dismiss its lack of popularity outside New York. As far as hip New Yorkers were concerned, if people didn't like punk, that meant that they were just revealing their middle-class origins.

In his inimitable way, Wolfe distinguishes two stages in the careers of the abstract expressionists whose careers were made by critics. First came the Boho (from "bohemian") Dance, which meant acceptance by one's peers and by critics. Then came the Consummation, i.e. commercial success, in which critics announced the Next Big Thing to the general public. The decentralizing tendencies of the seventies created an atmosphere in which you could become a star while retaining your anti-middle class attitudes in the Boho Dance. This is in fact what most of the punks did.

There were two exceptions to this generalization about New York punk. One is Blondie, a group who truly lived in squalor and poverty, paid its dues, learned to play, and deserved success when it came. The other is the Ramones, who assimilated the garage-band sound. They have as much of a feel for good-time sound as the Beach Boys do, as anyone who has seen their wonderful movie *Rock 'N' Roll High School* (1979) knows. The title song for that movie, like their clever "Teenage Lobotomy," expresses teenage fantasies and teenage frustrations while maintaining an ironic distance from them. Maybe it's because the Ramones are from unglamorous Queens that they have a genuinely populist quality.

In New York the main thing was presence; if you had that, and looked and acted like a star, you were one—at least for fifteen minutes. Isabelle Anscombe and Dike Blair make a good point when they say that, "American punk has more to do with boredom than with unemployment; it bears a closer allegiance to comic books than politics."[8] Not so in London. In London, the main thing was passion. If the New York punks were dripping in irony, irony was just was London punk lacked. Unlike American punk, British punk expressed real grievances and real suffering. Debby Harry and the other members of Blondie chose to live in poverty; the London punks wanted nothing more than to escape from the grinding poverty of the gray suburbs which oppressed them. Commenting on the hopelessness of this environment, Caroline Coon says, "It's in London's suburbs where the contrast between the promise of a better future and the reality of the impoverished present is most glaringly obvious."[9] So most of them had no choice but to go on the dole, which is British for welfare. Sometimes they even went hungry. It is very moving to read what Joe Strummer of the The Clash said about what the Anarchy in the U.K. tour meant in terms of food: "We were eating Holiday Inn Rubbish, but it was two meals a day. And when I got off the coach we had no money and it was just awful. I felt twice as hungry as I'd ever felt before."[10]

Unlike American punk, British punk represented a development of an earlier working-class movement, the skinheads. The skinheads, who appeared in late sixties and early seventies, adopted a look consisting of heavy boots, pants held up by suspenders, tatoos (even on their foreheads and lips), and very short hair. When they went to Brighton on bank holidays or to football matches in large groups, they created an intimidating effect, which was what they intended. Yet for all their bravado in asserting working-class pride, they were fighting a losing cause; time was definitely not on their side. Nick Knight, a British photographer who did a wonderful photo essay on the skinheads, observes that, "The irony is that the skins in trying to be 'authentic' have ended up reviving an idea of working class culture which is frozen at precisely the point when a 'real', 'authentic' working class identity was being positively eaten away from outside."[11] For all its passion, the skinhead movement never had a chance. Its decline coincided with the decline of a favorite British working-class pastime, football.

In fact, the absence of football as a symbol of class solidarity made the music more important than it had ever been before. Music among the British punks filled the vacuum which football had left. Moreover, they realized that they no longer had to be passive spectators, for rock 'n' roll had always meant self-assertion of one kind of another. In this sense, the key punk song is the Sex Pistols' "No Feelings," especially the line which Johnny Rotten screams over their version of the wall of sound, "I'm in love with myself," What we have here is an assertion, not of a political program, but of the discovery of what Daniel Yankelovich called personal entitlement. The Sex Pistols made a terrific impact because through them their audience discovered that they didn't have to go through their lives saying "sir." It was as though they had discovered the working-class equivalent of black pride, and had realized that they didn't play the equivalent of Uncle Tom to their betters—or to their peers, either. Entertaining can seem like tomming for people whose social identities are precarious, so they came on like entertainers who didn't want to entertain. After seeing them for the first time, Coon noted:

"What impressed me most...was their total disinterest in *pleasing* anybody except themselves. Instead, they engaged the audience, trying to provoke a reaction which forced people to express what they felt about the music. Quite apart from being very funny, their arrogance was a sure indication that they knew what they were doing and why."[12]

Billy Idol neatly expressed punk's discovery of narcissism when he confessed, "I went straight into a band from in front of a mirror where I posed rock 'n' roll style."[13]

The punks called attention to themselves with their clothing as well as with their music. The torn clothing which they wore, like the tattered shirts, the chains wrapped around their bodies, the safety pins in their cheeks, said something of great importance. The provocative clothing of the punks symbolized their position in the rigid British class system, which offered them no future, and very little present worth mentioning. Yet it also had an ambiguity which caught the eye of novelist Alison Lurie. As she says in her book *The Language of Clothes*, "The punk style was a demand for attention, together with a cry of rage against those who should have paid attention to these kids in the past but had not done so." The trouble was, "At the same time, other aspects of the Punk Look appealed not only for attention, but for the love and care that we give to very small children, especially injured ones." Lurie concludes, "It was this double message, as of a viciously angry, miserable baby, that made the Punk Look so deeply disturbing. Most new styles cause only surprise, scornful amusement or admiration; the Punk Look made people in

Britain feel rage, guilt, compassion and fear simultaneously; it was fashion moving toward political protest, possible political action."[15]

Nevertheless, the people who describe British punk as a political style oversimplify the music by neglecting its relationship with the past. "No Feelings" owes a debt to that great earlier anthem of personal entitlement, "Get Off of My Cloud," just as "Get Off of My Cloud" itself owes a debt to "Blue Suede Shoes." Similarly, the infamous "Anarchy in the U.K.," which went to #2 despite being banned, owes a debt to "Paint It Black" as surely as Black Sabbath's "Paranoid" does.

British punk has another relationship to the past as well. In its stress on working-class macho, on personal entitlement, and on the symbolic role of clothing, punk represented a further development of Mod, and thus a further development of the music of the most important Mod group, The Who. The most explicit evidence for this is the song "Generation X," by Billy Idols's band of the same name, which is a reply to "My Generation." The Who had great significance for all of punk, but especially for the Sex Pistols. But that is not to say that the Sex Pistols are derivative from The Who as the New York dolls were derivative from the Stones; they have a more active, more creative relationship with The Who because they *reply* to The Who with passion and creativity of their own.

For all its importance in the sixties, The Who's music had limited themes and used limited melodic devices. To simplify that music even further in the name of populism and anti-elitism is to leave one's self very few possibilities indeed. But if the performers themselves knew only three chords, then they were no "different than anyone," as Dylan once put it. Coon unwittingly paraphrases Andy Warhol very neatly when she writes, "When, for months, you've been feeling that it would take ten years to play as well as Hendrix, Clapton, Richard (insert favorite rock star's name), there's nothing more gratifying than the thought, 'Jesus, I could get a band together and blow this lot off the stage!' "[15] Thus the punks tended to obsolesce the distinction between performer and artist, just as disco did. They did not fully understand what egalitarianism meant, though, for it created an unexpected dilemma. The problem was that they acquired a following with a style whose appeal came at the price of further development. The Sex Pistols had no future in more ways than one.

The story goes that Malcolm McLaren first noticed Johnny Lydon aka Johnny Rotten because his teeth had turned green from neglect. We can think of his failure/refusal to brush his teeth as a form of body art which involved externalizing one's self-hatred as hatred of physicality in general, and/or women in particular. The Pistols were true to their working-class roots in the misogyny which they expressed in "Bodies." Only if you believe that all protest, everywhere, is inherently good can you deny the validity of Ellen Wills' objection to this aspect of punk: "The punk rockers were scarcely defenders of the family, of tradition, but like pseudo- populist politicians they tended to equate championing the common man with promoting the oppression of women."[16]

Wills' comment points up the internal self-contradiction which limited punk as surely as its musical style did. On one hand, its protests would not have taken on such genuine passion if they had not grown out of narrow-minded, sexist working-class attitudes. On the other hand, such passion turned out to be indistinguishable from self-indulgence and self-hatred. Sid Vicious turned out to be just that—vicious. Not heroic, not inspiring, not courageous. Just vicious.

Fortunately, British punk meant more than excitement in a few clubs and big sales in safety pins. British punk produced one of the great bands of the seventies—The Clash. If rock 'n' roll is a universe, The Clash and the Sex Pistols are different planets. Where the Pistols are parochial, The Clash are cosmopolitan. (Three of the four members of The Clash had gone to art school.) Where the Pistols have only one style, The Clash have many. In this respect, they remind a thoughtful listener of no one so much as Led Zeppelin. What Led Zep was to heavy metal, The Clash were to punk. The Clash grew out of punk, with militant songs like "White Riot" on their first album, but they soon transcended their milieu. Of course, some people said that punk died the day The Clash signed with CBS, but we can easily recognize here another version of the purist attitude which denounced Dylan for playing an electric guitar. In Tom Wolfe's terms, true punks feared the genuine popularity of the Consummation.

You can hear three different styles on The Clash's second album, *London Calling*. First, there is the nostalgia style, as in the rockabilly "Brand New Cadillac." (Fifties nostalgia was popular in England in the late seventies, which is why Declan McManus' manager insisted that he take the name Elvis Costello, and why the Stray Cats broke first in England, and then in America.) "Hateful" is reminiscent of Bo Diddley, "Wrong 'Em Boyo" takes off from "Stagger Lee," as "Revolution Rock" takes off from "Stand By Me." Second, there is the jazz style, as in "Jimmy Jazz," a song which Rickie Lee Jones could do justice to. Third, there is the reggae sound of "Rudie Can't Fail."

The Clash's interest in black music led them to reggae, which had the same significance for British musicians in the seventies as the blues had had for British musicians in the sixties. Both styles came from oppressed groups with whom British kids felt an affinity. By the early seventies, reggae had become the favorite music of the skinheads, and The Clash picked up on it.

This heady stylistic mix becomes even more complex on *Sandanista!*, an album which is comparable to *The Wall* and *The River* in the way it brings the seventies to a close. This triple album contains no less than thirty-six songs, and shows The Clash to be a confident, mature group. They are still experimenting with jazz ("Look Here" and "Broadway"), and they have discovered the synthesizer, which they use in a surprisingly melodic way, as on "Up in Heaven (Not Only Here)."

The Clash toured America for the first time in 1979, and the experience profoundly affected *Sandanista!* The title of the first cut, "The Magnificent Seven," comes from an American movie, and other song titles such as

"Washington Bullets" and "Broadway" have American references. "Washington Bullets" lists examples of American militarism, but matches "Washington Bullets" to "Afghan bullets"; The Clash explicitly compare the two superpowers on "Ivan Meets G.I. Joe." If the Beatles' "Bungalow Bill" on the white album deals with the American mystique of violence in a fairy-tale setting, The Clash deal with the same attitude in specific historical settings.

Another American reference of more than passing interest is "Hitsville U.K." Berry Gordy called Motown's first headquarters "Hitsville," and in fact "The Magnificent Seven" owes something to the first song with a social conscience on Motown, Edwin Starr's "War." Moreover, the song "One More Time" asks the question "Can I get a witness?" The fantasy that Hitsville would come to the U.K. so that the boys and girls would not be alone was not an idle one, and was more or less realized when Dave Robinson and Andrew Jakeman formed Stiff Records in July of 1976. While acting as tour manager for Jimi Hendrix in the late sixties, Robinson had been impressed by the vitality of American regional labels, which is how Motown started out, and took them as a model. (The British are usually amazed at the decentralization of American life.) Stiff adopted Motown's marketing philosophy of putting out only those singles which had a good chance of success. The label released about one single every two weeks, and 30 per cent of them charted.[17] Those are excellent numbers for a small British label. In addition, the promotion department at Stiff raised the writing of hype to a fine art, which was no less an achievement than getting all those singles on the charts, if a less profitable one.

Some things don't change in British rock 'n' roll, and one of them is the intense media deprivation which British kids feel because they have no equivalent of Top 40 radio. Thus, The Clash's *London Calling* harks back to *The Who Sell Out* in its interpolation of radio announcements and in its social commentary in the lyrics. The Clash continue the album/radio station analogy on *Sandanista!* when they begin "Lightning Strikes (Not Once But Twice)" with a rap from WABI, a New York reggae station. Just in case somebody missed the point the proper voice of a BBC announcer begins "Version City"— and plays the record at the wrong speed. In addition to "Lightning..", "The Magnificent Seven" and "Version City," use the rap with which The Clash first became familiar in 1979. Since this is The Clash, they don't camp up their use of rap style, as Blondie does on "Rapture," but bring to it their usual sensitivity and inventiveness.

In its ambition, in its stylistic variety, and in the theme of the encounter with America, *Sandanista!* invites comparison with the white album. We hear on both albums the results of the complex attraction/repulsion which British musicians feel for America, and perhaps The Clash included a collage of tape effects, "Mensforth Hill" to remind us of "Revolution 9." Even the possibility of such a comparison suggests that if British punk did nothing but produce The Clash, all the agitation and strange outfits would have been worthwhile.

Notes

[1]Cf the comment by Lester Bangs in his book on Blondie: "I know Deborah's game. She, like Chris, has been to Andy-School, and sometimes I think she may have learned her lessons better than he." Lester Bangs, *Blondie* (New York: Simon and Schuster, 1980), p. 66.

[2]Quoted in Suzi Gablik, *Has Modernism Failed?* (New York: Thames and Hudson, 1984), p. 43.

[3] Myles Palmer, *New Wave Explosion*, p. 17.

[4]Ellen Wills, *Beginning to See the Light* (New York: Wideview Books, 1982), p. 90.

[5]Tom Wolfe, *The Painted Word* (New York: Farrar Straus and Giroux, 1975), p. 18.

[6]Quoted in *ibid.*, p. 52.

[7]*Ibid.*, p. 82.

[8]Isabelle Anscombe and Dike Blair, *Punk!* (New York: Urizen Books, 1978), p. 90.

[9]Caroline Coon, *1988. The New Wave Punk Explosion* (New York: Hawthorn Books, Inc., 1978), p. 70.

[10]Quoted in *ibid.*, p. 4.

[11]Nick Knight, *Skinhead* (London: Omnibus Press, 1982), p. 30.

[12]Coon, *1988*, p. 4.

[13]Quoted in Bruce Dancis, "Safety Pins and Class Struggle: Punk Rock and the Left," *Socialist Review*, Vol. 8, No. 3 (May-June, 1978), p. 73.

[14]Alison Lurie, *The Language of Clothes* (New York: Random House, 1981), p. 163.

[15]Coon, *1988*, p. 14.

[16]Wills, *Beginning to See the Light*, p. 90.

[17]See Bert Muirhead, *Stiff. The Story of A Record Label 1976-1982* (Poole-Dorset: Blandford Press, 1983), p. 6.

Chapter 28:
A Channel of One's Own:
Michael Jackson and MTV

Like 1959 and 1969, 1979 was a year in which death signalled a change in musical style. Almost exactly ten years to the day after Altamont, 11 kids were crushed to death as they tried to get into a Who concert in Cincinnati on December 3, 1979. Although there was great public outcry in Cincinnati, and many lawsuits, no nationwide soul-searching followed these deaths like the nationwide soul-searching which followed Altamont. Yet no less than Altamont, this concert marked a change in attitudes and served as a harbinger of change in popular entertainment. 1979 marked the end of another era of innovation and the beginning of another era of assimilation. This era lasted a little less than the usual five years, giving way by mid-1983 to another era of innovation, the key to which is the simultaneous emergence of MTV and Michael Jackson.

To return to that cold night in Cincinnati in 1979, the problems started with "festival seating," a promoters' euphemism for "no reserved seats." Festival seating means that the kids have to stand outside for hours. In Cincinnati, only two of the many doors to the Coliseum were opened, and the 11 kids who died were literally crushed to death. There's an irony here; they died not from bad drugs or from rioting, but because of the situation. In his book, *Are the Kids All Right?* investigative reporter Jack Fuller shows that no one person was to blame for these deaths, although promoter Larry Magid engaged in sharp practices, and Pete Townshend made some callous statements about the disaster. Fuller gave his book a subtitle, "The Rock Generation and Its Hidden Death Wish," and cites some medical evidence that every rock fan ought to know about. It turns out that listening to hard rock has an immediate effect on the body, and one that's easy to demonstrate. You do it by standing in front of your stereo with one arm held out parallel to the floor. As you play different kinds of music, a friend notices the amount of effort it takes to pull down your arm. Many musical styles actually invigorate the body and make it stronger. Dr. John Diamond, who devised this test, discovered that only one musical style weakens the body, and makes it easier to pull your arm down: hard rock. The heart of rock 'n' roll is the beat, of course, and Dr. Diamond found that the stopped anapestic beat, consisting of two short beats and one long had an especially debilitating effect on the body. It is exactly this beat that gives such force to the music of The Who and the Stones—as in "sat-is-FAK-shun."

Only in one case does the stopped anapestic beat make the body stronger. Put on a hard rock album from the seventies, stand with your arm straight out, and say things like "I hate life and people. I want to be sick. I want to die." Your arm will become stronger. Hard rock, then, greatly reinforces negativity and a death wish, which explains why the Sex Pistols made such a terrific impact. The negativity of Johnny Rotten's lyrics worked together with their wall of sound style to create tremendous energy. As their career showed, it was negative energy, but it was undeniably energy.

The physiological evidence is plain and incontrovertible: Hard rock reinforces negativity and promotes self-destruction. The deaths of Bryan Jones, Janis Joplin, Jimi Hendrix, Jim Morrison, and Keith Moon all suggest as much. Fuller concludes, "Through six weeks of compulsive listening to the hard-rock albums prior to the concert, many of the crowd can arrive for a concert hypercharged emotionally, in a waking trance, and not even aware of it. By the time psychoactive drugs or alcohol or both get working the post-hypnotic state can deepen, and the behavior can become more irrational."[1] What happened, then, at Cincinnati happened because the negativity in the kids' heads caused them to act more irrationally in a difficult and stressful situation than they would have otherwise, and 11 of them died. Despite what The Who said, the kids were not all right, and rock 'n' roll helped to kill them.

It's easy to find other reasons for thinking of 1979 as a year of change; for one thing, it marked the beginning of a recession. A number of promoters lost big money when they put on concerts that summer, and profits declined for both CBS and Warner Brothers.[2] The dollar volume for the industry as a whole declined by 11%.[3] This decline continued in 1982, when one of the top-selling, and most creative albums of the year, John Cougar's *American Fool* sold less than half as many copies as REO Speedwagon's *High Infidelity* from the previous year.[4] As usual, technological and demographic changes were making a difference.

The record companies were suffering from decentralization in the form of private taping; people were taping friends' albums or albums off the air. More important, though, was the major post- *Star Wars* phenomenon in the entertainment industry, video games. Video games were taking millions of dollars that kids would otherwise have spent on records. Entertainment was moving inside, to safe places like arcades in shopping centers.

The kids who were spending money on music were buying fewer and fewer albums; they were going for cassettes. Cassette sales went from 31% to 40% of all units sold between 1981 and 1982. By 1984, cassette shipments increased by 30%, while album and EP shipments dropped by 13%.[5] Cassettes were to albums what 45s had been to albums in the fifties; the sound quality wasn't nearly as good, but cassettes were convenient and portable. Now that more and more cars had tape players, you could listen to tapes while cruising, and it was easy to change tapes while stopped at a red light.

One of the second-generation heavy metal bands, Def Leppard, was primarily a cassette group; when *Pyromania* went platinum, cassettes sold better than albums by a ratio of six to four.[6] The group's appeal to high school and junior high school kids reminds us that in style as well as in name, they are an anagram of Led Zeppelin, and that they are to Led Zeppelin what the Monkees were to the Beatles. It is because they have a younger audience that Def Leppard has done so well in spinoffs like T-shirt sales.[7]

If the kids were spending less money on music, the baby boomers were hardly spending any money on music at all—they had mortgage payments to worry about. The demographic revolution produced by the baby boomers was coming to an end, at least as far as music was concerned; this is the principal social meaning of that flawless movie *The Big Chill*. College enrollments dropped steadily, and the average age of the American population rose as the very last of the baby boomers graduated. More and more of them decided that blue jeans looked grungy, and the sales volume for Levi Strauss jeans levelled off in 1980, and dropped precipitously in 1984.[8]

The baby boomers were buying some cassettes—video cassettes. The boom in sales of VCRs was in large part created by married couples who wanted to watch X-rated video cassettes at home. In the eighties Americans were more and more looking for home entertainment, and that meant television, since television now offered the choices of network, cable, cassette, and games.

It is difficult to exaggerate the importance of television in American life today. Only when a trend, or a person, appears on network television does that trend or that person take on meaning for the country as a whole. Not for nothing do advertisers put labels on their products which say, "As Advertised on TV!" They know that if people have seen it on TV, that makes it real. This capacity of television has obsolesced the much-discussed difference between image and reality.

What goes on network television becomes real in a way that makes debate irrelevant. Recalling the way the assassination of President Kennedy and its aftermath dominated television for days, David Marc writes:

During all of this, the mystique of the U.S. Constitution notwithstanding, television was in charge of the country. The possibilities of coup d'etat or some other radical development of the assassination were controlled by network telecast. The mere fact that Walter Cronkite was narrating the event suggested that no serious damage had been done to the structure of the state. After three days of such programming, TV turned the reigns [sic] of power over to Lyndon Johnson, and *Perry Mason* came back on the air. Television had demonstrated its central position in American culture to a degree that was no casual matter.[9]

Still, the fact remains that Walter Cronkite did not hold elected office, and that fact means that until the election of Ronald Reagan, television and the formal structure of American government remained distinct. And of course, television and government grew sharply hostile to each other during the Nixon years. We didn't have a single President who was really good on television between Kennedy and Reagan. But the election of Ronald Reagan in 1980, and his great victory in 1984, signified a reapproachment between television and government, for the most important thing about Reagan is that he is good on television.

Why is it that Reagan is "The Teflon President"—that none of the many scandals of his administration stick to him? Why is it that Reagan can maintain his extraordinary personal popularity, while polls often show that a majority of Americans disagree with his policies? Why is it that Reagan had no coattails in the 1984 election? I know of no better way to answer these questions than to quote McLuhan again: "The medium is the message."

The content of what Reagan says—his "stands on the issues," as the political cliche has it—has minimal importance in comparison to the fact that he is good on television. In fact, being good on television is now the most important function of any President. After the horrors which we saw on the news in the sixties, after the Watergate hearings, and after the televised nightmares of the Iranian hostage crisis, Americans needed a reassuring presence on television. And they got one in the person of Ronald Reagan. He satisfied the needs of an enormous audience; he succeeded where Nixon failed. As for leadership, he hardly needs to exercise its substance, because he is so good on television. What conservative philosophy he has is hardly more than an actor's sense of what the audience needs. What his audience, i.e., the electorate, needs is a head of government who reigns but who does not rule and thereby affirms his commitment to decentralization. Or, as John Naisbitt has said, "Ronald Reagan is riding the horse in the direction the horse is going."[10]

Many young voters voted for Reagan in 1984 because he was good on television, and they could not imagine a world without television. Only what is on television is real to them, and that brings us to MTV and Michael Jackson. The coming together of rock 'n' roll and television brings to a close a 30 year cycle during which they were separated even more than television and government were opposed to each other.

It is now generally accepted that MTV helped to produce a megastar, Michael Jackson. Just as the separation of music programming from television helped to produce Elvis Presley in the fifties, so now the merger of music programming and television has helped to produce Michael Jackson. Like Bing, Frank, and Elvis, Michael has experienced what may be called Liftoff. Liftoff is popularity which goes off all the usual scales and becomes an obsession. The Beatles experienced Liftoff, and perhaps the Supremes did, but no singles act between Elvis and Michael did. Dylan didn't in the sixties, and David Bowie and Bruce Springsteen didn't in the seventies. Now that *Thriller* has sold more than 30 million units worldwide, we are beginning to understand that The Michael Jackson Liftoff has far-reaching implications.

When Liftoff occurs, it is related to the appearance of a new ethnic group in entertainment, and/or to technological change. In the case of Michael Jackson and MTV, it is related to the new use of a previously existing medium. Just as AM radio had existed for a long time before Top 40 appeared, so television had existed for a long time before MTV appeared. And when MTV did appear, it was as an extension of advertising. In the seventies, disco showed executives that it was possible to break groups without airplay on radio; this practice continued in the use of video promo clips in clubs around the country. In fact, various groups such as the Stones had been making video promos for some time, and some old videos from the sixties show up on MTV from time to time as "Closet Classics." If the sixties obsolesced the distinction between high culture and popular culture, the eighties have obsolesced the distinction between commercials and entertainment. To mention just one example, Southside Johnny's commercial for Miller beer is much more enjoyable than many supposedly non-commercial videos.

Not surprisingly, MTV resulted from a great deal of marketing research by Warner-Amex Satellite Entertainment Corporation, the parent organization of MTV. MTV first appeared on August 1, 1981. At first, it had limited distribution to only about 4 million viewers. Still, it was helping to break Duran Duran and Culture Club in out-of-the-way places like Tulsa. MTV's big move came over a year later on September 1, 1982, when MTV came to New York and LA, where decisions are made in the entertainment industry. Then came *Thriller*, and the rest is history.

The addition of sight to sound on MTV has changed many things, but it has not done away with hype. Hype is thriving in the bands of the eighties, the kind that college radio stations play. Two examples must suffice here. Haircut 100's Nick Heyward once said, "A pop band at the moment is really about small things, like socks and vests and nice hair and the way the singer's eyebrows are shaped." Spandau Ballet's Gary Kemp topped that one by saying, "In fact, the music is irrelevant. The people in our clubs are more important."[11] In fact, the music is not irrelevant at all, but something *is* happening here, as the final tetrad chart shows.

MTV

Enhances:	Obsolesces:	Retrieves:	Reverses Into:
Visual Qualities	Music Only Formats	Narrative	Video Cassettes

The remainder of this chapter will work through the implications of this table.

The most obvious thing to do in music video is to show the performers in a concert setting, so a lot of directors have done just that. Sometimes the concert setting is real, and sometimes it is faked with varying degrees of success: Van Halen's "Jump" works well, but Bruce Springsteen's "Dancing in the Dark" works less well. Another possibility is to create a pure stylistic exercise, a succession of striking visual images, none of which lead anywhere. This is what Russell Mulcahy did for Stevie Nicks in the "Gypsy" video.

Another possibility is to take the album cut and add to it a narrative which is not present in the music alone. Two of the most effective examples are "Come Dancing," by the Kinks, and "Sharp Dressed Man," by ZZ Top. In both cases the video tells a story which is not present in the lyrics to the song. The video for "Come Dancing" is set in a provincial dance hall, no doubt very much like the ones in which the Kinks started out. The video tells the story, entirely without words, of a fortyish man (played by Ray Davies) who looks out of place and who falls for the hat check girl. The band plays a more active role on "Sharp Dressed Man," when ZZ Top intercedes for a kid up puts on his tuxedo but who can't get into the dance. The distinctive red coupe which has appeared on other ZZ Top videos pulls up, though, and out come three phenomenally sexy girls who take our hero in tow.

In "Sharp Dressed Man" and "Legs," director Tim Newman has created for ZZ Top something unique: A series of trademarks for the group which serve as the identification and structure for any number of three or four-minute sitcoms. Newman gave the group a collective Robin Hood persona; the performers don't *do* anything but stand to the side and make a golf swing motion like Johnny Carson's, and dangle a ZZ Top key chain. A kid gets into distress of one kind of another, and when the distinctive cherry red coupe appears, we know that salvation is on the way. These videos are thematically and visually satisfying, and represent brilliant solutions to the problem of what to do with performers who don't move well.

Marshall McLuhan once said that the content of any medium is another medium, and although we now understand that this is not exactly a universal truth, it often applies to rock videos. We can say that the content of many rock videos is a movie, which provides a visual structure absent in the music. The following table gives some indication as to how this works.

Act	Video	Movie Source/Reference
The Rolling Stones	"Under Cover of the Night"	*Missing* (1982)
Billy Joel	"Pressure"	*Poltergeist* (1982)
David Bowie	"Let's Dance"	*Un Chien Andalou* (1928)
Duran Duran	"Hungry Like the Wolf"	*Raiders of the Lost Ark* (1981)
The Ramones	"Psychotherapy"	*Alien* (1979)

Even this brief and incomplete table suggests that horror and adventure movies often supply the visual content for rock videos, and it's easy to understand why. These are the movies which have the most dramatic and arresting images. Inevitably, movie history has great significance for rock videos.

This is where Michael Jackson comes in. His justly famous "Thriller" video is an homage to horror movies, and at one point he sketches a movie screen in the air with his fingers to make sure that his date gets the point. Similarly, the choreographic style for "Beat It" consciously derives from *West Side Story* (1961). But the video integrates movie history with the performance on the TV screen; it doesn't just add a visual track to an audio track. It's an essential part of Michael's appeal that he seems to have gotten it all together.

Just think of what he does dramatically in "Beat It" and "Thriller." "Beat It" begins with a shot of him lying on the bed in his room, singing. But he soon rushes out, and separates the gangs who are about to rumble. Although he dances with them, he is not one of them. He is both with them, and not with them. Very much the same thing happens on "Thriller." If "Beat It" derives from *West Side Story*, then "Thriller" derives, less directly perhaps, from that classic thriller *Dr. Jekyll and Mr. Hyde*, in the Victor Fleming version from 1941 which starred Spencer Tracy and Ingrid Bergman. In the video sometimes Michael is the good guy out on a date with his girl, and is just as threatened as she is when the monsters encircle them. But sometimes he is one of the monsters. In this, his Mr. Hyde role, he has those green cat eyes in, his jacket is torn, and his carefully coiffed hair is mussed. In both of these major videos, then, he both belongs and doesn't belong.

Like the myth of Frankenstein and his creator which preceded it, the myth of Dr. Jekyll and Mr. Hyde creates a dramatic image for the schizophrenia of the modern world. We are, and have been, fascinated by split personalities because they speak deeply to the split which we sense within ourselves. Michael's capacity to combine these oppositions within a single persona thus has great appeal, for we think that if he can do it, so can we.

Although he lives at home, and is part of a large family, Michael is essentially alone. Although he sings *about* Billie Jean, he does not sing *to* Billie Jean. And we know what happens to his date on "Thriller." The success of Michael's persona as someone alone could happen only in the age of movies like *Flashdance* (1983), which celebrate the self for its own sake. In turn, *Flashdance* came after such major movies of the seventies as *Annie Hall* (1977) and *The Electric Cowboy* (1979), in which a boy and girl meet, fall in love, and then go their separate ways. To understand how radical a change Michael's isolation represents in a musical context, we need to take note of Jane Feuer's observation in *The Hollywood Musical* that music, dancing, and love were inseparable in the classic Hollywood musical of the thirties and forties. In such movies as *Dames* (1933) a boy and a girl meet, fall in love, and put on a show. The showbiz setting provided an obvious justification for the musical numbers, and as a result, "The triumph of couple and show that dominated the classical period was so much taken for granted that by the early 1950s, the most ordinary Hollywood musical assumed the dualism automatically."[12] Like so much else in the fifties, though, this dualism of couple and show changed after Elvis made it big. Elvis' movies such as *Loving You* (1957) and *Jailhouse Rock* (1957) celebrate the self and stardom, not love and music. This trend continues through the Beatles' movies, which are notable for their absence of love interest, and reaches a certain culmination in *The Rose* (1979). Rock stardom is so intense and so exclusive that it cannot sustain a relationship. Hence, Michael can successfully represent aloneness. Moreover, his aloneness clarifies the way his persona combines four oppositions of personal attributes.

I. Child/Man

The Bible says, "When I became a man, I put away childish things." But the days when we could so clearly define our identities has passed. After all, the refrain of "My Generation" is, "Hope I die before I get old," and Dylan wished that we might stay forever young. Michael has the promise of doing just that. It is part of Michael's continuity with the sixties, and especially with the Beatles, that there are elements in him of both the Child and the Man.

He is a man in that he is phenomenally rich, and has impressive musical achievements, even if Quincy Jones did give him a lot of help with *Thriller*. He is brave and forceful, unafraid to dash into the thick of the fray in the video for "Beat It." Michael Jackson is not a wimp. But he is not a mature man, either, and he often acts out his role as a Child in his public appearances. When he accepted his umpteenth Grammy for narrating the record version of *E.T.* (1982), he said, no doubt sincerely, that it was the one that meant the most to him. And at both the Grammys and the earlier American Music Awards, he sat with Emmanuel Lewis, the diminutive child star of *Webster*. As for Michael's future, one hears that Stephen Spielberg may direct him in a new version of *Peter Pan*.

One episode from the video for "Say Say Say," which he made with Paul McCartney, plays up Michael's role as a Child. After the Mac and Jac show has arrived at the hotel, Paul is shaving, and Michael playfully dabs a bit of shaving lather on his cheek, although he obviously doesn't need to shave. It is something boys do as they imitate their fathers, and this gesture marks the distinction between Michael's roles as a Child and as a Man. Indeed, Paul and Linda seem to act as Michael's parents in the video.

In "Say Say Say," as in the other videos, Michael both belongs, and doesn't belong. As part of the con he leaves the show wagon to mingle with the crowd. Then he takes a sip of the Paul's patent medicine, and turns into a he-man (another play on the Child/Man opposition). He later joins Paul on stage, and they dash off together after the show. As Michael hops on to the wagon, a girl hands him a bouquet of flowers, thus reversing the famous and much-discussed scene at the end of Chaplin's *City Lights* (1931), where Charlie hands the girl a bouquet. This reference to *City Lights* is not an idle one, for Michael himself has said that he idolizes Chaplin. The hat and cane which Michael used with such aplomb on the Motown 25th Anniversary Show came from the Little Tramp.

When you think about it, it's obvious. Michael has Chaplin's consummate physical grace, and his ease with himself. But it is part of the Tramp's melancholy that he is always alone, that he walks off down the road with his slouch turning into a swagger even though he has failed to get the girl yet again. One cannot separate the Tramp's innocence from Chaplin's sexless film persona. Whatever Chaplin's off-screen behavior may have been, on screen he is the most sexless of all our major stars. Like the Tramp, Michael is immensely attractive, but still sexless.

While he was still legally a child, Michael appeared in *The Wiz* (1978), Motown's remake of the Judy Garland classic *The Wizard of Oz* (1939). Like Michael, Judy Garland became a star as a child, and the Child constituted a significant part of her persona. The trouble was, her persona did not allow for growth, and her career in the fifties was often a lament for lost innocence. I mention Judy Garland here because her self-destructive personality anticipated the self-destructive personalities of rock stars. This similarity may explain the reappearance of her *A Star Is Born* which came out at the very beginning of the rock era in 1954, in a rock version starring Barbra Streisand and Kris Kristofferson (1976)

Judy's fate may await Michael. Unless he becomes more of a Man, and less of a Child, his ability to perform will suffer, and at forty he could find himself singing "Billie Jean" as a lament.

II. Man/Woman

This second opposition in Michael's persona does not so much contradict the first one as complement it. You first sense the feminine quality in his sexuality when you watch him lead the gang in the "Beat It" video in a series of aggressive bumps and grinds. Then, after doing this classic stripper's move, he...flashes the audience. There's no other way to describe it. He turns to face the camera, and whips open the sides of his unbuttoned jacket, only to close them again. Then, too, there's a suggestion of traditional stereotypes of feminine sexuality in the cover photo for *Thriller*, where Michael sprawls langorously before us in his white suit with a couple of curls artfully arranged across his forehead. And let's not forget that Michael is the first rock star in history who had a nose job.

Once we realize that Michael is as much Woman as Man we start to understand why he has "Come along at the right time." The obvious examples here come from movies: Julie Andrews as a woman pretending to be a man pretending to be a woman in *Victor/Victoria* (1982), and Dustin Hoffman as a woman in *Tootsie* (1983). If your taste runs to lightweight farce, there's Michael Keaton in *Mr. Mom.* (1983) And with the bizarre Grace Jones, the decadent Alice Cooper, and the ever lovable Boy George on display at the 1984 Grammy show, there was sexual ambiguity all over.

The point is that for some time now movies, and popular culture in general, have been dealing with the ambiguities of our sex roles in this day of house husbands and magazines which advertise maternity clothes for the professional working woman. Yet Michael's androgyny enables him to avoid the whole problem.

This androgyny of Michael's is not new, even among rock stars. David Bowie was probably the first major rock star with an androgynous persona, but Mick Jagger also prances to mind as someone who learned to dance by watching Tina Turner, and who preens himself like a caricature of a woman onstage. Mick even poses as a cheap hooker on "Tattered": "I can't give it away on Seventh Avenue." And before Mick, and the picture of The Stones in drag, there was Elvis. Specifically, there was Andy Warhol's *Elvis*, which turns him into such a pretty boy that he comes across as feminine, even if he is holding a six-gun in each hand.

So Michael's androgyny represents a culmination of the ambiguity which previous superstars have hinted at; but now that ambiguity finds a resonance in a much larger audience. If the opposition Child/Man enlarges Michael's audience to include children, the opposition Man/Woman enlarges it to include teeny-boppers. Girls between the ages of 10 and 14 are starting to discover boys, but they're still uncertain about the whole thing, so they like stars who are a little like themselves, a little feminine. They definitely do not want an idol who is a macho man. In the late seventies, this section of the market was putting pictures of Shaun Cassidy and Scot Baio on its walls; by 1984, it was Michael Jackson.

III. Good/Evil

But Michael is not a performer with limited appeal, like Shaun Cassidy, and he is not a sitcom star like Scott Baio. What keeps him from coming on like a wimp is the suggestion of evil in his persona. The suggestion of evil balances the goodness of his Child image, and of his role as a peacemaker in the "Beat It" video.

At both the American Music and the Grammy awards, Michael wore tuxedo pants, a sequined red tunic, dark glasses—and a single black glove on his right hand. He wore a single white glove on his right hand in his video for "Billie Jean," thereby starting a fad at junior high schools all over the country. So what is going on here? Is this self-indulgence, like the way Jon Voigt appeared on the Academy Awards show without a tie a few years ago? No, Michael's carefully created costume had both a source and a definite function.   That single black glove comes from *Star Trek II. The Wrath of Khan* (1982). In that movie, the bad guy out to get Admiral Kirk and all the other good guys is Khan, who leads a band of hippies in his quest for galactic revenge. Ricardo Montalban plays Khan as a loon, and to show just how loony he is, he wears a single black glove on his right hand. This eccentricity nicely conveys to us that Khan is unbalanced. Most people didn't notice how Montalban created that effect, but Michael did. Yet when Michael wears a single black glove, it creates balance, not imbalance, because of the implicit goodness in the Child part of his persona. As Paul McCartney once said in an interview shown on MTV, "Nice fella, Michael; talented, too." That image as a nice fella, as a mere Child, could stifle Michael as it stifled Judy Garland. He seems to have some awareness of this danger, and so is creating room for growth in his persona.

Surely some such consideration explains his dual role as a good guy and as a bad guy in the "Thriller" video. After Michael alternates between retreating from the monsters, and dancing with them, an alternation signalled by appropriate changes in his clothing and appearance, the video builds to a climax when the girls retreats to a house. In a time-honored tradition, she finds no safety there because the monsters start breaking through the windows and even the floor. Then the evil Michael bursts through the door. We get a shot from Michael's point of view as the girls retreats to the couch, becoming more and more panicky as the tempo of the music gets faster and faster until.... We get a shot from her point of view of Michael as a good guy, without the cat eyes and tattered jacket. "Whew," we sigh, "It was all a dream." Michael seems to confirm this when he puts his arm around the girl, and says, "Let's go home." And just as we are relaxing at the thought that we were right about Michael all along, he turns to us—and he has those cat eyes in again.

So we *were* wrong about Michael; we were limiting him by dismissing him as sweet and harmless. That delicately featured face and sweet voice conceal, and occasionally reveal, a demonic quality which is not illusory but inherent in him. That is to say that by helping us to recognize a demonic quality in him, he is also recognizing that quality in ourselves.

Yet danger lurks for Michael here, too, and it comes from his church, the Jehovah's Witnesses. Just as Donny and Marie Osmond's Mormon beliefs have limited their careers, so Michael's beliefs as a Jehovah's Witness may limit his. Not many people know that in May of 1984, an article carrying Michael's name appeared in the magazine of the Jehovah's Witnesses, *Awake!* The author of this article renounced the "Thriller" video, saying, "I realize now that it was not a good idea." Jehovah's Witnesses do not believe in demons, and thus this statement is consistent with official doctrine. The problem, of course, is whether Michael actually wrote the article, or whether someone wrote it for him. Reporters have had no success in finding out the truth. Whatever the truth, the fact remains that the puritanism of the Jehovah's Witnesses runs counter to the age of licence in which we live, and Michael is eventually going to have to come to terms with this contradiction.[13]

IV. Singer/Dancer

In the lyrics to "Billie Jean," Michael quotes Mama's advice that he shouldn't "go breaking young girls' hearts." This line gives us a clue to the importance of Michael's Motown heritage, because it sounds so much like the advice which Mama gives the young lover in the first Major Motown hit, the Miracles' "Shop Around." The Motown tradition has proven crucial for him in other ways as well. For one thing, there's the role that Diana Ross has played as Mother to Michael's Child. For another, there's the Motown tradition of dancing as a visual accompaniment to singing. From the very beginning, Berry Gordy put his performers into sweat shops and trained them with an eye to television appearances. But the black and white tapes of the Temptations and the Miracles that you sometimes see on nostalgia shows look very dated. The trouble is, the performers' neatly synchronized movements nowadays make them look more like marionettes than anything else. Motown performers have little of the flash and fervor which the best black singer/dancers like James Brown and Tina Turner have shown. Michael has flash and fervor to burn, though. Another way of saying that Michael "came along at the right time" is to say that his combination of talents as both a singer and a dancer makes him very well suited for MTV. Michael is the first superstar about whom we can make such a statement, and in turn that means that rock videos are heir to the legacy of Hollywood musicals in terms of style.

Sammy Davis, Jr, once said in an interview that he saw something of Fred Astaire in Michael's dancing, especially in his turns. This link between Michael and the king of the Hollywood musical hints at the way Michael is of his time while transcending it as well. What Michael does, and the way he does it, relates to an opposition in film styles familiar to every film student— the opposition between the montage style of Sergei Eisenstein and the invisible editing whose best-known proponent was Andre Bazin. Before we can understand Michael's role in the history of visual music, a brief digression is therefore necessary.

Bazin wrote primarily about the films of Jean Renoir and Orson Welles, emphasizing their long takes and unobtrusive cuts. Although he probably didn't realize it, his ideas apply equally well to the musicals of Fred Astaire and Ginger Rogers. Many of their dance numbers, for instance, are done all in one take of seven to ten minutes. Such long takes require the consummate professionalism which Fred and Ginger always had; they allow the dance numbers to develop, and they also allow the inevitable romance to develop as well.

When the Southern tradition began to replace the New York-Hollywood tradition in the fifties, the film-making style began to change, too. Critic Dave Kehr has stated the problem very well: "The limited emotional range of high-energy rock makes it difficult to express feelings that fall short of absolute ecstasy or inflamed passion; there are few halftones in the music, which means that virtually every number must be a climax. And when a narrative is composed only of climaxes, it can't function. There's no room for the buildup of feelings, no room for dramatic translations."[14] Kehr makes the point that these features of rock 'n' roll made for problems when Richard Lester was planning *A Hard Day's Night*: "He had to make a musical with four lead performers who couldn't dance, and his montage—with its rhythm, energy, and exuberant effects—gave a sense of dance movement to a musical that otherwise would have been without one.[15] That is to say, Lester reached back over Vincente Minelli and Busby Berkeley to Eisenstein's theories of montage, which emphasized quick cuts and unusual camera angles. Since Eisenstein himself created the film in the editing room, he could, and did, use amateur actors. His style, then, amounted to a democratization of filmmaking. Among other things, the rock revolution represented democratization as well, so Lester was able to make a brilliant film with the Fab Four by adapting montage, and montage rapidly became assimilated into the style of the sixties.

Since Eisenstein's startling cuts and camera angles demand attention, they lend themselves readily to advertising. (In fact, his greatest legacy is probably in television advertising.) Not coincidentally at all, most of the directors of rock videos went from film school, where they studied Eisenstein's films, to directing commercials, where they applied Eisenstein's style, to directing rock videos, where they developed that style even further. Their problems resembled Lester's in that they were working with performers who couldn't dance or act, so they made a virtue of necessity; they drew on Eisenstein's distinctive and readily identifiable style. But what they didn't acquire was Eisenstein's insistence on discipline, and the resulting coherence in the montage of his shots. So directors often shot videos like Eisensteins gone crazy with a zoom lens, cutting more or less at random from a close-up of a cymbal to a close-up of a guitar to the close-up of the lead singer's sweaty face.

To return finally to Michael, what is unusual about his videos is that their visual style offers a marked contrast to most of what we see on MTV. First of all, the director has no problem integrating the performer into the video since the performer is a consummate dancer. Both "Beat It" and "Thriller" tell a story which develops tensions and builds to a climax. For these reasons, the director has no need for the usual montage style of rock videos. Rather, Michael's videos have generally invisible editing with few quick cuts and predictable camera angles. It makes no sense to photograph an extraordinary dancer fronting wonderful ensemble work in such a way that we can't appreciate what's going on, and Bob Giraldi was smart enough not to do that.

Appropriately, then, "Thriller" is a self-contained work which tells a story by confronting two different genres—the horror movie and the musical. It is not concert footage jazzed up with tricky camera angles, and it is not a video in which the musicians create a backdrop, however effective, for the narrative. Since Michael sings his own song and dances to his own music, he had complete involvement in it. It is this completeness that makes the video so satisfying, for his multiple talents as both singer and dancer solve the problem of what to do with the video portion of MTV.

Michael is thus the complete performer of the eighties. Eventually the standards which he is setting for this new contemporary art form are going to make people get tired of watching singers jump around on stage or cavort in odd settings. They will want the integration of songwriting, singing, and dancing which—so far—only Michael can bring off.

And what of the future? No doubt MTV and the distinctive MTV style will continue for some time to come, just as Top 40 did in the fifties. But styles change rapidly in the latter years of the twentieth century, and it is already possible to imagine that MTV will reverse into video cassettes with complete narratives, just as the three-minute single reversed into the concept album in the sixties. Julian Temple, director of the Kinks' "Come Dancing," among other videos, once made this comment: "For rock video to progress, it'll have to get to where the movie musicals of the forties were, when directors and composers worked together to create a vital third entity from the music and visuals. It'll have to become more of a two-way street between directors and musicians."[16]

In 1984, there were straws in the wind that rock was being assimilated into narrative contexts of various kinds. Linda Ronstadt was singing Puccini, Roger Daltrey was doing Shakespeare, and Sting had an acting role in *Dune* (1984). More and more, people were thinking of records as soundtracks—Prince's *Purple Rain* is the most obvious example. Two or three sound-tracks were released each week, and some fourteen of them went platinum. Most indicatively of all, each of the five songs nominated for an Academy Award had gone to #1 on the pop charts. This had never happened before.

In 1984, MTV was affecting not just commercials and movies, but even prime time network shows. *Simon and Simon*, as well as *Knight Rider*, have occasionally used rock songs, but the show which most successfully integrates music and narrative is *Miami Vice*. The director of *Miami Vice*, Michael Mann, has said that his show and MTV are "first cousins." Journalist Emily Benedek writes that, "Their common ancestor, according to Mann, is the concept of sound as counterpoint to visual images that was formulated by the revolutionary Soviet filmmaker Sergei Eisenstein in the late 1930s."[17] And of course it was *Miami Vice* that used ex-Eagle Glenn Frey's song "Smuggler's Blues" as the basis for an episode, with Frey himself playing the role of the smuggler. In this prime example of the integration of rock into narrative structures, the show used the song not while the credits rolled, but as counterpoint to, and commentary on, the action. So "Smuggler's Blues" became something like a Wagnerian leitmotif, just as Jan Hammer's incidental music for the show often does.

It seems unlikely that at any time in the immediate future MTV will program the longer works which the integration of rock into narrative structures promises. This situation raises the possibility that acts will make their own full-length video cassettes with their own music, acting, and special effects. One obvious advantage which these cassettes would offer is the absence of the censorship which MTV's mass audience imposes; on full-length cassettes the acts would be free to deal with the sex and violence which have informed so much great rock 'n' roll.

Thus, MTV is yet another of the innovative uses of technology which has led to innovations in music, and in popular culture in general. Technology is not, and never has been, a neutral, passive ground for the personalities of the performers. On the contrary, it names the game which the performers play—and we get to enjoy the game.

Notes

[1] Jack Fuller, *Are the Kids All Right?* (New York: Times Books, 1981). p. 240.

[2] See "A Crack in the Record," *Forbes,* September 3, 1979, p. 14.

[3] *Time,* February 15, 1982, p. 37.

[4] See Al Clark, ed *The Rock Yearbook 1984* (n.p.: Virgin Books Ltd., 1983), p. 10.

[5] Debby Miller, "Cassettes Outsell LPs in So-So Year," *Rolling Stone,* July 5, 1984, p. 41.

[6] Jeffrey Peisch, "Cassettes Now Outselling LPs," *Rolling Stone,* November 24, 1983, p. 59.

[7] See Patricia Bates, "Def Leppard at head of pack in touring and T-shirt jungle," *Amusement Business,* September 3, 1983, p.4.

[8] I take this information from Nancy Yoshihara, "Faded Glorias," *Columbia Tribune,* August 26, 1984, p. 63.

[9] David Marc, *Demographic Vistas,* p. 134.

[10] John Naisbitt, *Megatrends,* p. 109.

[11] Quoted in Stuart Coupe and Glenn A. Baker, *The New Rock 'N' Roll* (New York: St. Martin's Press, 1984), p. 6 and p. 7.

[12] Jane Feuer, *The Hollywood Musical* (Bloomington: Indiana U. Press, 1982), p. 89.

[13] See Ari L. Goldman, "Modern Culture Tests Faith of Jehovah's Witnesses," *New York Times,* August 29, 1984, p. C15.

[14] Dave Kehr, "Can't Stop the Musical," *American Film,* May, 1984, p. 36.

[15] *Ibid.*

[16] Quoted in Michael Shore, *The Rolling Stone Book of Rock Video* (New York: Rolling Stone Press, 1984), pp. 121-122.

[17] Emily Benedek, "Inside Miami Vice," *Rolling Stone,* March 28, 1985, p. 85.

CODA

During the period 1954-1984, the media made rock 'n' roll into an international language. This was a period of great technological change, and therefore was a period of great stylistic and cultural change as well. In the fifties, the wild-eyed Southern boys burst into national consciousness on 45 rpm records, and then the brilliant British rockers made the transition from 45s to 33 1/3 albums. By the seventies, rockers had the audacity to compete with television. Decentralization and historical consciousness played off against each other to create remarkable and often confusing stylistic diversity. MTV brought this era to a close by obsolescing the music only formats which had created rock 'n' roll in the first place. Throughout this period the Southern tradition with its complex mixture of mostly black but also white music provided rich and seemingly inexhaustible inspiration for musicians of different backgrounds. The religious and hedonistic elements of the Southern tradition have helped to bring about what now seem like permanent changes in American consciousness.

In very general terms, these are some of the most important features of thirty years of rock, 1954-1984. But, as I have insisted all along, rock didn't come from nowhere, and didn't even come exclusively from the Mississippi delta—it was inherently and inevitably related to the history of American popular music in general. Since this is the case, the clarification of what rock 'n' roll was should help us to understand other eras of American popular music as well. The analogy which comes to mind is Freud's concept of the analyst as archaeologist; once one layer of the past has been cleared away, a second one appears.

A new era in American popular music began with the Jazz Age, which may be said to have gotten underway in 1924. On the evening of February 12 of that year, a distinguished audience gathered at Aeolian Hall in New York. Musicians as different as John Phillip Sousa and Igor Stravinsky had come to hear the Paul Whiteman Orchestra, attracted by the scheduled premiere of a new work by an up and coming composer—George Gershwin's "Rhapsody in Blue." As Gershwin's biographer David Ewen has said of the audience that cold night, such notables "Rubbed elbows with song writers, song pluggers, vaudevillians, stars of musical comedy, and the rank and file of jazz devotees in what surely must have been the most polyglot audience to attend a concert in Aeolian Hall."[1] The diversity of the principal work of the evening matched the diversity of the audience. One Hugh C. Ernst explained in an introductory address that, "Mr. Whiteman intends to point out, with the assistance of his orchestra and associates, the tremendous strides which have been made in

331

popular music from the day of discordant Jazz, which sprang into existence about ten years ago from nowhere in particular, to the really melodious music of today."[2] Ernst's stilted diction reveals both what was going on, and how uncomfortable people were with it. Jazz didn't come "from nowhere in particular"; it came from New Orleans, and black musicians brought it up the Mississippi to Chicago, and then to New York. Moreover, for people like Ernst, the only real music was the smooth, melodic music of composers like Victor Herbert, and jazz was acceptable only insofar as it could be made melodic. As one reviewer of "Rhapsody in Blue" said condescendingly, "Mr. Gerschwin will bear watching; he may yet bring jazz out of the kitchen."[3]

Something very important began with "Rhapsody in Blue"—the interplay of the Southern tradition with the New York-Hollywood tradition. Of course, it is not enough to say that Gershwin adapted jazz forms into a rhapsody. What matters for the history of American popular music is that the mass audience *liked* the results, for Paul Whiteman's recording of "Rhapsody in Blue" went platinum, which was an extraordinary sale at the time. If we think not in terms of raw numbers but in terms of market penetration, the sales of "Rhapsody in Blue" in the twenties were the equivalent of the sales of *Thriller* in the eighties.

Gershwin once said that no matter how much time he spent with the rich and famous, he had "something of the tenement" about him. He thus represents the enduring source of creativity in American popular music, its impurity. The impurity of his work reached a culmination in his masterpiece *Porgy and Bess* (1935), which combines black spirituals and vernacular music with operatic forms.

Gershwin was not the only great Tin Pan Alley composer who mixed the Southern tradition with the Hollywood tradition, for we find something similar in the work of Jerome Kern. The American musical theater came of age with Kern's *Showboat* (1927), which incorporates elements of Southern music in some of its great hits. "Can't Help Lovin' Dat Man," for instance, is marked "Tempo di blues," and has unusual blues harmonies.[4] After the black members of the cast heard "Ol' Man River," sung by Paul Robeson for the first time, they repeatedly assured Kern that it was a folk song they had heard as children! As this incident suggests, for the great songwriters of the day, it was not just a matter of whites exploiting black creativity—although there was plenty of that—but also a matter of gifted whites responding sensitively to black creativity and assimilating it for themselves. As one more instance of the cooperation of blacks and whites in this show, it's worth mentioning that a black man named Will Vodery did the vocal arrangements.

In addition to the premiere of "Rhapsody in Blue," another very important event in the history of American music occurred in 1924. In September of that year Louis Armstrong came to New York to play with Fletcher Henderson at the Roseland Ballroom. The big city blacks snickered a little at Louis because he looked like a hick, but they stopped snickering as soon as he started to play. As a matter of fact, his impact on black musicians was simply overwhelming—the story goes that a number of them were so stunned at hearing this authentic American genius for the first time that they couldn't eat or sleep for several days.

Louis' arrival in New York has exceptional importance not just because he was a phenomenal virtuoso. Louis brought authentic New Orleans jazz, and authentic blues, to New York at a time when hardly anyone, black *or* white, knew what the authentic article sounded like. Louis' biographer James Collier makes the point that no matter how gifted such major figures in jazz history as Duke Ellington and Fletcher Henderson were, they did not come from the South, and had grown up in middle-class families with middle-class values. "They had little firsthand experience with the music of the sanctified church and none whatsoever with the work song or the blues that grew out of it. It is important to keep clearly in mind that jazz was not endemic to American black culture as a whole but was produced in New Orleans and spread from there. Northern blacks had to learn about it the same way whites did."[4] As a result, "It was [Sidney] Bechet and Bubber Miley in the Ellington band, Armstrong in the Henderson band, who taught the Eastern blacks what jazz was."[5] However, if men like Ellington and Henderson didn't know what jazz was, they knew a great deal about classical music, about which Louis knew nothing, of course, and they proved to be remarkable synthesizers of these disparate traditions and styles. All of this only goes to show yet again the importance of impurity in the history of American popular music.

George Gershwin and Louis Armstrong; a Jew from New York, the son of a Russian immigrant; and a black from New Orleans raised mostly by his grandmother, a former slave. Gershwin went South, to South Carolina, when he was working on *Porgy and Bess;* Armstrong went north, first to Chicago, and then to New York, to make his fame and fortune. Their careers represent the way immigrants played off against each other the various strands of American music which had generally remained separate before 1924. In their different ways, they brought the South all the way to New York.

Thus, we have two thirty-year periods, 1924-1954, and 1954-1984. As a very broad generalization, we can say that an interplay between the Southern tradition and the New York-Hollywood tradition occurred throughout both periods. The difference is primarily one of emphasis.

From 1924 to 1954, the New York-Hollywood tradition with its emphasis on melodic love songs remained dominant. Still, the Southern tradition in the form of various jazz styles remained alive and well, but it was primarily restricted to live radio and to records. Consistent with the dominance of the New York-Hollywood tradition was the dominance of a media complex of network radio, movie studios, and major record labels which transmitted the music.

From 1954 to 1984, a decentralization of the media occurred. Top 40 and progressive FM stations, independent labels, and long-playing albums helped to bring about the dominance of the Southern tradition. Probably the crucial element in the whole period was the appearance of the electric guitar, which gave the blues a volume which it had never had before. Yet the New York-Hollywood tradition never died out; it went to television where it thrived under the aegis of Perry Como, Mitch Miller, and Lawrence Welk.

Very generally, the New York-Hollywood tradition represents melody, and the Southern tradition represents rhythm. Music needs both melody and rhythm, and America needs both the New York-Hollywood tradition and the Southern tradition. Neither is going to die out, and the assimilation of rock 'n' roll into narrative contexts suggests an assimilation of these two traditions. The production of laser discs, with their extraordinary sound reproduction, and their high resolution video capacity, may prove to be the ideal medium for innovative musical creativity in the future.[6]

Notes

[1]David Ewen, *George Gershwin, His Journey to Greatness* (Englewood Cliffs: Prentice-Hall, 1970), p. 77.

[2]*Ibid.*, p. 81.

[3]Quoted in *ibid.*, p. 81.

[4]James Lincoln Collier, *Louis Armstrong, An American Genius* (New York: Oxford U. Press, 1983), p. 118.

[5]*Ibid.*, p. 119.

[6]The best comments published so far on the integration of audio and video are to be found in an unusual place—a stock recommendation. Lee S. Isgur, a researcher at Paine Webber, has written a well-informed, insightful paper on this process. Showing an astute understanding of the way technology structures popular entertainment, Isgur isolates a "key event": "In October, 1984, Pioneer Electronics began selling in Japan a laser disk player capable of playing a laser disk of any diameter (5,8 or 12 inches) and encoded form (video images, audio sound and/or digital information).... We believe multi-purpose laser disk players eventually will be installed in most households—in much the same way that three-speed phonographs triumphed over single-speed 33 1/3, 45 or 78 rpm players thirty years ago." (Lee S. Isgur, "The Third Wave: The integration of Audio With Video," privately printed research paper for Paine Webber, dated January 17, 1985, p. 2.

Index

335